MW00770478

Detective
Ellis H. Parker

AMERICA'S SHERLOCK HOLMES

By Grandson Andrew Sahol & Russell Lloyd

Note: All pictures or newspaper clippings in this book are from the Parker/Sahol family
collections.
Copyright Pending
Contact: tellrussl@gmail.com
Print ISBN: 978-1-09839-361-8
eBook ISBN: 978-1-09839-362-5

TABLE OF CONTENTS

INTRODUCTION

Note: *The words of* **Andy Sahol** *will always be italicized in this book.*

RUSSELL LLOYD ON ANDY SAHOL:

"Andy is the last person left who can tell the true Ellis Parker story. He is closer to Ellis Parker than anyone else could ever be. He has compiled the memories of his family and has spent years researching his grandfather's life."

ANDY SAHOL ON HIS SORROW:

"Everyone loses someone. Everyone has sadness. Everyone deals with pain sometime in their life. What is very sorrowful is when these things are inflicted upon a person, and they don't come naturally. That's what this story is about. And that is what my book is about. The hardest thing in life to accept is death and sorrow. Even harder to accept is when this is put upon you by an outside source." Andy Sahol on his sorrow)

ANDY SAHOL'S DEDICATION:

"I dedicate this biography to my grandfather, Detective Ellis H. Parker Sr., my uncle Ellis H. Parker Jr., and especially to my loving mother, Lilyan Parker Sahol (Ellis H. Parker's daughter). I miss her every day. I am also dedicating it to the other siblings and descendants of Ellis H. Parker to recognize the pain and suffering we (his family) endured. I hope it will bring some peace to everyone and find peace for him. This book is the truth. As much as I know, I don't think anyone can expect more." (Andy Sahol)

WHY IT WAS IMPORTANT FOR US TO WRITE THIS BOOK

Andy Sahol and I (Russell Lloyd) wrote this book with only one goal, to shed light on one of America's most significant law enforcement officers so that the body of his work can be appreciated. That man is Detective Ellis H. Parker, frequently referred to as "America's Sherlock Holmes." Which was and is still deserving praise, indeed. The book is written to debate foregone conclusions about the Lindbergh case or the evidence revealed at the trials or in the following years. We will strive to reproduce Detective Ellis H. Parker's thoughts, conclusions, and investigations about it and present his lost papers that have been recently found. The case's classic interpretation can be read in hundreds of books, magazines, and online websites. The media has made sure that the players and characters are all well known. Charles Lindbergh, his family, his in-laws, employees, and the New Jersey State Police come to mind first. Then there is the arrest, the trial, and the execution of Bruno Richard Hauptmann.

The official and only record of the case can be found in the Hauptmann trial manuscript. Anything else is speculation or theories presented to generate profit via book publishing, which there is nothing wrong with. That being said, the writers of this book are convinced that Detective Ellis H. Parker solved the Lindbergh baby kidnapping case and delivered the only signed confession. The one signed by Paul H. Wendel.

Andy Sahol on the Lindbergh case & Paul Wendel: "*Ellis Parker, when he talks about the Lindbergh case, felt it was criminal. He believed that Hauptman was innocent of the baby kidnapping. Period. He regularly wrote that the abduction and the distribution of the ransom money were two distinct and different crimes. "Paul Wendel thought himself more intelligent than everyone, even himself. My Grandfather knew that Paul Wendel was a con artist and that Wendel's reputation went back very far. Wendel had graduated from law school and had earned a druggist license. He lost his right to practice law for improper conduct and his druggist license for fraud. He once tried to sell Al Capone, a technology whereby gasoline could be made from water. His intelligence contradicted him-self." "Paul Wendel was wanted on many charges. As many as 13 warrants were out for him while he testified at my grandfather's trial. That my grandfather was accused of conspiracy to kidnap this low life is unreal. My Grandfather was a man that had served New Jersey loyally as a Law Enforcement Officer for decades gaining great fame. It doesn't make sense. Governor Moore wrote a letter asking my grandfather to join the Lindbergh case investigation. He was performing that duty when arrested. It blows my mind how such a low life as Paul Wendel could silence my grandfather. Wendel was a man that had spent time in prison and at a mental hospital in West Trenton. By the way, a chisel matching the same description as the one found at the bottom of the ladder during the Lindbergh investigation had gone missing from the same hospital."*

ELLIS PARKER HAD THE RIGHT MAN.
IT WAS PAUL WENDEL

We think that Ellis Parker had the right man. Somehow Paul Wendel and his accomplice Isidor Fisch disposed of the Lindbergh baby. Alive or dead. But it does make some sense that the baby was killed before he was given to Paul Wendel. That baby couldn't have been lying there in the woods all that time. It would have been found sooner. Leaves only covered it. How credible is it that someone goes to take a piss and sees the baby? That area had been thoroughly searched many times. Including the night of the kidnapping and the day after. There was a Telephone line running nearby, right next to it. It would have been hard to overlook. Anybody following the cable during the searches would have likely seen it. It couldn't have been there that long. Nearby was a cemetery where many infants had been buried. Some about the time the Lindbergh baby was kidnapped. Maybe one was dug up as a replacement? Ellis Parker did not believe that the body found was that of Charles Lindbergh Jr. He pointed out that the baby was too big. The corpse was much shorter than the Lindbergh baby.

Andy Sahol on David Wilentz: "My grandfather was a great patriot and a brilliant man. One that should be honored today for all he accomplished. It was Wilentz that destroyed that. It is crucial that we know that the bad guy in this book is David Wilentz. Wilentz ruined the life of an incredibly good man for ambition, not the truth. It has been alleged that Wilentz bribed witnesses, fabricated evidence, and supported the perjury of more than one witness. Countless writers and investigators have doubted Hauptmann's guilt since his death. Wilentz put an innocent man to his death in the electric chair. David Wilentz then the New Jersey Attorney General, his cronies William Clark, John Quinn, and others withheld evidence that would have saved Richard Hauptmann from the electric chair."

Andy Sahol on the irony of his life: "The irony of everything that's happened in my life, especially in the last 25 years, is that I become engrossed with my grandfather. It is not just because of the countless books I read as they don't cover his life to any degree but also by discovering my family. My Uncle Edward comes to mind. He didn't talk about my grandfather's crime. Notice that I did not call it a kidnapping. It was a crime. My Grandfather was an exceptionally good person, loyal to his family. He spent a considerable amount of time with his son, Edward, teaching him about life and his passion for woodworking. My Grandfather learned to build furniture when he lived in Penny Hill with his parents. He was taught many other things while growing up there. He became well-rounded and especially loved hunting and fishing. When I started my intense study of my mother's life, I began to feel so much sorrow. I can't go on here. I remember so much now. It is hard to talk about it. There was a period during my investigation that I became severely depressed. As I traveled to visit the many archives that had information about my grandfather, I got deeper into everything that transpired with my grandfather, and it was troubling me. That was when I began to realize how much this was important to me. In 2007 I submitted a petition for My Grandfather's posthumous pardon and then again in 2008. I was turned down both times within a year. I then resolved that my mission wasn't to pardon him. You only pardon somebody for a crime or something they did wrong. My Grandfather never did anything wrong. I mean, never!"

THIS BOOK'S GOAL

THE READER MUST UNDERSTAND THAT this book is a product of Detective Ellis H. Parker's family, both living and passed, and his countless friends and admirers. It is the crowning achievement of the lifelong ambition of Grandson Andy Sahol. It is meant to set the record straight by shining the spotlight on the man's career known as America's Sherlock Holmes (Detective Ellis H. Parker). It describes the unjust conviction and imprisonment he suffered at the hands of Hauptmann's Prosecutor David Wilentz, Prosecutor John Quinn, and Judge William Clarke. Their conspiracy, creation, tampering, and manipulation of evidence during and after the Hauptmann trial and then again during the Parker trial led to Ellis Parker's guilty verdict, imprisonment, and death at Lewisburg Penitentiary.

It is based on our firm and unshakeable belief that Ellis H. Parker, most probably America's foremost Detective of his time and maybe all times, did solve the Lindbergh baby kidnapping crime. He did this by producing Paul H. Wendel's confession, a disbarred lawyer, a convicted perjurer, and a lifelong schemer. Detective Parker was wrongly convicted of the alleged kidnapping of Paul Wendel to obtain his confession by the same New Jersey State officials listed above that had a great deal to lose if Bruno Richard Hoffman's conviction was overturned or discredited. These officials had become world-famous and celebrated for their conviction. The execution of Bruno Richard Hauptmann has been called by many writers and scholars the greatest miscarriage of justice and misconduct ever carried out.

<u>Note</u>: If a translator had been provided to Hauptmann, he likely would have been able to defend himself better. There was a language barrier, and he often didn't understand what was told to him.

<u>Andy Sahol, on Ellis Parker's mental state at his trial:</u> *"My grandfather's faculties were still there during his trial. At some point, Prosecutor Quinn stated that he was acting irrationally. Ellis answered, "Why would an intelligent person, when he realizes the fruitlessness of his actions, continue?" You can easily understand his depression in this response. My Grandfather was not always in his right mind. Pop was accused of "winking" during the trial by prosecutor Quinn and even by Judge Clark. They didn't realize that Pop's winking and laughing was due to his medical condition. He was not always in complete control of himself. That's why in his later years, his friends, his family, and particularly Ana Bading would help express his thinking. Yet, his brilliant mind was still evident as he was usually ahead of them in his thoughts. He would need occasional reminding of things. Maybe in 1937, they did not realize that a condition like this should not be used against a person, I guess. My grandfather, at times, was confused and not fit for trial. But he was still intelligent enough to show his wit. When people would say something, he would make a remark that made them laugh. He was always ahead of the game. But then, at his trial, he was only even with the game, but he still had enough brilliance within him at this time to fight for himself. You must remember that in 1937 it was getting close to the end for him. He only lived until 1940.*

Even Quinn, the prosecutor, brought up my grandfather's 44 years of service during his trial. His words showed how good he could be and how wrong he could be. I don't know if that makes any sense. During the trial, my grandfather states that he just wanted to save the Lindbergh baby. He was pointing out that this goes back to 1932, in the very beginning. He claimed that he photographed the baby. There is no evidence of this. At the same time, he is contradicting himself. It was at this point in his testimony I realized why my Uncle Ellis Jr. did not testify. If they were both on the same par mentally, it would have helped, but I think that Ellis Jr. believed that if he swore to tell the truth, he would contradict his father, and they could be convicted of perjury. That is my theory of why my uncle did not testify."

The complicated case and life of all those surrounding the Lindbergh family and crime will be discussed in a never-ending search for evidence. The evidence is needed to establish support for old and new theories until the end of time. One thing is sure, Ellis H. Parker solved the Lindbergh case. He produced the only written and signed confession to the Lindbergh crime. The confession of Paul Wendel. We believe that the baby was handed out the front door to Paul Wendel and Isidor Fisch, either at the direction of or by Charles Lindbergh himself.

FORWARD

<u>Andy Sahol on January 2019:</u> *"My grandfather's story is almost unbelievable. This book will bring awareness of the humiliation, grief, destruction, and unwarranted prosecution of my grandfather and my uncle. I would like to think it will bring my family closure, but I doubt anything could.*

My mother passed away in 2002 from complications of Alzheimer's disease, not unlike the illness that took her father, Ellis Parker. During the last two years of Mom's life, she conveyed to me all the pain that she and my family had suffered and had endured in silence due to my grandfather's arrest and imprisonment.

Lilyan Parker, the daughter of Ellis Parker, was a beautiful woman inside and out. At the age of thirteen, she was a terrific athlete who won a swimming meet on Long Beach Island against Pennsylvania swimmers. She was also my fantastic mother, and I miss her dearly. I learned about her pain while suffering from the horrible disease of Alzheimer's. It was just like they say, her short-term memories faded away in the last few years, and then things that happened long ago came to the surface. Even with this horrible illness, she was able to teach me so much.

When she was in a nursing home, I would pick her up to take her out weekly for car rides. The trips always included a stop at the Mt. Holly Cemetery to visit my grandfather's grave. My Grandmother, Cora Parker, and my aunt Mildred are buried nearby in the same plot. As she stood there, she would grit her teeth in anger over what they did to my grandfather. I remember her telling me that my grandfather was a good man, and this, his trial, imprisonment, and death, should not have happened to him. I knew then that he was innocent, without a doubt. They not only had destroyed my Grandfather but his family as well. Their savings were taken from them, their home on High Street, and their house down the shore. That is why I am so determined to correct the record of my grandfather's life.

My grandfather passed away on the morning of February 4th, 1940. I never had a chance to know him. I was not even two years old when he died. I regret not knowing him. Now 80 years old, I am sometimes depressed due to my sadness when I think about my mother.

My mother believed that my grandfather knew that somehow Lindbergh was involved in kidnapping his child from the very beginning. More importantly, she told me that Paul Wendel had been feeding my grandfather information he should not have known for some years. It should be noted that Paul Wendel was the only person that confessed to the Lindbergh kidnapping. When allowed to withdraw his confession by Prosecutor David Wilentz, he took it.

My mother also blamed David Wilentz for my grandfather's jail sentence. She knew that Wilentz didn't personally prosecute my grandfather and my Uncle Ellis Jr. (her brother) in their trial. Still, Wilentz had set up the actual prosecutor, John Quinn, and Judge William Clark, with whom he had a remarkably close relationship. Wilentz became incredibly famous for sending Hauptmann to his death. World-famous, in fact. My Grandfather believed that Wilentz had orchestrated his indictment because of ambition. He had withheld information that would have helped Richard Hauptmann avoid the electric chair. Wilentz had a lot to lose if it was proved that he had sent an innocent man to his death. When Wilentz realized that my grandfather was determined to prove Hauptmann innocent, he wanted him silenced. He plotted against my grandfather after Governor Hoffman had granted Hauptmann a 30-day reprieve from his death sentence. The prosecution of Hauptmann and my grandfather were similar. Wilentz publicly controlled the Hauptmann case. He managed my grandfather's trial from behind the scenes. He was heavily involved in the arrest and prosecution of my Grandfather while covering up the mistakes he made in rushing to put Richard Hauptmann in the electric chair and my grandfather in Lewisburg Penitentiary, a place over 400 miles from his family and powerless. Wilentz had to go after my grandfather to silence him.

I believe that crucial evidence was manufactured and withheld in both cases. There is little doubt in my mind that Hauptmann was threatened with harm to his family. My Uncle's family (Ellis Parker Jr.) was also threatened. What other reason could make Hauptmann chose to die? The threat to his family is the only logical explanation of why Hauptmann didn't take the deals offered him to avoid electrocution. He only had to change his plea to guilty to prevent it and be paid thousands of dollars. He feared for his family the same way my uncle did when he was released from prison and threatened. Why was my uncle kept in prison another year and three months after my grandfather died? The only explanation is that Attorney General David Wilentz or higher officials feared him being on the street and continuing my grandfather's investigation.

Later in this book, you will learn of my grandfather's legendary letters that were thought lost until just over a year ago. Anthony Scaduto, in his excellent book, Scapegoat, wrote that he went to Mount Holly and interviewed the surviving Parker family members in 1975. I knew he talked to my Uncle Edward, trying to find the letters that my Grandfather had supposedly saved. I think it was my Aunt Betty who told him that the letters had been destroyed. I guess she had a good reason for that. Maybe she didn't want to deal with it. That would make sense.

The letters had been stored in her house for years. Her daughter, my cousin, Betty Jean Arrenson, found the letters in her attic after she died. She called me and said, "Andy, I think you should have these." I was astounded because there were 4 or 5 legal-sized boxes of letters and papers. We (co-author Russ Lloyd and I) were amazed by the admiration and love expressed for my Grandfather in these letters. Not only did I receive all the letters and papers but also the complete Hauptmann trial transcripts.

My Grandfather acknowledged every letter he received. Whether from the public, his friends, or politicians. His mail was incredibly overwhelming during the Lindbergh case. He received hundreds of letters weekly. He most often responded, "I assure you that I am only interested in Justice." These words are a tribute to Ellis Parker. A man who gave his life in the pursuit of that Justice he spoke of. The letters will be included in the second part of this book. They will shed new information and insight into my grandfather's life and the Hauptmann case."

LIVING WITH ELLIS PARKER'S GHOST

J. D. MULLANE WROTE THE following for his weekly column in the Burlington County Times on June 8, 2011.

Andy Sahol takes a seat in his living room, leans forward, and pleads the case for his dead Grandfather, Ellis Parker.

My Grandfather is innocent. He went to prison, and how is it for a detective to die in prison? That's where he died. You know that, right? How's that for miscarriage of justice? It should never have happened. My Grandfather knew who kidnapped Lindbergh's son, and it wasn't Bruno Hauptmann. It was Paul Wendel, and Wendel confessed to it. It's here, in my research. All this, here. All this. You just have to read, connect the dots.

Sahol speaks interrupted for almost 20 minutes. On TV tables are stacks of papers, photocopied court documents, memos, old newspaper clippings, books, binders.

It's all in here. Look. You have to read them," he said, looking, paging, reading.

Sahol is 72. He is a retired troubleshooter for PSE&G. He is a widower who lives in an age-restricted development in Florence, NJ. He has spent 13 years trying to get a presidential pardon for his late Grandfather.

"My goal is to clear him," he said.

Detective Ellis Parker is largely forgotten, but he was a living legend in Burlington County. He served as the county's chief Detective from 1894 to 1937. His pipe smoking and fiddle playing earned him a reputation as a homespun hick, but he wasn't. His crime sleuthing brought international fame. He was called "the world's greatest living Detective," a real-life Sherlock Holmes. It was not an exaggeration.

Parker solved 200 murders and sent 300 criminals to prison. He had no high school diploma, but he was brilliant at sorting fact from fiction and, as a friend once said, "making one fact bear the weight of another, and another, until he had a logical structure."

Andy put it this way: "He was doing forensic CSI stuff 100 years ago,"

Take the case of the Pickled Corpse. In October 1920, two men were suspected of robbing and killing a bank courier. Two weeks later, when the body was found near a Burlington County pond, an examination of the corpse indicated the courier had been dead a day or two. The suspects' alibis checked out. Scores of people had seen the pair in the days and weeks after the courier vanished.

Detective Parker's instincts said the courier had been dead longer than that. He discovered that Hemlock trees around the pond had enriched the water and soil with Tannic acid, preserving the body and making it seem as if the courier had been dead only a day or two. The killer confessed.

Then came the Lindbergh murder in 1932. The toddler son of Charles Lindbergh, the world's most famous aviator, was kidnapped from his bedroom in Hopewell, Mercer

County. State investigators kept Parker out, although he desperately wanted in.

Richard Bruno Hauptmann was executed for the crime. Parker believed the culprit was Paul Wendel, a doughy, middle-aged Trenton Lawyer with a shady past. He became obsessed with Wendel. Parker employed "investigators," including his son, Ellis Jr., to kidnap and torture Wendel to coerce a confession, according to John Reisinger's 2006 book, "Master Detective."

The Parkers were tried, convicted, and sent to the Lewisburg Federal Penitentiary in Pennsylvania. Ellis Sr. died seven months later, in February 1940. He was 68. Ellis Jr. was released in 1941 and later pardoned. He never discussed the case again.

Andy Sahol is in his bedroom, poring over more stacks of research documents.

"I see it as my duty to my family to set the record straight, to get me Grandfather pardoned. President Clinton didn't answer me. President Bush said he wasn't entertaining pardons. Oh – see this paper here? My Grandfather had thrombosis of the left hemisphere of the brain. That qualifies him for an insanity defense."

Sahol is up, off to another room with another table laden with more papers. He passes a large painting of his grandfather, ghostly and dapper in a dark suit and broad trimmed hat.

He flips through documents saying "Here" and "Look" and "See?"

"You just have to look. Connect the dots," Andy says. "It's all right here. It's here, in all of this. In my heart, I know."

THE STORY CONTINUES ON AUGUST 8, 2020 (TOLD BY RUSSELL LLOYD)

A lot of time has passed. Andy Sahol is now 81 years old. He has suffered some severe setbacks and has been hospitalized several times, but he still has the energy and desire needed to set the record straight on his grandfather's incredible life. Thankfully, he has regained his health.

But something is different. Andy no longer believes his Grandfather Ellis Parker and his uncle Ellis Parker Jr. require pardons. Why?

Andy Sahol Answers: "*Because they were never guilty of a damn thing!" Andy tells me. "They were innocent and deserved an acquittal, not a pardon. A pardon is only possible when there is an admission of guilt. They never admitted guilt, and my research proves they were not guilty. The sentence needs to be reversed; they were innocent of any crime. It is a fact that my grandfather solved the Lindbergh case.*"

"*Paul Wendel was the kidnapper, and he either killed the baby or took the wrap for someone else. He even signed a confession! Claimed, his family helped! Who does that? Hauptmann was only guilty of extortion and money laundering. He was executed because David Wilentz wanted to become famous for solving the case. Then Wilentz needed to silence my Grandfather and my uncle. It was the same trial all over again. Manufactured evidence was used to obtain guilty verdicts on Hauptmann, my grandfather, and my uncle.*"

"*I have new evidence now to prove what happened. We have recovered the "ELLIS PARKER LOST FILES." They were thought to have been destroyed by my Uncle Ellis Parker Jr. Anthony Scaduto, author of Scapegoat, traveled to talk with my Uncle Eddie in Hainesport in the mid-1970s. Eddie told him that he didn't know anything about the files but that Ellis Junior's second wife, Betty, might know something. Scaduto learned that Ellis Parker Junior was told to burn the files by my grandfather. My Grandfather said to him that he was worried that people would be hurt if they came out.*"

In his book, Anthony Scaduto tells of his search that took him to Mt. Holly, New Jersey. He describes meeting with Eddie Parker, Detective Parker's son. After telling Scaduto that he had no idea where the papers ended up, Eddie suggests that he contact Ellis Parker Junior's second wife, Betty, his widow who had remarried. Betty was living in Clearwater, Florida, with her new husband. Scaduto telephoned Betty, and she told him that her then-husband Ellis Parker Junior had destroyed the papers just as his father had requested before his death.

In Scaduto's book, he wrote that Betty told him, "They've been destroyed."

After Scaduto replied, "Oh my god, no," Betty continued, "I'm afraid so. My husband was so discouraged about everything that happened to him and his father. After that, the Wendel thing blew up in their faces. He ordered me to burn everything after he died."

Scaduto asked, "but why?"

"Ellis told me that no good will come out of this now. It's too late. No one will ever believe that Hauptmann is innocent, and my father was right. So, I burned the papers after my husband died."

Disappointed, Anthony Scaduto gave up on the search.

Betty (now Mrs. Blair Rodman) maintained her Mount Holly residence while residing in Florida and visited home often. In 2017 Andy Sahol received a shocking call from Betty's daughter, Betty Jean Arronson. Betty Jean was cleaning out her late mother's home in Mount Holly to get it ready for sale. She called Andy to tell him that she had found several boxes in the attic that he should have. After bringing them to his home in Florence, New Jersey, Andy discovered that the boxes contained the long thought destroyed files of his late Grandfather, Detective Ellis H. Parker.

Andy Sahol adds: "*The lost files of my grandfather Ellis Parker contain enough new information to change the conception of history. My Grandfather presented the signed confession of Paul Wendel to the prosecution. Wendel was the only person to confess to the kidnapping and murder of the Lindbergh child. Wendel repudiated his confession after being offered a deal by the Hauptmann prosecution led by David Wilentz. Wendel would be rewarded beyond his wildest dreams. All his past transgressions, sins, outstanding warrants, and criminal charges would be lost. Paul Wendel would be free to write about his involvement in the Lindbergh case for large sums of money, as he had often talked of doing. It was an offer he could not refuse."*

THE LINDBERGH-HAUPTMANN AFTERMATH BY PAUL H. WENDEL

In 1940 Paul Wendel attempted to profit on his Lindbergh case notoriety by publishing "The Lindbergh-Hauptmann Aftermath. The publisher was Loft Publishing. I suspect there were less than a dozen copies printed. It is near impossible to find an original today.

Mark W. Falzini (author & archivist for the New Jersey State Police Museum) was kind enough to provide me with a copy of the book. Marks' books on the Lindbergh case and other subjects are highly recommended.

Wendel opens his book by dedicating it to the Hon. Wm. F. X. Geoghan (District Attorney of Kings County) and too Francis A. Madden (Assistant District Attorney) and the Law Enforcement Officers who had solved the Lindbergh kidnapping case.

Wendel will have you believe that he was sacrificed by his friends Ellis H. Parker Sr., Ellis H. Parker Jr., and Anna Bading (Ellis Parker's assistant). Wendel claims that Ellis Parker held him captive until he was forced into confessing to a crime that he did not commit, calling it the vilest fraud in American History. By doing so, Bruno Hauptmann could go free, and Ellis Parker could get the credit for solving the Lindbergh case. This would aid Ellis's close friend, NJ Governor Harold Hoffman. Hoffman's ambition was to become Vice President of the United States and for Ellis Parker to replace J. Edgar Hoover as Chief of the Federal Bureau of Investigation.

Wendel described his 15 years of questionable friendship with Ellis Parker beginning in 1920. Wendel tells of assisting Ellis Parker in the Louis Lively case, the John Brunen murder case, and several others. His claims of deep involvement and importance in Ellis Parker's successful arrests are ludicrous. Any intelligent individual with knowledge of Wendel's life would laugh at the absurdity of this. Wendel was nothing more than Ellis Parker's stool pigeon and a snitch.

Wendel then, conveniently, begins to tell the story of him warning that Ellis Parker was violating the suspect's rights that he was holding. How convenient is this, considering that Wendel contends that he was held against his will by Parker? Wendel describes an occasion where he read a law book to Ellis that defined the accused's rights. Wendel was referring to his claim of false imprisonment and denial of rights. Quite convenient, don't you think?

Wendel writes that on the night of the Lindbergh kidnapping, March 1st, 1932, he was in his Laboratory all day and evening, experimenting with gas and heat absorption. Ellis Parker noted that innocent people have difficulty remembering the details of where they were or what they were doing in long past days. The guilty will take the time to fabricate alibis in great detail.

Wendel describes his invention that was to be purchased by the infamous Al Capone. This invention would be capable of turning water into gasoline. It sounds like the proposal of a fool to me. What idiot would present such a preposterous thing to Al Capone of all the people? Paul Wendel writes that he did! Wendel also contends that he was attempting to use these contacts to obtain the Lindbergh baby's return. Supposedly Ellis Parker told Wendel that you could get anything you want from Governor Hoffman if you do this. Wendel tells of Ellis Parker offering him the cash to purchase the baby. Wendel, a man that can only be described as an opportunist, conniver, and schemer, would have you believe that he turned the opportunity down.

The balance of Wendel's book describes his imprisonment, his plots, and his plans. The description of what he suffered is self-serving, as you would expect. His lengthy explanation and details will bore you to death.

In many parts, it reads like a weak attempt at horrible literature or fabricated storytelling.

Andy Sahol, on his Grandfather's Death Certificate: "*I got my grandfather's Death Certificate from the Lewisburg Penitentiary. In the document, I learned that his death was caused by thrombosis of the brain's right hemisphere. To support this, I hired a forensic expert to investigate. It was a bit of money, but it was worth it because I have it in writing now. His disease was progressive. A tumor might have ended his life instantly, but this disease coming from years back shows the slow deterioration of my grandfather's brain and why he eventually died on February 4th, 1940.*"

Andy Sahol's comments on Judge Clark's Actions in Court: "*Clark was insulting the witnesses. They brought up the Rancocas Rum and Gunning case. My grandfather was never involved in that. Their reason for doing this was to have the jury question my grandfather's character. They wanted to throw some dirt at him. They were desperate. Maybe they read something in the newspaper that alluded to his involvement, but he wasn't. He was never charged with anything in his life until this trial. The incredible thing was what Judge Clark said when testimony was going to refer to the Lindbergh case. He interrupted and said that the Lindbergh case had nothing to do with Parker's case. Nothing to do. Now, my opinion is that it had everything to do with it. Here again, Clark broke every rule of ethics in this trial; he testified numerous times, which is unethical. He did not allow witnesses, for instance, like my Grandfather's Doctor, that would have testified to his poor health.*

Over the last 20 years, I have unsuccessfully submitted petitions to pardon my Grandfather posthumously. I was turned down twice. Finally, I realized that this wasn't my goal. A pardon forgives somebody for doing something wrong. Ellis H. Parker never did anything wrong. So, I am not even interested in a pardon anymore. I want the public or the people in a higher power to realize that this man deserves much more. He deserves exoneration, period.

All this happened when I was young. My mother told me about how the imprisonment of my grandfather shocked and saddened the family. I came to know my grandmother Cora (Ellis Parker's wife) after my Grandfather's death. She lived until 1965. After my grandfather was imprisoned for all those years, and after he died, the family had to take care of my mother because everything was lost during the trial. Each of them did their part; my aunt Helen, for instance, was a child when her brother (Ellis Jr.) and my Grandfather were arrested. She never married and worked at Bell telephone for years. She helped all she could and lived with her mother (my grandmother) to care for her. That's another tragedy.

The people behind the arrest and my Grandfather and uncle's trial were supposedly respected officers of the court. They destroyed the life and reputation of the most well-known, respected, and successful law officer that the United States may have ever known.

My Grandfather was tried for the conspiracy to kidnap Paul Wendel. Judge Clark said the Lindbergh case had no bearing on my grandfather's trial. That was not a true statement because the Lindbergh case had everything to do with it and to do with my grandfather's demise.

My Grandfather's prison number was 8735. My uncle Ellis Parker Jr's number was 8736. I initially wanted to title this book # 8735. I have strong feelings about this number, and I have thought about its meaning for many years. I want people to look at the number and say, "who is this # 8735? What does that number mean?" I want them to find out by reading this book and learning about the injustice of it.

In my research, I found the most unbelievable thing, and it goes to prove that my Uncle Ellis Parker Jr. was threatened with harm. That information came from his daughter Kay Rodgers. She told me that he had refused many times to talk about his imprisonment and trial because "no good would happen if we pursued this." Late in his life, he told Kay, "Harm could come to many innocent people."

On top of that, I learned that my uncle was due for parole on June 21st, 1940, which was only five months after his father's, my Grandfather's death. Unbelievably, I have definite proof that my uncle was not released for parole until October of 1941. They, in effect, kept him one year and three months longer than he should have been. Uncle Ellis could have been paroled a year and three months earlier than he was. The only viable reason for this is that someone higher up decided against his release and wanted to see him held longer. All this again points to Wilentz's fear of releasing my grandfather. I also believe that he threatened my uncle for the same reason. My cousin Kay (Ellis Parker Jr's daughter) thought this as well. What other reason could there be for him to have stayed in prison? There was letter after letter from the Attorney General down and from the US Pardon Attorney stating that he was eligible for parole only five months after my Grandfather died.

My Uncle Ellis Parker Jr. and his second wife, Betty, lived on Mount Holly's Canal Street after being paroled from prison. It had to be around 1942. MY Aunt Betty was a schoolteacher that walked home after school each day. More than once, an unknown visitor would be waiting on her front porch claiming to be the Lindbergh baby. It shows you just how famous the whole Lindbergh case became. Unfortunately, it also reminded them of the tragedy of it all.

Interestingly, I was at the University of Penn hospital with my wife one time many years later. She was there to be treated by one of their doctors. When done, we were standing at the counter, waiting to make a follow-up appointment. I overheard two men whispering behind me. Incredibly, one claimed, addressing the other, that he was the Lindbergh baby! This was just out of the blue. He had no idea who I was and did not realize that I was listening to him or that I was connected to the case through my grandfather. It still hurt to be reminded about it after all those years."

HOW IT MAY HAVE HAPPENED ON MARCH 1st, 1932

THE CRIME OF THE CENTURY occurred on March 1st, 1932. An American night that will live in infamy to be discussed and argued over until time ends. It is also a night that Detective Ellis H. Parker will always be linked to. This is unfortunate.

It was a damp, dreary night in Hopewell, NJ, when the young infant Charles Lindbergh Jr. was taken. What happened that night and the following day is well documented. Although Anne Lindbergh was scheduled to return to her parent's home in Englewood, NJ, she had changed her mind because she was concerned that her son, Charles Lindbergh Jr., was coming down with something, maybe only a cold, she hoped. The Lindbergh family and servants would stay in their newly built Hopewell mansion rather than chance tiring the baby with the long car ride back to her parent's home. Her husband, the world-famed aviator Charles A. Lindbergh agreed. Later that evening, the nursemaid went to check on the baby she had put to bed. To her horror, the baby was missing from the crib. She called out in alarm.

Now aware that his child was missing, Charles grabbed his rifle to search the grounds. Failing to find his son, the aviator, came inside the mansion to await the police. Local officers were first to arrive; next was newly appointed Colonel Norman Schwarzkopf, head of the New Jersey State Police, walking in to assume command.

After introductions, the Colonel told Charles and Anne, "We need to search for the baby quickly. Time is of the essence." After searching all through the night, Colonel Schwarzkopf told the Lindbergh family, "I have sent for Detective Ellis H. Parker, the world's most famous Detective. He is being driven from Mount Holly to help us find Charles Jr. It's about an hour from here. Surely you have heard of him?"

Anne, who was hysterical and crying openly, "Oh yes, of course, please get him here as soon as possible. I just want my baby."

Her husband, Charles, remained calm. Anne Morrow Lindbergh once stated that her husband Charles never cried.

Charles "Norman, do you think that is necessary? Can't we keep this to ourselves? In a small circle. It might be easier to control the efforts of everyone that way." Motioning to the door, "It's like a circus out there already."

Norman Schwarzkopf responds, "Parker is excellent, Sir. Extremely qualified and experienced. Probably the best in the world."

Charles "Maybe so, but I think there will be too many chiefs with him here. You know, too many cooks spoil the stew? You and I can organize the investigation without anyone else. You are capable, don't you think?"

Anne "Charles, are you sure? Think again. This is our child we are speaking of. Not a stolen car or money."

Charles, looking sternly at his wife, "Stop contradicting me. Keep your mouth closed, woman! I know what is best."

Raising his voice, Charles turns to Schwarzkopf to say, "Call off the car with Parker, right now, Colonel. Understand? I don't want him here. We don't need him. It is my child that is missing, and I will make the decisions."

More on the Night of March 1st, 1932

On that March evening (3-1-1932), at approximately 9:00 PM, the 20-month-old Charles Augustus Lindbergh Jr. was either carried down a ladder resting against the Lindbergh's Hopewell mansion, or he was silently taken from his crib and handed out the front door. Grandson Andy Sahol is sure that Detective Ellis H. Parker believed it was the front door and that the baby was handed to Paul Wendel and Isidor Fisch. It will never be known if the child survived that trip. If the child were known to be dead before leaving the Lindbergh estate, the Ransome request would be worthless. The kidnappers would be inclined to remove the baby's body if he was accidentally dropped on the way down the ladder.

Who did this will always be discussed and disputed by everyone except the family of Ellis H. Parker and his Grandson Andy Sahol? In 1936 Paul Wendel told Ellis Parker that he took the baby to his home in Trenton, NJ, to be cared for by his wife and children. Amazingly, Paul H. Wendel would later admit in his confession that the Lindbergh baby later died in his arms in his confession.

Andy Sahol: "*I want the reader to know that my grandfather didn't believe it was a kidnapping; it was a crime. There is a difference. My research and my grandfather's letters all point to that. When we look at the crime, the reader should put himself at the Lindbergh home that night and the following day. You, your wife, and the servants are in the room when Colonel Schwartzkoph informs you that a trooper has been sent from the Penn's Neck barracks to Mount Holly. He is to bring my Grandfather, Ellis Parker, America's Sherlock Holmes, to the Lindbergh estate. Picture this scene; someone in the room vetos bringing Ellis Parker to the mansion. The trooper sent for Ellis Parker is recalled. Who would order this? Not the servants. Not the wife (Anne Lindbergh). She didn't even open her mouth when Charles was around. Wouldn't she, the mother, have wanted the great Detective, only 30 miles away, there to find her baby. The mob guys? Why were they even there? Schwartzkopf? He was the one who sent for Ellis Parker. It had to be Charles Lindbergh. What did he fear? What had he done?*

I know that my wife would have demanded that Ellis Parker be brought there immediately. I think the reader would agree. No one has ever proved what exactly happened that night and the next morning, but so many books tell us that Schwarzkopf was a pawn in Charles Lindbergh's hands. If this were to happen today, the husband and wife would be placed in separate cars for

*independent questioning at the police station. Any great detective would have
done that, and Ellis Parker was the Greatest Detective."*

FROM THE ELLIS PARKER LOST FILES

SQUIRE JOHNSON'S REPORT TO COLONEL SCHWARZKOPH ON
3-10-1932, REGARDING THE LADDER

On March 10, 1932 (9 days after the Lindbergh baby was kidnapped), Squire Johnson, the Assistant Director of Construction, Division
of Architecture, wrote to Colonel Norman Schwarzkopf, Superintendent
of New Jersey State Police, detailing his inspection of the ladder found at
the Lindbergh home. Johnson shockingly concluded that the ladder was
constructed by two different men, one lefthanded and one righthanded.
He reported that the ladder was made approximately one month before
the crime.

Johnson wrote that the most surprising thing was that a 3-foot-long
piece of maple, of identical size and quality as used in the dowels for assembling the ladder, was discovered in the corner of Lindbergh's library by
Sargent Gardner and Squire Johnson that day (3-10-1932).

Johnson also wrote that the plane (tool) being held at the New Jersey
Police Headquarters was not the plane used on the ladder. Johnson's opinion was that the ladder was not well made, and that the maker was not well
trained. He also wrote that the ladder was challenging to navigate. It was considerably more difficult to descend than to ascend if both hands were not free.

A copy of this letter was found in Ellis Parker's Lost Files by his
Grandson (Andrew Sahol). It is a smoking gun contradicting much of the
conclusions later disclosed by the Lindbergh investigation team. It brings
doubt about Hauptmann's being the lone ladder builder. Was he also alone at
the crime scene? Why did Colonel Swartzkoph ignore all this information?

About an hour after the child was discovered missing by the Lindbergh
family and staff, Charles Lindbergh placed a call to the New Jersey State Police

in West Trenton, NJ. He told the duty officer, Trooper Dunn, that his child had been kidnapped. He then began his investigation and never relinquished control of it.

Colonel Schwarzkopf let this happen. He had previously worked at a department store as a security guard with little experience in law enforcement. Also, Schwarzkopf and Ellis Parker had some previous disagreements. But he was able to set them aside with so much at stake. This was the one case that had to be solved. Schwarzkopf knew the world was watching closely. He needed the help of the single best Detective in the world regardless of his past relationship with Ellis Parker. It was the right decision. The life of a child was at stake.

Trooper Horn never did arrive at the Mount Holly Parker home. He was told to turn around at some point. That order could have only come from Schwarzkopf himself. But remember, Schwarzkopf wanted Ellis Parker there. The only person that could have overruled him was the baby's father, Charles Lindbergh. Why would Lindbergh override Schwarzkopf and not have the world's most significant Detective help recover his child? Imagine being faced with a suddenly missing child and not being able to do something about it? Unbelievably, Lindbergh turned down World Famous Detective Ellis Parker's assistance while his weeping wife stood by him desperate for her missing child? Who makes that decision unless he has something to hide?

CHARLES LINDBERGH, ALEXIS CARREL, EUGENICS, THE HOLOCAUST, & ADOLPH HITLER

Charles Lindbergh and Alexis Carrel had become close friends in the early 1930s. Lindbergh later considered Carrel his best friend. They shared views, worked on inventions together, and purchased island homes next to each other off France's coast. They shared personal, political, and social perspectives.

Carrel was a French biologist and surgeon awarded the Noble Prize in 1912 for Physiology/Medicine for pioneering vascular suturing techniques.

Working together on the project, Carrel and Lindbergh invented the perfusion pump that made open-heart surgery and organ transplantation feasible.

The red flag about Carrel's relationship with Lindbergh is his suspected connections to the Nazi Party and Adolph Hitler. Before Carrel's death, he was attacked in the newspapers over his relationship and collaboration with the Nazi regime. He was indicted but died before the trial could start. Lindbergh preserved and promoted Carrel's ideals even after his death.

Carrel and Lindbergh championed the Eugenics Philosophy. Eugenics is the study of how to arrange reproduction within a human population to increase heritable characteristics. Francis Galton developed eugenics to improve the human race. It fell in disfavor only after the perversion of its doctrines by the Nazis. Carrel advocated that humanity would be better guided by a group of intellectuals that would incorporate Eugenics. Charles Lindbergh subscribed to the teachings of Eugenics, and he believed in the breeding of healthy children. After WWII, Carrel was accused of helping the German command to implement Eugenics. He advocated using lethal gas to rid humanity of "defectives" before the Nazis put it into practice. Many Americans believed that the Third Reich used the Eugenics theory to justify the murder of approximately 6 million Jewish people during WW2.

Charles Lindbergh stood against those Americans who wanted to join the fight against Germany in Europe. Public opinion turned on him when he accepted Nazi awards (the German Service Cross) pinned on him by Herman Goring. In 1941 Charles Lindbergh accused the Jewish race of being behind America's drive to enter the war. He urged the US to stay out of the fight with Hitler. Charles Lindbergh was an admirer and ally of Adolph Hitler, and it has been alleged he arranged a residence in Berlin to spend the duration of the war near his idol. Winston Churchill, a friend of Lindbergh, was furious when he learned of Lindbergh's isolation speeches.

Hitler was arguably the evilest man of our lifetime. He was the architect of the "Master Race plan." In one speech, Lindbergh predicted that Germany would win World War 2. In another speech, Lindbergh blamed the British, the Jewish, and the Roosevelt administration for pushing America into the war.

For being a Eugenic, Lindbergh was later believed to be supportive of the Holocaust. Anti-Semitism was a running theme in many of Lindbergh's speeches, where he blamed the Jews for the outbreak of the war in Europe. In one horrible instance, Lindbergh said, "Their (the Jews) greatest danger lies in their large ownership in our motion pictures, our press, our radio, and our government."

Could Charles Lindbergh have been embarrassed by what he considered a "defective" son? A son that may have had physical or mental limitations or deforming childhood maladies? Much like Joe Kennedy's family faced when they lobotomized intellectually disabled daughter Rose Marie?

Charles Lindbergh may have been embarrassed by his son's health issues to the point that he didn't want the world to know of them. Lindbergh's obsession with Eugenics may have been his motivation to arrange his son's disappearance or death. He may have wanted only to hide his son away from the public, not to see him dead. The thought of this is detestable, mainly if Lindbergh couldn't accept that he had fathered a defective child. He may have been embarrassed by his son's health issues to the point that he didn't want the world to know it. That is a horrible thought, but it has been suggested as a motive. Charles Lindbergh believed in the science of Eugenics. He joined the society, and he donated money to them.

Lindbergh was also an advocate of non-intervention, supporting the Antiwar America First Committee, which opposed American aid to Britain in its war against Germany. He resigned his commission in the United States Army Air Forces in 1941, after President Franklin Roosevelt publicly rebuked him for his views. This is a sobering thought when we question Lindbergh's character and consider the possibility of his involvement in his son's disappearance.

Another reason for questioning the character of Charles Lindbergh was revealed just after he died in 1974. Lindbergh was accused of leading a double life with three mistresses in Germany. Amazingly two of them were sisters! The real irony of this is that both sisters suffered walking disabilities because of childhood illness. Lindbergh's legal American wife, Anne Morrow Lindbergh, supposedly knew all about this and that his mistresses had born Charles seven children. Sometime later, a few of the children came forward to claim that Charles Lindbergh had fathered them after finding pictures of him and his love letters addressed to their mother in their attic. Three of them published a book titled "The Double Life of Charles Lindbergh." They submitted to DNA testing to verify their claims. The Lindbergh family has consistently refused to comment on this.

FROM THE ELLIS PARKER LOST FILES

CHARLES LINDBERGH EMPLOYED TWO MINOR UNDERWORLD CHARACTERS

The following came from the pamphlet "The Lindbergh Case # I" found in Ellis Parker's files:

"An eccentric old lecturer from Fordham University, John F. Condom (Jafsie), became the Lindbergh's official emissary. But not before two minor underworld characters, Selvy Spitale and Irving Bitz, had offered their valueless services and for a time employed."

This may be evidence that Charles Lindbergh knew and was associated with the underworld. The kidnapping case and the characters in it may have been influenced or directed by organized crime.

We (Andy Sahol & Russell Lloyd) share our opinions in the following sections:

THE NIGHT OF THE KIDNAPPING, LINDBERGH IN CHARGE, THE STAFF'S PROFIT MOTIVE

On the night of the kidnapping, we believe that the ladder was placed outside under Charles Lindberg's order. He was home that night early to set this up; the family was not usually at the new mansion except on weekends.

Lindbergh had planned the kidnapping and organized the whole night himself. He didn't want Ellis Parker because he feared him and didn't want to risk facing Ellis Parker. Ellis might easily have seen that the guilt was Lindbergh's. Ellis would have suspected him immediately. We don't think that the baby was Ann Lindberg's child; maybe it was her older sister Elizabeth's baby. Charles had dumped Elizabeth after several months of dating. We also suspect that the baby was dead before that night. The kidnapping may have been a staged coverup. Lindbergh had organized and controlled this whole thing. He wanted to cover up what he was doing. The people in the household were deadly afraid of him. They died long before Lindbergh did, many in suspicious circumstances. That is why they didn't try to capitalize on their knowledge with books and interviews in later life for profit.

ON THE LADDER

The ladder could have been any ladder. I think the whole controversy over the ladder has been overdone. The baby was handed out the front door.

ON RICHARD HAUPTMAN'S CRIMES

Maybe Hauptman's only crimes were to build the ladder and pass the ransom money? It is as if someone had gone to the Morrow home to measure for it. It adjusted to the upper and lower windows there perfectly. Could it have been intended for the Morrow home? Was the plan initially to have the baby taken from the Morrow home? Did Charles Lindbergh change his mind? Did he realize that the remote location of his new home would be less risky? Less chance of being witnessed. Less staff on hand to control? The ladder was designed for use at the Morrow home. It did not fit the Lindbergh's windows. I believe that the ladder was moved to the Lindbergh home from the Morrow home. Lindbergh still needed a ladder to set up the fake kidnapping at his new home, so he took it. I don't think anybody climbed the ladder that evening. I think the baby was handed out the front door, and I doubt he was alive. I think the baby was handed to Paul Wendel and Isidor Fisch.

THE OBITUARY OF DETECTIVE ELLIS H. PARKER

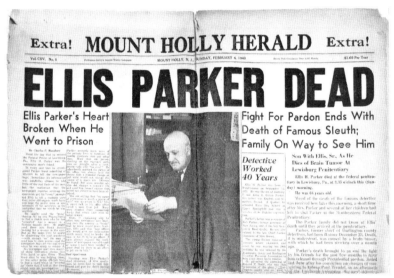

The following stories were reprinted from Detective Ellis H. Parker's hometown newspaper,
The "Mount Holly Herald." They ran on the day he died. The long-gone paper was his greatest
fan, and he of it. (Copy was saved by the Sahol family)

EXTRA!

MOUNT HOLLY HERALD
Mount Holly, NJ, Sunday, February 4, 1940

'ELLIS PARKER DEAD'

Ellis Parker's Heart Broken When He Went to Prison
by Charles C. Hansberry

Until the day that he entered the federal prison at Lewisburg-Pa., Ellis H. Parker was the newspaper man's friend. In every case that he investigated; Ellis Parker found something of interest to tell the newspaper boys. Sometimes his information was indefinite; ofttimes he told little of the real facts of the case, but the realization that the newspaper reporter covering the case "must" get his story prompted Ellis to tell a readable yarn that never did anyone much harm and kept the public more or less informed of his activities in the particular case on which he was working.

He might send the gang chasing far up into Pennsylvania to find a Dutch cook who had "revealed" was a suspect in a famous murder case. He might send them into South Jersey looking for a woman in the case. But at the same time, he might be shadowing the real murderer with enough "on" the man to send him to state prison. The newspaper boys got the real story when he was ready to release it.

No newspaperman ever resented these wild goose chases that Ellis loved to give them. They knew that he was helping them, as few other police officials have, find the story while he "covered up" facts that, if told at the time, might ruin his investigation.

Only once in Parker's long life of investigating did the case get away from him and land on the front face of the newspapers before he was ready. That was the Lindbergh-Hauptmann-Wendell case. Breaking about his ears that were heard to Frisco back and back, this case ruined his life, landed him in prison, and probably hastened his death.

34

Ellis went to Lewisburg last summer outwardly facing the world with courage, but his heart was broken. Whether or not he had erred will be debated as long as the Lindbergh kidnapping is remembered. The dockets of the federal courts say that he was convicted of "conspiracy to kidnap."

Was Keen Observer

A keen observer of all that transpired in Burlington County, Ellis Parker probably knew more of the private lives of hundreds of nearby residents than any other man. More than one person, starting on the wayward path, was set straight after a confidential talk with "the chief." He relentlessly pursued the duties of his office but always held the theory that the criminal charge or jail term would not change the course of a man's life. Ofttimes, he found that some sensible advice did change a person's life and send him toward success that would not otherwise have been attained.

The old saying that "an ounce of prevention is worth a pound of cure" was an axiom in Ellis's life. A short talk in his office often saved a man from jail. Many were stopped from committing deeds that would have been labeled crimes.

Once, in explaining why he often sent newspaper men hustling over the country on "leads" that the new would prove fruitless, Ellis said that "Any officer who would give out information which would tend to hinder the case, is not fit to be an officer. I have always enjoyed the confidence of newspapermen, although, at times, I have been "needled" a great deal by them in an effort to get me to talk."

Real Sportsman

Gunning was Ellis Parker's chief diversion. A true sportsman, he loved best to visit Egg Island and gun for ducks during the season. "Sportsmen are the best type people in the world to do business with," Parker once said. "A sportsman is better qualified to do business than any other; if he is a gunner for Quail, he must make a quick decision and be accurate in aim, and when a person is accurate, he becomes proficient in his work."

"The Sportsmen are a liberal class of people," Parker said. "It is impossible to do business with an extremist. It does not matter which way they are, you never can convince them against their will, and they will not listen to reason; therefore, you are only wasting your time."

The attitude of communities toward crime has much to do with criminal control, Parker believed.

"The majority of people in every community think an officer is paid to take care of that community." Ellis once declared. "This is true, but no community needs to be infested with evildoers if it doesn't want to be. An officer is clothed with authority and has a right to arrest with the execution of writs, etc., but without the assistance of the public, his powers are limited. If the public will be fair and assist him, and if there is someone in the community who was undesirable, something could be done about it. It rests with every community what goes on in it. An officer should be protective rather than an oppressive force. If he can keep the people regulated and out of trouble, he is doing the community some good. An officer never becomes any bigger than his friends make him, and without friends soon strikes his level. To have the people's confidence, this is the most viable asset; an officer can have."

Detective Worked 40 Years

Ellis H. Parker was born in Wrightstown on September 12, 1871. He was the son of Anthony J. And Anna E. Girton Parker. His father was English, and his mother was French. A Quaker, he attended First Day school at Upper Springfield and was a member of the Hicksite organization.

Parker's father was a cousin of Joel Parker, former governor of New Jersey, and of the late General E. Burd Grubb. He was also related to the late Chief Justice Gummere of New Jersey.

The young Parker received a common school education, and when he was nearing his 20thbirthday, he was selected by the Monmouth, Ocean, and Burlington Counties Pursuing Association to help trace down horse thieves.

He attracted the attention of Eckard P. Budd, who was the prosecutor of Burlington County. He was offered Burlington County Chief Detective's position, the position he held until his suspension following charges in the Wendel case.

A peculiar thing happened to Ellis Parker in his early days. He aimed to be a great musician, and he played the violin for dances, accompanying a harp player for a few years. He started to play for dances when he was 14 years old. A short time later, he was robbed twice. A man, working for his father, robbed the home and stole all young Ellis's belongings. Parker got them back, having hunted the thief himself.

Then he had his horse and wagon stolen, and that irritated him. It was after he had recovered the horse and buggy through his detecting efforts that the pursuing association asked him to be one of the "pursuers."

It was then that young Parker started to study the state in which he lived. He prided himself on his knowledge of New Jersey, its people, and its conditions throughout his life. He once said that "the state was larger to me in my early days than the world is today."

Parker was married in 1900 to Cora E. Giberson, of Manahawkin. There were 15 children born to them, seven of whom are now living.

During his service as County Detective, Parker had an average of 4000 reports a year on various matters wanting his attention, with about 1000 cases investigated each year. In his years of service, he handled about 40,000 criminal cases. He investigated 236 murders and obtained confessions in all but 10 cases.

For many years Parker was consoling with detectives and investigators throughout the country. He assisted in many significant cases in various counties of the state and other states. In many, his name did not figure.

The only organization of which Parker was a member, outside of sportsman's organizations, was Mount Holly Lodge of Elks, No. 848.

Fight for Pardon ends with Death of Famous Sleuth; Family on the way to see him.

Son with Ellis Sr., as he dies of a brain tumor at the Lewisburg penitentiary.

Ellis H. Parker died at the federal penitentiary in Lewisburg, PA., at 3.35 o'clock this (Sunday) morning.

He was 68 years old.

Word of the death of the famous Detective was received here later this morning. A short time after Mrs. Parker and several of her children had left the visit Parker at the Northeastern Federal Penitentiary.

The Parker family did not know of Ellis's death until they arrived at the prison.

Parker, former chief of Burlington County detectives, had been ill since December 23rd. It is understood that death was caused by a brain tumor, with which he had been stricken with over a month ago.

Parker's death ended the fight by his friends for the past few months to have him released through a presidential pardon. He was jailed last June after his conviction on charges of conspiracy to kidnap Paul Wendel, in the aftermath of the Lindbergh kidnapping. The aged Detective left Mount Holly for the Federal Prison on June 22, 1939.

Under the constant care of his son, Ellis Parker Jr., who was also convicted of the Wendel charges, the Detective's condition became worse day by day during the past two weeks.

When it was first revealed that Parker was in a serious condition, members of the Parker defense committee, organized here to aid the Detective, sent petitions containing the names of 8000 signers to Washington.

Harry Green, Newark attorney who represented Parker, filed the petitions, along with several hundred personal letters written by officials and friends of the Detective, with the federal Board of Pardons. Immediate action had been hoped for, but at the time of the Detective's death, no word had come from Washington.

In one of the last letters that he wrote to Mount Holly, Parker said, "I hold no malice toward anyone. I believe in God and always will. I had never lost faith."

Parker was serving a term of 3 to 6 years in prison.

Late in July, he suffered a knee injury in a fall at the prison and was in the hospital for a short time. On July 28th, Green conferred with Attorney General Murphy in Washington in the first step toward a pardon move. On November 2nd, a federal indictment against the Parker's in Brooklyn was dropped. At the time of Ellis's death, a New York State indictment still stood against him.

Recently, a move was started to secure a pension for Parker, but court action failed.

INTRODUCING DETECTIVE ELLIS H. PARKER

Grandson Andy Sahol stands in front of a portrait of Grandfather Detective Ellis H. Parker (9-12-1871 to 2-4-1940). It was painted by Andy's cousin Steve Ferenzi.

<u>Andy Sahol:</u> *"Why is my Grandfather Ellis Parker important? Because you can rate him up with the most significant American detectives of all time, real ones, like the Pinkertons, William Flynn, Raymond Schindler, Dave Toschi, Izzy Einstein, Moe Smith, Johnny Broderick, and William Burns. All Americans should remember him and honor his legacy. Particularly the members of the Law Enforcement Community. I have heard it said that Ellis Parker solved 1000 cases during his career, with over 300 of them deemed major or capital crimes*

in which he usually obtained a signed confession. He did much more than that; thousands of his less serious cases were never documented. My Grandfather would work 24 hours a day to protect the public. It was his nature, part of his plan".

Detective Parker of Mount Holly, NJ, was commonly referred to as America's Sherlock Holmes during his lifetime. It was meant as a compliment. When he heard it, he would reply, "Unlike Sherlock, I am a real flesh and blood detective. Not a fictional character." His fame reached across America from coast to coast and then the oceans.

 In 1935 Detective Parker sat down with Fletcher Pratt to collaborate on the book " The Cunning Mulatto." Detective Parker solved 288 of the 300 major crimes he investigated. Author Pratt picked 12 of them to describe in the book. They were serialized in many newspapers to be read by millions. Detective Parker's fame spread across the United States from coast to coast. This is a great place to start if you want to learn about Ellis's crime-solving abilities and ground-breaking techniques. His unparalleled record of solving crimes earned him recognition from organizations like Scotland yard, the Surete (Detective branch of the French police), and many other countries. Unfortunately, this book is long out of print and sells for high prices when found.

INTERESTING FACTS ABOUT THE PUBLISHING OF THE "CUNNING MULATTO

Fletcher Pratt visited Ellis to gather information in Mount Holly. Ellis gave him the information, newspaper, and magazine articles needed for the book. Ellis was surprised when he later learned the Pratt had completed the book.

Ellis withdrew his consent to publish the book on 7-29-1935 in a letter to Fletcher Pratt. Author Pratt brought a representative of the publisher to see Ellis. Ellis agreed to issue the book for a percentage of the sales. In a meeting with Harrison Smith of Harrison Smith and Robert Haas, Inc., Ellis gave his permission to publish on 7-31-1935. The royalty rate was .125 per book (5%), which sold at $2.50 each. It was also disclosed that newspaper rights had been negotiated for newspaper excerpts.

On 8-6-1935, Harrison Smith wrote Ellis to express his pleasure with the book. He wrote, "After talking with you the other day, I was firmly convinced that if I ever committed a crime, it would not be within the borders of your county!"

Several copies of the Cunning Mulatto were mailed to Ellis on 8-21-1935 by Louis Bonino of Harrison, Smith & Robert Haas (the publishers). The book was published on September 16, 1935.

Detective Parker received numerous written requests for autographed copies of the Cunning Mulatto after its release. He also received multiple requests for public appearances and book signing events.

In a letter of 1-30-1936, The McClure Newspaper Syndicate advised Ellis that The Cunning Malatto was to be serialized by The McClure Newspaper Syndicate. It would appear in American Detective Magazine and some newspapers. McClure requested that Ellis provide another serial. Seth Bailey of The McClure Newspaper Syndicate wrote Ellis about his writing for them permanently. Ellis turned down the offer to concentrate on his Detective work.

WIP Radio of Philadelphia reviewed The Cunning Mulatto over the air on 10-23-1935 at 2:45 PM.

Royalty statements came routinely from Random House.

Andy Sahol learns about Ellis Parker's health from Fletcher Pratt's book:
"I learned more about my grandfather's health problems when I read Fletcher Pratt's book The Cunning Mulatto. Pratt came closest to any writer could describing my grandfather's brilliant life and career. He mentions in his book

that he had gone to see my grandfather while researching it. He found my grandfather in bed wearing a bathrobe. My Grandfather told Pratt that the reason he was in bed was that Doctor Harold E. Longsdorf had advised him that he wouldn't live 2 weeks if he didn't get some rest. Pratt's story showed me how far back my grandfather's illness had begun. It hadn't happened in one or two years. It had started at least seven years before his illness took him. The reader must remember that my grandfather only lasted seven months in prison before he died on 6-29-1939. His doctor's testimony might have kept him out of jail and maybe my uncle as well."

An Issue: The word "Mulatto" in the book title and story was picked by Fletcher Pratt to describe one of the criminals arrested by Detective Parker. "Mulatto" is defined as a person with mixed white and black ancestry. The word is considered offensive in this age. If the book is ever republished, the title should be changed to show respect for everyone.

Andy Sahol: "I think that the Cunning Mulatto was the most accurate and realistic rendition of my grandfather's work and his cases. It showed how good my grandfather was at being a Detective. The cases in the book were "as told by Ellis Parker" to Fletcher Pratt. We are getting the cases firsthand. The book was remarkably successful and led to magazine stories, radio interviews, and lecture opportunities. My Grandfather received regular royalty checks to prove ownership. A few years back, I hired a lawyer to get the rights back, but Fletcher Pratt's family had renewed the copyright before it ran out. The copyright will expire in 2030. Since the book openly acknowledges that the stories are "as told by Ellis Parker," I believe I have the legal right to use them any way I feel fit."

 ## FROM THE ELLIS PARKER LOST FILES

FROM THE AMERICAN MAGAZINE, DECEMBER – 1930

In December 1930, Arthur C. Bartlett wrote about Ellis Parker for The American Magazine. He titled the article "The Smartest Criminals Spring

Their Own Traps" and then added, "famous small-town Sherlock Holmes explains why."

Bartlett starts out with Ellis Parker's first case's widely repeated story, the theft of his own horse and buggy while performing at a barn dance. Bartlett declared, "The discovery of the theft was the exact moment Ellis Parker the fiddler turned Detective." Bartlett wrote, "He got his man, and he has been getting them ever since. Bartlett also notes that Ellis Parker had handled one hundred and seventy-six murder cases, out of which he only failed to get a conviction on just twelve. Of the twelve, he had confessions from seven. But four of them were women, Ellis explains, the jury didn't want to hang women, so they acquitted them. The other three cases had extenuating circumstances.

Bartlett pointed out that Ellis Parker didn't put the screws on suspects; he didn't believe in the rough stuff. Ellis told Bartlett, "I've never struck a man in my life while trying to get a confession. That sort of confession doesn't mean a thing."

One of Ellis's more well-known cases was described in the article. The one where Ellis was able to determine that a man shot in his own bed was, in fact, shot by his wife, who was reporting the crime. Ellis fed her a better alibi after disputing the one she had just told him. She then changed her story to agree with Ellis's new alibi after proving that she had also been in the husband's bed. She changed her fabricated story. Ellis concluded, "An intelligent person who commits a serious crime always gets a story ready to tell. This one wasn't perfect."

A pretty little girl was reported missing. Days had passed before Ellis became interested in the case. His search of the young girl's home found nothing. He turned his attention to a neighbor whose young son had often played with the girl. Ellis had discovered that the neighbor had a criminal record. Ellis searched this house without incident. Ellis knew something didn't make sense, so he had a local blacksmith make him a pointed iron rod. Ellis took the rod to the neighbor's basement and prodded the packed earth, which hadn't look disturbed, foot by foot until the rod sank easily. He had found the young girl's grave.

Another, "The Fort Dix Murder," was a famous Ellis Parker case. A dead Army Sargent was found on the Fort Dix grounds. He had been missing for over three months. Ellis decided to interview each member of the dead man's company with not much to go on. He asked, "Where were you that night?" Now remembering where you had been three months ago is difficult for most anyone. It was difficult for all but one man. Without hesitation, one private recited his activities down to the smallest details for the day in question. "The story was too good to be true," Ellis remembers, "No man on earth could recall so many details. I knew right then I had my man."

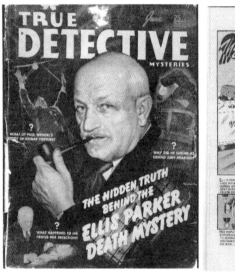

The above shows how Ellis Parker's abilities brought him fame and recognition. Detective Parker was featured in many newspaper articles, books, magazines (the above example is the cover of True Detective magazine), and even comics (The example is from EC Comics-Crime Patrol).

Andy Sahol points out: *"There should be a statue of him in Mount Holly to acknowledge his contributions to law enforcement. "He was a genius," said Grandson Andy Sahol of his Grandfather Ellis H. Parker, "who lived in houses that still stand on High and Garden Streets in Mount Holly. I admire him. He's become my role model in every way. I feel his presence in me. I picked four codes of his to emulate:*

1.) *Simplicity: he strived to be uncomplicated.*
2.) *Patience; do a slow analysis of each situation.*
3.) *Intelligence: use the intelligence that is around you.*
4.) *Perseverance; never give up.*

That's how he lived his life. That's why he was a brilliant Detective."

FROM THE ELLIS PARKER LOST FILES

More on The Cunning Mulatto

We found a copy of TIME Magazine (The Weekly Newsmagazine) in Ellis Parker's lost files. It wasn't until reaching the next to last page of the September 16, 1935, edition that we understood why. TIME had included a favorable review of "THE CUNNING MULATTO and OTHER CASES OF ELLIS PARKER, AMERICAN DETECTIVE." The book was credited to writer Fletcher Pratt, but it was a book that contained case stories as told by Detective Ellis Parker. Ellis received royalties from this book for many years. The subsequent fame led to him receiving offers to write additional descriptions of his cases for Newspapers and other magazines. The cases described in THE CUNNING MULATTO were serialized in Newspapers throughout the United States and around the World. National Crime and Police magazines competed for his co-operation on cover stories. Ellis was also offered opportunities to speak at many functions and be interviewed on the radio. All the exposure led to Ellis becoming famous as he worked on the "Crime of the Century."

TIME, September 16, 1935

68

fashioned tableau, with symbolic figures representing Poverty lurking miserably on one side of the stage while heedless Wealth dances with frantic unconcern on the other. An imposing volume, beautifully bound and illustrated with five full color reproductions of Artist Wight's portraits, *South* has much to recommend it: careful descriptions of characteristically lovely Southern scenery; sensitive evocations of feminine moods; a number of memorable conversations that are witty even if faked. But these graces are effectively nullified by Artist Wight's dogged determination to cram the whole boiling South into one volume.

Clinical Cases

THE CUNNING MULATTO AND OTHER CASES OF ELLIS PARKER, AMERICAN DETECTIVE—Fletcher Pratt—*Smith & Haas* ($2.50).

For 42 years Ellis Parker, round, short, grey-haired and good-natured, has been a practicing detective in Mount Holly, N. J. (pop. 6,573). He has worked on about 300 cases, principally crimes of violence. According to Fletcher Pratt, "he is probably the best detective in America if not in the world." Last week Author Pratt, heretofore recognized as a historian (*Ordeal by Fire*), offered a volume containing accounts of twelve of Ellis Parker's more sensational successes. Less a batch of detective stories than a collection of analyses of human behavior in moments of crisis, *The Cunning Mulatto* is obviously modeled on the tales of Sherlock Holmes, with Author Pratt in the rôle of Dr. Wat-

son asking intelligent leading questions. Although he tells little of his personal life, Detective Parker began trapping criminals because of his anger when his horse & buggy were stolen. Believing that people in times of stress act accord-

ELLIS PARKER
. . . started his career without his horse & buggy.

ing to a few readily recognizable patterns, he was seldom led astray by strange but meaningless combinations of circumstances developed after a deed of violence. Some cases:

¶ Bradway Brown, supposedly murdered for revenge or blackmail, was killed by robbers who were traced when Detective Parker noted that similar robberies were following the main highways.
¶ Louis Lively, mulatto brush-maker who had the habit of cutting little girls' throats, was trapped when Detective Parker noted that Lively always used the same type of false tips to mislead police.
¶ David Paul, Camden, N. J. bank messenger, disappeared with $40,000, was thought to have run away until his lack of preparation for flight seemed suspicious. Detective Parker found that Paul was murdered by old cronies whose crime was almost perfect.
¶ The man who killed John Brunen, circus-owner, to get his business was suspected by psychologist Parker because his alibi was so good. Innocent people usually do not remember exactly what they did on the night of a crime.

Pain & Punishment

BOXING IN ART AND LITERATURE—William D. Cox—*Reynal & Hitchcock* ($5).

When Aristotle in *The Nicomachean Ethics* pointed out that boxers find "the crown and the honors" of victorious combat pleasant, but that "receiving the blows they do is painful and annoying to flesh and blood," he expressed an attitude toward pugilism that has been held by most of the writing men since his day. The 37 authors whose fragmentary observations are included in *Boxing in Art and Literature* seem as a rule to approach it with a strange air of mingled respect and disdain, as if striving to find some intel-

During over 40 years of service, Detective Parker came to be called America's Sherlock Holmes. He was a brilliant and celebrated New Jersey Law Enforcement Officer. For 67 years, his reputation was legendary. His 68th and final year was heartbreaking and should not be his final judgment. But for being asked to investigate the Lindbergh Kidnapping Case by the Governor of New Jersey, Detective Parker would have spent his last years in honorable retirement with his loving family. Instead, Detective Parker agreed to help with the case and ultimately died in the Lewisburg, PA Federal Penitentiary after a deeply flawed trial for a crime he did not commit.

ELLIS PARKER'S EARLY LIFE & FAMILY

The Legendary Detective was born to his Quaker parents on a Wrightstown, NJ site that would later become a military base known as Fort Dix. Ellis Parker's conduct as a dedicated husband, father, and Detective was a testament to the Quaker teachings of peace, humility, community, kindness, and respect his parents exposed him to.

Andy Sahol: "My Grandfather's father was Anthony J. Parker, of English descent. His wife (my Great Grandmother) was Anna E. Girton Parker of French descent. Anthony was my Great-Grandfather. His father (my Great-Great-Grandfather) was Marcus Parker. Marcus Parker fell at the Battle of Monmouth during the Revolutionary War. Anthony Parker (Ellis's Dad) owned and operated an Inn named "The Parker Hotel & Rest Stop" for many years. The Inn was about 100 yards from the Dix military base. Anthony was a cousin of Joel Parker, former governor of New Jersey, and of General E. Burd Grubb. Anthony was also related to Chief Justice Gummere of New Jersey.

I still have copies of the Parker Inn's liquor and commodity licenses in my home. Inns and Hotels were actively monitored and regulated in those times. With his wife Anna E. Girton, Great Grandfather Anthony would frequently hold auctions to sell off the land, raw materials, horses, and houses. They would cater for weddings and many other affairs. They could earn a decent living from this.

My grandfather Ellis H. Parker was born on September 12th, 1871, in Tilton Hospital. It is incredible to me that he was born in a hospital. Not many of the Parker's were. Tilton Hospital was within walking distance of the Parker Hotel. Grandfather attended the Quaker First Day School in Upper Springfield, and he joined the Hicksite organization. The Hicksite was a liberal branch of the Quakers. There wasn't much of a school system then. I think he was mostly homeschooled, focusing on his reading, writing, and arithmetic skills. When he was only ten or eleven years old, he left school, 4th grade, I think, to help his family with finances. Everyone was expected to contribute.

My Grandfather grew up learning his father's (Anthony Parker) businesses. He began by assisting with the cleaning and maintaining of the two rooms offered at the Inn to travelers. Many of these travelers were on their way to Philadelphia from New York. Unfortunately, Hotel owners were limited by law to providing just two rooms for overnight accommodations in the early years. It was the town's way of controlling growth to keep undesirables away.

My Grandfather's (Ellis Parker) older brother was Howard Parker. Howard was 11 years older than Ellis. After Howard, there was Anthony (named after his father), sisters Carrie and Emily-Sarah. The youngest of the five children was my grandfather, Ellis.

The Inn and the land my grandfather was born on was known as Penny Hill. Penny Hill is now known as Wrightstown, NJ. Only a stone's throw away from Wrightstown is the military base now known as Fort Dix. When Fort Dix was opened, it was initially called Camp Dix. The opening of Dix grew the surrounding areas quickly. The Parker Inn & Hotel became very busy and successful quickly.

A lot of my descendants are buried in Wrightown's Cemetary. Their headstones still stand. They had settled in the area, many near Freehold, New Jersey.

My Grandfather became an excellent horse rider early on in his life. But he did have some setbacks. He was kicked numerous times, resulting in some very ugly bruises.

All my grandfather's years of attending to horses resulted in his reluctance to use automobiles when they were introduced. Even after the automobile became America's number 1 choice for transportation, my Grandfather still preferred the horse."

The young Ellis Parker received a common school education, and when he was nearing his 20thbirthday, he was asked by the Monmouth, Ocean, and the Burlington Counties Pursuing Association to help track down horse thieves. Then noticing his success, he was offered Burlington County Chief Detective's position by Prosecutor Eckard P. Budd. Ellis held this position until he was suspended following the Paul Wendel court case years later.

A peculiar thing happened to Ellis Parker in his early days. He longed to be a great musician, and he played the violin for local dances, accompanying a harp player for a few years. This began when he was only 14 years old. A short time later, he was robbed twice. While working for his father, a man broke into the Parker home and stole all of young Ellis's belongings. Ellis Parker got them back, hunting down the thief himself.

It was then that young Ellis started to study the state in which he lived. Throughout his life, Ellis prided himself on his knowledge of New Jersey and Burlington County, its people, and its conditions. He once said that "the state was larger to me in my early days than the entire world is today."

Ellis Parker's music career continued with him playing the fiddle at home for hours on hours. He was about 16 or 17 at the time. Wanting to continue developing his talent Ellis helped organize a 3-piece band consisting of friends. The group would meet for practice in Brindletown, NJ. They named themselves "The Brindletown Orchestra" in 1989 after the town. Ellis Parker was the Fiddler, Joe Raymond strummed the Harp, and Jake Walker picked the Banjo. The "Brindletown Orchestra" rehearsed and learned the popular tunes of the day. They were willing to travel anywhere that they could get the opportunity to perform. It was often at any of the hundreds of popular barn dances being held in those days for socializing. "The Brindletown Orchestra" became quite proficient at their craft and grew very well known as a result. They were well-liked and sought after. They remained a performing unit until 1897, when Ellis Parker left to become a detective.

At Left is Ellis Parker with Anna Bading in Ellis's preferred mode of transit.

Understand that this was in the day before automobiles changed our world. The primary means of transportation in Ellis Parker's youth was by horse. Horses were a sign of success back then, and they were crucial to the economy. Stealing them would often end with the culprit hanging from a tree with a noose around his neck. Most horses were attached to a buggy. Ellis Parker loved to travel this way. After time had passed and automobiles had taken over the streets, Ellis still proudly preferred to travel by horse and buggy. It was not uncommon to see Ellis Parker riding about Mount Holly on his carriage, ignoring the automobile traffic.

Ellis Parker would travel to the band's performances on his horse and buggy, leaving it outside the barn until the concert was over. After one lengthy gig, a tired young Ellis Parker emerged from the barn to find his horse and buggy missing. The criminals soon found out that this was the wrong horse and buggy to steal. Ellis was very distraught over the loss. At this young age, using his innate wits, Ellis investigated the crime and uncovered the culprits. His common sense, reasoning, and deductive abilities were already well refined.

Ellis found his horse and buggy intact, very quickly. The news of his success traveled fast. The Burlington County Pursuing Society society, hearing of Ellis's horse and buggy incident and other similar achievements, offered him (at the tender age of 20) a position. He was to be employed on a case-by-case basis, helping to catch thieves and other criminals, particularly horse thieves, while working from Mount Holly. The Society couldn't afford a full-time investigator at the time, but Ellis became a professional by accepting this position.

Andy Sahol: "_There were other Detectives in New Jersey back then, but they were scattered about with great distances between them. Burlington County was almost like a Cowboys and Indians film back then. Everyone could do almost anything they wanted. Crime was common, especially horse theft, and my grandfather had his hands full._"

After distinguishing himself, Ellis H. Parker was hired in 1897 as the first full-time Chief of Detectives for Burlington County, New Jersey. He moved into the Mount Holly County Courthouse office located just next to the Prison on High Street. Ellis Parker could look over the impressive Prison (opened in 1811 and now a museum) from his Courthouse office.

At left is The Mount Holly (Burlington County) courthouse. Ellis Parker's office is on the 2nd floor.

At right is the Mount Holly prison built in 1811.

Over the next 40 years, Ellis Parker's desk would become surrounded by file cabinets containing his notes on each of over the 300 major crimes he had worked on. His evidence safe was also in a prominent position and is still on display in the Mount Holly Prison. Ellis truly treasured his loyal assistant, Anna Bading. Anna was a talented detective herself, helping Ellis organize everything for most of his years. In some ways, Anna can be defined as Ellis's Watson (of Sherlock Holmes fame).

At left is Ellis Parker's famous evidence safe. It is still on display in the Mount Holly prison museum.

At right is Ellis Parker with Anna Bading (his Watson of Sherlock Holmes fame).

<u>Andy Sahol:</u> *"Ellis Parker was a Detective looked down on by professional law enforcement as somebody who had not received formal training in investigated techniques. Yes, he was quite the folk hero," noted Paul W. Schopp, a professional historian who lives in Riverton, NJ.*

Ellis Parker solved 288 of the 300 major crimes he investigated, racking up an almost impossible conviction rate. The cases were filed in his office. During Ellis's career, he sent many criminals to prison, the gallows, or the electric chair. The gallows were conveniently located in the yard behind the Mount Holly Prison, and just a short walk away. When and if you visit there, you will feel the electricity in the air that sends chills up and down your spine.

Ellis's competence at solving complicated crimes gradually became well known to reporters and newspaper readers. Ellis was named the "Sherlock Holmes of the United States" (Holmes was a fictional English book character first introduced in 1891) because of his impressive record. He wisely friended reporters and frequented Newspaper offices to keep the public informed of his progress during exciting, complicated, or unusual cases. Ellis would often cleverly create, and release wanted posters to local Newspapers to locate or capture suspects or escaped prisoners.

The story of the last execution at the Burlington County Prison is a tale retold many times. It was the double hanging of Rufus Johnson and George Small. The two men were convicted of Murdering Florence Allison of Moorestown, an English-born governess, at her refuge for homeless children. Arrested within days by the famous and celebrated Detective Ellis H. Parker, the men were hung on March 24, 1906, two months after the crime. A piece of the rope used for the execution still hangs in a prison hallway.

Andy Sahol: "_My Grandfather solved the Johnson-Small case in a few days. On his way to the gallows, Johnson said to my grandfather, "I hold no malice to you, Mr. Parker." He said that because, during his arrest, a mob had tried to lynch him, and my grandfather handcuffed himself to Johnson to prevent it._"

Ellis's unparalleled record of solving crimes earned him recognition from organizations like Scotland Yard (in England), the Surete (the Detective branch of the French Police), and many other countries. He was credited with solving crimes by deduction without leaving his desk. Detective Parker only had to examine the data and the evidence to identify the suspect. Ellis was also a profiler before profiling was universally recognized. He either invented or refined the good cop-bad cop technique and the use of chemical analysis in crime-solving. Ellis turned Science into a vital law enforcement tool. When called in 1920 to investigate a body found in water, he sought help from a chemist. Detective Ellis learned that the acidic content of the water had helped preserve the remains. This meant that two men that had been eliminated as suspects were ruled back in. The pair soon confessed.

It was Ellis Parker's idea to create a Rogues' Gallery in the Mt. Holly County Jail. He wanted all the imprisoned criminals photographed and any future criminals as well. Ellis rightfully reasoned that such a photographic record would be helpful when investigating future crimes. He was ahead of the times with this idea.

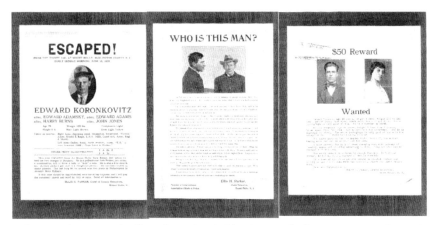

Above are three examples (from the Andy Sahol family papers) of how Detective Parker took Wanted Poster creation to a new level. He became well known in law enforcement circles for it.

Ellis was a short, stocky, bald man except for a small mustache and a fringe of hair that turned white as he aged. He was exceptionally agile, robust, and powerful. Ellis's strength and fitness would prove helpful more than once during arrests that went sideways. One death-row prisoner broke free while being led to the prison yard scaffolds to meet his maker. He made it up and over the prison wall to flee down Burlington-Mount Holly Road. Ellis caught up and overcame the criminal from behind, tackling him to the ground. The errant felon was cuffed and returned to the prison yard. There he met the hangman's noose and his maker in short order.

Ellis Parker's hobby was hunting. He spent most of his spare time at the Egg Island gun club. Duck hunting was his primary sport. While in Mt. Holly, he whiled away his leisure time at the Elks Club; otherwise, he was at his home on High Street, directly opposite the county jail.

During his many years in Mount Holly, Ellis operated a garage at King and Washington Streets, a pool room, and a Tobacco store that stocked his preferred pipe tobacco and cigar brands.

Ellis smoked a pipe throughout his adult life and was partial to a cigar. He was rarely seen without carrying his pipe. His tobacco of choice was "Sir Walter Raleigh." He preferred to use wooden matches to light it. Ellis was known to forget to shave when engrossed in a complicated case. Each day's highlight was taking his lunch at the Mount Holly Elks Club, which was only a short walk from his office. Elk members could eat and drink, but faithful to his Quaker teaching, Ellis never drank. Seated in the club, Ellis would spend his time reading the Trenton Evening Times and any other newspaper he could get his hands on. Newspaper reading was a passion of his. He would also enjoy playing cards with the other Elks members. These pursuits helped to relax him and re-energized Ellis daily, keeping his wits and deduction abilities sharp. Ellis had been one of the first two charter members (along with Blanchard White) to be initiated into the Elks' Order on April 23, 1903.

At left is Ellis Parker with his always present pipe and sometimes with a cigar.

At right is Ellis at his favorite pastime, the reading of the daily newspapers.

<u>*Andy Sahol:*</u> *"My Grandfather used a lot of common sense and the media to his advantage. Newspaper reporters. He would stop by their offices, frequently*

keeping them apprised of his cases and progress. I think the editor of the Mount Holly Herald was a close friend. Sometimes he would plant items to help identify or flush out criminals in hiding."

In the later years of his life, Ellis made the wrong decision by becoming involved with the Lindbergh case. It quickly became known as the "Crime of The Century" baby kidnapping case due to the resulting publicity and intense media coverage.

<u>Andy Sahol</u>: *"Unfortunately, the real story of The Crime of The Century is buried with my grandfather."*

THE CRIME OF THE CENTURY
HOW THE LINDBERGH CASE WAS REPORTED TO THE PUBLIC

<u>Note</u>: Following is a description of "The Crime of The Century" while unfolding in the 1930s. This book's writers do not believe that Bruno Richard Hauptmann was guilty of kidnapping the Lindbergh baby or being at the Lindbergh home that night. We will present as much evidence as possible later in this book as we can to support our opinion. Still, the age of the evidence will forever make it impossible to prove anything conclusively.

The media and many authors began to reexamine the case in the 1970s. This reexamination is still going on today. It is now a generally accepted opinion that Bruno Richard Hauptmann was most likely innocent of the kidnapping but was guilty of passing on the ransom money. Detective Ellis Parker strongly felt this way. Why did Hauptmann choose to accept the death penalty when given an alternative? The only logical reason is that his family was threatened if he did not. Only an organized criminal organization would have this power over him.

<u>The Story as Told to The Nation</u>: Lindbergh's young namesake was taken from the Lindbergh home on March 1st, 1932. Two months later, the infant,

Charles Lindbergh Jr., was found dead on the side of a nearby road by a truck driver. The nation was shocked and appalled. The crime became the most significant news story of the century. The arrest, the conviction, and the execution of Richard Hauptmann did not change this. The nation continued to grieve for many years.

At the time of the kidnapping, Charles Lindbergh was the most famous man in America. His aviation feats had made him as famous as President John F. Kennedy would become many years later. Lindbergh had moved to his North Jersey mansion to escape a media that was desperate for photographs and stories of his family. He wanted to raise his son in private.

Lindbergh (from Minnesota) had presented himself as a shy man caught in the headlight of fame. This only made the public want him more. He was followed everywhere. Pictures and stories about the young child circulated in the nation's newspapers until those of the crime replaced them. The ladder used to reach the nursery became such a symbol that ladders were manufactured as toys and souvenirs. Every facet of the Lindbergh family and those that serviced them found its way to the front pages. Each of them was considered a suspect.

When Betty Gow discovered that the baby was missing at 10:00 pm that night, she rushed to Charles Lindbergh in his study. Lindbergh immediately called the police to say, "My son has just been kidnapped."

The arriving Troopers found a ladder left behind in 3 pieces used to reach the 2nd story window. A troubling ransom note was found in the baby's room, demanding $50,000 with instructions to wait for contact.

Everyone in the United States wanted to help. Offers, suggestions, advice, tips, leads, and suspects' names were on everyone's lips. Family members, servants, friends, and acquaintances were interviewed by detectives. The newspapers ran stories every day to keep the nation informed.

The kidnappers arranged to meet John Condom (dubbed Jafsie) to deliver the $50,000 ransom payment. Jafsie had offered to be an intermediary. The meeting took place in a Bronx cemetery. Charles Lindbergh was also there, and later (at trial), he would pick out Bruno Richard Hauptmann as the man he heard speaking. He had only heard two words at the Cemetery. "Hey, doctor."

Hauptmann was discovered and then arrested by the Brooklyn police for spending some of the ransom bills identified by serial numbers. Additional currency bills were recovered in his garage. The German immigrant Richard Hauptmann insisted he was innocent, declaring that his friend Isidor Fisch had given him the money for safekeeping while visiting his family in Germany.

The Hauptmann trial was held in Flemington, NJ. Over 10,000 people assembled daily in the streets surrounding the courthouse daily.

Hauptmann was found guilty on February 13, 1935. He was sentenced to death. He was offered a reduction in sentence and suspension of the death penalty if he would change his plea to guilty. He was also offered money for his family. He still refused.

In a surprising development, Detective Ellis H. Parker delivered a signed confession to the crime. Paul H. Wendel had confessed that he had taken the baby from the Lindbergh home. New Jersey Governor Harold H. Hoffman ordered a stay of execution to review and investigate the new evidence.

Bruno Richard Hauptmann was eventually executed on April 8, 1936. While still insisting on his innocence.

OPINION: BRUNO HAUPTMANN GOES TO HIS DEATH PROCLAIMING INNOCENCE

Bruno Hauptmann willingly allowed the State of New Jersey to electrocute him. The thing that troubles me the most is why would a guilty man choose death over life? And why would he not take the money offered to confess that would ensure that his wife and child would be provided for?

Hauptman professed his innocence until his death. Could it just be that he was innocent? Or was his wife and child threatened with harm? Hauptman's history and connection with criminals could explain why he went to his death silently. History has shown us that there was and maybe still is a code of silence. Snitches are shunned. The Jewish code of Mesirah forbids the reporting of crimes, and the Mafia code Omerta demands silence with a warning of consequences.

On March 1, 1932, an American national celebrity and "hero" Charles Lindbergh's 20-month-old son was kidnapped from the 2nd story of their newly built mansion in Hopewell, New Jersey. A ladder was found leaning on the house just under the nursery by the arriving police officers.

At right is Charles Lindbergh Jr., shortly before he was taken from the Lindbergh estate.

The initial investigators found a ransom note, but they had no leads to the baby's whereabouts. On March 15th, 1932, New Jersey Governor A. Harry Moore wrote to Detective Ellis Parker, asking for his help. Ellis Parker agreed. On May 12, 1932, the Lindbergh baby's presumed body was discovered not far from the Lindbergh home, dead of a massive skull fracture. The nation was in shock.

At left, the baby's remains are discovered not far from the Lindbergh home.

At right is the shocking photo sto-
len from the Trenton NJ morgue
where the child's body was taken
after being discovered. Charles
Lindbergh had his son cremated
after seeing this image. Shortly
after that, he released his son's
ashes into the air from his airplane.
Lindbergh described his reason for doing this as that he was afraid that his son's
burial site would be disturbed by souvenir hunters.

<u>Something to think about</u>: "There are hair samples from the Lindbergh child's last haircut and from the corpse, but science does not make possible a positive identification based on hair samples alone." This excerpt was taken from **Bruno Richard Hauptmann: Killer or Victim?** By Peter Yerkes, April 9, 1978, Today Magazine, The Philadelphia Inquirer.

<u>QUESTION</u>: The art of DNA analysis has exploded since 1978. Where are these samples now?

Late in 1934 German immigrant, Bruno Richard Hauptmann was apprehended by the police. He had foolishly passed some of the bills (currency) that had been given to the supposed kidnappers by Charles Lindbergh in payment for the baby's release. Hauptmann was soon prosecuted as the sole suspect by the State of New Jersey.

RICHARD HAUPTMAN AND ISIDOR FISCH LAUNDERED THE RANSOME MONEY

Ellis Parker wrote many times in his letters that he didn't believe Hauptman did anything except work with Isidor Fisch and help launder the money.

At left is Richard Bruno Hauptman's Trenton jail photo.

Andy Sahol: "My Grandfather, Ellis Parker, when he talked about the Lindbergh case, felt it was criminal. He believed that Hauptman was innocent of the baby kidnapping. He regularly wrote that the kidnapping and the distribution of the ransom money were two distinct and different crimes. Everyone wonders why Hauptmann went to the chair without talking? There is a simple explanation. At the time, anybody could threaten you or your family. I believe that Hauptman's family was threatened. He was warned not to open his mouth to anybody, or his wife and son would suffer for it. Sounds like the Mob, doesn't it?"

The Lindbergh case remains in dispute to this day. Suspects, theories, and conclusions are a dime a dozen. Even Lindbergh himself was suspected because his baby son had been diagnosed with rickets, and supposedly this troubled him. Doubted because rickets was common at the time. One of the baby's nannies (minders) committed suicide (by drinking arsenic) when the police came to question her a second time. That makes us wonder about a possible conspiracy in the house. The scheme could have even included the baby's parents or other members of the Lindbergh's staff. It may sound cruel, but this possibility has been raised many times over years.

At the left is Violet Sharp, seated next to her sister. What was she so guilty of? Violet took her own life with arsenic rather than being questioned again by the police. It was well known that arsenic poisoning was an excruciating way to die.

Yes, the stakes were high. Ellis Parker would love to have been the Detective who solved the Lindbergh case. Who wouldn't have? His fame would last forever, and he was obsessed with finding the real killer. But Ellis's behavior and conduct during his life make one doubt that he would have ever manufactured false evidence willingly. The record of his life and character speaks out loudly. Had Ellis refused NJ Governor A. Harry Moore's request to look at the case, Ellis would have lived out the rest of his life with his reputation intact.

At right is the cover of "Scapegoat." The book was written and published by Anthony Scaduto in 1974. It is the best and most compelling book ever written about the Lindbergh "Crime of The Century" case. Author Anthony Scaduto was a New York Post investigating reporter. He wrote many other successful books before his death in 2017. The conclusions made in this book are dead on and backed up with in-depth research and first-person testimony. Since this book's publication, more than enough information and new evidence have been uncovered to justify an official reopening of the case. Scapegoat is far and away the best book ever written  about the "Crime of the Century." It would not have been possible for us to create this book without the information found in Scapegoat.

Analysis: Bruno Richard Hauptmann was not the Lindbergh baby kidnapper. He was framed with no chance of a fair trial. Even his requests for lie detector tests were refused. Despite all this, the case has never been officially reviewed.

In the "Scapegoat" book, Murray Bleefeld states after being asked by author Scaduto about the killer, "Did you catch him?" Bleefeld replies, "We sure did. His name's Paul H. Wendel. A disbarred lawyer, very brilliant, but a psychopath. Paul H. Wendel. Remember that name. Paul Wendel was a man who believed everybody in the world had done him wrong, and he was going to show the world he was smarter than everybody else by kidnapping the baby of the world's hero, the Lindbergh baby. Paul H. Wendel killed that baby, not Richard Hauptmann. Hauptmann had nothing to do with it."

In addition to forever challenging the historically inaccurate record of Richard Bruno Hauptmann's life, Scaduto also corrects history's false judgment of Detective Ellis H. Parker. If Wilentz hadn't destroyed Ellis Parker's reputation with false evidence and threats, Ellis Parker would have been forever celebrated as one of America's most brilliant crime solvers and law enforcement officers.

The evidence presented by Scaduto in his book clearly exonerates both Hauptmann and Parker. Scaduto brings to light Prosecutor David Wilentz's disgraceful behavior meant to ensure his own reputation and fortune. David Wilentz had used any means he could to discredit Detective Parker and silence him forever. His motive? Simply to justify his new fame and enrich his future. Not to see that justice was served.

On page 15 of Scaduto's book, he describes asking Murray Bleefeld in a phone call about his role in the Lindbergh kidnapping. Murray tells him that Ellis Parker hired him to catch the real Lindbergh baby kidnapper. Murray then names the kidnapper as Paul H. Wendel, calling him a disbarred lawyer, a very brilliant man, and a psychopath.

Murray explained that Paul Wendel was a man who believed everybody in the world had done him wrong. He was going to show the world he was more intelligent than everybody else by kidnapping the baby of the world's hero, the Lindbergh baby. Murray stated that Paul H. Wendel killed the baby, not Hauptmann and that Hauptman had nothing to do with it. Hauptmann was just a dumb carpenter who became the fall guy. Murray adds that he had gotten a confession from Wendel for Detective Parker and Parker's son, Ellis Parker Jr., with the help of his own brother-in-law.

Later in the book (page 27), Scaduto writes that there was something very strange about New Jersey officials' passionate and obscene haste to kill Hauptmann legally and close the case.

On page 65, after the Lindbergh baby's body was found, Allen Hynd (a magazine writer) wrote that Ellis Parker, who was sitting out the case because it was in an adjourning county, had been getting information from his friends in the NJ State Police. They told Ellis it was rather curious that the body had not been discovered earlier, as the area had been thoroughly searched numerous times.

Andy Sahol: "_Scaduto's book is the best book of all those written about the Hauptmann case. It establishes that the trial was a farce, organized, and directed by the prosecution to send an innocent man to death. Since it was published, the Lindbergh trial's reputation and those responsible for it are in great doubt. Scaduto says it like it was. He interviews each subject and draws his conclusions. His main source was Murray Bleefeld, who supposedly worked for my grandfather. Bleefeld's testimony in my grandfather's trial led to the guilty sentence and imprisonment. He put my grandfather in prison. Amazingly, in Scaduto's book, he admits that Detective Ellis Parker solved the case and called out Paul Wendel as the man responsible for the Lindbergh baby kidnapping plot, just as my grandfather had claimed. That was quite a turnaround for Bleefeld. So many things stink in this case. Two things more than others: Hauptman never kidnapped the baby. My Grandfather never kidnapped Wendel._"

Paul Wendel confessed that he did take the Lindbergh baby down the stairs and out the front door that fateful night. The Scapegoat book and many others agreed that Richard Hauptman might have been guilty of lesser crimes and did not act alone. Hauptmann was well-connected and aware of the crime when arrested. He was only guilty of money laundering, and it is doubtful that he was at the Lindbergh Mansion on the night of 3-1-1932. There are altered workplace documents (and court testimony) that place him at work during that day and visiting his wife's place of employment, a Brooklynn bakery, that night. Ellis H. Parker was and still is considered a genius Detective by many.

Grandson Andy Sahol is convinced that Paul Wendel carried the baby from the mansion, as he had confessed doing, and that Detective Ellis Parker did solve the "Crime of The Century." Paul Wendel, before and after the Lindbergh case, led a life of deception. He got a sweet deal to change his story and turn on Ellis Parker. The Hauptmann prosecution team's ambition resulted in the wrongful conviction of Ellis Parker with the bonus of avoiding being convicted for the abduction and death of the infant. He most certainly would have replaced Richard Hauptmann in the electric chair. It was a pretty sweet deal for Wendel. The Lindbergh case made many of the prosecution team and the trial witnesses world famous. Doesn't it strike you strange that the Hearst newspaper management paid for Richard Hauptmann's defense while damning him as a baby killer in all their papers? Very convenient. Hearst newspapers enflamed the general public to near hysteria while making the prosecution team famous, righteous, and just. The prosecution team was made heroes with their pictures and photos viewed continuously in the newspapers around the world. This made them media stars. They had much to lose if it was proven that they had sent an innocent man, Hauptmann, or just a bit player to his death. This was exactly what Ellis Parker, in concert with Governor Harold Hoffman, was close to proving. They did get a short stay of execution.

The Police were under enormous pressure to solve this sensational crime. When evidence was lacking, they planted it, falsified it, or persuaded witnesses to lie on the stand. There is proof of many witnesses reversing their original statements during testimony. Charles Lindbergh himself suddenly recognized Richard Hauptmann's voice as being the same one he had heard months before from a distance. Hauptmann had spoken only **two** words then. This emotionally charged moment at the trial was immediately evident on the jury. That moment, more than any other, was the catalyst to having the jurist voting Hauptmann guilty.

Andy Sahol, on the Travesty of Justice: "As in the Hauptmann trial, there is a travesty of justice in my grandfather's trial. If we look at Judge Trenchard's charge to the Jury in the Hauptman trial and then Judge Clark's charge to the jury in my grandfather's trial, they are similar. They used the same tactics and are manipulative. All legal scholars agree that the Lindberg-Hauptmann trial *was one of the worst examples of American Justice ever. I have many articles on that, like that of Professor Allan Dershowitz, whose book "America on Trial" described the case as just that."*

At left is Paul Wendel, a very suspicious character. Ellis Parker was right. There is more than enough reason to believe that Wendel was in on the Lindbergh baby snatch and at the Lindbergh home on the night of the crime.

Many witnesses called to testify against Hauptmann were promised a share of the reward for doing this by officials. Or they had taken it upon themselves in hopes of a profit. Evidence was planted framing Hauptmann with the lies spoken in court.

If you don't think that a trial of this magnitude could be fixed, think about this. Since 1973, approximately 162 people that had been sentenced to death have been exonerated. This is per the Death Penalty Information Center. Records were not being kept before 1973.

The "Crime of the Century" was the single most corrupt prosecution in American history. The persecution of Ellis Parker was a further disgrace and was criminal.

Andy Sahol: "Paul Wendel played my grandfather. Maybe he didn't confess anything at first, but Wendel now had someone to vent to. I doubt anyone else wanted anything to do with him, but my grandfather used him for information. That was what my grandfather's relationship with him was about. He was suspicious of Wendel. Especially when Wendel offered his help to find the Lindbergh baby. Wendel was a con artist from the beginning."

Paul Wendel, a savory character that Ellis had known for years, showed up at Ellis's Mount Holly office with an offer to share inside information that could help find the Lindbergh baby. This information would come from

Wendel's "connections," meaning the Mob (organized crime). Of course, Wendel, a disbarred NJ lawyer, and criminal wanted to be compensated for this information.

Wendel was a con artist from the beginning, throughout his entire life. He earned a law degree that was later taken away. His druggist license was also suspended when fraudulent activity was discovered. Wendel had on his record convictions for perjury and many other crimes before the Lindbergh kidnapping. He continued his life of poor judgment for his entire life. Paul Wendel lived a deceitful life long after the Lindbergh case had faded from the nation's headlines.

In 1945 the New York Times reported that the 58-year-old Wendel was charged with practicing medicine without a license.

The headline read: **KIDNAPPING VICTIM ACCUSED OF FRAUD, Paul H. Wendel to Face Trial of Practicing Medicine Without License**
(From the New York Times April 25, 1945)

Paul H. Wendel, a 58-year-old former New Jersey Attorney, who became nationally prominent about a decade ago because of his connection with a fantastic phase of the Lindbergh-Hauptmann case, was arraigned before Magistrate John D. Mason in Bay Ridge Court yesterday afternoon charged with practicing medicine without a license.

Wendel was in New Jersey Psychiatric Hospital in Trenton for a year before the kidnapping. The hospital had the same chisel that was found at the Lindbergh mansion under the ladder. That chisel could have come from the Hospital.

The baby was found on the route back to Trenton. Wendel used the same route when he took the dead baby back. This is not a route that Hauptman would have used.

Unfortunately, Detective Parker's examination of additional leads, including those provided by Paul Wendel, was at odds with and challenged the official NJ prosecution led by David Wilentz. Wilentz had publicly convicted Hauptmann as the one and only perpetrator, sentencing him to death.

Andy Sahol on the Lindbergh Case Stamp of Approval: "The trial of my grandfather and uncle was a stamp of approval for the Lindbergh case. There was no way David Wilentz wanted my grandfather to solve the Lindbergh case. He was working ferociously in the background to make sure that my grandfather was found guilty. Proof of that, in my mind, is that Wilentz and Clark sat on the Appeals Courts together."

Andy Sahol: "I think that Paul Wendel was handed the baby at the front door. Or it could have been handed to Isidore Fisch, who was with Wendel. There was a conspiracy in that mansion. Be sure of that. It is probably something that can never be proved because so much time has passed. It had to be an inside job. It could have been Violet Sharp, or it could have been someone else, but somebody handed over the baby, either alive or dead. It is only common sense. Was this at the direction of Charles Lindberg? Could it be that he was covering up a family accident or tragedy where the baby was deliberately killed? Or did Charles Lindbergh want the baby hidden because of his shortcomings? Did he say, "Let's get rid of the baby, call Wendel?" This is the type of thing I am wondering. I think my grandfather was too. I believe strongly that Paul Wendel is the bad guy and that the confession he gave to my grandfather was legitimate. My Grandfather was right. Wendel's confession described the best route to the Lindbergh estate. He even wrote the route into his confession! Hauptman prosecutor David Wilentz threw out this confession. Another suspicious thing is that David Wilentz visited Paul Wendel at 4 Mile Colony Hospital, recovering from his alleged kidnapping ordeal. I believe that Wilentz's real mission was to grill Wendel. This visit was never acknowledged in court, but it is significant. During this meeting, Wendel most likely told Wilentz he was going to turn himself in. Hearing this, David Wilentz had no choice. He had to stop him."

FROM THE ELLIS PARKER LOST FILES

The following was taken from a newspaper clipping that Ellis Parker obviously felt was important enough to save. The clipping had been sent to him by a private citizen.

WITNESS PUTS ISOBOR FISCH AT LINDY SCENE

New York Daily News – Thursday- March 5, 1936

Witness Puts Isidor Fisch at Lindy Home

By Robert Conway (staff correspondent of the news)

Trenton (March 4) Isidor Fisch, the dead friend whom Bruno Richard Hauptmann accused of leaving him $15,000 in Lindbergh ransom money in a shoebox, was placed squarely on the scene of the Sourland Mountain kidnap-murder by an affidavit which Gov. Hoffman's investigators obtained today.

Alfred Hammond, a crossing watchman for the Reading Railroad, was the eyewitness who implicated the little Jewish furrier now dead. Hammond swore that members of the New Jersey State Police deliberately ignored his sensational identification.

The middle-aged watchman who was guarding the grade crossing at Hollows Corner, approximately a mile from the Lindbergh estate near Hopewell, NJ about the time of the kidnapping on March 1, 1932, declared he first told the authorities of a suspicious car and the occupants immediately after the crime was committed. Following Hauptmann's arrest in the Bronx in September 1934, State Troopers questioned him again, showing him several photographs.

Identified Pictures

"One of the pictures was Isidor Fisch." Hammond declared in a statement now in the Governor's possession. "That was when they showed me a lot of photographs, most of them of Hauptmann in the Barracks at Wilburtha, New Jersey."

"I said that is the man (pointing to the Fisch portrait) who was sitting in the back of the machine." And the State Police detective said, "Nothing doing."

Trooper Ignored Story

Q. Exactly what did the State Trooper say to you when you told him it was Fisch you saw in the back of the car?

A. He said it couldn't be because Fisch died broke in Germany.

Q. What else?

A. The Trooper insisted Fisch couldn't have been implicated in the case. He acted as if he wanted to drop the subject if I couldn't identify Hauptmann's picture.

Hammond was just as positive that Hauptman, awaiting execution the week of March 30 for the murder of Charles Augustus Lindbergh Jr., was not one of the three men in the car.

On eight or nine successive days prior to March 1, 1932, when the baby was stolen from its nursery, the watchman saw the mysterious car. This fact is confirmed by records in the State Police files on the Lindbergh case. Col. H. Norman Schwarzkopf, head of the State Police, admitted today.

Certain It was Fisch

The driver of the mystery car, which Hammond described as a five-passenger sedan of a peculiar bluish-green tint, looked like an Italian. The same man, whom he is sure was Fisch, always rode in the back seat. The car always appeared between 7:30 AM and 8:00 AM in the morning, coming from the Lindbergh estate toward Hopewell, and first attracted his attention because it bore a New York State license.

Note: The above story is complete and identical to that published on Thursday, March 5th, 1936, in the New York Daily News. It reported that Isidor Fisch had been sighted at the Lindbergh kidnap scene the night of the kidnapping (March 1st, 1932). Alfred Hammond, a crossing watchman for the Reading Railroad, was an eyewitness that had seen Fisch and other occupants in a car at Hollows Corners, which is approximately 1 mile from the Lindbergh estate. We suspect that Paul Wendel was one of those other occupants. Paul Wendel had a history with Fisch that included Wendel's being represented before he lost his law license.

Detective Ellis Parker had long suspected that Isidor Fisch was more heavily involved in Charles Lindbergh Jr's kidnapping than the many investigators had believed. We found several letters addressed to the Detective from John Harrington. Harrington was attempting to arrange Fisch's exhumation (in Germany) for Parker to take his fingerprints.

Meanwhile, in the USA, Ellis Parker spoke with several undertakers to determine if it was feasible that Fisch's fingers were preserved enough for accurate results. The opinions were inconclusive.

This information supports our belief that Paul Wendel and Isidor Fisch were handed baby Charles A. Lindbergh Jr. out the front door that night by his father. And it supports our contention that Detective Ellis H. Parker had solved the case with Paul Wendel's confession, the only suspect to ever confess to the crime.

Detective Ellis H. Parker exposed the relationship of many years between Paul Wendel and Isidor Fisch. Detective Parker suspected that Fisch accompanied Wendel to the Lindbergh mansion the night of the crime.

New Jersey Governor Hoffman sought to delay Hauptmann's execution to give Ellis Parker time to investigate Wendel and the Lindbergh case. To combat this, the Grand Jury dropped all charges against Wendel and ordered that the execution of Hauptmann be carried out. Hauptmann was strapped into the Electric chair on April 3, 1936, then eternally silenced. Hauptman was a man that had professed his innocence from the beginning.

At left is the New Jersey Electric chair that took Richard Hauptman's life. It is still displayed at the NJ State Trooper's Museum in Trenton, NJ. A visit to the museum is highly recommended.

Andy Sahol: "*David Wilentz, then the New Jersey Attorney General, his cronies William Clark, John Quinn, Norman Schwarzkopf, and others withheld evidence that would have saved Richard Hauptmann from the electric chair.*"

Ellis and his son, Ellis Jr., were accused of conspiracy to kidnap Paul Wendel and crossing state lines to hold him captive. The irony of this is that when released from his alleged captivity, Paul Wendel asked to be driven to Ellis Parker's home in Mount Holly, thereby crossing over state lines to make it a federal case! The car's driver was Murray Bleefeld, who was later offered a deal to testify against the Parkers to avoid kidnapping charges.

During Wendel's captivity, he signed a 25-page confession to the Lindbergh baby kidnapping and described the body's disposal! So, maybe Ellis Parker did solve the Lindbergh kidnapping? Wendel even implicated his wife and children in the plot! What type of man does that? Subsequently, Wendel recanted his confession to claim that he had been forced to write it under duress. Ellis Sr. and Ellis Jr. were indicted for Wendel's kidnapping and transportation over state lines. New Jersey Judge William Clark presided over the trial. Clark should have recused himself for having a personal relationship with Wendel, but he didn't.

FROM THE ELLIS PARKER LOST FILES

<u>Note</u>: The following letter was written to David Wilentz by Paul Wendel five days after he was released from the State Colony in New Lisbon, NJ, where he had gone willingly to rest at the suggestion of Ellis Parker. We believe that David Wilentz instructed him to write this letter after meeting with him either at the New Lisbon Colony or shortly after being released. The grammar of the letter has not been corrected. It reads exactly as the copy we retain. If you compare this letter and the confessions he wrote, it is hard to believe his torture claims. It reads like a calculating, guilty man looking for a way out after he has confessed the truth. Notice that Wendel is still looking for "The Big Score" of a million dollars. That was always his goal throughout his whole life—the life of an evil con artist.

March 29, 1936

Mr. David Wilentz, Trenton, NJ

Dear sir,

This is to inform you that I knew nothing about the kidnapping and murder of Charles Lindbergh Jr. and was never on the Lindbergh property.

I know nothing about the crime except what I read and heard.

I did sign several false statements, which implicated me. I was forced by torture and brutal treatment In New York, where I was detained from February 14 to February 24, 1936, from that date until today, I was detained by Ellis Parker Jr., at the State Colony at New Lisbon, N.J., under guard, two in the day and extra at night.

I pleaded with Ellis Parker Jr., Dr. Jones to get in touch with the Attorney General of New Jersey, Colonel Schwarzkopf, and Pros. Hauck and I ask if he did not deliver me to the above to return me to Mercer County, he kept telling me that he would act and not before when he got ready. Ellis Parker, who I thought was my friend, tried to tell that Pros. Hauck and Attorney Wilentz would be supersealed (superseded?) by any he would name because Gov. Hoffman assured he would do so, that I was to plead guilty with a lawyer that confession would be used, and I could write a story that I had been out of my mind and suddenly come to and realized what I had done which startle not only the medical but would make me a million dollars and my family could live easy the rest of their life. Parker promised me that the Attorney General Wilentz, Pros. Hauck or Justice Trenchen would not try the case that Governor Hoffman was Governor, and he would appoint anyone Parker asked him to. He said he would appoint Pros. Eastwood and have a special Grand Jury appointed to indict me, and then if it were tried in Hunterdon that he would speak to Judge Robbins about it, and I would get the benefit of it (meaning his friendship with Judge Robins). I knew that Parker was trying to do me harm, so I built up a defense for myself. I could show Pros. Hauck and Attorney General Wilentz just what was going on. I ask for law books, which were brought to me, and I wrote to showing him that Governor Hoffman could not supersede Pros. Hauck or Wilentz. I told Parker that the lie wanted me to plead to something I did not was out of the question. I told him after he had informed that I would plead guilty so that the Court would look ridiculous and make a laughingstock out of Attorney General Wilentz and Col. Schwarzkopf and State Police.

Sg. Paul H. Wendel

H. W. Bradley, Sheriff

Under Sheriff C. J. Milltop

Thomas Conrad, Special Deputy, Mercer County, Trenton, N.J.

<u>Note</u>: On top of this, Paul Wendel had been previously convicted of perjury, was a former mental patient, and was currently a fugitive for several embezzlement counts and the passing of bad checks. Yet, he was the prosecution's star witness against a law officer and public servant with 45 years of exemplary service. It is also unbelievable that Wendel was given luxury accommodations (paid by the prosecution) for months while awaiting the trial.

<u>Andy Sahol</u>: "The irony of this was Paul Wendel, the man whose testimony helped convict my Grand Father would visit him at his Mount Holly house whenever he was in trouble. My mother, her brothers and sisters, and her friends remembered him coming to the door. Wendel accused my grandfather of being the mastermind of a plan to kidnap him and coerce a confession over ten days by torturing him."

FROM THE ELLIS PARKER LOST FILES

DANIEL W. LYONS (U.S. PARDON ATTORNEY) LETTER TO PAUL H. WENDEL REGARDING HIS REQUEST THAT EXECUTIVE CLEMENCY BE GIVEN TO ELLIS H. PARKER DATED ON MAY 5, 1939

The relationship between Ellis Parker and Paul Wendel was complicated. No more significant example of that is finding out that Paul Wendel wrote President Franklin Delano Roosevelt asking him to grant Executive Clemency to Ellis Parker. Daniel M. Lyons (US Pardon Attorney) wrote back to Wendel on May 5th, 1939, advising him "no application for Executive Clemency is pending at this time." Lyon's closed his letter adding, "the contents of your letter have been noted and will, of course, be considered in connection with any action taken on a petition for Executive Clemency."

FROM THE ELLIS PARKER LOST FILES

In Detective Ellis Parker's lost files, we found a 75-page document titled "The Lindbergh-Hauptman Aftermath," written by Paul H. Wendel. It was written to profit from his involvement in the Lindbergh case. The publisher was Loft Publishing. I suspect that there were less than a dozen copies printed. It is near impossible to find an original printing today.

Unfortunately, the copy we found was incomplete and nearly unreadable. Mark W. Falzini, author & archivist for the New Jersey State Police Museum, was kind enough to provide me with another copy. Mark's books on the Lindbergh case and other subjects are highly recommended. The displays and archives he organized at the museum are a must-see if you are reading this book. We consider Mark one of the world's leading experts on the "Crime of the Century." Marks' books on the Lindbergh case and other subjects are highly recommended.

Wendel opens his book by dedicating it to the Honorable Wm. F. X. Geoghan (District Attorney of Kings County) and Francis A. Madden (Assistant District Attorney) and the Law Enforcement Officers who solved the Wendel kidnapping case.

Amazingly, this is a first-person description of Paul H. Wendel's alleged abduction written by himself. It includes a note that places Paul Wendel at the Towers Hotel in Brooklyn, NY. Nowhere are the names of Wm. Geoghan or Francis Madden included or anything about their contribution to solving the Wendel kidnapping case.

In the manuscript, Wendel tells of the many years' relationships with Detective Ellis H. Parker, beginning in 1920 before he details his kidnapping under Parker's direction. Wendel accuses Ellis Parker of performing treacherous deeds to gain wealth, power, and position so that Harold Hoffman could become the Vice-Presidential candidate in the coming election. Wendel suspected that Detective Parker was anxious to replace J. Edgar Hoover as Chief of the Federal Bureau of Investigation after the election. The manuscript contains descriptions of numerous cases that they had collaborated on. Wendel calls their relationship a union and claims that they were equals. Wendel also claimed to have been Parker's legal representative and hired as his investigator for $5000 a year.

Wendel writes that Parker told him that this would be his last case and that the baby's triumphant return would make him famous in retirement.

In the manuscript, Wendel tells a lengthy story claiming that he had gone to Chicago to negotiate with Al Capone's representatives to arrange the Lindbergh child's return to Detective Parker. For the safe return, Detective Parker was allegedly offering a pardon for Al Capone that would be obtained with the help of Charles Lindbergh's father-in-law Dwight W. Morrow. Morrow was a former Ambassador to Mexico, a US Senator, and a partner at J.P. Morgan. He died in 1931 as one of the richest men in New Jersey.

When the possibility of a reward for the baby's return was discussed, Wendel claimed he didn't want a reward.

Wendel will have you believe that he was being sacrificed by his friends Ellis H. Parker Sr., Ellis H. Parker Jr., and Anna Bading (Ellis Parker's assistant) for political gain. Wendel claims that Ellis Parker held him captive until he was forced into confessing to a crime that he did not commit, calling it the vilest fraud in American History. By doing so, Bruno Hauptmann could go free, Ellis Parker could get the credit for solving the Lindbergh case. Ellis's close friend, NJ Governor Harold Hoffman, would increase his chances of becoming President of the United States.

Wendel describes his 15 years of questionable friendship with Ellis Parker beginning in 1920. He tells of assisting Ellis Parker in the Louis Lively case, the John Brunen murder case, and a number of others. His claims of deep involvement and importance in Ellis Parker's successful arrests are ludicrous. Any intelligent individual with knowledge of Wendel's life would laugh at the absurdity of this. Wendel was nothing more than Ellis Parker's stool pigeon and a snitch.

Wendel then, conveniently, begins to tell the story of him warning Ellis Parker that he was violating a suspect's rights that he was holding. How convenient is this, considering that Wendel contends that he was held against his will later by Parker? Wendel describes an occasion where he read a law book to Ellis that defined the accused's rights. Wendel was referring to his claim of false imprisonment and denial of rights. Quite convenient again.

Wendel writes that on the night of the Lindbergh kidnapping, March 1st, 1932, he was in his Laboratory all day and evening, experimenting with gas and heat absorption. Ellis Parker noted that innocent people have difficulty remembering the details of where they were or what they were doing in long past days. The guilty will take the time to fabricate alibis in great detail.

Wendel describes his invention that was to be purchased by the infamous Al Capone. This invention would be capable of turning water into gasoline. It sounds like the proposal of a fool to me. What idiot would purport such a preposterous thing to Al Capone of all the people? Paul Wendel writes that he did!

Wendel also contends that he was attempting to use these contacts to obtain the Lindbergh baby's return. Supposedly Ellis Parker told Wendel, "if you do this, you can get anything you want from Governor Hoffman." Wendel tells of Ellis Parker offering him the cash to purchase the baby. Wendel, a man that can only be described as an opportunist, conniver, and schemer, would have you believe that he turned the opportunity down.

The balance of Wendel's book describes his imprisonment, his plots, and his plans. The description of what he suffered is self-serving, as you would expect. His lengthy explanation and details will bore you to death. In many parts, it reads like a weak attempt at horrible literature or fabricated storytelling.

Much of the manuscript describes Wendel's alleged confinement and torture in New York, designed to force him into a false confession.

He tells of needing the money and then thinking of kidnapping the Lindbergh baby for ransom. The "Crime of the Century" was all his idea. Wendel recalls building the ladder in his basement and tells of his actions on the kidnapping night. It is in detail. He alone wrote and created the Red Circle on the ransom note.

Upon arriving home that night with the Lindbergh baby, Wendel writes of handing it to his wife's arms and his kids' help with baby's care until he could return it for a significant profit. However, while in his family's care, he amazingly blames the baby's death on natural causes. Wendel then tells of burying the baby on Mount Rose Road.

Wendel concludes the manuscript by describing his return to Mount Holly to see Ellis Parker and being lodged at the New Lisbon Four Mile Colony, a State Hospital for feeble males.

The following was reported by The Cattaraugus Republican (New York) on 4-1-1936

Paul Wendel, a 49-year-old former lawyer and druggist and who now lists his business as «salesman," was at the New Lisbon state colony for the feeble-minded for a short time before he was turned over to Mercer County authorities and charged with the Lindbergh murder. The head of the state colony said Wendel came to the hospital with Detective Ellis Parker and signed a paper stating that he was entering «voluntarily" and «treated as a guest."

WHY WAS ELLIS PARKER INDICTED FOR KIDNAPPING PAUL WENDEL?

Detective Ellis H. Parker's troubles began when he started investigating the disappearance of the Lindbergh baby. Charles Lindbergh Jr. was kidnapped in Mercer County, a county where the famous Detective Parker had no jurisdiction.

Note: The Lindbergh property was in 2 New Jersey counties. The front door was in Mercer County, but much of the property was in Hunterdon.

An order was issued by the New Jersey State Police to bring Detective Parker to the Lindbergh home on the night of the kidnapping. For some unknown reason, the order was rescinded before it could be carried out.

When we (the writers of this book) recovered the lost files of Ellis Parker in 2018, we found his feelings about the crime repeated in many of his writings. Ellis Parker wanted only one thing: to recover Charles Lindbergh's son and return him to his parents. Certainly, he wanted to solve the case because he didn't believe that Hauptmann was guilty, but his passion was to reunite a son with his parents. Sadly, he was never able to accomplish that. Even after discovering the supposed baby's body in the woods near the Lindbergh home, Ellis questioned whether the body recovered was that of the Lindbergh child.

Ellis couldn't accept Bruno Richard Hauptmann's guilt after his arrest. At the urging of his close friend, NJ Governor Harold H. Hoffman, elected in 1936, Ellis investigated "The Crime Of The Century," using his and the Governor's' resources.

NJ State Police Director Norman Schwarzkopf, New Jersey Attorney General David T. Wilentz, and Charles Lindbergh himself demanded that Bruno Richard Hauptmann be held accountable for the Lindbergh baby kidnapping and death. They conspired to allow no doubt, organizing a rush to judgment for Hauptmann. They worked to block and discredit every attempt by Detective Parker to continue his investigation using any means available to support their guilty contention without regard to conflicting evidence or reliability. There is every reason to believe that much of the evidence used was fraudulent and contradictive. They viewed Detective Parker as the only threat to the Court's guilty verdict and Bruno Richard Hauptman's subsequent execution. The personal credit heaped upon Wilentz, and Schwarzkopf afterward made them rich and famous. Today, many experts wonder why they had rushed Hauptmann to judgment even after so much conflicting evidence had surfaced.

Hauptmann's arrest and the trial were called "the most bungled police job in history" by Governor Harold Hoffman soon after he dismissed Norman Schwarzkopf from his office with the NJ State Police. Since the Hauptmann trial, numerous authors, journalists, and even the American Bar Association viewed the trial as a media circus. After the trial, the American Bar Association voted to ban cameras from courtrooms. It was the most spectacular and depressing example of improper publicity and professional misconduct ever presented in an American criminal trial. How could you consider this a fair trial for Hauptmann? Especially one the ended with his death penalty. Over the years, a modern consensus has developed that Hauptmann was a "Scapegoat," supported brilliantly by Anthony Scaduto's book of the same name in 1977.

After the execution of Hauptmann, these now powerful men turned their attention to Detective Parker. Parker had to be silenced at any cost, not in the interest of justice, but to protect their newfound celebrity.

Paul Wendel and Detective Parker had a long history described as a professional friendship, but it was on Parker's terms, as he was no fool. The Detective saw him as a source of information, using his underworld contacts to gather information to help solve crimes.

FROM THE ELLIS PARKER LOST FILES

PROFESSOR MUSHROOM SENDS A CANADIAN NATIONAL TELEGRAM TO ELLIS H. PARKER

Someone under Professor Mushroom's alias is reporting to Ellis Parker via a Canadian National Telegram on 4-26-1936. Professor Mushroom informs that he has been searching for John "Scotty" Gow (the chief of the old & new Purple Gang or the M.P.A. as he calls it) and has learned he is still alive. He states that Gow does what he pleases and gets Police protection here and everywhere. The Professor also informs Ellis that he has written 9 or 10 letters to Governor Hoffman and wonders if the Governor has shared them with Ellis.

Note: Paul Wendel communicated with Detective Ellis Parker using the alias of Professor Mushroom on many occasions. This telegram referred to the Purple Gang. The Purple Gang, also known as the Sugar House Gang, was a criminal mob of bootleggers and hijackers with predominantly Jewish members. They operated in Detroit, Michigan, during prohibition in the 1920s. The gang came to be Detroit's dominant criminal gang. Excessive violence and infighting caused the gang to destroy itself in the 1930s. You can't always believe what Paul Wendel tells you, but in this instance, it does bring to light that Wendell was connected to organized crime.

FROM THE ELLIS PARKER LOST FILES

A total of 27 letters or Telegrams were found in Ellis H. Parker's files dated from early March 7, 1932, through November 14, 1935, written by Paul Wendel. The two men remained in constant touch for these years. Wendel's affection for Ellis was apparent as he told Anna Bading to make sure the boss (referencing Ellis) took his medicine. Ellis Parker was also fond of Wendel, and he wrote him in a style as you would to a good friend or relative and describe family outings or fishing trips to him. Wendel was also telegramming Ellis during this period and would make trips to visit Ellis at Mount Holly's office. Wendel became very familiar with the entire Parker family. Because Ellis suspected that his mail was being monitored, Wendel would use aliases. Wendel would use aliases such as Doc, Investigator 48, Paul, Herman, K.7, Dorothy E. Wendel, A, Albert-7, D, and Mrs. W. Wendel. He addressed many of his letters to Ellis Parker's assistant Anna Bading to throw them off. Many of these letters were merely acknowledging that Wendel was investigating issues that dealt with the Lindbergh case or talking with associates about the same issues.

Wendel had many contacts from all walks of life, including organized crime.

Ellis asked Wendel to get information from his contacts to help him find the Lindbergh baby. Again, we see that Ellis Parker's primary focus was to find the baby. Finding the guilty kidnapper was secondary to him. Ellis cared about the baby first.

Ellis began to suspect Wendel when the information he brought to him was beyond the accuracy he expected. Ellis eventually reasoned that Wendel knew way more than he should have. Wendel was incredibly involved in the Lindbergh case leading up to the interrogations that resulted in his confession.

Wendel referred to contacts in Chicago. He did use the word "mobs" in his communications or "Societies." It can be suspected that the Chicago reference was to the organization run by Al Capone. In one letter, Wendel tells of being near to finalizing a deal to have the Lindbergh baby returned. In another letter, Wendel mentions obtaining details about each member of the household. It is most likely that it was the Lindbergh household he referred to. Another letter told of 2 New York men of interest. A very interesting letter talked of Wendel being 90% sure the baby would be returned, providing that a promise of no prosecution would be kept. In another, Wendel wrote, "I am sure the Colonel (Schwarzkopf) will be glad to have known him (Ellis) soon. In another letter, Wendel asked for Ellis Parker Jr. to call him. Later Ellis Jr. would be accused of kidnapping Wendel. In another, Wendel asked for Ellis's help for Morris Perlich. The Grand Jury in New York had recently indicted Perlich, and it may be thought that Wendel was intending to help one of his contacts. Most of Wendel's letters were intentionally vague, and many were addressed to Bading to keep the communications secret. One light moment was when Wendel asked if Ellis was enjoying his new teeth. In some letters, Wendel addressed Ellis as "The Boss." When addressing his letters to Anna Bading, he would infer that Ellis was "your father." Wendel wrote that he "was on the job." It may be that Ellis Parker's letters were more likely to be intercepted by the Hauptman prosecution team's moles. In Wendel's final letter, he asked for a job, possibly with the Highway Department.

Related information: In 1936, Paul Wendel worked for the election of Harold Hoffman. We learned that Wendel often used his son for errands and meetings. On 11-13-1934, Anna Bading sent her condolences to Paul Wendel when learning of his mother's death and his father's injury.

Convicted of perjury, suspected of fraud numerous times, and then disbarred, Paul Wendel had a very poor reputation. Wendel asked Detective Parker for help in getting his law license restored. Unable to accomplish this,

Ellis began to use Wendel as an investigator for some of his cases, including the Lindbergh kidnapping. At some point, Detective Parker realized that Wendel knew too much about the Lindbergh crime to have not been involved. Detective Parker began to suspect that Wendel had participated in the actual crime, the one he was investigating.

Parker then turned his investigation onto Wendel. There is reason to believe that Wendel went to Brooklyn willingly to be questioned after he admitted that he was a crime participant. Ellis promised to use his powerful contacts, along with Governor Hoffman's cooperation, to spare Wendel the jeopardy of a death penalty and possibly shorten his time of imprisonment if he did. Parker may have promised Wendel assistance writing his confession to reduce his exposure to harsh punishment. In his original draft, Wendel admitted holding the baby in his arms when he dropped the infant to his death. He had also included descriptions of his family's role in the kidnapping plot exposing them to arrest and prosecution unnecessarily.

When Ellis Parker presented Paul Wendel's surprising confession to his longtime friend NJ Governor Harold H. Hoffman, the successful Bruno Richard Hauptman prosecuting team was shocked and alarmed. Their newfound celebrity was in jeopardy. The conviction of Hauptmann and his impending execution was placed in great doubt. The Governor immediately ordered a stay of execution so that there would be time to review the Wendel confession given to him by Detective Parker. In the confession, Wendel described his abduction of the Lindbergh baby in great detail.

It should be noted; Paul Wendel signed three separate confessions. These confessions were revised later by Ellis Parker and his assistant Ana Bading to cast Wendel in a more forgiving light and to eliminate any chance that Wendel's family members would be charged as accessories in the Lindbergh baby kidnapping.

·

Andy Sahol: I believe that Paul Wendel was involved in the kidnapping from the very beginning and that his confession was genuine. I believe strongly that Wendel was guilty. My grandfather got his confession, and it was genuine. It was not forced during Wendel's captivity, as claimed by the Prosecution in my grandfather's trial. The confession was withdrawn only because of David Wilentz's intense pressure on Wendel. I was in my thirties when I figured this out. My aunt was still alive then, and she confirmed that none of my family believed what Lindbergh said. I think that Wendel did handle the baby and that he did take it to his house.

After he completed writing his confession, Paul Wendel was ready to leave Brooklyn. He requested that he be driven to meet with Detective Parker at his Mount Holly, NJ home. Wendel considered the Detective, a close friend that could be trusted. After the meeting with Parker, where he revised his confession with Ellis Parker's assistant Ana Bading, Wendel agreed to be taken to the New Lisbon, NJ, 4 Mile facility at Ellis Parker's suggestion for rest and recovery before surrendering himself. Ellis Parker chose the facility because he had several friends working there.

At some point, Prosecutor David Wilentz (also the New Jersey Attorney General) either visited Paul Wendel at the 4 Mile State Colony in New Lisbon, NJ, or at someplace close to it. Wendel admitted that he had agreed to be taken to the 4 Mile facility at Ellis Parker's suggestion after surrendering himself to Detective Parker in Mount Holly and confessing to the Lindbergh baby abduction. The 4 Mile facility accepted disabled, mentally challenged individuals or those that needed behavior modification assistance.

Hauptmann Prosecutor David Wilentz sought out and visited Paul Wendel either when he left the 4 Mile facility or shortly after that. During his approximate 2-hour meeting with Wilentz, Wendel either decided to withdraw his confession to the Lindbergh kidnapping or was convinced by Wilentz to do so. It is only reasonable to suspect that Wilentz promised to release Wendel, which he did, and protect him from future charges as payment for his cooperation. Wendel either claimed, or he was threatened to claim, that he was forcibly imprisoned, beaten, and tortured to write the confession while being held a prisoner in Brooklyn, NY by Ellis Parker Jr., Murray Bleefeld, Martin Schlossman, and Harry Weiss.

<u>Note</u>: Any bruises on Wendel's body (if ever seen) were probably self-inflicted.

There were still open warrants for Wendel at this time. He was never prosecuted, so they most likely disappeared after Wendel agreed to testify against the Parker's.

It is only reasonable to suspect that Wilentz promised to release Wendel and protect him from future charges if he rescinded his confession of the Lindbergh baby kidnapping and testified to his forcible imprisonment by the Parkers. This maneuver by Wilentz sped up the process of executing Hauptman, most likely an innocent man.

THE TRIAL IS SET UP TO BEGIN

ON APRIL 6, 1937, PAUL Wendel's kidnapers, Harry Weiss and Martin Schlossman, were sentenced in New York Federal court to, from 20 years to life, at Sing-Sing prison for their crime. The trial was called a sequel to the recent Lindbergh baby murder case tried in Flemington, NJ. Murray Bleefeld's fate was to be decided at a later date. There was no indication of when that would be.

New Jersey Governor Harold Hoffman had declined to permit the Parkers' extradition for the New York trial. The Parkers, however, were soon to face similar Federal charges in New Jersey. Murray Bleefeld was the third man accused of aiding Detective Ellis H. Parker Sr., his son, Ellis H. Parker Jr., Harry Weiss, and Martin Schlossman in abducting attorney Wendel and extracting from him a false confession to the kidnapping of Colonel Charles A. Lindbergh's son. The Wendel confession had delayed the Bruno Richard Hauptmann execution for three days.

Wendel had been abducted in Manhattan on February 14, 1937. He was then taken to Brooklyn and held until February 24, 1937, against his wishes. There he was allegedly tortured until he confessed to the kidnapping of the Lindbergh baby. He described being transferred from his Brooklyn imprisonment to Detective Parker's home in Mount Holly, NJ. Soon after his release, he repudiated his confession to the kidnapping.

Before sentencing, both Weiss and Schlossman claimed to be innocent.

During the trial, Murray Bleefeld testified that they were all acting under the direct orders of Detective Ellis H. Parker.

Attention now turned to the location of Detective Parker and son, Ellis Jr.'s trial. Both the Prosecution and the Defense argued for the location they deemed most favorable to their case. The Parker defense presented the Federal statute that permits trial in the home county of the accused. Mount Holly was preferred, and a resolution by the Burlington County Board Of Freeholders that was adopted offered the use of the County Courthouse in Mount Holly.

On April 14, 1937, Judge William Clark denied a change of venue motion for the trial of Detective Ellis Parker and his son. The defense had previously argued that the recently enacted Lindbergh law had made the crime punishable by death. A Federal statute ensured that anyone facing the death penalty had the right to be tried in his home county. In this case, Burlington County. The defense motion was a tactical move that failed because the prosecution had already announced that they would not seek the death penalty in Parker's case. Judge Clark ruled that the death penalty could only be relevant if harm had come to the individual held captive according to the new federal law. Judge Clark also pointed out that he could not believe that the defense team realized the consequences of the motion putting the Parkers in danger of the death penalty.

After the threat of having the trial held in Brooklyn or Philadelphia, the defense agreed to have the trial take place in either Trenton or Camden in Burlington County, NJ.

On April 13, 1937, the Philadelphia Circuit Court moved to block the Parker trial in Newark. This was the eighth legal move made to block the trail from Newark. This action opened the way for the trial to be transferred to Mount Holly, Trenton, or Camden. There was a conflict over where most of the incidents described in the case had taken place. Brooklyn or Burlington County?

In a surprise, Parker's attorneys abandoned their opposition to the trial being held in Newark on April 19, 1937.

On April 19, 1937, it was agreed that the trial would commence on April 27, 1937, in Newark, NJ. It was apparent that the Parker attorneys feared that the trial would be held in Brooklyn if they did not capitulate. The Brooklyn trial would be dangerous for the Parkers, and their consent included a demand for a "Bill of Particulars." The defense had served a list of 70 questions to Federal District Attorney John Quinn several weeks before asking him to explain in detail the charges in the indictment. The Parker defense continued to press for the plot data during the following weeks.

On April 26, 1937, Judge William Clark announced that he would preside at Ellis H. Parker's trial. Parker, chief of Burlington County Detectives, his son, and three others are charged with violating the "Lindbergh Law."

THE TRIAL OF DETECTIVE ELLIS H. PARKER

FROM THE ELLIS PARKER LOST FILES

ON ELLIS PARKER'S DEMEANOR AT TRIAL, PROTECTING GOVERNOR HOFFMAN

Ellis Parker purposely discounted Governor Harold Hoffman's role at trial. He stated that he did not name Paul Wendel to the Governor to protect him when reporting the confession. Parker and Hoffman's relationship went back for many years. They were fast friends. Their friendship was important to Ellis. Hoffman had spoken at the 1934 Testimonial Dinner organized to honor Detective Ellis Parker's career held at the Log Cabin Lodge in Medford Lakes, NJ. One of Ellis Parker's greatest strengths was that he was loyal and kind to his friends.

A trial of this nature is often a battle of wits. Defense and Prosecution lawyers attempt to trick witnesses into mistakes. It is a chess match. Ellis was thoughtful and deliberate when his turn came. He was up to the task. He balked at many questions. His answers were often non-committal, like: "I didn't check that." and "No, sir. I was perplexed about what to do." In addition to: "I wasn't impressed. I don't know why. As far as actual work is concerned, I didn't do much."

His best response was: "This was an awful predicament. I didn't want to do what was wrong; I wanted to do what was right."

Note: This information was from an unidentified newspaper clipping found in Ellis Parker's Lost Files.

FROM THE ELLIS PARKER LOST FILES

FUGITIVE WARRANT ISSUED TO ARREST DETECTIVE ELLIS H. PARKER

Ellis Parker was arrested on a Fugitive Warrant issued by the Kings County New York Grand Jury. The warrant was issued by District Attorney William F. X. Geoghan (of Brooklyn) after an indictment of Ellis Parker for Paul H. Wendel's kidnapping. Wendel was a disbarred Trenton, NJ Lawyer.

Wendel's "confession" was responsible for the delay in the execution of Bruno Richard Hauptmann. Wendel's confession was later repudiated.

Detective Parker was sitting on the Mount Holly Elk's Home porch when Louis Bornham of the New Jersey State Police Detective Bureau served him. Assistant District Attorney Francis A. Madden of Brooklyn accompanied him.

Ellis, with his Attorney, James Mercer Davis Sr. demanded his constitutional right of being taken before the nearest Justice of Peace, which, in this instance, was John Throckmorton of Mount Holly. Throckmorton fixed bail at $500, which Ellis paid himself.

District Attorney William F. X. Geoghan said he would prepare extradition papers at once, but that action would be delayed until Governor Harold Hoffman returned from the Republican National Convention in Cleveland.

Ellis Parker Jr. was also under indictment on the same charge and was a fugitive from justice.

<u>Note</u>: The above was taken from a newspaper clipping found in the Ellis Parker Lost Files. Ellis knew the arrest was coming that day. He had his attorney with him when he was served.

At right is Ellis Parker and Anna Bading arriving for court in Newark, New Jersey.

<u>Andy Sahol</u>: *"My Grandfather and my uncle (Ellis Jr.) were tried in Newark, NJ, by Judge William Clark. Grandfather's lawyers had argued unsuccessfully for a change of venue to the place of the so-called crime, Mount Holly, NJ, as was the common practice. The trial incredibly saw over 250 witnesses called, most of them sympathetic to my grandfather, his brilliant law enforcement career, and his service to the public. At sentencing, Judge Clark spoke out against the practice of presenting character witnesses, particularly public officials. He felt the defenses' purpose was to influence the jury as if Ellis Parker's amazing life and career no longer mattered."*

At left is Ellis Parker Jr. with his father, Ellis Parker Sr. sitting on the Mount Holly, NJ courthouse steps.

Ace Detective Parker and his son, Ellis Parker Jr., were convicted in Judge William Clark's court. Ellis, Sr. was sentenced to a six-year term. Ellis Jr. was sentenced to a 3-year term. They were both sent to serve their time at the Lewisburg, PA Federal Penitentiary on June 30, 1937. Detective Parker, now close to his 67th birthday, was in rapidly failing health due to the trial's strain and seeing his family fortune spent to finance his defense.

Andy Sahol on Judge Clark being biased st Ellis Parker's sentencing: "One of the tragedies here, which is shown by my grandfather's trail, is that Judge Clark was biased against him. First of all, Judge Clark should have been recused for 3 or 4 different reasons. One of the saddest things was when the defense wanted to present Doctor Longsdorf (Ellis's physician) for his medical testimony. Judge Clark refused, saying, "Ellis Parkers' health had nothing to do with the crime." Can you imagine that today?"

At Left is famed Detective Ellis Parker with grandson William Fullerton at one of the shore properties that he was forced to sell off to finance his defense.

Andy Sahol: "When my grandfather went to prison, my uncle Eddie became the house's head at only 18 years of age. The trial had put my family's two breadwinners in jail, my grandfather and my uncle, Ellis Jr. It gets you sick to your stomach. They lost everything. My parents and the other family members had to take care of my Grandmother because she suddenly had no income. Everything had been spent on her husband's defense. Ellis Parker put over 40 years of service in, risks his life, and they take everything from him. That's the *sickening part of the story. That's what I am angry about, what they did, they crucified him, to put it mildly.*

The Judge presiding at my grandfather's trial, Judge Clark, was cruel and vicious. Along with NJ Attorney General David Wilentz, they robbed him of everything. Wilentz did not want my grandfather on the Street, so when Judge Clark read the sentencing, it reads like he was a mass murderer or serial killer. You must look at that carefully and put it into context. It shows that Clark was prejudice towards my grandfather. Judge Clark chastised my grandfather at the sentencing, suggesting that my grandfather took advantage of his position. My Grandfather was as unselfish and as honest a man as you could ever meet. If anything, it was Judge Clark and NJ State Attorney General David Wilentz taking advantage of him.

I cannot prove that Attorney General David Wilentz or Judge Clark knew that my grandfather was slowly dying during his trial. Still, Clark would not allow medical testimony about his condition. He said it was not relevant. His erratic behavior was noticed yet never investigated.

I hired a forensic expert in 2006 to give testimony and report to me on this, it cost me a lot of money, but I did confirm that he had the disease, thrombosis of the right hemisphere, and slowly destroying him before the trial. His condition was not acknowledged during the trial. They wanted my Grandfather jailed and silenced so that he could never dispute the execution of Bruno Richard Hauptmann. The court should have been told of my Grandfather's illness; if it had been, I doubt his trial would have been continued. They prosecuted a defenseless man, a man that should have been in a hospital instead of a courtroom. My Grandfather was finally diagnosed with his disease at the Lewisburg Penitentiary, where he was incarcerated after the guilty verdict. It is on his death certificate, although it was too late. The conviction was based on a recently enacted law, a law passed to deter children's kidnapping as a direct result of the Lindbergh case. Not criminals with lengthy rap sheets like Paul Wendel. The injustice is a stain on America. My Grandfather was later found to have a cerebral thrombosis on the right side of his brain. It was responsible for his decline.

I (and Forensic Phycology experts) believe it affected his judgment and that it should have been taken into account by the authorities. I'm angry at the way it was handled. My Grandfather's condition was not allowed to come out during the trial or sentencing by those running it. They blocked it. Even after the trial, when a pardon was proposed, the same individuals fought it. They wanted assurances that he was dying first. What were they afraid of? My grandfather had become increasingly childlike and insecure during his final years. He lost his photographic memory, and other county workers were compensating for him. He was rambling and argumentative when he had always been calm, collected, and precise. He met every criterion of diminished capacity. He should have never been tried. None of us are the same when reaching his stage of life. God forbid that anyone suffers from dementia, but it is a very common medical condition that strikes with no mercy. Should we forget that individual's contribution to law enforcement and society?"

FROM THE ELLIS PARKER LOST FILES

7-17-1939

From: Ellis H. Parker

To: Cora E. Parker, 509 Garden St., Mount Holly NJ

Note: Ellis Parker wrote this letter to his wife Cora from the Lewisburg, PA Prison, about 7 months before his death. In the letter, Ellis longed for his home and his family. He expressed comforting words to his family. It is apparent that Ellis was still well enough to manage his affairs.

Dear Wife,

I received a letter from Charlotte and Edward and was awfully glad to hear everyone is okay. Tell Ed to keep the junkman outside of the place at the Bay, as I don't want anything taken from there.

Tell Lew McFarland we both want to be remembered to him, Clara, and all the rest, and if the time ever comes when he can visit us, I will notify you, and you can tell him. Ed also sees Pat Dolan and tell him I still consider the Dolan family among my best friends.

On Saturday morning, I was sent to the office to sign the note. I am willing to sign power of attorney to mama, Anna, or anyone if you think it is necessary to expedite affairs, so you can have the papers made up and send them, and I will sign and return them.

Thursday, Friday, and Saturday of last week, I was off my food, and I felt bad, but I feel a great deal better this morning.

Yesterday I slipped and wrenched my knee, and I am limping this morning. Now don't forget, you, Ed, and Charlotte write as often as you can tell us all that is going on. I see by the press, Cain has returned from the West.

Thank Hannah for us and tell her she has got to attend to my affairs until I return. I read about Marshall winning and I know what that means to her. Tell her to write to Harry Green, our lawyer, and tell him we are waiting for him every day. Tell Harry to remember us to his force and Mike and Bill and tell Hannah keep you posted how things are going, and you let us know.

If Anna or little Herman make any big fish catches, why just throw them down for us. I will close with a prayer for all, and may God bless everyone.

From your husband,
Ellis H. Parker, # 8735

FROM THE ELLIS PARKER LOST FILES

ELLIS PARKER'S LETTER OF 7-4-1939 TO HIS WIFE CORA PARKER FROM LEWISBURG PENITENTIARY

Ellis enjoyed communicating with his family and friends while he was incarcerated at the Lewisburg Penitentiary. When writing home, he took the time to express his concern for Cora, the children, and his pets. He worried about the long trip Cora would have to endure when visiting. "I would be worried more if I knew you were coming than if you stayed home." He asked Cora to kiss all the children for him, and he spoke of missing his mother's rice pudding and pies. "He closed with, "We remain, praying nothing will happen until we are reunited again."

Before he took a turn for the worse, Ellis Parker was visited by Mount Holly city clerk Clay W. Reesman, a longtime family friend. Ellis told Clay, "I hold no bitterness in my heart against anyone, and I still hold steadfast faith in God. Once we get out of here, we intend to forget this whole affair and discuss it with no one. "As they left, Ellis shouted to Mrs. Reesman, "Be sure and call Mom. Tell her I am all right."

Many friends, luminaries, politicians, and law enforcement officers of the era convinced of Ellis's and his son's innocence pleaded to President Franklin Delano Roosevelt for clemency. Over 8000 persons signed the petition. Unfortunately, before mercy could be put in motion, Detective Parker died behind bars at Lewisburg 6 months later, on February 4, 1940.

At right are the flowers placed on his grave by hundreds of the people who turned out for Ellis's burial ceremony to honor his life. Cora was reunited with her husband in 1967.

Dave Kimball-VP of the historic Burlington County Prison Museum Association: "When Ellis Parker died, the New York Times ran an obituary on him, and they don't run obits on County Sheriffs."

Courier-Post newspaper obituary: "It was an inglorious end to the most brilliant career in crime-detection history, outside the annals of fiction."

Andy Sahol: "My grandfather passed away on February 4th, 1940. I never had a chance to know him. I was not even two years old when he died. I regret not knowing him. Now at 80 years old, I am sometimes depressed due to my sadness when I think about my grandfather and my mother."

On the left is the grave of Detective Ellis Parker and his wife Cora in Mount Holly, NJ. Cora was reunited with her husband in 1967.

At left is the gravestone of Ellis Parker's loyal assistant Anna (Yoos) Bading. She lived a long and productive life. Her contribution to Detective Parker's success was enormous. Anna was buried in 1972 next to her husband, Herman Bading. Herman spent some time working for Ellis Parker and later as a New Jersey State Trooper.

Anna Bading on Ellis H. Parker and the strength of his many friends: "An officer never becomes bigger than his friends make him. Without friends, he soon strikes his level."

Andy Sahol: "I don't know the names of all the people that worked for my grandfather. I wish I did. I am sure they were very competent. My Grandfather's success was due to their support. I have read that the people that worked with him and for him told great stories about him. He was respected and looked up to. I think I take after him. We are both prone to cluttering. He was competent and meticulous with a steel-trap memory from the start of his career. My mother told me he was calm yet boisterous, when need be, depending on the circumstances. I liked to call him Pop. All his siblings affectionally called him that. He was such a loving and caring person. He helped everyone he could during the depression. My Grandfather had built and sold houses in a disadvantaged section of Mount Holly. He held the mortgages. Instead of demanding payment, he told my uncle Eddie and Ellis Jr. to find ways to help them. To me, this is one of the things that make me the proudest of my grandfather. Not the many cases but the fact that he was a good person and loved people."

A PETITION TO ASK FOR THE POSTHUMOUS OVERTURN OF ELLIS H. PARKER'S CONVICTION OR AN EXECUTIVE CLEMENCY (POSTHUMOUS PARDON)

On February 7, 1940, a final heart-wrenching letter arrived at the White House:

My Dear Mr. President:

Just recently, I wrote to you, asking executive clemency in the case of Ellis H. Parker, Senior, of this town. The Supreme Being, in all his infinite mercy (sic), has relieved you from that responsibility. Mister Parker passed away in the Eastern Federal Penitentiary at Lewisburg, Pa: this very morning.

Yours Truly,
Robert F. Myers
Mount Holly, NJ

Before Ellis Parker's death (in 1940), petitions were started by his friends and admirers asking for an executive pardon or clemency. One of the petitions was estimated to contain 6500 signatures. Just before Ellis's death, letters and telegrams rained down on the White House beseeching President Franklin D. Roosevelt to pardon Chief of Detectives, Ellis H. Parker, Sr. from such notables as:

Senator William H. Smathers

Colonel Mark O. Kimberly, Superintendent, New Jersey State Police

Robert Peacock, Assistant Attorney General Of New Jersey

Commissioner George DeB. Kein, The Port Of New York Authority

Howard Eastwood, Prosecutor of the Pleas of Burlington County, New Jersey

Samuel Borden, The Farmers Trust Company

George B. Bitting, Surrogate, Burlington County's Surrogate Office

Joseph G. Buch, Chairman, Crippled Children Commission

Rudolph Thielen, Imperial Detective Bureau

County Detective Benevolent Association Of New Jersey

The New Jersey State Assembly of County Detectives

Major Clifford R. Powell, Forty-Fourth Division, Trento

Robert Turner, President, Mechanics National Bank of Burlington

Dr. Harold E. Longsdorf, Superintendent, Mount Holly Mental Hospital

John B. and Dorothy Roe Lewis, Publishers, Daily Enterprise

Hon. Frank A Hendrickson, Judge, Burlington Co. Common Pleases Court

Charles C. Hansbury, Editor, The Mount Holly Harold

Russell M. Stoddard, Mount Holly Coroner

Alvin D. Sweeney, Structural Trades Alliance of Burlington County

Walter I. Dill, Vice President, Union National Bank and Trust Company

Francis H. Reed, Jury Commissioner, Burlington County

F. Geo. Furth, Sherriff, Burlington County

Frank M. Ryan, Managing Editor, Courier-Post Newspapers

S. I. Newhouse, President & Publisher, The Newark Ledger

This list of above notable law enforcement, judicial, media, financial leaders and others, reflects the respect and admiration those who had dealt with Ellis H. Parker had for him. Ellis was a life well-lived. His contribution to the development of law enforcement, criminal pursuit and capture, and criminal prosecution was un-measurable. He should be acknowledged and honored for this.

According to a New York Times article that appeared the day after Ellis Parker's death, Judge Clark (presiding Judge at Ellis's criminal trial) had vowed, "…if a legal precedent could be found for a posthumous pardon, he would give consideration to a recommendation for it." Prosecutor Quinn concurred. He, too, would recommend the posthumous pardon.

FROM THE ELLIS PARKER LOST FILES

In the February 6, 1960, edition of **The Levittown Times newspaper,** Mrs. Anna Bading talked about working with Detective Ellis H. Parker when announcing her retirement after 41 years of service. Although remembered as his secretary, she could be described as the fictional Doctor Watson to his Sherlock Holmes. This newspaper clip was found in the Lost Files of Ellis Parker. It must have been placed there by someone who was in possession of the files at that time.

"BALD EAGLE OF THE PINES" RECALLED BY THE SECRETARY WHO WILL RETIRE SOON

Anna described Ellis Parker as a great detective because he understood human nature. In addition, he possessed a keen understanding of the people around him and the criminal mind's workings. Mrs. Bading continued to note that Detective Parker excelled as a sleuth because he always was on the alert mentally and physically even when he sat for hours at his desk. She remembered that he would sit at that cluttered desk for hours, drawing on one of his pipes, staring at a mall spot on the wall. Mrs. Bading stated that she started working for Detective Parker in December of 1919. I was with him until the day he left to enter the federal penitentiary at Lewisburg, PA, where he would die on February 4, 1940, of a brain tumor. Anna described Ellis Parker as a short bald man, usually wearing a coat or a tie. He spoke with a twang like many of Burlington Counties Pine Barron natives. He smoked that same strong-smelling pipe every day.

"He would use colorful words and phrases even when he wasn't angry!" she chuckled. Despite everything, she asserted he was a soft-hearted person who believed in actual rehabilitation of criminals. He would seek pardons and paroles for criminals he had been instrumental in convicting. Countless times he saved misguided youth from jail sentences. Before his ill-fated role in the Lindbergh case, detective Parker would receive an average of 4000 case reports a year, leading to almost 1000 cases investigated each year.

Ellis was a shrewd and tenacious sifter of fact, rumor, and clues while on the case. He often resorted to a homespun brand of psychology. He managed to look like a typical motion picture version of the slow-moving, bungling, County police official. But appearances can be deceptive, as many found out.

He thought faster than many criminals. That is why so many police officials made the trip to Mount Holly from all parts of the world. He once solved a murder case in California by reading correspondence from the West Coast police and also from officials in Greece where the suspected slayer had fled.

Ellis possessed a deep sense of fair play as was attested to by convicted Rufus Jackson, a murderer, who on his way to the gallows, told Ellis, "I will be dead in two minutes. You have been fair to me."

Ellis was always interested in keeping friends. He performed favors for the influential and the "man on the street" without regard to position.

"An officer never becomes any bigger than his friends make him," he once said. "And without friends, he soon strikes his level. To have the people's confidence, this is the most viable asset an officer can have."

Had he lived longer, he would have spent the days with his large family, and Ellis would have chatted with "the boys" at the Elks club, where he was a daily visitor.

Ellis H. Parker Jr. was paroled on October 17, 1941, after serving two years of confinement. He was granted a full pardon on January 30, 1947, by President Harry Truman. But sadly, it was too late for Ellis H. Parker Sr. who had died in 1940 after exhausting his savings, selling his properties, and all his investments to finance his defense. His descendants are suffering this loss to this very day.

This 2006 book, written by John Reisinger, was instrumental in creating an explosion of interest in Ellis Parker. "Master Detective, the life and crimes of Ellis Parker, America's Real-Life Sherlock Holmes" is an excellent source of information for anyone who wants to expand their knowledge of Ellis's life. However, we must caution you that Reisinger's book talks about the Lindbergh baby case in detail. His book is far from the definitive look at the case or of Ellis Parker's life. We disagree with his conclusion that Ellis was "A Good Man Gone Bad." Or that Ellis had committed any crimes. Mr. Reisinger has sided with the public record, but we believe it will be proven to be a flawed record.

Andy Sahol: _"John Reisinger came to me, and I gave him a lot of material for Master Detective. He brought his wife Barbara to my home in Roebling, NJ. They are charming people. I don't think that John did all the research that he should have. His work reflected the opinions of those times when the crime occurred. Most of the modern books conclude otherwise. I lent him my copy of the Cunning Mulatto and some other books. He had never seen the Cunning Mulatto before. I wanted him to help bring my grandfather's life to light. I was hurt when he portrayed my grandfather as a flawed man. But I was happy when the book was published because it did bring my grandfather's life into modern times. It generated a lot of interest in his career and his place in history and has given me a chance to right the misconceptions."_

OPINION: How sad is it that John Reisinger (author of The Master Detective) said he visited the Mount Holly Courthouse, and no one in the Court House knew where the great detective's office was located or had ever heard of him? By now, you know that Ellis H. Parker was known as America's Sherlock Holmes and should be remembered as possibly America's greatest Detective of all time. Parker's participation in the Charles Lindbergh baby kidnapping case was his downfall and led to his unjust imprisonment. The public has since forgotten about his nearly 50 years of exemplary service, which we intend to correct with this book. What a shame that DNA was not available at that time. Bruno Hauptmann would have lived a long life, and Ellis Parker would have had a statue erected in Mount Holly to honor him. Most importantly, Ellis Parker would have died peacefully surrounded by his family instead of in Federal prison.

There were many reasons to expedite the death of Richard Hauptman for the Lindbergh kidnapping. Reputations and future promotions would go to those men that accomplished it. Their haste is suspicious. Richard Hauptman must have had help if he was involved. A quick end to the case was necessary to favor the reputations of those that apprehended him. Ellis Parker did not believe that Hauptman acted alone. This made Ellis very unpopular with those that wanted swift justice and wanted to enhance the standing and reputation of those who had high political ambitions. Appointment to high offices was at stake. Was there a conspiracy to keep Ellis in prison as long as possible? It seems that a pardon would only be considered if there was proof that Ellis was terminal.

When Ellis was tried for transporting Paul Wendel over state lines, the chief prosecution witness was the previously mentioned Paul Wendel, a disbarred NJ lawyer, and career criminal. In his confession, he told of witnessing the Lindbergh child's death. Amazingly, the judge at Ellis Parker's trial (judge Clark) was acquainted with Paul Wendel, his father, and his family. Surprisingly he did not recuse himself from the case. Paul Wendel's entire life was full of poor decisions. Mr. Wendel had been previously convicted of perjury and had spent time in the NJ State Hospital for the Criminally Insane. He also had outstanding warrants for fraud, embezzlement, and passing of bad checks. The warrants were still outstanding while he testified before the court that was deciding Ellis's fate. It is possible that he was promised immunity for his cooperation and testimony.

Andy Sahol, on his Grandfather's Jury Selection: "The Jury selection I believe was illegal. For instance, Lawyers for Paul Wendel and Murray Bleefield were on jury selection for my grandfather's trial. How is that?"

For many frustrating years, the Parker family has been requesting that Ellis H. Parker receives a posthumous pardon like his son, Ellis H. Parker Jr., did. We now believe that Ellis H. Parker's conviction should be vacated instead of pardoned. We want to see this happen soon for Ellis Parker's grandson Andy Sohal and the entire Parker family. Andy has been working passionately to see justice done for many years. This burden weighs heavily on him and all of Ellis's descendants. It is a tragedy that Ellis H. Parker is not remembered and celebrated as one of the United States' most significant law enforcement officers. In 1937 the then Prosecutor of Burlington County, Howard Eastwood, removed Ellis Parker from his county detective's long-time job. After Ellis's conviction, he said, "His unusual career as an enforcement officer merits recognition as does his 40 years of loyal and devoted service to Mt. Holly and Burlington County."

Andy Sahol: "What happened to my grandfather is simple to understand. Who among us has not experienced sorrow, pain, or suffering when another individual with a sinister goal deliberately pursues it at our expense? He should be honored; It's my goal to free him completely. Not just have him pardoned but put on a pedestal where he belongs."

FROM THE ELLIS PARKER LOST FILES

Note: The following letter was mailed by Robert R. Bryan, a lawyer representing the widow of Richard Hauptmann (Anna Hauptmann), to Lillian Sahol, daughter of Detective Ellis H. Parker, on January 14, 1985. It was sent many years too late to help her husband, Bruno Richard Hauptmann, or Detective Ellis H. Parker. The American Public and the media had found the conviction of Bruno Richard Hauptmann questionable. The consensus was now convinced that Hauptmann was a "Scapegoat," just as writer Anthony Scaduto claimed in his brilliant book of the same title.

Robert R. Bryan

2169 Union Street

San Francisco, California 94123

415-563-1211

1-14-1985

Mrs. Lillian Sahol

21 - 7th Avenue, Roebling, NJ 08554

Dear Mrs. Sahol:

As you may be aware, I represent Mrs. Anna Hauptmann, the 86-year-old widow of Richard Hauptmann. She was executed in 1936 for the Alleged murder of Charles A. Lindbergh, Jr. My 13-year investigation, including the review of over 200,000 pages of previously suppressed governmental documents, establishes that the authorities knowingly prosecuted an innocent man. Truly the "Trial of the Century'; was one of the greatest judicial frauds in the history of American jurisprudence. Consequently, we are in litigation to right this terrible wrong.

Recently I have been contacted by several people in New Jersey regarding your late father, Mr. Ellis H. Parker. As a consequence, I have reviewed that aspect of the case and remain convinced that his conviction was a gross miscarriage of justice. Mrs. Hauptmann remembers Mr. Parker as being an unusually fine, honest, and kind person. It would be nice if, during the course of our efforts to exonerate Mr. Hauptmann, that your father's name is also cleared.

I certainly am most interested in any helpful material and comments you might have.

Your understanding will be appreciated.

Yours very truly,

Robert R. Bryan

cc: Mrs. Anna Hauptmann

THE ELLIS H. PARKER BIOGRAPHY

PART TWO:
THE LOST FILES

THE "LOST FILES OF ELLIS Parker" were recovered by Ellis Parker's grandson, Andy Sahol, in 2017. They are important historical artifacts. The long-believed destroyed letters had been missing for over 80 years. Written between 1932 and 1940, the letters tell the Lindbergh baby kidnapping story, often called "The Crime of the Century" by the countless Americans who were inspired to write him. They are placed in loose chronological order here to read like a novel dramatizing the case's issues. The grammar was not cleaned up or corrected.

American grammar and writing were much different in the 1930s. Considerably fewer words were used, and grammar often took a back seat to correctness. A few times I made grammar corrections to the text when it was not readable or understandable. Many of the letters were typed onion skin copies. Because of age, these letters would crumble in your hands. They were not legible when photographed, so they are reproduced here. Thankfully, most of the letters could be read.

It was often necessary to repeat information in our notes to explain the conclusions reached in these outstanding long-lost letters.

ABOUT THE ELLIS PARKER LOST FILES

An Explanation of the recovery of Detective Ellis H. Parker letters and papers in 2017

Additional information found in these files is not meant to lead our reader to a new conclusion about the "Crime of the Century." That has been done in countless books and millions of sites online. Ellis Parker's letters and files are important because they represent information that he felt was necessary to save for later research or investigation. Legendary Detective Ellis

H. Parker was known to leave no stone unturned, and he was well organized. He self-taught himself to be a thorough and complete investigator during his brilliant career. That and his distinguished record of conviction was the reason he becomes known as "America's Sherlock Holmes" and "The Sly Fox."

The letters found in the Lost Files are not validated in any way. We can only tell you that Ellis Parker saved them, indicating that he was interested in preserving them. Some of the information presented by those writing to Detective Parker is ridiculous, but some are very thought-provoking. I have attempted to research some of the allegations when possible. The American public was invested and passionate about the Lindbergh case. That is why it became the "Crime of the Century." You can sense that in these letters.

Only letters of significance have been reviewed here. Ellis Parker received many others of support and personal nature. Many were written to support him during a time of injustice (his arrest and trial). They wrote to condemn and to praise him for imprisoning Paul Wendel. Some included resumes and offers of assistance for payment.

One persistent writer, Beatrice Potter, of Worcester, Mass, wrote Ellis often with theories on the Lindbergh case and others. She enclosed countless newspaper clippings relating to these other matters of interest and the Lindbergh case.

Following are some loose notes that were included in the lost files we found:

- Isidor Fisch was accused of laundering money for bootleggers with the assistance of Richard Hauptmann.

- A prediction that the kidnapped baby could not have died on the night of March 1, 1932, because the stars and moon were not aligned correctly, but it was not a good night for babies.

- That Violet Sharpe's sister was working at the McCabe Apartments in Englewood, NJ that night in easy communication with each other.

- Lindbergh wouldn't allow his servants to be questioned. They were English and very loyal.

- A statement that The New Jersey police have to have a witness and Attorney General David Wilentz must win the Hauptmann case.

- That the real culprit can be discovered by finding the bootleggers that were Isidor Fisch's companions.

- That Richard Hauptmann loved money.

- That it wouldn't have cost much to keep Hauptmann in jail for another year instead of executing him while there were still doubts.

- That the bootleggers warned Richard Hauptmann that his wife and baby would die if he told the real story.

- That Richard Hauptmann was very affectionate with his wife and son.

- Richard Hauptmann was told that the whole USA Government couldn't keep them alive if he tells.

- 9-8-1936 letter marked from Irving Green, son of W. Jones. The writer wanted Ellis to identify the man in Room # 221 of the Pennsylvania Hotel in NYC that had occupied the room on January 4 through 7, 1936.

- On 12-8-1935, Ellis received a letter from the Secret Society for Justice Cleveland. Ellis was warned that if he was the means of freeing Hauptmann from the chair, your scalp will be taken. Hauptmann is guilty and should die for his crime.

- On 1-27-1935, George E. Flemming of New York City wrote to tell Ellis Parker that he had a way of returning pardon power to the Governor of New Jersey, giving him the ability to spare Hauptmann.

*These and other stories follow in **THE ELLIS PARKER LOST FILES***

PAUL H. WENDEL & HAROLD H. HOFFMAN SECTION OF THE ELLIS PARKER LOST FILES

<u>Note</u>: The following section of the **ELIS PARKER LOST FILES** concentrates on the two most important personalities in Detective Parker's investigation of the Lindbergh kidnapping.

<u>Paul H. Wendel</u>: Who confessed and signed his confession to the kidnapping of the Lindbergh baby. Wendel was for many years associated with Ellis Parker as an investigator and confident. Eventually, Ellis realized that he knew too much to be innocent of the crime.

<u>New Jersey Governor Harold G. Hoffman</u>: Was a lifetime friend and ally of Ellis before and after his election to office. The relationship went back many years to begin when the Governor was a child. Ellis and Governor Hoffman's father were close friends.

PAUL WENDEL SECTION
PAUL WENDEL'S LETTERS, 1932 TO 1935

A total of 27 letters or Telegrams were found in Ellis H. Parker's personal files dated from early March 7th of 1932 through November 14th, 1935. The two remained in constant touch for these three years. Paul H. Wendel wrote them. Wendel's affection for Ellis was apparent as he told Anna Bading to make sure the boss (Ellis) took his medicine. Ellis Parker was also fond of Wendel, and he wrote him in a style as you would to a close friend or relative and describe family outings or fishing trips to him.

Wendel was also telegramming Ellis during this period and would make trips to visit Ellis at Mount Holly's office. Wendel became very familiar with the Parker family. When communicating with Ellis, Wendel would use aliases such as Doc, Investigator 48, Paul, Herman, K.7, Dorothy E. Wendel, A, Albert-7, D, and Mrs. W. Wendel addressed a good number of these letters to Ellis Parker's assistant Anna Bading. Many of these letters were merely an acknowledgment.

Wendel was investigating issues that dealt with the Lindbergh case or talking with his associates about the same problems. Wendel referred to contacts in Chicago. He did use the word "mobs" in his communications or "Societies." It can be suspected that the Chicago reference was to the organization run by Al Capone. In one letter, Wendel tells of being near to finalizing a deal to have the Lindbergh baby returned. One letter mentioned obtaining details about each member of the household. It is most likely that it was the Lindbergh household being referred to.

Another note told of 2 New York men of interest. A very interesting letter talked of Wendel being 90% sure the baby would be returned, providing a promise of no prosecution was kept. In another, Wendel wrote, "I am sure the Colonel (Schwarzkopf) will be glad to have known him (Ellis) soon. In another letter, Wendel asked for Ellis Parker Jr. to call him. Later Ellis Jr. would be accused of kidnapping Wendel. In another, Wendel asked for Ellis's help for Morris Perlitch. The Grand Jury in New York had recently indicted Perlitch, and it may be thought that Wendel was intending to help one of his contacts. Most of Wendel's letters were intentionally vague, and many were addressed to Bading to keep the communications secret. One light moment was when Wendel asked if Ellis was enjoying his new teeth.

In some letters, Wendel addressed Ellis as "The Boss." When addressing his letters to Anna Bading, he would infer that Ellis was "your father." Wendel noted that he "was on the job." It may be that Ellis Parker's letters were more likely to be intercepted by moles of the Hauptman prosecution team. In Wendel's final letter, he asked for a job, possibly with the Highway Department.

Wendel worked for the election of Harold Hoffman. Wendel used his son for errands and meetings.

Note: On 11-13-1934, Anna Bading sent her condolences on Wendel's mother's death and his father's injury.

FROM THE ELLIS PARKER LOST FILES

Paul Wendel (alias Paul Wendler) History of Bounced Checks

In Ellis Parker's files, we found a document listing 44 checks that bounced in 1932 and 1933, totaling $5263.07.

Information obtained by inquiry at the Cheltenham National Bank, Cheltenham, PA., through Harold S. Ashworth, concerning a man giving Paul H. Wendler's name, supposed to be Paul H. Wendel, of bad checks that had been passed by the said Wendler and came through this bank.

The account was opened on June 12, 1932. Paul Wendler put a note through Cheltenham National Bank for $190.00 and skipped out September 15, 1932, opened an account for $430.00

Note: The fact that Ellis Parker retained this information in his files indicated that Ellis knew exactly what he was dealing with regarding Paul Wendel. Wendel never fooled Ellis, nor did Ellis ever wholly trust him.

FROM THE ELLIS PARKER LOST FILES

THE LABOR NEWS
TRENTON NEW JERSEY
WENDEL IN LUXURY WHILE VICTIMS SUFFER

The Trenton newspaper "The Labor News," on October 22, 1936, ran an article titled "Wendel In Luxury While Victims Suffer." The article told that Paul Wendel Jr. (the son) attempted to satisfy the victims of his father's embezzlement indictments with an offer of $250 to each. He told them, some living in poverty, that he doubted they would be seeing any funds from their case and would be wise to take his offer. His father, Paul Wendel Sr., was still living on the state of New Jersey since his testimony during the Lindbergh and Parker trials.

The country was startled by the confession that Ellis Parker obtained as Hauptmann's execution drew near. Wendel then claimed that he had been kidnapped and that his confession had been forced.

Ellis Parker was arrested and then tried, along with his son Ellis Parker Jr. in the United States Federal Courts (Newark, NJ) for conspiracy. At the trial, Wendel claimed that the confessions (there were 3 of them) had been forced. Murray Bleefeld and Harry Weiss testified that they believed that Wendel was the kidnapper of the Lindbergh baby. While held in Brooklyn, he broke down, buried his face in his hands, and told Bleefeld that he had kidnapped the child. Wendel went into so much detail that they were both convinced he was telling the truth. Ellis Parker testified that Wendel's written confession, in his handwriting related such details as would only be known by the guilty man.

There was never any evidence that Ellis Parker was motivated by anything other than good faith. Ellis was not interested in money. Ellis spent a considerable amount of his own funds to investigate. He never tried to make money, publicize his activities or sell stories to newspapers or magazines as Wendel did. He turned down countless offers and refused large sums of money for his stories.

FROM THE ELLIS PARKER LOST FILES

PAUL H. WENDEL & ELLIS H. PARKER COMMUNICATIONS

Received: on 3-7-1932
From: "Doc" a Paul Wendel alias.

In touch with you about someone, I explained to you about. Had first conference which up to now was successful. Conference again later. Will keep you advised.

It was mentioned to ask whether you had a letter direct from the principals to ask you if you would do what you are doing. My answer was that you can get it. They want to help if it is possible to obtain success. It was told they would leave no stone unturned if I could produce according to my explanation made to them as per your conversation this morning. They asked for the detail information names that might be attached names of the entire household, and people who generally come to the home.

It was suggested that you inform your principals to deal only with you for the time being, and you will deal through me. Any promise we make, we must keep because I do not want to hurt my standing.

Expect to see you in person soon.

Note: This is an example of the communications between Paul Wendel and Detective Ellis H.

FROM THE ELLIS PARKER LOST FILES

Received: 3-15-1932

From: INVESTIGATOR 48

Attn: New York, New Jersey

To: Ellis H. Parker, chief

I beg to report that I have had a conference with some people who are acquainted with the information that I seek.

It will be necessary to get some assurance for the Council to act upon showing a correspondence between the father and you, or the president and you. There must be mentioned in this that it is desired to have you use your utmost influence and knowledge to try and obtain the missing baby.

I have been given a 90% assurance that if the same is returned, the baby, no doubt, would be returned according to your instructions. This was said after I showed them the clipping of the father that he would not prosecute if the return was made.

I am holding messenger awaiting your decision.

Regards, INVESTIGATOR 48

<u>Note</u>: It is suspected that INVESTIGATOR 48 was Paul H. Wendel. Wendel was then working for Ellis Parker at his direction, as he often did.

FROM THE ELLIS PARKER LOST FILES

Date: March 16, 1937

Postmarked: 3-16-1937 (Providence, RI)

Addressed to: Chief of Detectives Ellis H. Parker, signed by M. Greene.

The writer contends that the Lindbergh baby (named Bobby) was alive and accompanied by a tall, blonde woman who answered to the name Daisy. She pleads for Ellis to believe her. The baby was gone the next morning (March 2, 1932), but he had supposedly told the writer that he was going to a school in Miami, Florida. The writer states that he/she was in New York for three weeks around the night of the crime, visiting from Providence, RI. He or she (undetermined) claims to have spoken with Mrs. Hauptman and some of her former neighbors. She recalls that a gang stopped at the rooming house on West 86th street the night of March 1, 1932, with the baby. Two of them answered the description of Paul Wendel and his daughter.

Regards,

M. Greene

Note: Charles Lindbergh Jr. was born on 6-22-1930. He would have been approximately just three months short of turning six years old. It is possible that he was speaking at this age. The fingering of Paul Wendel is interesting.

FROM THE ELLIS PARKER LOST FILES

Date: 3-28-1927

To: Joseph Linarducci

c/o Prosecutor's Office

Dear Joe,

I am enclosing you a bill in the Mandamus proceedings and ask that you send a check for $118.36 to Paul H. Wendel, 13 North Stockton St., Trenton, NJ.

Ellis H. Parker

Chief of Detectives

NOTE: This dates Ellis Parker's relationship with Paul H. Wendel back to 1927. In the attached bill, Wendel is referenced as Paul H. Wendel, Esquire, confirming that he was a practicing attorney at this time. Wendel would be disbarred (suspended) later.

FROM THE ELLIS PARKER LOST FILES

Paul Wendel's Later Career as A Book Writer

Paul Wendel took to writing after the Lindbergh years instead of being incarcerated or executed for the Lindbergh baby's kidnapping and death as he should have been. It would be one thing if he had writing talent, but I don't believe that he did have that ability based on my reading of only his Lindbergh book. There is no doubt in my mind that Paul Wendel was a genius. Unfortunately, he used it for self-gain and evil purposes. He added the title "Written by Dr. Paul Wendel" to his medical books at some point. He fancied himself a Chiropractor, although the science of Chiropractic Art was at a very early stage. I think that Paul Wendel was using "Chiropractic

Art" as just another of his cons. The legitimate practicers of the Art today would be well advised to avoid any connection to Paul Wendel, in my opinion. Amazingly these books still have value to collectors.

Here is a list of books authored by Paul Wendel that I found online. I can't vouch for the accuracy:

- Wendel tells all: "My 44 days of kidnapping, torture, and hell in the Lindbergh case. (1936)

Note: The above is the only book I was able to read.

- Naturopathic pharmacopeia, Naturopathic physicians guide (1950)
- Die Sprachen Argentiniens Im Online-Diskurs, Analyse Ausgewahlter Suchmaschinentreffer (German Edition)
- Die Ubersetzung Von Phraseologismen Aus Dem Roman Small Gods Von Terry Pratchett Ins Spanische Und Deutsche (German Edition)
- Tijuana. Fremd- Und Selbstbilder Einer Stadt Und Ihrer Bewohner (German Edition)
- Father Kneipp's health teachings: Instructions in water cleansing, breathing, food, herbs, earth and sunshine (1947)
- Bloodless surgery, with technique and treatments (1945)
- Brief guide to naturopathic gynecology (1949)
- Seven days of rightful living: A brief discussion on right living, with remarks on food, exercise, bathing, constipation, indigestion, and a word to mothers (1949)
- Standardized Naturopathy: The Science and Art of Natural Healing Poster (1951)
- Naturopathic Farmocopeia - Naturopathic Physicians Guide Paperback
- Standardized Naturopathy-sciences and Art of Natural Healing Hardcover (1951)

FROM THE ELLIS PARKER LOST FILES

THE FRIENDSHIP & LOYALTY BETWEEN HAROLD HOFFMAN & ELLIS PARKER

Harold Hoffman and Ellis Parker were the best of friends. Not only was Hoffman a featured speaker at the Medford Lodge dinner honoring Ellis, but he also wrote frequently to his friend. An exchange of letters in May 1935 occurred on the occasion of Herman and Anna Bading's wedding. Hoffman sent Ellis a picture of the bride and groom given to him by Herman Bading on 5-1-1935. "I thought that you might like to have this photograph, as once in a while, you can look at it and derive some inspiration." Hoffman was pictured in between the married couple holding a sign that read Motor Vehicle Act." At the time, Hoffman was the Director of the Motor Vehicle Division. This was before his election as governor.

Ellis wrote back the next day (5-2-1935). "I beg to acknowledge receipt of your letter, enclosing a photograph of a bashful and blushing bride, from whom, it is suggested, I may derive some inspiration. Now, between thee and me, I'll tell the cockeyed world, it doesn't take a bride to inspire me."

"In studying the expression of the groom, his face plainly tells me that he is already suspicious of his bride, but I doubt if the bride can repeat what a bride once said: I know the length of yours, but you don't know the depth of mine. And then there was another little brand-new bride, who got down on her knees to say: Now I lay me down to sleep. And the groom said: Oh Yea-?"

The friendship and loyalty between these two friends continued until Ellis Parker's death and after.

THE TESTIMONIAL DINNER

A no better indication of Ellis Parker's reputation and career can be found than the Testimonial Dinner held on Tuesday, May 11, 1934, to honor Chief Ellis H. Parker, of Burlington County Detectives at the Log Cabin Lodge in Medford Lakes, New Jersey. Ellis was honored by the assembled diners. Speakers included Prosecutors, Judges, the President of the New Jersey Senate, a member of the Republican State Committee, and the then Commissioner of New Jersey's Motor Vehicles Department, Harold Hoffman. Harold Hoffman was a close friend of Ellis's who would later win an election for New Jersey Governor.

The notice was made by New Jersey Justice Joseph B. Perskie in his charge to the Burlington County Grand Jury: "They shall tender him that dinner for the outstanding services which he has rendered to this county and state. In my opinion, he has well-earned it, and I join in the felicitations and good wishes of his many friends. I personally wish him long life and continued life of useful service."

The Riverton Police Department, the Norristown Police Department, the Pennsylvania Police Department, the Philadelphia County Detectives, the Pennsylvania Railroad Police, the Merchantville Police Department, and the New Jersey State Police all made special mention of their respect and admiration. The Philadelphia Evening Bulletin sent well wishes to a superior sleuth, a grand fellow, and a dependable friend.

FROM THE ELLIS PARKER LOST FILES

GOVERNOR HAROLD G. HOFFMAN, ELLIS H. PARKER'S FRIEND, HIS ROLE IN THE LINDBERGH CASE AND HIS LIFE AFTER IT

After being elected, Governor Harold Hoffman asked his friend, Ellis H. Parker, to re-investigate the Lindbergh case. He had great doubts about Bruno Hauptmann's guilt. The previous Governor, A. Harry Moore had put Ellis Parker on the case. Harold G. Hoffman visited Bruno Hauptmann unannounced at his prison late in the evening of October 16, 1935. They talked for more than an hour, with Hauptmann maintaining his innocence the whole time. Anna Bading was brought along because she was a stenographer and fluent in German. Anna was Ellis Parker's assistant and often referred to as Ellis's "Watson," like the Sherlock Holmes right-hand man, Watson. This visit is what is most remembered about the youngest New Jersey Governor ever elected (he served from 1935 to 1938). The visit reveals the Lindbergh baby kidnapping case's enduring power and fascination, known forever as the "Crime of The Century." This moment overshadowed Hoffman's military service and his rank of Colonel when discharged, returning to his position of Director of the New Jersey Unemployment Commission.

Hoffman wrote his thoughts about the Lindbergh case in a series of articles published by Liberty Magazine. He noted that the baby's corpse was never positively identified as Lindbergh's son.

Years later, On February 2, 1950, Hoffman appeared on the popular TV show, What's My Line. Life was good for Hoffman until March 18, 1954, when New Jersey Governor Robert B. Meyner became aware of some missing sums. Hoffman was suspected of embezzlement. He was suspended from his position while an investigation began. Unfortunately, former governor Harold Hoffman suffered a fatal heart attack on June 4, 1954; he left behind a letter addressed to his daughter admitting guilt. At first, she destroyed the letter but later reconstructed it at Attorney Harry Green's recommendation.

In 1985 23,633 documents relating to the case were found in the garage of Harold Hoffman's former home. Hoffman had taken them for review and never took them back. After the discovery, Hoffman's widow sued the state, claiming that they had contributed to her husband's death by allowing a miscarriage of justice in the Hauptmann execution. Her case failed.

FROM THE ELLIS PARKER LOST FILES

In the lost files, we found a letter that Detective Parker wrote to Harold G. Hoffman, Commissioner of motor vehicles, Trenton, NJ. On May 27, 1932, containing the following:

> I am more than ever convinced that the baby found is not the Lindbergh baby, and I am positively certain that the person spoken of is the real person.

> His mental condition is such, that it cannot be forced. Twice he has taken Anna for a short ride. I firmly believe he wanted to tell her, but that his heart failed him. He did, however, say, "you must tell the boss to realize that this isn't like an officer going after a criminal. This is giving something up that you can still be arrested for." This convinces me that there is still fear within him, as he said to me personally, "If you were to deliver this baby back, undoubtedly you would be arrested. Perhaps summoned before a grand jury, as those people have arrested Curtis, have tried to get Peacock, and the chances are they will try to arrest Condom. What are you going to do about it if they should arrest you?" I told them that they didn't dare arrest me because the governor had written me a personal letter and asked me to interest myself in the case. I would tell them that the baby was left at my place, and I know what my rights are when I am summoned before he Grand Jury and I would not waive them. So far as I was concerned, they could go to hell as I wouldn't talk. This seemed to satisfy him, but at that, I can see that he is a little suspicious.

> There is only one thing I can do, and that is to play him until such time as he will give it up.

Furthermore, I've decided should I get possession of it, to immediately notify you and instead of taking it to its home where they were all waiting for it, to take it to Englewood, in another County, which will throw them all out of gear. Undoubtedly, the Prosecutors in the other two Counties would cooperate with anything they would suggest, and this would beat them at their own game.

I don't want you to lose faith in this matter because after learning what I have, I'm convinced that I am right.

Signed,

Detective Ellis H. Parker

Note: This letter is a smoking gun and one of the most significant found in the Lost Files. Harold Hoffman was Commissioner of Motor Vehicles before he was elected Governor of New Jersey. His friendship with Ellis Parker went as far back as his childhood. Ellis was a close friend of Hoffman's father who shared his love of hunting. Governor Hoffman agreed with most of Detective Parker's theories on the Lindbergh crime. He also believed that Richard Hauptman was not guilty of the crime and that the body found was not that of Charles Lindbergh Jr. Hoffman urged Parker to investigate thoroughly. Detective Parker refers to a 3rd party in the above letter that we are sure was Paul H. Wendel. It is a damning piece of evidence because this is the same Paul Wendel who confessed in writing to the baby kidnapping.

Ellis Parker wrote this letter on May 27, 1932. The baby was kidnapped on March 1, 1932. The Anna referred to in Ellis Parker's letter was Anna Bading, his trusted assistant and confidant. Anna is often compared to Sherlock Holmes's Watson. She had nurtured a strong relationship with Wendel, who trusted her. This biography's writers strongly believed that Wendel is guilty of the Lindbergh baby's kidnapping and death.

FROM THE ELLIS PARKER LOST FILES

Note: Ellis Parker wrote the following sometime after the Lindbergh kidnapping and before his trial (5/5/37) and imprisonment. A period of 5 years. It clearly shows that Ellis still processed all his sleuthing abilities and facilities at this time. His health would deteriorate later, leading to his eventual death at the Lewisburg Federal Prison on 2/4/40. Ellis's assumptions and conclusions make sense. Many countless writers have reexamined the Lindbergh case to agree with him. Ellis's paper (below) starts with his theory on how people become criminals but then goes deeper into his thoughts on the Lindbergh case. This is reproduced here exactly as Ellis wrote it.

EARLY AND LATER CHANGES IN LIFE

As studied by Detective Ellis H. Parker.

Boys and Girls between the age of 12 and 13 years have a complete change in their physical life. Boys' voices change, and Girls' mensuration period starts, and they change from Boyhood into manhood and girlhood into womanhood. This is a very dangerous part of their lives, so far as crime is concerned. Statistics show that the largest percentage of crimes are committed under and up to the age of 22 years. If the Boy and Girl can be guided and regulated through this period and kept away from crime, it would diminish crime, and the crime wave which we have now, would not exist.

Then the change, later in life, seldom begins earlier than 40 years; it takes place in both sexes but has never been known much in criminal work.

When this change comes, sometimes the victim will wander away: and they won't know who they are, and they are classed as amnesia victims. Some will commit suicide; others will go insane; practically no two are ever handled alike. Some women will have good husbands and family and go with anything or anybody, and their friends do not understand. It seems as though a thread in their brain has snapped, and their whole life becomes changed. It is similar to apoplexy or paralysis. A great many subjects who have these sudden changes, later die of apoplexy or paralysis. I have known men to have accumulated a fortune and, in two or three years, run through with the whole business. They would go with women who were not fit to carry their wife's shoes, and their friends would not know what it is all about. It has been said that a person would live the life of a good citizen for fifty years, and under the impulse of a moment, become a criminal. This is because this change has taken place in their lives, and when that change does take place, they turn to be criminals. They become obsessed with the idea that they are supreme; that there is nothing in the world that they cannot do and that they are smarter than anyone living. They will plan and perfect the most perfect crimes. They have the "Doper" backed off the earth, as far as "Gut" are concerned, and they will go into their crimes, with the deepest Cunning and Scheming. It is said by the physiatrist that they are more or less victims of catatonic dementia praecox, the form in which cycles of extreme lethargy and extreme mental and physical activity, and they can plan and execute a most cunning type of schemes and of course are animated be a disordered emotional condition.

In order to discover those subjects, when a crime is committed, one must hunt for the unnatural things which have been done around the crime. One of the unusual things about the kidnapping of the Lindbergh baby, as I see it, it was the HOTTEST thing anyone could have done in the world, as he was idolized and loved by the public in general. He was living among friends and admirers. Had Lindbergh's baby been stolen around St. Louis, where he came from, there might have been the element of jealousy but surrounded by friends as he was, that would eliminate all jealousy, in my opinion. If the Kidnappers had stolen the President of the United States, a portion of the People would have been satisfied, B U T in this instance; Everyone frowned upon it. I believe outside of the kidnapper himself that there was absolutely no one, no matter who he was, but who frowned upon this Crime. That would indicate to me, a person of this Type did this job.

The next significant thing which in my judgment is unnatural was the Ransom Note. This Note, I understand, demanded $50,000; If this had been regular kidnappers, the demand would have been higher, owing to the fact that they were wealthy people. In nearly all cases of organized kidnapping, grown people are kidnapped; they don't kidnap babies. When they specified certain denominations of money, as I have before, this shows the scheming- cunning mind, and planning which I have referred to above. If I had

$100,000, given to me in $5,000 bills, I could and anyone else could, without detected, dispose of them. This again shows me clearly that it is a person of the type referred to. Oft times a person highly educated and whose standing in the community is of the best, has this change. It overcomes them, and this is the type who can do these crimes and get away with them. No one who knows them would ever suspect. They realize all of this, and they glorify in their acts. They get a thrill, they get the news over the radio, they get the Press accounts; in fact, they get a lot of fun out of it. They know they have the world by the ears, and no Officer has any right to work on a case where it is committed by this class of crooks except as Officer who has thoroughly studied them. They might steal the baby and might demand a Ransom and might not be in need of the money at all, as I said before. They glorify in doing something that would mystify the World, and they seem to get fun out of it.

The establishment of Police Headquarters at the Lindbergh home was the greatest mistake that could ever have been made, as the moment that was done, the door against information was closed. Lindbergh had become the idol of the American Public, so much so that wherever he went, to the theatre or ball game, people were so anxious to see him, they annoyed him. Not that he didn't appreciate their glorifying in him, but it was a hindrance as to his own pleasure, and that was the reason he selected this place, which he did, for his home, so that he would be left alone, to enjoy life. There is no question in my mind that this individual realized all of that. They thought that when Lindbergh found that his baby was gone, and the Note left for him, that he would deal with them directly and that he would consummate the deal, and that no one in the world would know about it. B U T the police got there when the note was discovered, and the case BLEW UP. Lindbergh was shut off from any contact he might try to make.

Don't forget that this type of criminal when they do any job, think over every detail before doing it, and when they attempted to make contact, they shut every door behind them, and if you attempt to check on them, YOU WILL LOSE THEM.

FROM THE ELLIS PARKER LOST FILES

STATE OF NEW JERSEY

DEPARTMENT OF STATE POLICE

SPECIAL REPORT OF INVESTIGATION

Station: Penn's Nook   Troop: G   Date: March 2nd, 1932

Report of: Sgt. C. J. Campbell #344

Subject: Investigation Kidnapping of Col. Lindbergh's son.

On this date returned to Station from policing the basketball game at Trenton, NJ. Learned that Col. Lindbergh's son had been kidnapped at 10:30 A.M. Detective Haussling arrived at this Station left at once with Detective Haussling for the Lindbergh home. Arrived there and met Lt. Wils. Was relieved of the investigation and returned to the Station as investigation was being handled by Capt. Lamb of "B" troop.

At 10:14 A.M. this date, a message came over the teletype for a man from this Station to go to the Lindbergh home and notify Detective Horn to get in touch with Ellis Parker, detective of Burlington County. Left Station for Col. Lindbergh's home. Arrived there and was advised by Sgt. Haussling that Detective Horn had left two hours previous for Ellis Parker's office. At this time, Capt. Lamb instructed me to take a Trooper and go to the Mercer County Airport and meet Major Lamphier and go up in a plane and if I noticed anything suspicious in vicinity of the Lindbergh home to drop a message. Took Trooper Walter Schindler with me on this call. Proceeded to Mercer Airport and met Major Lamphier went up in plane at 12:30 P.M., made numerous circles in vicinity of Lindbergh's home at about 500-foot altitude saw nothing suspicious around any farmhouse, visibility was excellent looked all over woodland. Dropped message at Col. Lindbergh's home to this effect. Returned to Mercer Airport at 1:45 P.M. and then returned to

Col. Lindbergh's home and reported this. At this time was detailed by Col. Schwarzkopf to clear traffic on road leading to Lindbergh home as it was jammed up. Cleared up traffic and left Trooper Jackson to keep traffic moving. Returned to Station.

Left Station 7:00 P.M. with Trooper Atkinson to Col. Lindbergh's home as information had been received from Lt. Hays of New Brunswick Police through a Joseph Goldberg of 175 Baldwin Street, New Brunswick had seen a suspicious car part of re. 3-K-3 5—N.Y. with 3 men and a small baby in it about 2:00 A.M. this date. Our car in route to Newark, N.J. and last seen of it was on South Street, Newark, N.J. thought this information may be of some value. Also received information from Jeff Lifgren of Kingston that a Ford sedan reg. 7A74-77 N.Y. was seen by him on the Lincoln Highway on March 1st, about 2:00 A.M. thought this may be of value. Took this information to Hopewell and turned over to Major Schoeffel. Was detailed to return to Station and await arrival of Newark Detectives and transport them to Hopewell to work on case. Returned to Station, met with Detectives, and transported them to Col. Lindbergh's home.

Note: This is American "History in The Making," for sure. You are in the car with the first Police officer called to investigate the Lindbergh baby's kidnapping. I love that Trooper Campbell tells us that he was assigned to Police the basketball game at Trenton, NJ. For some reason, that makes it more real for me. It is genuine proof that Detective Ellis Parker was sent for. I don't believe that could have occurred without Charles Lindbergh's approval. Col. Schwarzkopf's admiration and loyalty to Charles Lindbergh has been well documented. Charles made the final decisions. Col. Schwarzkopf carried them out.

Of particular interest to me is the sighting of a suspicious car on Baldwin Street, New Brunswick, with three men and a baby in it. Could they have been on their way to Paul Wendel's home? Wendel later confessed to Ellis Parker of taking the baby to his home. If this is so, it would have been wise for them not to drive directly there from the Lindbergh's Hopewell mansion.

FROM THE ELLIS PARKER LOST FILES

Note: The following documents either were intended to be published in the daily newspapers or they were. I can't be sure. Detective Parker had a favored relationship with reporters and even the owners of many New Jersey newspapers. Both these articles were most likely typed in Ellis Parker's office in Mount Holly. The original and the onion skin copy was intact in the manner Ellis's secretary Ana Bading usually favored. They are a window into Ellis's deductions and investigations and early thoughts on the 'Crime of The Century.'

EVENING BULLETIN - MARCH 4, 1932

"PARKER OFFERS AID IN FINDING BABY"

Hopewell, N.J. March 4: Ellis H. Parker, whose name has been synonymous with New Jersey criminal investigation for many years, today said he is ready to help find Charles A. Lindbergh, Jr.

The famous chief of Burlington County Detectives said: "If the prosecutor of this county is willing to permit me, I would be only too glad to give what assistance I could." He added that he was not as yet been asked to aid in the search.

"I have been following the case with the greatest interest from the outset," Parker declared, "But of course, the only info I get is from the newspapers."

"Judging from that, I would very emphatically say that this was an inside job. It was the work of persons who knew their business and evidently was plotted and carried out with the utmost efficiency, unfortunately".

"Certainly, the persons who did this were thoughtful enough to realize that as soon as the crime was discovered, they would be hunted as few human beings ever have been. They must have had some forethought that they would be pitting their wits against the combined police powers of the entire country. Yet there were sufficiently sure of themselves to go ahead with the job."

"This fact would immediately stamp them as exceptional criminals with keen minds or else downright fools, and I don't think the latter guess would be correct."

"There is one thing that is to the advantage of the police and leads me to believe that the Lindbergh baby may not be many miles from his home."

"The is the kidnappers had no way of knowing just when their crime would be discovered. It might be five, ten, 15 minutes after the baby was taken. So that what they eventually had planned to do and did was to get a safe hideout as quickly as possible".

"There is a possibility that they may have moved further away the next day, but would be running a big risk, with every road guarded."

Many unusual points have arisen during the investigation, and more probably will be met. Every case has something different from any other, and the usual extremes to which criminals go in trying to cover their tracks oftentimes are the very things which hasten their arrests".

"The ladder that was used, for instance, is a queer type. From what I have been able to learn, part of it is well-finished, with rungs fitted neatly to the uprights, while one section is crudely done, the boards being nailed on. The fitted-in rungs are uniformly spaced, but the nailed boards are irregular and rather wide apart.

The fact that it was in three sections, while possibly signifying this was done to carry it in an automobile, does not prove the point. That may have been done so that the ladder could be hidden in someplace where at full length, it could not be kept without attracting attention.

There is no doubt that other clues, which the police think best not to make public, are being diligently followed. It is impossible to analyze this case from the outside.

Personally, if I were in Colonel Lindberg's place, and it was my baby, I would pay the money to the kidnappers first and get the baby back, then do what could be done later."

PUBLIC LEDGER – May 14, 1932

LINDBERGH ERRED IN DEALING WITH GANG, PARKER ASSERTS

The Lindbergh kidnapping clearly shows the folly of dealing with the underworld, and the necessity of going to the police immediately in such cases, Ellis H. Parker, chief of Burlington County detectives and widely known crime expert said today at his office in Mount Holly.

Chief Parker declined to give any theories regarding the crime because he had no official connection with the case and was not in possession of all the facts.

"But I will say this about the case," he continued. "In the first place, the Lindbergh's never should have paid any ransom whatsoever or had any dealings with the underworld. If I'd been in charge of the case, there would have been no ransom paid."

It was suggested to the chief that Colonel Lindbergh had perhaps over-ruled the State police on the ransom question.

"If I'd been in charge, then, I'd have withdrawn from the case altogether. When we've got to the point where we've got to stoop to deal with these gangsters, then the whole police force ought to resign and deal with the underworld on the basis of so much cash per case settled."

"In the second place, the State police never should have been put in charge and should have refused to handle it. Don't you think New Jersey detectives and police are as good as any in the country?"

"Why did they call in outside help? They had the State County Detectives Association; they had the authorities of Mercer and Hunterdon County. As chief of detectives in Burlington County, I've never yet been officially notified the baby was stolen, and all I know I've learned from the press. The way the case has been handled is a disgrace to the state and the Nation."

FROM THE ELLIS PARKER LOST FILES

Letter dated March 10, 1932

To: Colonel H Norman Schwarzkopf, Superintendent of New Jersey State Police

I respectively submit herewith summary of my investigations in connection with the ladder used in the abduction of Charles A. Lindbergh, Jr.

I am dispensing with a detailed description of the ladder in-as-much as this has been previously submitted.

Indications are that this ladder was constructed by two different persons. The two smaller portions, in my opinion, were constructed by a left-handed person, in-as-much-as the saw cuts on the rungs of these two sections, by virtue of the splintering or break which occurs at the bottom of every saw cut, indicate that they were sawn by a person who wielded the saw with his or her left hand. The large section does not show such indications, and the rungs were sawn by a keener saw than was used on the two small sections. With the exception of one runner piece which bears indications of having been sawn with a rip saw and then planed, I believe the 1 x 4 runner pieces to have been parts of a crate used in shipping machinery or some similar object or material. It is possible that these pieces were part of a crate used for protecting bathtubs in transit.

The daub of red lead which appears on one of the broken runner pieces should bear out this opinion, in-as-much-as red lead is the material used almost exclusively by plumbers, steamfitters, or other persons engaged in mechanical work or the installation of machinery.

The previous theory that this material had been incorporated in crates used to transport farm machinery to Percy Van

Zant of Blawnburg has been disproven by investigation, which has, no doubt, been reported to you by Sergeant Gardner.

The large portion of this ladder is the only portion liable to have come in contact with anything during its transportation to the Lindbergh home, and this larger section bears evidence of having been fastened to or had contact with some object or surface bearing oil or grease during said transit.

The ladder is not well constructed from the standpoint of mechanical or structural details; it being weak in several respects; particularly in the matter in which the various sections are joined together to make a whole and the handling which the ladder has been subject to since its discovery makes it impossible to ascertain approximately how many times it has been subjected to use.

Material of a similar grade and age has been found at the Institution dumping grounds, State Village for Epileptics at Skillman. I understand that Captain Lamb discovered and submitted a piece of similar grade and age bearing a red lead mark identical with that on the ladder.

This ladder has been recently made, and I would place its age as having been made within approximately one month before the crime.

It might interest you to know that a 3' long piece of maple of the identical size and quality as that used in the dowels for assembling this ladder was discovered today in the corner of the Library in Colonel Lindbergh's home by Sergeant Gardner and the writer. This material is commonly used for forming the core for reals on which wheat or corn binding rope supplied to farmers is rolled. It is also used as a core for rolling oilcloth. It is not a common material, neither is ¾" size a common size.

The plane offered for my inspection at the New Jersey State Police Headquarters in Trenton is not the plane with which the aforementioned runner forming part of this ladder was planned with, but the chisel found at the scene of the crime is the same size as the chisel used in constructing the ladder and pending the receipt of magnified photographs of the chiseled portions of the ladder and the chiseled piece, it is possible that this is the same tool used in constructing the ladder.

The ladder is not well made. It seems to be the product of a person who is perfectly familiar with the woodworking details, but who has had no training in such work. The angle of the nails driven through the rungs into the large section of the ladder alone indicates this, as also does the distance between the rungs of all sections of the ladder. The relation of the angle of the saw cut to the machine evened edges of the rungs on the two smaller sections of the ladder further indicates that these cuts were made by a left-handed person. This theory, I believe, is further borne out by the fact that the ladder had been placed on the right-hand side of the Nursery window, which would be the normal side for a left-hand person to work from. A right-handed person wishing to apply pressure to the window, for the purpose I believe the chisel was taken to the house for, would place the ladder in a position where he or she could use their right hand.

The break in the handle of the chisel is recent and might have been done during the construction of the ladder. It is entirely possible that the hand of the person constructing the ladder was injured when this took place.

The material used for the runners or upright pieces of various sections of the ladder is a cheap common variety of yellow pine and is not the size or grade commonly used in building construction. It is more commonly called boxwood, and as I have previously stated is used for the construction of crates. The rungs of the ladder are of a better-quality white pine and of a grade and size sometimes used in building construction. I do not believe that this material was used for crating, with the exception of one piece, which shows evidence of having been machine nailed.

This would be an extremely difficult and if not impossible ladder for a short person or a tall person unversed in climbing to have negotiated. It is considerably more difficult to descend a ladder of this description then to ascend, particularly if both hands are not free.

I have endeavored to give all details pertinent to my investigations. If further details are required, I will be glad to submit same upon your advice.

Squire Johnson, Assistant Director of Construction. Division of Architecture and Construction.

Note: Squire Johnson wrote this report to Norman Schwarzkopf on March 10, 1932, only nine days after the abduction of the Lindbergh baby on March 1, 1932. You cannot read this report or evaluate it without coming away with respect for his intelligence and organized thoughts. Who gave this report and when it was given to Detective Ellis Parker is unknown? Squire's Johnson opinion that the ladder was not well made is significant as Bruno Richard Hauptmann was considered a master carpenter. Johnson also noted that the quality of the wood was inferior. Wouldn't an experienced carpenter, as was Hauptmann, have used higher quality wood for safety?

The most significant conclusion made in the report was that two people had constructed the ladder, one of them being left-handed and the other right-handed. That is a smoking gun. If two people created the ladder, then isn't it plausible that two people were also at the scene of the crime? The discovery in Colonel Lindbergh's library of a 3-foot-long piece of Maple the identical size and quality used in the dowels for assembling the ladder is perplexing. It is not sure when it had been placed there or if this information leads to a definite conclusion. Why Lindbergh was not asked about this wood at some point is beyond reasonable.

On February 5, 1935 (as reported in the New York Times), Squire Johnson reversed his theory on the ladder to state that he now believed that only one person had built it. This astonishing announcement removed suspicion that Hauptmann had an accomplice in the construction of the ladder and at the scene of the crime. At the Hauptmann trial, the Prosecution asserted that Hauptmann was the lone builder of the ladder and the only man guilty of taking the Lindbergh baby.

Questions on the Squire Johnson report were asked of Colonel Norman Schwarzkopf while he was on Flemington's stand the same day. Johnson's repudiation was a significant triumph for the Prosecution that had consistently contended that Hauptmann was alone. I must wonder if the Hauptmann prosecution threatened Squire Johnson to change his opinion. Naturally, they did not call him to testify during the trial. An understandable tactic for the Prosecution but not for the Defense.

FROM THE ELLIS PARKER LOST FILES

Office of Prosecutor of the Pleas of Burlington County

Mount Holly, New Jersey

HOWARD EASTWOOD, Prosecutor

ELLIS H. PARKER, Chief of Detectives

TELEPHONES, Day - Mt. Holly 144, Night – Mt. Holly 145

May 27, 1932

Harold G. Hoffman

Commissioner of Motor Vehicles, Trenton, N.J.

Dear Commissioner: -

I am more than ever convinced that the baby found is not the Lindbergh baby, and I am positively certain now that the person spoken of, is the real person.

His mental condition is such that he cannot be forced. Twice he has taken Anna for a short ride. I firmly believe he wanted to tell her, but that his heart failed him. He did, however, say, "You must tell the boss to realize that this isn't like an Officer going after a criminal. This is giving something up that you can be arrested for". This convinces me that there is still fear within him, as he said to me personally, "If you were to deliver this baby back, undoubtedly you would be arrested. Perhaps summoned before a Grand Jury, as those people have arrested Curtis, have tried to get Peacock, and the chances are, they will try to arrest Condon. What are you going to do about it, if they should arrest you?" I told him they didn't dare arrest me because the Governor had written me a personal letter and asked me to interest myself in the case. I would tell them the baby was left at my place and I know what my rights are when I am summoned before a Grand Jury, and I would not waive them, so far as I was concerned, they could go to Hell, as I wouldn't talk. This seemed to satisfy him, but at that, I can see that he is a little suspicious.

There is only one thing I can do, and that is, to play him until such time as he will give it up.

Furthermore, I have decided, should I get possession of it, to immediately notify you and instead of taking it to its home, where they are all waiting for it, to take it to Englewood, in another County, which will throw them all out of gear. Undoubtedly, the Prosecutors in the other two Counties would cooperate with anything that they would suggest, and this would beat them at their own game.

I don't want you to lose faith in this matter, because, after learning what I have, I am convinced that I am right.

I learned yesterday, for a certainty, that they have never given any reward or even a letter of thanks to the people that were supposed to have found the child. This, in itself, is more than convincing that they are playing the game as I had written you in a previous communicating.

Very truly yours,

Ellis H. Parker

Chief of Detectives

Note: I believe that the only person that Ellis Parker could be describing is Paul H. Wendel. I was surprised that Wendel was suspected by Ellis as far back as May of 1932. Anna Bading, mentioned here by Ellis Parker, was very close with Wendel. They often talked and in great detail for some years. Ellis believed that he could recover the Lindbergh child with Wendel's compliance, and he confirmed that to Harold Hoffman. At this time, Hoffman was Commissioner of New Jersey Motor Vehicles but was looking forward to running for the Governorship.

Ellis wrote this letter only 87 days after the Lindbergh kidnapping. Wendel was already a suspect in Parker's mind and involved enough to know the baby's location. Ellis would later realize that he was looking into the eyes of the real killer of the Lindbergh baby.

FROM THE ELLIS PARKER LOST FILES

American Detective & Service Agency

Investigations CIVIL – CRIMINAL – INDUSTRIAL

HALL BLDG.

Cor. E. State and Ewing Street

TRENTON, N.J.

Office Phone 5767, Night Phone 5551 32097

January 8, 1934

Mr. Ellis Parker,
Chief of Burlington County Detectives,
Mount Holly, New Jersey.

Dear Mr. Parker,

In reference to the telephone conversation of Jan. 1st, this young man mentioned went away and as yet has not returned. He registered at the Hotel Sterling here in Trenton, on Dec. 27, 1933, and left on Jan. 2, 1934, saying he would be back on Jan. 4, 1934, the day we arranged for him to see you. He left two suitcases at the hotel and an unpaid hotel bill.

His name is Rathbun, he is an army man stationed at Cristobal, Panama Canal Zone, and is on a 42-day leave, his home is in Lansing, Michigan. He said he knew a lot about the Lindbergh case. I would like to know if you are going to check up on him or let us know if we can help you in any way.

I remain'

Very Truly Yours,
Russell Suozzo

Note: The life of a Detective is full of leads. During the years of the Lindbergh case, it must have been overwhelming for Detective Parker. This interesting lead came from a peer who either worked for or ran a detective agency in Trenton, New Jersey. After reading that, the young man left two suitcases at the hotel and an unpaid hotel bill, it seems suspicious. Especially after learning that he went on the same day, Ellis was supposed to see him.

FROM THE ELLIS PARKER LOST FILES

THE STORY OF ANNA HAUPTMANN September 1935

Anna Hauptmann (Wife of Richard) wrote an article or short book she titled "Story Of Anna Hauptmann" and dated it September 1935, sometime before her husband Richard was executed on April 3, 1936. She spoke lovingly of him and their life together. She shared some of the letters Richard had written to her while he was imprisoned and on trial.

Richard wrote to Anna frequently. This is one such letter:

"Dear Anny, you heard the testimony from those four people who saw me in the bakery in the evening March 1, 1932. They are four strange people to us, so nobody can say they are friends. You heard the witness of April 2, 1932, and the witness of November 26, 1933, despite all cross-examination from the prosecution in almost every instance to assail credence of the testimony of the witnesses that saw me in those three days, their testimony remained unshaken. Why the jury did not take their testimony into consideration, I do not know. Or is it that the word of a working man counts for nothing at all? I was not in a position to bring prominent people for my defense to the witness chair, but I think the word of an honest workman will go as far in the eyes of fair justice as any other person.

Another time he wrote about Mr. Hockmuth, a man of 87 years of age, who claimed that he had seen Richard Hauptmann near the Lindbergh home or a few miles away driving a dark green car on 3-1-1932. The night of the kidnapping. "My Car was never green," wrote Richard. "Hockmuth testified that I had a red face. Never did I have a red face."

Hauptmann also wrote, "I was never near Hopewell in all my life." And "In all my suffering, I sleep well and peaceful and have no fear of the future, then I know that the sandy foundation of which this case is built must and will fall."

Anna also told stories about Richard's kindness to others, his fondness for children, and his consideration for old people. If you had only known my Richard as I have known him…a loving husband…considerate of me at all times…a proud and happy father…and a good friend to everyone in need. This was the man that Mr. Wilentz would have you believe capable of committing the worst crime in the annals of crime…kidnapping and murdering a baby. I have marveled at Richard's lack of bitterness toward those responsible for his present position.

Note: So, if Hauptmann did not take the baby away from the Lindbergh mansion, who did? Detective Ellis H. Parker believed that it was Paul Wendel and Isidor Fisch.

FROM THE ELLIS PARKER LOST FILES

Written in 1935

New Jersey License 1935 E56402

This Jew has the same appearance of the fellow who was around the Lindbergh's place for several days prior to the kidnapping. I just ran into him and two confederates and trailed them, and I would swear they are the ones who were so suspicious. Who are these fellows? What is their business? From what I picked up recently, they are bad, and I don't care to have my name known, so I submit this to you, and I am sure you will get on a hot trail when you get this fellow. From what I understand, he stands in with the big shots at Newark, NJ, but I am not at liberty to tell who I am.

THIS IS A HOT TIP MR. PARKER. CHECK ON IT.

Signed, Anonymous

Note: I only wish we could get the Motor Vehicle record on this license plate from 1935. Maybe Ellis Parker did and eliminated this lead. But this was written in 1935. I wonder about that and why the writer waited so long to report it. That brings a lot of doubt.

FROM THE ELLIS PARKER LOST FILES

Subject: Emily Balas & Ellis Parker exchange of letters – 12-31-1935 to 1-30-1936

I learned from the Lost Files that Ellis Parker exchanged a series of letters with Emily Balas, who resided in the Saint James Apt. Hotel in Chicago. Ellis responded to her letters on December 31, 1935, January 21, 1936, and finally on January 30, 1936. Not much of importance was discussed in Ellis's first two letters. Emily because was asking for Ellis to grant her a private meeting since she had some vital information to give him. Ellis explained that it would be impossible for him to leave Mt. Holly at the time because of his responsibilities in the Lindbergh investigation. He also pointed out that all of the investigation costs were a burden. He assured Emily that if she wrote him with all the particulars, he would keep it strictly confidential.

In her final letter to Ellis Parker, Emily Balas apologized because she had learned that her suspicion that the Lindbergh baby was in a traveling stage act was incorrect. She spent the rest of her lengthy letter explaining why she had been suspicious of the baby and the stage act. It was an exciting read, but after her admittance, she was mistaken about the child, unclimactic.

Using this opportunity to speak about the missing Lindbergh child, in Ellis Parker's final letter of January 30, 1936, he wrote:

"I received your most interesting letter, and I have never felt certain that the child found was the Lindbergh baby. The morning after it was discovered, I went there and looked at it. The decomposition that had set in destroyed the body too much for the time it was supposed to have been there. Unless acid or some other ingredients had been applied to destroy it."

FROM THE ELLIS PARKER LOST FILES

<u>Note</u>: I found the following newspaper article online. They were not a part of the Lost Files. It is not the first time I have come across the story of someone willing to testify that they saw Bruno Richard Hauptman at Frederickson's Bakery the night of the kidnapping. Including his wife, there are three such reports. Surely this alone would warrant a life sentence for Hauptmann instead of ending his life.

Upon his arrest, Bruno Hauptmann was asked by the police where he was the night of the kidnapping (Monday, March 1, 1932). He told them he was at Christian Frederickson's Bakery on Dyer Avenue, in Brooklyn, until 9 P.M. Hauptmann explained that he met his wife Anna there, her place of employment, every Monday to walk her home after eating dinner. On the night of the kidnapping, they went to bed as soon as arriving home so that they could rise early the next morning.

I find it hard to believe the rush to convict him to a death sentence. Could the motive have been that if Hauptmann remained alive, he would eventually tell the whole story? Important men had that to fear. Their newfound celebrity would end, destroying their reputations and exploding careers.

Harry Ulig was a close and trusted friend of Bruno Hauptmann and Isadore Fisch. He testified at the "Trial of The Century" in 1932. Uhlig accompanied Fisch to Germany on the liner Manhattan on December 9, 1933. Fisch was going there to die. Bruno Hauptmann saw them off from the pier. During their investigation, the police found out that Fisch purchased his passport on the same day that the Lindbergh baby's body was discovered, May 12, 1932.

Healdsburg Tribune
Number 81, February 7, 1935

WITNESS AIDS ALIBI DEFENSE OF HAUPTMANN

Story Corresponds to that told by Mrs. Hauptmann
By United Press

FLEMINGTON, N.J., February 7, 1935----Walter Manley, pale and nervous from illness, bolstered the alibi of Bruno Richard Hauptmann today by swearing that the German carpenter was in Frederickson's Bakery in the Bronx on the night of the kidnapping of the Lindbergh baby. His story corresponded with that of Mrs. Hauptmann, who was a waitress there in 1932 and by several other persons who gathered in the little restaurant to eat Danish and drink coffee. Manley went shakily to the witness stand, and counsel for both sides made their questioning as brief as possible due to his recent illness. The courtroom got its first glimpse today of Henry Uhlig, a red-haired German youth, who was the closest friend of Isadore Fisch. Whom Hauptmann says gave him the $14,000 ransom money. Uhlig testified that Fisch frequently borrowed money and lost some of it in a pie factory project. He told of sailing for Germany with Fisch in 1933. But he denied knowledge of a package of letters and documents which Fisch is supposed to have left with his sister.

FROM THE ELLIS PARKER LOST FILES

Note: I am not sure when this was placed in the lost files. Siglinde Rach wasn't alive in 1935. And there was no West Trenton archive then either. It was most likely placed there at some other time, maybe accidentally. It doesn't matter because the interview did take place in 1935. Ellis Parker did moderate it, and Anna Bading did transcribe it. It supports the belief that Isidor Fisch was a significant player in converting currency for illegal profits and money laundering. A valuable talent to specialize in if you are a member or associated with a kidnapping gang, which Isidor Fisch most certainly was.

Submitted to the LKH Forum by Siglinde Rach

From files at the W Trenton NJ Archive

Statement of George Steinweg, taken at his office, 226 E. 86th Street, New York, on October 25, 1935.

By – Ellis H. Parker.

Stenographer – Anna E. Bading.

Q. Mr. Steinweg, when this fellow Fisch came here and purchased a ticket from you, according to the testimony, he paid somewhere around $1,000. All totaled.

A. Yes. The thing is this, when he was here, naturally, my young man and myself we never took any notice of what kind of money he paid, but to tell the absolute truth, the day when I read that when the girl in the movie claimed she got a yellow back and was told the Lindbergh money was not yellow back, but a yellow certificate, has a yellow stamp, or have only the yellow stamp I was reminded of the incident on the day when Fisch was here. Fisch was here in the morning. First, he came and made a deposit, I don't remember anything, but on the 14th of November, in the morning Fisch was here and brought about $1,000. I had an associate here in business, and he intended to go, the following spring to Europe, and used to come here always. His office is on 84th Street, and his name is Louis Gartner, 407 E. 64th Street. He used to come in and say, "if you have any gold, I will take it and take it over with me, and I get more for it." Then we were off of the standard, but it was not mandatory to deliver gold notes, and every day he used to come in, and on the 14th of November, I had quite a lot, and before noon he came in and took about $100. Or so from my young man and gave his nice fresh money and about a half an hour later he came back again and said, "If you got some more, give me some more," and I gave him another $100 or so and said "Give me more. You will take my check, and I said, "sure," and I remember that, and I took about $100 and put it in my own pocket. My wife's birthday is later in November, and I thought I would give it to her. They looked so nice and clean. And this incident with this Mr. Gartner, this check, I remembered it immediately because it was certificates. I had than my money a day or two later on and put it back, they were not gold notes, and thought my wife would not look at them anyway because they are not yellow on the back and Mr. Gartner kept them until the spring when it was mandatory to deliver the gold notes. The last day and that very last day, he went down to the Federal Reserve and gave them to the bank.

Q. Were they delivered under his name?

A. Under his name, Gartner. Federal Reserve on Pine & Wall and when the case came up with Bruno Hauptmann, some inspectors came to him apparently asking for income tax until all of a sudden, they gave him a little piece of paper and told him to write Faulkner and made him sign all kinds of names, Faulkner, Faulkner, Faulkner, whole pages full and happened to be the same day Federal Reserve had received Lindbergh's notice that he made a deposit of the money he got from me. That money he got from me on the 14th of November, on the day when Fisch paid here. I remember the incident and said, "Louis, gave me a check. Get that out. I know you gave me the cash, and besides, you gave me a check," and that is the check on the 14th of November, from Louis Gartner.

(Produces check, as follows: "New York, November 14, 1933, Manufacturers Trust Co., 1513 First Ave., Corner 79th Street. Pay to the Order of Adriatic Exchange, $150.00. (signed) Louis Gartner" Endorsed "Adriatic Exchange, 226 E. 86th Street, New York City".)

We had more and deposited some, and recently I spoke to the man in the bank and said, "Did you have trouble too? Did you ever get any of the Lindbergh money?" He said, "Yes, they were here, but we couldn't check that up, nothing that you could trace that." I wanted to see if it was on the 14th it was deposited, and there was a $500. cash deposit on that slip, and if the Federal Reserve on the 14th of November also found in the deposit of the Corn exchange certificates, you have a closed case there. What he got and what I had and what I deposited there was about $1,000.

Q. What other money came in that day?

A. No big amounts. That was in the morning he was here. He came here and got checks for Uhlig. He paid for Uhlig's ticket as well as traveler's checks. Uhlig disclaimed it first, and later Uhlig said first he was here that day, and he was not here because Fisch was here alone and paid for Uhlig's ticket and also the traveler's checks, and then Uhlig said he felt Fisch owed it to him. Anyway, Uhlig called me on the telephone and said, "Mr. Steinweg, what shall I do? You know Fisch died, and he left some bundles with friends in the Bronx. How can I ship those things over," I said, "Mr. Uhlig, very simple, bring them here, and I will take care of that," and he said, "All right, I will see you the next day," and he did come and sent some money to his father, "40. A small amount and I said, "What did you do with the bundle," and He said, "That is all right. That is taken care of," and that was in the spring. Bruno was arrested in September, and that was months before, right after Uhlig returned. He called me up, and he denied he ever said it and how should I know there were bundles. He said, "Up with friends in the Bronx," and later, I asked him, and he said, "I didn't say it," and I said, "I told you didn't have to do anything. To put it in a big box, just put an address on, and I will ship them over. Cost you 12 cents a pound" "All right, he said, I will bring them down," and he came a few days afterward and said, "Oh, that is all taken care of," so he knew Fisch left bundles there. When he called me up, he said Fisch died. He said he paid for the ticket and then later he said Fisch paid it, but he owed it to him. My partner was stumped and had my man to sign the name of Faulkner and got the handwriting.

Q. Fisch had other money here?

A. Yes, sure. Of course, I didn't count it, but he had quite a lot. You should check up on deposits in the Yorkville National Bank for the 14th to 20th, and the Corn Exchange National Bank.

FROM THE ELLIS PARKER LOST FILES

1226 S. 26th St.

South Bend, Ind.

November 6, 1935

Ellis H. Parker

Mount Holly, N.J.

Dear Sir:

Some months ago, when I wrote my version of the American Detective's article "Why We Convicted Hauptmann," I didn't know to whom I would send it. That will account for the way it reads.

After reading in the paper that you were interested in this particular case, I decided to send it to you, for I wanted to send it to someone who would, in turn, help the Hauptmann's, for I have always felt sorry for them. I am sure he has been framed.

My theory may not be news to you, but if it is, use it. One thing more, if the child found was the Lindbergh child, then it was embalmed, for not one animal will go near formaldehyde. If it were not embalmed, dogs and other animals would have devoured and scattered it everywhere.

Please keep this article I have written strictly confidential and do not use it in any way except in an investigation.

Very truly yours,

Jack Le Krieg

Here is the article that was written by Jack Le Krieg:

I have read the article "Why We Convicted Hauptmann" in the April issue of the American Detective and have heard over the radio that Hauptmann's death verdict will not be rescinded. Having read of the kidnapping and then followed the trial throughout, I noticed some little details left out, and some statements not explicit enough, which is so important to the reader who thinks and goes deeper into it than the reader who just wants a thrill.

I think the verdict returned against Hauptman is preposterous. Of course, I am not blaming Adrin B. Lopez. It was not his verdict – he wrote it just as he got it.

Just think. Twelve persons on a jury, supposed to be intelligent, would willfully send a man to his death on such evidence. They want us to believe they went through all the evidence in eleven hours. I read every word of the kidnapping and trial. I had plenty of time to think over and study it, but they didn't. There was too much confusion there. I doubt if they remembered very much of the evidence brought out, true or untrue. There was plenty of both, and so much that wasn't told at all. I lived in that kidnapping and trial, and in the past years of reading fact stories and the murders and crimes that have been committed around my home, I haven't been a bad guesser. Richard Hauptmann never kidnapped or murdered that child any more than I did, and furthermore, WAS the child kidnapped?

I wish I were a good writer, able to write it just as I think. Well, anyway, here are some questions I would like to ask any detective.

1. Would any person murder a child, leave it within a few steps of a highway, and less than four miles from its home, exposed as it

was, and then expect to collect a ransom on a child that might be found any moment?

2. Why didn't they push the ransom before Condon entered the case?

3. In order to open the shutter, the kidnapper would have had to set the ladder at least one and one-half feet from the window, open the shutter, then go down again and move the ladder over on the shutters. The ladder nearly reached the top of the window, and at the point of getting on or off the ladder or window still, the ladder would be about two feet out from the sill. Now, if you think that is easy, just try it on a good ladder, without anything in your arms.

4. How did the kidnappers happen to get the right window the first time?

5. Would a kidnapper stop to take the pins out of the blankets when he could slip the child out without doing that?

6. Why didn't he leave the ransom note on the bed? You know it might have blown off the sill the way the wind was blowing that night.

7. Would Hauptmann take a 1x6" board out of his attic, rip it down to a 1x3 ½" when he could get one the right size where he was supposed to have gotten the others? It would have taken less time and work.

8. What would you do with $50,000 of "hot money," or what was left of it, that had been left in your possession by someone who had since died?

9. Would a man that has worked all his life, and worked with his hands, commit a crime of that sort?

10. Why did Violet Sharpe tell so many prevarications when the truth would have fit in better, and then commit suicide? Or did she commit suicide?

11. What was the police carpenter doing at the Hauptmann home?

12. Why wasn't the child's body found sooner?

13. Was the child's body there on the night of March 2, 1932?

14. If it was, why didn't the wild animals or dogs attack it?

15. Will any animal eat embalmed flesh?

16. Where was the kidnapping car parked on the many occasions it was supposed to be at Hopewell, including March 1, 1932?

Well, there are too many questions to ask. I could ask them for hours, which means there were too many important things left out, and such silly things put in when a man's life was at stake.

Suppose I was Lindbergh, and my wife was Ann Morrow Lindbergh. I had plenty of money, and my wife would inherit many times more. Born in wealth and raised in wealth – and you know how such children are raised. They never get very close to their parents until they are grown, and they don't care much for their parents by that time. Now suppose we had a child born to us that was not normal, and I knew he older the child grew, the worse it would become. My wife knew this too. Well, would a child like that cramp my style?

Some, of course, but my wife – well, she just couldn't take it. I know Lindbergh could not murder his child, and I will grant his wife wouldn't, but what was to stop them from putting the child in some home where he would be taken care of for the rest of his life, which might not be many years for an abnormal child. The keeper could be well paid and save many embarrassments for the parents. But how to do it?

You can see that a framed kidnapping is the only way. Sometimes I doubt if Lindbergh was ever cognizant of all the facts of the case. He always seemed too square a man for that, but no real mother would be away from her child as Mrs. Lindbergh was. Now coming back to the kidnapping, you must admit the ransom was never to be collected, and if Condon had never intruded, there never would have been anything to it. He, however, saw a chance for notoriety, and he went for it strong.

Betty Gow, Violet Sharpe, and Mrs. Lindbergh knew all about it, and as Isidor Fisch knew Violet Sharpe, it was easy for them to get together in collecting the ransom – a double-cross I call it – but they got it. Perhaps it cost Violet her life, one way or another, and Fisch couldn't find a "fence" for the "hot money," so he borrowed the money from Hauptmann and sailed for Germany, where he later died.

What would you do if you had been Hauptmann? Perhaps the same as him. After he found the money, he started to spend it in order to get back the money back he had loaned Fisch, and it was so easy he kept it up until he was caught. I think that is the only charge he is guilty of – spreading ransom money, and you or anybody else would do the same if they had the nerve.

Ellis Parker responded on 12-14-1935:

> December 14, 1935
>
> Jack L. Krieg,
> 1226 So. 26th Street,
> South Bend, Ind.
>
> Dear Sir: -
>
> Your letter received enclosing your article, which proved very interesting to me.
>
> I wish, at this time, to thank you for your interest in me and this matter, and may I state that I will keep your article in mind so that if any time anything arises, I can refer to it.
>
> Again, thanking you, I remain,
> Very truly yours,
>
> Ellis H. Parker
> Chief of Detectives

Note: An excellent letter. It makes you aware of how many theories and how complicated the Lindbergh case was. Item # 1 made me step back and think about the issue. You kidnap, then you either deliberately kill or accidentally kill the baby, then leave the body by the side of the road? Who does that and still expects to collect a ransom?

FROM THE ELLIS PARKER LOST FILES

<u>Note</u>: Following is a series of letters between Rudolph Thielen, Chief Justice Mr. Charles Evans Hughes, Harold Hoffman & Ellis Parker. Who was Rudolph Thielen? I found the answer to this question on Author Michael Melsky's website:

Michael Melsky is a highly respected expert on the Lindbergh case. Besides moderating the unique website, the Lindbergh Kid Nap Proboards. Michael has written three volumes of "The Dark Corners of The Lindbergh Case." The authors of this book strongly recommend them.

Rudolph Thielen was one of the Hauptmann Defense team's Handwriting Experts who Defense Attorney Edward J. Reilly never called to testify during the trial. Thielen studied handwriting, but he also graduated from a Detective School before starting the "Imperial Detective Bureau," located first in New York City and then later in Newark. Thielen offered New Jersey Governor Harold Hoffman his services gratis during Hoffman's re-investigation of the Hauptmann case because he firmly believed Hauptmann was innocent.

<u>Rudolph Thielen writes to Chief Justice Charles Evans Hughes on 11-6-1935</u>:

MEMO E.P. (Ellis Parker)

The Governor asked me to bring this to your Special attention. He believes that it is the "real McCoy."

Bill Lutz

325 East 64th Street

New York, N. Y.

November 6, 1935

Hon. Chief Justice Mr. Charles Evans Hughes

United States Supreme Court

Washington D. C.

Dear Sir:

Referring to the Hauptmann-Lindbergh kidnapping murder case, I have some very interesting facts to report, in order to save an innocent convicted man from going to the electric chair. I feel it is my duty to do this move in the first place as a good honest German American, second – because my own investigations have revealed, Hauptmann may have had something to do with the extortion of the money in this case, but never could have actually kidnapped or killed the Lindbergh baby.

Since 1932, I have been working on this case, - being a student of the investigation of crime and criminals – and I can assure you, and millions of other Americans will support this statement, that the snatching of the Lindbergh baby has been an inside job.

Unfortunately, Isidor Fisch is dead, but not only the "honor" of the dead should be protected, but we have to have also consideration for the living among us. I cannot help but be ironic when referring to Fisch and hope I will be forgiven since Fisch did leave a bad record behind, this I can prove, and also many others.

Now Fisch associated with the servants of the Lindbergh and Morrow household, there is an original picture in existence, showing the group mentioned, including Fisch, and this picture is now kept by a Private Detective here in New York City.

Same picture was given to Mr. Reilly before the trial had started, bet he never had it marked for evidence, the first unfairness to Hauptmann done by his own defense counsel, also Reilly neglected to have Fisch's latest police Registration Card from Germany in court, the card I received from German

Authority and handed to Hauptmann's chief counsel before the defense began to testify.

The cards handwriting – I claim as Reilly's former handwriting expert – shows similarity when compared with the original ransom notes, which were sent to Col. Lindbergh.

Fisch used to live with Violet Sharpe together as man and wife for a while in Lake Hopatcong, N. J.

Fisch has sold hot money here in New York City – one dollar for 60 cents. Fisch has given a large sum as a loan to people in Long Island in 1932 – the latter that practicably broke were after that able to open a new business, buy two more homes, and made twice a trip to Europe.

Before Fisch came to money, he borrowed $800. – from a friend but never returned same to the creditor. This friend wanted to testify in Court at Hauptmann's trial, but he said that he was warned by Police not to open his mouth.

Fisch was seen at the Cemetery on the night of April 2, 1932, when Dr. Condon passed the ransom money over to the extortionists – by the Cemetery guard Robert Riehl, but he again was advised by Police not to testify.

Violet Sharpe took poison because the Police wanted to question her. "Do you believe that?" I may say.

Ollie Whately, Lindbergh's butler, died. (What a coincidence.)

Henry (Red) Johnson was deported in a hurry. I would like to know why, since the kidnapping was not solved yet.

Again, Fisch was seen on the night of the kidnapping in the company of Violet Sharpe and a little baby on a ferryboat, so Peter Sommer – a former Police Department employee testified.

Violet Shape was seen on the same night being in a nervous state by the Hauptmann defense witness Mrs. Anna Bonesteel of Yonkers.

Mr. Scanlan – Hauptmann's double – came forward at the time of the trial and declared voluntarily he had been moving along in the vicinity of the Lindbergh home on the day of the crime and probably he must have been seen on that occasion by the two State witnesses Hochmuth and Whited who both put their finger on Hauptmann, pointing him out as to be the man they saw. Strange to say, this Robert Scanlan, a realtor of Melo Park, N. J., never was accepted to testify for the defense.

This – another hit against Hauptmann – shows clearly the willingness of the defense counsel to save their client from being prosecuted for a crime he never committed.

Old man Hochmuth could have been mistakenly convinced since the double did remember meeting him in the section of the Lindbergh estate on the very day of the kidnapping, so why wasn't Scanlan admitted to the stand, so that the matter could have cleared up?

There was another man who has resembled features of Hauptmann, this man also went to the Hopewell section during the time of February 28 to March 2, 1932. He was driving a truck, and on the truck was a ladder. The man, living in Islip Terrace Long Island, went out to get some trees from Hopewell. When he returned, there was not a single tree on his truck. I ask here: "Must one necessarily be a wood expert, to trace a ladder? Wouldn't a good investigator also do the trick, in order to get real and good evidence?"

Dr. Hudson's examination of the "kidnap ladder" resulted in not finding any of Hauptmann's fingerprints, and according to science, they would have been found should the accused have handled it.

Dr. Condon, the "States Witness," had long before admitted that he never would be able to point out "John" once he even refused to identify Hauptmann as to be the man, at least he needed time to think it over.

A Bronx juror Mr. Whaley once slipped out with the same statement, and he was threatened to be jailed by District Attorney Foley of the Bronx.

It took Col. Lindbergh a long while to "recognize" Hauptmann's voice to be the one he heard near the Cemetery while he – Lindbergh – was sitting in his car, three hundred feet away from the spot where ransom money was passed over to "John." All he heard of the conversation between Condon and "John" was "Hello Doc!" and then Condon entertained the extortionist for almost an hour. Does your honor believe that? Would any criminal – when facing his payoff – stop to think that long? There is one point where the U.S. Supreme Court must stop to think, before judging too hastily, I do not believe in fairy tales anymore, and I hope you neither cannot be fooled with.

Mrs. Lindbergh had told the jury, she found nothing at all disturbed in the baby's room right after the crime. Now I cannot help to think whether or not Betty Gow put the Baby to bed. Besides, when does the nurse now stay in Scotland, why doesn't she return to the United States, where prosperity seems to have past the corner? I hope her conscience isn't bothering her.

Henry (Red) Johnson, Betty Gow's former sweetheart, was a sailor, we must keep that in mind. A sailor easily has a chance to cross the ocean if he wants to. So, I ask – has that man settled down in Norway, or is this only a stray story like so many the public has glanced at?

In 1933 a man about 25 years of age with reddish hair came from Boston to see his two friends in a rooming house on the Eastside of Manhattan. He rented a room in the same house and claimed to be all through with work. He stated to have been working for a family in Massachusetts, then his employer suddenly died and left him in their will 35,000 dollars. It would be very easy for any State official to trace this case down, also any other smart investigator given legal authority could handle it. This "servants" name was Johnson. He stayed not quite a week, left in a hurry when the proprietor wanted to call the Police. His former address in Boston is known to me, I even keep letters in my hands revealing that address. Those letters were given to me by the owner of the rooming house mentioned above.

Another of the many pieces of information that was given to me by a woman in West 51st Street Manhattan. She signed a sworn statement, which contains a revelation of a plan made by two Armenians Nishan Sarkiskian and Matos Leylegian, in 1929. These two members of the Tashnag Club – now serving a life sentence for the murder of the late Archbishop Leon Touraine - laid plans to kidnap the Lindbergh baby even long before the child was born. In her affidavit, the woman admits to have overheard their plans, including also the one killing the later stabbed Archbishop. The woman never did believe (her two brothers) would really have the intention of killing anyone. But they did so finally.

In May 1933, a woman left the United States on a German liner for Germany. That woman confessed to have been living in Buffalo, N. Y. She was in fear to be killed by her husband, of whom she knew too much as he was in on the Lindbergh kidnapping. I had the women traced by German Authority and found after she had been staying in Berlin in an Asylum for the poor about six months, the American Consulate General gave her Baby a free ticket to return to the United States. This person also easily could be found, her right name is recorded on my list.

On May 1, 1933, a man went up to the Federal Reserve Bank here in Manhattan to exchange his gold certificates (tens and twenties) for silver bills. He gave his name a J. J. Faulkner and his address as 537 West 149th Street. Now, this same section of Manhattan has been the busiest and active in connection with the Lindbergh baby kidnapping. The Lindbergh baby was brought to a rooming house at West 145th Street in the late evening of March 2, 1932. It was a couple who rented a large eight-dollar room for the two of them and "their" Baby. The Baby's hair was cut short with a machine, its head only showing blond stubbles. Its feet were some standing turned inside, the child made the impression of being lost and helpless, did not seem to notice when its "daddy" called him by name "Walter" but was alarmed when addressed by a woman (landlady) using the name Charles. The Baby was dressed only in nighties, it never was to leave the room during the (couples) one week stay, no person would be permitted to enter the room except the landlady when she made the beds, the latter again being under constant watch of a bunch of rough-looking men, as soon as she attempted to leave the house.

On the first night, the newcomers had company, it was a redhaired woman, and a New York Policeman in full uniform, they spoke, or better were behaving very suspicious, fright was written over their faces since they knew that people in the house were aroused about the presence of the Lindbergh baby

– which at the time had already been declared kidnapped, the landlady kept her chin up, acted dumbfounded in order to be permitted privilege with the hidden child. And that woman succeeded in her effort. The new tenants gave their names as Mr. and Mrs. B. Homes, both having a hard-striking feature of being Irish, also the redhaired woman and the policeman – who anytime could be pointed out by the above-mentioned landlady. The latter, still in a state of fright – wants me to keep her name out, until a better and real honest independent lawyer takes up Hauptmann's defense, or whom an effort is made by the U.S. Supreme Court to demand a new trial for Hauptmann.

To the above statement, - sworn and signed by said landlady – I must add that during the same week, - the first week of the Lindbergh baby's disappearance – two men were found murdered in New York City, who tried to earn a reward for pointing out the Baby's fate. These two men lived in the same house, where the Baby was held. Miss Hermina Koerner, - who held four letters written by a tenant of Dr. Condon – signed by 4 different names, written however by one person and one letter from Miss Mary Peacock ---- could have been a star witness for the defense, yet – this lady was ignored.

Asst. Attorney General Joseph Lennigan of New Jersey has been continuously drunk when assigned at the Hildebrecht Hotel in Trenton on January 12 and 13, 1935, to keep watch over the studies we defense handwriting-experts made over the original ransom notes. He attempted to frighten and frame us off the stand in the most disgraceful manner, and when he did not succeed, he expressed himself to be wishing Hauptmann would commit suicide. Who gave him the order to act the way he did? I trust Your Honor agrees with me, and I say such actions are illegal and cannot be tolerated with.

District Attorney Foley of the Bronx has framed me off the stand (so I was told by Reilly) the reason known to me is – he had a personal grudge against me for bringing his own friend into the Bronx Court on a criminal assault charge.

Mrs. Braunlich – another of our defense handwriting staff – complained in the presence of the other members of said staff, she was sent home from Flemington by Reilly because she rejected his intimate attentions upon her.

This same report I have sent to the two former and now presiding gentlemen of the American Bar Association, Mr. Earle Wood Evans of Wichita, Kansas – Mr. Scott M. Loftin of Jacksonville, Florida – and Mr. William L. Ransom in Chicago, Illinois, who promised drastic action against wrongdoing members of the Bar.

My offer to help solve the Lindbergh Kidnap "Murder" case was ignored by the Director of the U.S. Government Bureau – Mr. J Edgar Hoover.

Your Honor: May I assure you – and I trust you will take my report under consideration – that Bruno Richard Hauptmann is victimized, so my appeal goes to you, to grant this man a new trial.

With my highest regards,

Rudolph Thielen

Note: The above report was prepared for the Honorable Chief Justice Mr. Charles Evans Hughes of the United States Supreme Court by Rudolph Thielen. It is complex and fascinating. The investigation of the "Crime of the Century" will never be completed. It, much like the report of Rudolph Thielen, is too complex to find a consensus. Too many years have passed for verification. It is a fantastic read and incredibly thought-provoking.

Of all the things I read about the case, one thing stands out the most and has never been explained to my satisfaction. It is the alleged suicide of

Violet Sharpe. I am still shocked by this after all this time. I say "alleged" suicide because some think it could have been murder. I can accept all the theories, all the evidence, and all the explanations except this one. Something is afoul here.

Randolph Thielen writes, "Fisch used to live with Violet Sharpe together as man and wife for a while in Lake Hopatcong, N. J." This statement is unproven, but it comes from a very skilled investigator trusted by an American Governor and the famous Detective Ellis Parker. Thielen also discloses that Fisch was seen with Violet Sharpe and a baby on the kidnapping night.

The following note dated 11-7-1935 was found in the Lost Files:

From: Pittsburg, PA

Written by: Anonymous

Anonymous writes a confession letter. The writer admits to killing the baby because Lindbergh was mean to some young boys.

The following note dated 12-9-1935 was found in the Lost Files:

12-9-1935

From: Elmira-NY

Written by: Anonymous

Knows a man that will tell all about the kidnapping after a few drinks.

A second note dated 12-9-1935 was also found in the Lost Files:

12-9-1935

From: New York

Written by Anonymous

Anonymous overheard two German men say the baby is dead before the body was found.

Rudolph Thielen writes to Governor Harold Hoffman on 12-11-1935:

25 East 84th St.

New York, N.Y.

December 11, 1935

Ref: to Hauptman Case

Hon. Mr. Harold Hoffman

Governor of the State of New Jersey

State Capitol in Trenton, N.J.

Dear Sir:

Much has been said about the case in which Bruno Richard Hauptmann is involved. I have done my best and still try to save this man from any undeserved punishment.

As a former handwriting expert, in this case, I used to co-operate with the defense staff, have studied the original ransom notes in Trenton, and must say that they have been written by two persons, but it was not Hauptmann, it was not Bruno. Take a look at this picture, the latest German police registration card of Isidore Fisch. It shows he has written some of the ransom letters – beyond doubt. The original of this picture is in my hands, which I have studied for over seven months and compared with the ransom notes.

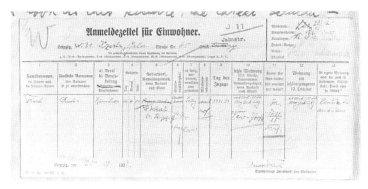

I have also studied another handwriting, and it proves to show the most startling results.

However, before making a statement, I prefer to confer with other handwriting experts on the matter, or to get in touch with your office, if it can be arranged.

I am sure today that it is of true fact, Bruno R. Hauptmann never had much of a help from anyone until the case reached your office.

My service as an expert to study handwriting had been accepted by Edward J. Reilly at first, then he has neglected to represent the defense properly and has chased all his Assistants home for no reason at all.

My investigation I have done mostly by myself and have spent my own money because I was surely interested in the case.

Within, you find my report to Chief Justice Mr. Charles Evans Hughes of the U.S. Supreme Court. Please read it carefully. It will help to solve the case in about a month or so.

I gladly will give the State of New Jersey all the co-operation to bring the guilty party's so far to confess to the crime.

This for today, and I hope that ignorance now will play a lesser part in the case. I trust since the matter is in your hands, I will be able to work out my plans more freely.

I assure you that I have the sincere wish to serve Justice and not to complicate things more as they

have been.

With my highest Respect yours,
Rudolph Thielen

Note: The above subject letter was written on 12-11-1935 by Rudolph Thielen and mailed to then N.J. Governor Harold Hoffman. It was immediately re-mailed to Ellis Parker with a note attached that said the Governor believes that this is the "Real McCoy."

In this letter, it is revealed that the writer (a former handwriting expert in the Hauptmann case) believes that two people wrote the ransom notes and that one of them was Isidor Fisch. He also asserted that Hauptmann did not write them. He supported this opinion by enclosing a sample of Fisch's handwriting that he got from Germany. Thielen disclosed that he had given this same information to Hauptmann's defense and U.S. Supreme Court Chief Justice Charles Evans. He had not received a response and remained suspicious about the reasons.

As explained in a previous letter, Rudolph Thielen was one of the Hauptmann Defense team's Handwriting Experts who Defense Attorney Edward J. Reilly never called to testify during the trial.

Thielen studied handwriting, but he also graduated from a Detective School before starting the "Imperial Detective Bureau," located first in New York City and then later in Newark. Thielen offered New Jersey Governor Harold Hoffman his services gratis during Hoffman's re-investigation of the Hauptmann case because he firmly believed Hauptmann was innocent.

Ellis Parker and Governor Harold Hoffman were suspicious of Isidor Fisch from the beginning of the case. We have reason to suspect that Isidor Fisch accompanied Paul Wendel to the Lindbergh home to take the baby.

Rudolph Thielen writes to Detective Ellis Parker on 4-18-1936:

> 55 West 75th Street,
> New York, New York.
> Susquehanna 7 – 8852
> April 18, 1936.

> Mr. Ellis Parker,
> Mount Holly, N.J.

> Dear Sir:

> I am one of Mr. Leo F. Meade's men doing some investigation in the Lindbergh kidnapping case. Today I had a telephone conversation with Mr. Meade, and he promised to get in touch with you and as soon as possible, hand over to you a statement that I have collected.

This statement was made by Mr. Friedelmeier, and in it, you will find the mentioning of a Russian who used to travel and do business with Isidor Fisch. Today Friedelmeier stated that he is positively sure that Wendel is the man who posed as the Russian. Friedelmeier has been threatened several times by strangers since he told his landlord (whose name is Isidor Kahn) about Wendel.

Enclosed you will find a sample of the material (which was supposed to have been stolen) that Russian sold to Friedelmeier in 1932.

If you will get in touch with me or send one of your men to my house, I shall be glad to give you all the necessary assistance. Please telephone before you send anyone to see me in order to be sure that I will be at home.

Very truly yours,

Rudolph Thielen

P.S. Attached to Mr. Friedelmeier's statement, you will find a label which is of importance.

Note: This is another confirmation of someone seeing Paul Wendel and Isidor Fisch working together. Most likely on a scam or a "get rich quick" scheme. Their relationship went back years before the Lindbergh kidnapping and long before Attorney Paul H. Wendel was disbarred. Ellis Parker suspected that together they played extensive roles in the Lindbergh kidnapping.

FROM THE ELLIS PARKER LOST FILES
THE EVENING SUN, BALTIMORE, MARYLAND
FRIDAY, DECEMBER 6, 1935

Detective and Governor Probe Hauptmann Case

TRENTON, N.J. - Governor Hoffman today announced that Parker, noted Burlington County detective, was "under the definite impression that Bruno

Hauptmann is not the man" responsible for the Lindbergh kidnapping. Parker has gained, considerable fame by solving a number of crime mysteries.

Ellis Parker Rated as One of Shrewdest Detectives

Lindbergh Case Prober Declares "I Can Tell a Guilty Man When I See One" - Insists He Merely Uses His Head

By John Ferris (Associated Press Staff Writer)

Mount Holly, N.J., Dec. 6 – Ellis H. Parker, who is making an independent investigation of the Lindbergh kidnap-murder, has won a reputation as one of the shrewdest detectives in the United States.

He likes to work alone, and he prefers his own methods. He has had a remarkable high percentage of success. In the middle of an important investigation, one day, about a dozen years ago, Parker remarked, "I can tell a guilty man when I see one."

A Simple Statement

None of his listeners doubted him. It was not a boast. It was a simple statement of fact. He was working on the murder of John Brunen, the circus owner of Riverside. Publicly the case appeared to be far from solution. Parker was keeping his own counsel, but those interested in the case knew there was something in the wind. It was nearly two months later that Parker, having wound up his fine-spun thread of reasoning, announced that the case was solved, and it was.

Parker, they say, had never laid a hand in anger on a suspected man. His manner is paternal, solicitous. He speaks gently; he is never emotional. He has a keen analytical mind. His record is proof of that.

Has Arrested Hundreds

He solved the murder of Davis Paul, the playboy Camden bank messenger, who vanished with $75,000 in checks and cash October 1920. He solved it because he "guessed" that Paul's body had been preserved in a cedar swamp creek and that he had died long before other authorities believed.

In his career, this short, stocky, grizzled man with the pipe has made hundreds of arrests and, in nearly every homicide case, has seen his prisoners convicted. Men and boys have confessed to him, for this 62-year-old man invites confidences by his kindly manner. Chicken thieves and horse thieves, petty bandits, vengeful murderers, all have fallen into his trap.

First Case Was His Own

His first case was strictly personal. As a young man, he played the fiddle at country dances. Someone stole his horse and buggy, he tracked down the thief, and his success so delighted him that he turned detective.

A little more than a year ago, he traced a man from California to Greece without leaving his office. People said it was uncanny. Parker said it wasn't. He was merely using his head.

<u>Note</u>: Ellis saved this newspaper article in his files. Included was a photo of Ellis Parker at his desk on a telephone. Also, there was a photo of Governor Harold G. Hoffman signing a document at his desk. In the upper right hand of the newspaper article was the notation, "Dear Ellis, my mother sent me this from Baltimore."

FROM THE ELLIS PARKER LOST FILES

Written on December 6, 1935

PENNSYLVANIA STATE BREWERS' ASSOCIATION

2311 PHILADELPHIA SAVINGS FUND BUILDING
PHILADELPHIA, PENNA.

Chief Ellis Parker

Burlington, N. J.

Dear Chief:

I see by the newspapers that you are working on the Lindbergh case, and I'm certainly glad to hear that because I know now that something definite will come to light.

Chief, I owe you a lot and feel grateful for what you have done for me. You probably recall my working on the case for the Camden Courier and the Philadelphia Record, which was through your recommendation.

The short while that I was on the case, I had several leads, one of which seemed very important to me at the time which I turned over to Col. Schwarzkopf, and never heard any more about it. This lead came from a bootlegger named Tony Sansone, who told me that his small daughter, by a common-law wife, was kidnapped about a year or so before the Lindbergh case by a mob from Brooklyn N.Y. and held for $10,000 ransom. The Kidnapping took place about three miles from the Lindbergh home.

I have a newspaper clipping showing his common-law wife seated in the District Attorney's office on a murder charge as she had killed a man in Brooklyn N.Y. over the Kidnapping.

Chief, this information was given to me in confidence by Sansone, and while he was drunk and if you think this information can help you, I can give you the story in detail, and I believe we can still reach Sansone and also have the newspaper clipping in my possession.

As you see by the letterhead, I am connected with the Pennsylvania Brewers Association of Pennsylvania. I have been their investigator for the past two years, and indirectly you were responsible in my getting this position and for which I feel grateful.

When you suggested my going with the William J. Burns Detective Agency, I did at the time, and through the agency, I made a contact in this office. You probably know Mr. Bergner, formally of the Bergner & Engle Co, of Philadelphia and at present, he is also the Mayor of Avalon, N.J., and the head of the Pennsylvania Brewers.

Chief, if you think this information, I have can help you, just let me know where and when I can see you, and I'll gladly do it. If there is any information that you need in Pennsylvania or in any way that I can be of any help to you, please do not hesitate to call on me as I would like to show my appreciation for everything, so hoping to hear from you,

I am, respectfully yours,

Frank J Acker

Note: Frank J. Acker (1881-1959) resided in Philadelphia for most of his life. He enlisted in the Army to serve during World War II. He went to college for two years and was employed as a Policemen, detective, and other public service positions during his lifetime. His affection for Ellis Parker is evident. I get the feeling that Ellis was considered a mentor.

My search for Tony Sansone was inconclusive. A Tony Sansone connected to the St. Louis bootlegging gangs can be found on the internet, but I found it impossible to be confident he was the same man referred to as the bootlegger by Frank Acker in his letter. There are reports (The Decatur Herold August 14, 1924) on the internet that Tony Sansone of St. Louis, Missouri, was the owner of a truck set ablaze containing fruit and illegal alcohol. When contacted by Police, Sansone told them that his vehicle had been stolen. He was cleared of prohibition charges. I also found a St. Louis Star newspaper article describing Tony Sansone as a pallbearer during a Gangster's funeral in 1927.

I would like to believe that Frank J. Acker's letter is essential. I wish I could have found anything written about his daughter's Kidnapping, as claimed by Tony Sansone, or his claim that his common-law wife was arrested for murder, but I did not. It should be remembered that a lot of time has passed.

Frank J. Acker has a long history of Detective work, thanks to Ellis Parker's recommendations.

FROM THE ELLIS PARKER LOST FILES

December 6th, 1935

Mr. Ellis Parker
Mount Holly, N.J.

Dear Mr. Parker:

This is not a "nut letter," and neither is it one that promises to solve the Lindbergh case. However, it may serve to remind you of certain facts which may have slipped your mind.

I worked on the case for many months while a member of the staff of the World-Telegram. I recall meeting you one day in your office and I believe Squire Johnson accompanied us. Since then, I have left the World-Telegram and now am in the motion picture business.

The only reason for writing you is to repeat certain of the things that came to my attention. Colonel Schwarzkopf insisted they meant nothing. Probably they did not, but because of the fact that the newspapers quote you as saying the sentence referring to "the telephone wire" is significant, then there may possibly be some significance in this.

As I said, probably not, but here it is:

Almost directly to the rear of the place where the body was found, a demented war veteran by the name of Schiapelli lived. This place also was near "the telephone wire." I do not recall the spelling; the wording I give here is about how it would be pronounced.

Skirting around that territory, I wondered about the inhabitant. Using more or less direct methods, I investigated, and I found the following:

1.) In the rude shack where this man lived, we found a set of Beck Brothers tools. Missing was the chisel of the size used on the ladder.

2.) The man was a carpenter of sorts, and the front portion of this shack was cluttered with wood of all sizes and shapes. To my untrained eye, it greatly resembled the wood used in the ladder. If my memory is correct, I showed a sample to Squire Johnson and he confirmed my judgment.

3.) In the lean-to attached to the building, I came across a veritable mound of junk – bedding, wood, boxes, etc. Digging beneath it, I came across a green sedan. This man told me, or rather told me later, that he had not used his automobile for about two years. However, the battery of this car was in good shape because the lights snapped on, there was gasoline in the tanks and the tires were inflated.

The place was a shamble. I recall that the man apparently slept upon a low lounge upon which there were piled many layers of blankets and comforters. Beneath one layer, I found a pile of dirty socks; beneath another, and deeper down, was a well-oiled shotgun carefully wrapped and tied; and so on.

These facts I duly reported to Schwarzkopf, but he insisted that they meant nothing, that his flat feet had checked into them and decided this man was not concerned. It is entirely possible and even probable that he was correct, but there still remain doubts because I don't believe the Colonel and his men could find an over-sized bull in one-acre pasture at noon of a sunny day.

There is another angle, and one which of necessity must be handled with the utmost discretion if it ever does come to light. That reason is that Squire Johnson might feel the lash of official censure if he were brought into it.

Johnson, you will recall, was the wood expert first called in to make a report on the wood in the ladder and the construction of the ladder. To the best of my memory, he made two reports. It happened that a copy of his second report came into my hands, but not the first. I know that the one I had was the second because, in the first paragraph it referred to an earlier report.

However, the prosecution and Schwarzkopf declared that there was no first report, and it was reported to me indirectly that he was informed it would be to his best interests – he has a State job –not to mention it. I am not certain of these facts; they are only hearsay. Perhaps they are of interest.

I do not know whether you were correctly quoted when you said you believed Hauptmann is "not the man" or is "not alone in this crime." If you said the latter, then I extend to you my congratulations because such is my sincere belief.

I do not believe there is anything additional that I might tell you. Should you, however, desire at any time to communicate with me, my address is

George Daws
Warner Brothers
321 W. 44th St.,
New York City.
The telephone is Chickering 4-2200.

Needless to say, I desire only that justice be served. I have no ax to grind, hate personal connection with any public inquisition, and am actuated solely by the thought that the few bits of fact and rumor I picked up long ago my serve you.

Please accept my best wishes,

Sincerely,
George Daws

Ellis Parker responded to George Daws on 12-12-1935:

December 12, 1935

George Daws
Warner Bros.,
321 W. 44th St.,
New York City

Dear Mr. Daws: -

Your letter of the 6th received, and it was awfully nice to hear from an old friend.

I have to refrain from discussing this case, which I have done all along. I realize the newspapers are having a good time. They wanted it for the long time, and I am perfectly cognizant of the fact of what is going on, so far as the press is concerned. After the storm is over and the smoke has cleared away, and you are in the district, stop in, and I will discuss it with you.

Very truly yours,

Ellis H. Parker
Chief of Detectives

Note: George Daws seems to have disappeared entirely after composing his letter. I could not find any other record of him on the web. The information disclosed in his letter on Squire Johnson is interesting. Daws leads you to believe he had a relationship with Squire Johnson. The Johnson report's most significant thing is that his stated opinion was that two people worked on constructing the ladder.

Surprisingly, Johnson revised his view while the Hauptmann trial was ongoing, although he did not testify at the trial. Johnson chooses to proclaim that he now believed there was only one person that had constructed the ladder.

The Hauptmann prosecution never strayed from projecting Bruno Hauptmann as a lone suspect in the Lindbergh crime. They dismissed any other solution to the crime, and there were many. However, it should be remembered that Hauptmann was not arrested until 9-14-1934, a full six months after Squire Johnson's report to Schwarzkopf. We believe that Johnson was directed to issue a 2nd report because later, the Hauptmann prosecution and Col. Schwarzkopf even went so far as to declare there was no first report. A suspicious and tangled web there.

This is just another of the unexplained reversals by the Hauptmann prosecution. We do not think there was ever a worse investigation or court conduct in American Justice's annuals. The prosecution's behavior can be understood. They wanted personal glory. The Defense was just incompetent; it was beyond explanation or fathoming.

It is hard to dismiss George Daws's testimony in this letter. The search of the grounds of Schiapelli's property, who was described as a demented war veteran, yielded items that are too coincidental to the Lindbergh case to dismiss easily. Daws accuses Schwarzkopf of insisting it was nothing after having the property searched by his officers. Schwarzkopf decided that he had no concern about Schiapelli. Given the stakes, the investigation of the possibly greatest crime in history, shouldn't Schwarzkopf have been more diligent in his exploration of this lead? Was Schwarzkopf the wrong man to lead the investigation, or was he overruled by Charles Lindbergh?

FROM THE ELLIS PARKER LOST FILES

December 6th, 1935

HERBERT S. MIKESELL
AMERICAN AND FOREIGN Scientific, Confidential Service
RICHMOND, INDIANA, U.S.A.

Mr. Ellis Parker
Special Investigator c/o Governor Hoffman, Trenton, N.J.

Dear Sir:

It is a lot of satisfaction to the public to know that the Lindbergh case will finally receive the attention of a real investigator not connected with a political office.

There are hundreds of expert investigators in this country and abroad who have the opinion that Hauptmann's conviction was not the final chapter that would be written into the records of the Lindbergh case. And you are not the only investigator whose services were refused and ignored in the case even when such services were offered gratis.

Personally speaking, I worked out more details of the case immediately following the crime than was introduced during the trial after the ransom money had established Hauptmann's identity in connection with the extortion phase of the case. But that part of it is history as my letters will testify if they are still on file, which is doubtful.

According to my deductions, the entire case was a typical Liquor-Ring gang job, and the methods employed, if closely compared and checked with other gang jobs, will yet go along ways in solving the case and bringing the guilty parties to trial.

Another angle I would check if I were on the job is the Condon phase. I often wondered just how much of that $50,000 ransom money went over the fence at the cemetery. Even if Hauptmann did receive it, he couldn't yell. He was short-changed without convicting himself for extortion. Condon has made a lot of expensive trips before and after the trial, which certainly cannot be charged to the Hauptmann angle without knocking hell out of Condon's own testimony at the trial. That Condon is a pretty smart fellow, and he's got iron nerves, but like all the rest of the smart boys, he has made a few dumb mistakes, and that's what gets the smart boys in the end.

If there wasn't any other evidence in the case to show that Hauptmann didn't kidnap the Lindbergh baby, but this one detail (A carpenter would have better sense than to climb up on as frail a ladder as that used in the Lindbergh snatch). He wouldn't risk his neck and the success of the crime on that detail, which he would be the most efficient in accomplishing.) no, Hauptman is not the man, yet his execution will relieve a lot of smart officials of more work and a hell-of-a-lot of disgrace just as the Tom Mooney case on the Frisco coast.

While I do not claim any powers beyond the range of common sense, I do not treat a human life in any other but a human manner, regardless of what that life is charged with. What a man owes, he should pay. But he should not pay some other account which he does not owe. There is a reasonable doubt that Hauptmann did not kidnap and murder the Lindbergh baby, and until it has been proven beyond a reasonable doubt that he did kidnap and murder the child, he should not be executed.

There is much that Hauptmann could tell in regard to the case which he has not testified, of that I am satisfied. But for that matter, there are in my estimation several additional persons who have not testified fully, and some of them were connected with the "inside" angle of the Lindbergh and Morrow homes.

We, the boys on the line who have had experience and training in the investigation of crime, realize that there is much to be done in this case. It is going to be plenty tough at this late stage of the game, but they have got a good man on the job in my estimation, one who does his work thoroughly and believe me we are all pulling for your success.

The complete solving of the Lindbergh case will restore in the public mind that a courtroom is a place of justice, whereas, at this stage of the case about the only impression which remains in the public mind is that it was the biggest show on earth and the biggest sell-out for the newspapers in the history of our criminal courts. Well, commercially speaking, it was a huge success, for those that got paid for their time, but it certainly won't encourage young America nor instill in young minds a respect of the courts nor a desire to aid in the maintenance of law and order, and it makes bad men worse if they haven't got a chance, why stand trial? And that makes them hard to take without somebody getting badly hurt.

Well, old man, sorry to have taken up your time with my ramblings. I just wanted you to know that there are a lot of us boys who are going to be badly disappointed if you don't turn this case inside-out, and it's the inside we want to hear about. The kids on the street corners know all about the outside, that's history.

Wishing you success, and knowing that you will be successful, I desire to remain,

Sincerely your friend,

H.S. Mikesell

#6-Howard Place Richmond, Ind.

Detective Ellis Parker responded to Herbert S. Mikesell on 1-31-1936:

January 31, 1936

Mr. Herbert S. Mikesell

#6 Howard Place

Richmond, Ind.

Dear Sir:

Your letter of December 6 has been received, and I deeply appreciate your writing me, although I am sorry not to have answered sooner, but as you undoubtedly realize, this case has kept me very busy. I appreciate the confidence you have expressed in me, and you, like many others, feel that there has been a mistake, and I hope that in the very near future, this case will be brought to a successful conclusion.

Again, thanking you for your confidence and trusting that I may again hear from you, I remain,

Very truly yours,

Ellis H. Parker

Chief of Detectives

Herbert S. Mikesell responded to Detective Ellis Parker on 2-3-1936:

February 3rd, 1936

HERBERT S. MIKESELL

AMERICAN AND FOREIGN Scientific, Confidential Service

RICHMOND, INDIANA. U.S.A.

Mr. Ellis H. Parker,

Chief of Detectives.

Burlington County, Mount Holly, N.J.

Dear Sir:

I have just received your answer to my letter of 12/6/36 and am very glad to hear from you.

To quote our old friend, "Will Rogers." About all I know, I read in the papers, however, according to their reports, which are given somewhat reluctantly, it appears that you are progressing as well as could be expected in a case which has gotten as cold as this one.

It is very seldom that I ever make any statements relative to court proceedings, which are in favor of the criminal, however, a good detective is just as proud of his work as a physician or any other professional man, and he values his reputation just as highly. When the job is done right, and the results are what would be expected by other associates with proper training and experience, he can then close the books and rest well at night. On the other hand, until the last detail has been balanced, the task is not finished, and an uncompleted or slighted job is of no good to anyone, while at the same time, much harm may result. It is because of the fact that I never could develop or reconstruct the case in my own mind, according to the available evidence, as the court found in this case; that made me boil up sufficiently to make some nasty sounding statements both orally and in the newspapers over a large section of this middle-western territory, and from your attitude and that of Governor Hoffman, I am confident that you both have about the same opinion as myself.

I began intelligence work in the United States Army in the year 1908, which is a few years past, and since that, I believe I have done about all classes of work from railroad detective to revenue department and immigration. So, when we old-timers fly off the handle, I guess we can be excused on the ground of old-age infirmities if for no other reason.

I went in for law for a two-year course of study and then completed four years in chemistry, and allied sciences, which has been a great help in every phase of the work and the public have become scientific-minded and demand that type of work as well as the courts throughout this section.

In addition to the public demand, a fellow has to meet competition in any profession or business, and this game of hide-and-seek is no different from the others in that respect.

If I would have had the Hauptmann assignment, I believe I would have started with the telephone call that removed the baby's nurse from the nursery at that particular time of the evening the crime was committed. That was no accident Chief. This fact is substantiated because of the other preparations which later developed. The ladder in readiness, the get-a-way automobile waiting, the criminals on the spot, the hide-a-way prepared, etc.

How in the hell anyone with common sense, could surmise that a slow-motion German boy who never did anything in his life but what he was caught before he finished the job, could plan and execute a job with the professional earmarks of this one is more that I can beat into this thick head of mine.

Whoever executed this crime not only had inside information as to the movements of the family and a plan of the house, forty-two windows according to my count from a drawing which was published in local papers, but they also had a thorough understanding of the land, roads, etc., of the entire section around the Lindbergh estate. In my opinion, that sailor boyfriend of the nurse-maid Betty Gow, and his associates, could just about clear up the entire case, while he is not in the country now, yet, his associates on the boat where he worked, could probably produce. At least that is where the trail leads unless I am blind as well as dumb.

Due to the fact that all preparations were completed and the criminals in readiness waiting for the signal that the way was clear and the fact that this fellow put thru his call at the moment everyone else was on his toes, is too strong to pass up as a coincident and with that boy on the line I can just about see the connections up to and including Hauptmann and his friend Fisch or whatever his name is. As for this boy

Hauptmann, he was just the fall-guy for the real boys on the job.

As to Condon and the rest, if I were Hauptmann's attorney, I would have their heads examined for sanity, and their eyes examined for color as well as distance and test their ears and memory of voices with German dialect. I'll gamble next year's salary that they cannot pick his voice out of twenty other Germans speaking broken English, three times out of five, with a one-week interval separating the tests, provided they are given a blind test or the suspects in another room removed from them at the time the test is registered.

I speak German, French, Italian, Spanish and Greek and I have a good memory, but I'll be darn if I could pick out a voice even in English if I had only heard the voice utter about four words and a year separating the original time from the test and I question anyone else possessing these superhuman qualities.

No matter whether Lindbergh's baby was handed out the window by someone within the nursery or whether the criminal entered and procured the child, that phone call which called the nurse from the room or gave her a good excuse for not being there at the time the crime was committed is the most important detail upon which to press an investigation. No matter what clues are outstanding, when you attempt to put them into the framework of the crime, they either mislead you, or they leave a wide-open space in the reconstruction of the crime, which nothing fits into excepting the phone call and the sailor back of it. That is the only sum-up I can get to save my life, and if I was sitting in Hauptmann's place, I'm dammed if I could see it any different.

Well, Chief, I never envied a man on an assignment yet in the profession, because I never was lucky enough to get the soft job, but my nose is just long enough to make me want to get my feet wet on this job, and I am darn sorry I couldn't have worked with you on it, and any other man who has a natural love for the game feels the same as myself.

The next time you see the Governor, you might mention that I started something with my newspaper articles in his favor. I have clipped about seventy from prominent papers in the last seven weeks. At least we got them believing that there are two sides to every story, and the story is not complete until both sides have been nailed together.

Best regards and success to you and the Governor, and when yours truly can step out of his way to be of any assistance, well, orders are orders.

Sincerely,

H.S. Mikesell

6-Howard Place, Richmond, Ind.

Ellis Parker responded a final time to Herbert S. Mikesell on 2-6-1936:

February 6, 1936

Mr. Herbert S. Mikesell

#6 Howard Place, Richmond, Ind.

My Dear Friend:

I received your communication of February 3 and read it with a great deal of interest, as oftentimes, other's thoughts are very beneficial. I appreciate more than words can express, your confidence in myself and the Governor, the latter, the Governor, has been criticized for publicity and political purposes, that he did what he did. This is positively not true. I have known Harold Hoffman from a boy. He is what I consider a full-blooded American, a person of decision, and courage. He knows this case is wrong, and he does not care what his political future or any other future is. He will stand by his guns. No power on earth will sway him from the line of duty.

Several newspapers who have axes to grind one way or another are slamming him, but it is like pouring water on a duck's back, as far as he is concerned.

I have devoted more time and study to this case than any other case that I ever had, and I would have dearly loved to have had charge of it when it first occurred, as I positively know there would be a different picture today, but sometimes I have experienced in life that a lot of people (prosecution) play unknowingly a part in a great drama to be enacted later. I do not know whether you can read between the lines or not in this affair, but I trust that it will be that way. Of course, the people who play a part in the first place do not get much benefit when the real act takes place.

Thanking you again for writing me, I remain,

Very truly yours,

Ellis H. Parker

Chief of County Detectives

Note: Ellis Parker writes, "I would have dearly loved to have had charge of it when it first occurred, as I positively know there would be a different picture today." From his letter to Herbert S. Mikesell on 2-6-1936 commenting on him leading the investigation on the night of the Lindbergh baby abduction.

Andy Sahol and I (Russell Lloyd) have said many times that it was a tragedy that Detective Ellis Parker was not brought to the Lindbergh house the night of the kidnapping. His experience at a crime scene alone would have made it very difficult for the criminals to have escaped immediate identification. The baby's movement or his corpse would have been known that evening, and every member of the household would have been interviewed by an experienced detective that very night. The mountain of unanswered questions would have been pursued, and more questions designed to bring the truth out would have been asked. Instead of being trampled over, the grounds, and the evidence, would have been secured. Every lead dismissed by Norman Schwarzkopf and Charles Lindbergh at the crime scene would have been followed up on immediately under the direction of Ellis Parker. There was no one at the location that had his type of experience or record of success. We know that it was Norman Schwarzkopf that had sent for Ellis Parker. He knew his limitations. Who rescinded that order? The only person at the crime scene that had that much power was Charles Lindbergh. What was he covering up or afraid of being uncovered?

The intelligence and intellect of Herbert Mikesell (1889-1964) are readily identifiable in his excellent writings to Ellis Parker. His comments and suspicions are well thought out. His two letters here are some of the best written to Ellis Parker on the Lindbergh-Hauptmann case. Herbert Mikesell was an experienced investigator who had spent his whole life at it. His conclusion that the Hauptmann case did not meet the "*proven without a reasonable doubt*" consideration is frightening because Hauptmann was electrocuted "with doubt" only two months later. The conduct of the investigators and the prosecutors of this case will forever be a "black mark" on American Justice.

FROM THE ELLIS PARKER LOST FILES

27th Floor,

370 Lexington Avenue,

New York, N.Y.

Telephone Ashland 4-5600,

December 7, 1935

Mr. Ellis Parker,

Chief Investigator,

Burlington County, Mt. Holly, NJ

My Dear Mr. Parker,

I am very glad to see your name come into the Lindbergh case because, for a long time, I have been wanting to unbutton something, although I might be forced to button up against other powerful forces.

In reference to the kidnap note demanding $50,000.00 ransom, I understand that the original note was lost. This is most unfortunate if it is so.

I say most unfortunate because I consider it a great handicap in backing up what I am about to unfold to you.

As you have probably observed, the writing of the kidnap note reveal clear indications of script writings in my analysis of written forms in determining the parent system of the culprit's penmanship. I fail to find indications of the same system of writing in what is plainly seen the elementary penmanship of the convicted man—Bruno Richard Hauptmann, a man of grade school education.

I also find in the writing of the kidnap note a clear indication of simulation or imitation, in addition to the usual dissimulation of one's own identity in handwriting. The two acts of simulation and dissimulation carried on simultaneously was done by a better penman, and it seems to me that the simulation was done to cast reflection on the person who was eventually convicted of the murder of the infant, as the records now stand.

You have observed, no doubt, that there are several letters in the writing of the kidnap note that do not coincide with similar letters in Hauptmann's known or conceded writing, as well as in the extortion notes that followed the kidnapping. Some of these are the peculiar curving of the stem of "y" of "redy," and of the "y" of "mony." Another is observed in the incomplete stem of "g" of "making."

Of the small letters' "d," three are observed with the ovals completely disconnected from the stem, as in "d' of "redy," "d" of "and" and "d" of "deliver." My comparison of the several small letters "r" is most unsatisfactory.

The suggestion that the writer of the kidnap note is a scriptwriter—probably German—are observed in the writing of "redy," "After," "mony," "warn," "k" of "making," "public" and "for notify."

Other things I have observed is that the writer of the kidnap note is afflicted with some nervous manifestation, and, physically, is not a person of "After" and "making."

I could go on picking on the writing of the kidnap note into many bits but with the original note reported lost, according to my information from the press, I do not know what good I might do at this time, especially in the face of powerful Prosecution, the testimony of many handwriting experts considered to be leaders in the profession, and the fact that Hauptmann did write the extortion notes, my reason for remaining silent. In the meantime, I have never accepted the convicted man as the actual writer of the kidnap note. With more than thirty years as a handwriting examiner, and more than fifteen years in the service of the Protective Committee of the American Bankers Association, my eyes tell me that the kidnap note is not only a dissimulation of one's identity but a good simulation of the writing of an intended dupe.

In concluding, I can only say this: Find the original note, if possible. Otherwise, doubt if what I have in mind can be demonstration with justice. Do not hesitate to call me.

Yours very truly,

Hubert R. Erlbrookes

Handwriting Examiner

<u>Ellis Parker replied on December 14, 1935:</u>

> Hubert H. Erlbrookes,
>
> 27th Floor, 370 Lexington Ave., New York, N. Y.
>
> Dear Sir: -
>
> Your letter received, and I deeply appreciate your inter-est in writing me. I also appreciate your offer to be of assis-tance, and you can rest assured, if the opportunity presents itself, I shall be only too glad to call on you.
>
> I also wish to thank you for your expression of confidence.
>
> Again, thanking you, I remain,
>
> Very truly yours,
>
> Ellis H. Parker
>
> Chief of Detectives

<u>Note</u>: The first thing that is obvious to me is that Ellis Parker felt the same way about Hubert H. Erlbrookes's letters. I think that Erlbrooke's opinions and conclusions influenced his thinking.

The thing that jumps out at me is the disclosure that the Prosecution lost the original ransom note. I refuse to accept that it was lost. I think it was deliberately destroyed by someone that had a lot to lose if Hauptmann was acquitted. The Hauptmann case is a horrible miscarriage of justice that America should have been ashamed of. Yes, Hauptmann had something to do with the ransom money, but Ellis Parker was confident that he was never at the Lindbergh residence, that night or any night. He did not kidnap the baby, and Bruno Richard Hauptmann should not have been sentenced to death in the Electric Chair.

FROM THE ELLIS PARKER LOST FILES

<u>The following is a Telegram received by Ellis Parker on December 7, 1935:</u>

WESTERN UNION

PF90 36 DL 7 EXTRA=S1 NEW YORK NY DEC 7 159P

ELLIS PARKER

PROSECUTORS OFFICE OY=

WOR WOULD LIKE TO EXTEND INVITATION TO YOU TO DISCUSS HAUPTMANN CASE WITH GABRIEL HEATTER NOTED COMMENTATOR STOP BELIEVE COULD ARRANGE TIME AT YOUR CONVENIENCE WOULD APPRECIATE ANSWER COLLECT=

JERRY DANZIG SPECIAL FEATURES WOR

1440 BROADWAY NEW YORK.

Detective Ellis H. Parker responded on January 23, 1936:

Jerry Danzig

1440 Broadway

New York, N.Y.

Dear Friend:

Some time ago, I received a telegram from you but neglected to answer it. I know Gabriel Heatter very well, and I have the highest regard for him. I often listen to him on the radio. It would be very unethical for me to discuss any case, especially a case such as this.

I interest myself in this case on the side of Justice only not to commercialize in any way. All of my investigations have been at my own expense. I hold a human life above everything. My only interest, in this case, is one of Justice. I am not inter- est in publicity or politics or any of the things that have been mentioned. I have even read where I wanted to be the head of the State Police. I wouldn't have the job if it was handed to me on a silver platter. I have no more interest in Hauptmann than I would any individual, and I am sure that the Governor is sincere in his stand, as he is the type that when he thinks he is right, he speaks, it wouldn't matter what position it placed him in before the public. He is honest in his convictions and is, in my judgment, a true American, one of decision and courage to back it.

Thanking you, I remain,

Very truly yours,
Ellis H. Parker
Chief of Detectives

Note: Significantly, Jerry Danzig would contact Ellis Parker. Ellis's fame was peaking. The United States was identifying his contributions as a law enforcement officer. It is a shame that Ellis turned down the opportunity but understanding Ellis's character and his dedication to law enforcement, does make sense. Although Ellis was in media demand during his life, he always focused on his true love, American Justice.

Jerry Danzig had a successful career in the golden age of radio broadcasting for many years. He worked with Martin & Lewis, Ed Sullivan, and many others. In his career, he rose to become Vice President in charge of Radio Network Programs of the National Broadcasting Company (NBC). In 1947 the US State Department sent him and other top Radio officials to visit the Soviet Union. There they studied and exchanged information on media production. Later in his life, Danzig served as a special assistant to Nelson A. Rockefeller.

According to Wikipedia, Gabriel Heatter (1890-1972) was an American radio commentator whose WW II ear sign-on was "There's good news tonight." He was only bested in the industry by Walter Winchell and Edward R. Murrow. That Ellis Parker was asked to appear with Heatter is high praise indeed. Heatter covered the trial of Bruno Hauptmann. When Hauptmann's execution was delayed, he ad-libbed while awaiting word on when it would occur. His professionalism under pressure and his ability to keep the audience informed without resorting to sensationalism earned him critical praise.

In his response to Danzig's telegram, Ellis Parker's real character shines. His creditability, his honesty, and his integrity are recognizable. Ellis Parker was an American original that should be remembered and celebrated. That is my goal, writer Russell Lloyd, and the purpose of Ellis's Grandson, Andrew Sahol.

FROM THE ELLIS PARKER LOST FILES

Envelope addressed to: Hon. Ellis Parker, Mt. Holly, Burlington County, New Jersey

Post Date: 12-7-1935
Postmark: Zip 19352, Lewisville, Pa.

Re: Bruno Richard Hauptmann

The writer comes in contact with many people and has heard many arguments, pro and con in the Lindberg case, some of which should be looked into before you take a man's life. About a week after Hauptman was arrested, I happened to be in a store in New York. The man who waited on me said to me, "Do you know that man over there?" referring to an elderly man who had collected around him a crowd of people near the door and who seemed to be lecturing to or haranguing the crowd. I answered him, "No." "Well," he said, "You evidently don't read the newspapers, that's Dr. Condon of Lindbergh fame." I looked at the man, amazed that there should be any mistake about Hauptmann's identity. I said, "Dr. Condon, DON'T YOU KNOW HAUPTMANN?" He turned deliberately around and said, "Yes, I know him NOW (emphasizing the "now"), and so would you IF YOU SAT ON THE BENCH AND TALKED WITH HIM MORE THAN AN HOUR AS I DID THE OTHER DAY." Writer: "Well, I think if I gave a man $50,000, I would know him the next time I saw him."

Dr.: "I didn't give him $50,000; I gave him $30,000, came back with $20,000, and the police said that was my part of the graft." Writer: "perhaps the baby is not dead." Dr.: "Oh, yes, it is, I am the only man in this world who has a picture of that dead baby, and the newspapers wanted to pay me magnificently for it, but I had so much sympathy for that poor mother that I would not sell it." Then he started to tell that Lindbergh was one of the "greatest men this generation has produced," but I was not interested and ran out. A short time after that, I was in a movie. I think it was in Jamaica – "The House of Rothchild." A picture was thrown on the screen of Dr. Condon, and it was the identical man who talked with me a short time before. People whom I met, almost without exception, think that Hauptmann is getting too rough a deal. You have not evidence enough to convict him. Supposing it should happen to be the truth that the boy Frisch left the money with Hauptmann. There is nothing superhuman about that. Some people have gone so far as to say that Dwight Morrow's disinherited son stole the baby together with Violet Sharp, etc. They were trying to get money and accidentally dropped the baby. Anyway, there must have been some great urge behind the suicide of that young girl. Also, did not Dr. Condon swear on the witness stand that he knew Hauptmann when he saw him in an automobile. Is it true that Mrs. Lindbergh swore on the stand that the baby was normal?

A friend of many years standing, a man of intelligence and integrity, told me of a colored man employed by the Lackawanna Railroad at Hoboken. He told me at intervals of six months apart that he was certain that this colored man knew all about that baby. It seemed that this colored man is a sort of a caretaker of the Morrow home when it is empty. He was recently given a six months' leave of absence by the

Lackawanna Railroad to go to Panama. My friend would like to know where he got the money to go with, for of himself he had no money. I think this would stand looking into, and my inquiry could be corroborated through the Lackawanna.

The other day, the "News" I think it was, published Hauptmann's eyes, saying they were the eyes of a murderer. Well, well, my lifetime of handling people does not make me agree with them. If I were giving the palm to anyone, as far as eyes are concerned, I would give it to Betty Gow.

Yours for fair play,

PS: My friend tells me that the colored man laughs whenever anyone talks about the Lindberg baby and says he wouldn't be surprised if the baby was still alive.

On 12-14-1936 (1 week later), Ellis Parker received a 2nd very similar letter from the same anonymous writer. This time signed "Yours truly for justice"

Envelope addressed to: Hon. Ellis Parker, Mt. Holly, Burlington County, New Jersey

Post Date: 12-14-1935
Postmark: Zip 19352, Lewisville, Pa.

Re: Bruno Richard Hauptmann

Note: *The first paragraph of this 2nd letter (following) is identical to the first.*

The writer comes in contact with many people and has heard many arguments, pro, and con in the Lindberg case, some of which should be looked into before you take a man's life. About a week after Hauptman was arrested, I happened to be in a store in New York. The man who waited on me said to me, "Do you know that man over there?" referring to an elderly man who had collected around him a crowd of people near the door and who seemed to be lecturing to or haranguing the crowd. I answered him, "No." "Well," he said, "You evidently don't read the newspapers, that's Dr. Condon of Lindbergh fame." I looked at the man, amazed that there should be any mistake about Hauptmann's identity. I said, "Dr. Condon, DON'T YOU KNOW HAUPTMANN?" He turned deliberately around and said, "Yes, I know him NOW (emphasizing the "now"), and so would you IF YOU SAT ON THE BENCH AND TALKED WITH HIM MORE THAN AN HOUR AS I DID THE OTHER DAY." Writer: "Well, I think if I gave a man $50,000, I would know him the next time I saw him." Dr.: "I didn't give him $50,000; I gave him $30,000, came back with $20,000, and the police said that was my part of the graft." Writer: "perhaps the baby is not dead." Dr.: "Oh, yes, it is, I am the only man in this world who has a picture of that dead baby, and the newspapers wanted to pay me magnificently for it, but I had so much sympathy for that poor mother that I would not sell it." Then he started to tell that Lindbergh was one of the "greatest men this generation has produced,"

Note: *From this point, the 2nd letter differs.*

But it was 7:30 P.M., and I was in a great hurry and not attaching the importance that I should have attached to this controversy, I went out.

There is no question that the Doctor intended to tell me that the only reason he knows Hauptmann was because he sat and talked with him recently and that he did know him otherwise.

This information was sent anonymously to Mr. Riley during the trial. I even called Judge Fawcett's office up before Mr. Riley came into the case and told them about it.

I am a Protestant Christian, and you can believe that I am telling the truth. If Dr. Condon was "joshing," then he should be made to stand by his "joshing." He was given a public talk, and it should be assumed that he was telling the truth.

Another thing that seems to me to be a great negligence, to say the least. The baby had a little woolen shirt sewed upon him because his chest was "wheezy" with a cold. He was pinned in a blanket and yet with at least five grown people in the house, he was so neglected that robbers could come with ladders, enter the house, fall off the ladder with the baby and make a crash, there was a dog there that obligingly did not bark, although I understand that he was a species of dog that would not do anything else but bark and the baby dd not scream from fright. He might have been chloroformed, but that takes time.

Yours truly for justice,

Copy to Col. Charles A. Lindbergh

Note: "Colored man" (used in the first letter) is a term I would not use myself. I find it offensive. I only included this term to remain accurate to the original letter.

I can believe that this man ran into Dr. Condon when visiting New York City. Condon was up and around the neighborhoods of the city often.

The connection between Dwight Morrow Jr. and Violet Sharp is interesting. If the baby was dropped as described, it might explain her suicide. She couldn't live with the guilt.

The anonymous writer is obviously angry with Dr. Condon for not acknowledging he was "joshing" in the New York store. Is there a code I am unaware of that covers when a stranger approaches you in a New York City store? When a dog is supposed to bark, I think, based on my dog, it is very unpredictable. The only time I can safely predict my dog will bark is when I am waving food in the air.

FROM THE ELLIS PARKER LOST FILES

THE PARKER HOUSE

BOSTON, MASSACHUSETTS

Glenwood J. Shepard

President and Managing Director

Postmarked, New York Station on Dec. 7, 1935, in a Providence Biltmore, Rhode Island envelope

Dear Mr. Parker:

I know you are a man of great intelligence and discernment. I also believe if I was a man, I could have been a detective.

I have from the beginning of this Lindbergh case – believed Condon the worst old hypocrite that ever lived – Why have they not seen thru him? I cannot imagine all this time, the real villain and Master Mind of the whole terrible plot – it was he and no other, who went to the library and found the symbol – and had in mind all the time he would get most of the ransom money – he knew the confidence Colonel Lindbergh had in him and took advantage of it.

Hauptmann was his tool – I am not excusing Hauptmann for whatever he did – but he is not the criminal – everything points to Condon, and I believe you know it – only get him and his bodyguard.

Hauptmann has been threatened (if he told the truth) his baby would be killed – no one but Condon at the back of it – everyone will soon know Condon the degenerate has the rest of the ransom money – planned the whole diabolical kidnapping and has kept Hauptmann silent – Oh, I pray God he will get his punishment – I am sixty years old and studied the case from the beginning – am a true American and could stake my life, Condon is the criminal –

Yours in Truth…

Note: Condon, or JAFSIE, was not a popular man. The public did not believe him sincere. He was deservedly high on everyone's list of suspects. The way he became part of the case was strange from the beginning. Condon placed an advert in the newspaper and was immediately trusted as the Lindbergh spokesperson. Yeah, we all got that. Makes sense. Right?

I can't let this line pass without comment: "I also believe if I was a man, I could have been a detective?" Thank God for women's empowerment! Anna Bading, Detective Ellis Parker's right hand, or Watson to his Holmes, was every bit a detective and indispensable to Ellis Parker.

FROM THE ELLIS PARKER LOST FILES

Windber. Pa.

Dec. 7th, 1935

Governor Harold Hoffman

Trenton, N.J.

Subject. Commonwealth vs. Bruno Richard. Hauptmann.

Dear Governor:

With some hesitancy, lest my motives might be misconstrued: am writing as to the public's general feeling, in this section, regarding the case of Bruno Richard Hauptmann, the peculiar circumstances surrounding him, the shady evidence, and the Jury that convicted him.

"I have no interest in Hauptmann but am prompted to write by reason of experience and having something in common as to the faults and sad realities in our common law procedure.

The general feeling here is that the Jury, playing to the galleries, was too anxious to convict, without reasoning that the evidence might have been in many ways manufactured, and the very action of the Jury after the conviction to large degree proved the fact. The limelight of convicting and flirting for the stage seemed the greatest object of the Jury, and the display was very nauseating to the people, and when the people got a chance to get a word in, the stage jury was silenced.

I personally followed the case fairly and carefully, and considering errors, mistakes, and probable misconceptions came to the conclusion that, aside from possession of the ransom money, the balance of the evidence in the main easily could have been invented and assumed.

I am an engineer, architect, also experienced in carpentering, and had more than 50 years of practical experience in lumbering and investigation, and from a reasonable point of view, say, that the ladder, or rather the two ladders, was not made by a carpenter, but was likely built by someone with less practical workmanship than Bruno Richard Hauptmann, any man that had any carpenter experience can square boards and fit a small ladder, without square, plane, or rule in a better manner than the ladder shown in the picture. Now here is a strange thing, when all the other workmanship was so crude in making this ladder, why? Was a plane used to make a neat job for a ladder to be used but once for kidnapping purposes? And what was the necessity of the two ladders, when it was proven that the ladders would not support man and baby possible weighing nearly 200 pounds? "What could have been the motive of two ladders"? And if one ladder was built after the kidnapping, and there was similarity as the workmanship and make of the two ladders, by what reasoning can anyone think that both ladders were not built until after the fact in the case? Hauptman certainly did not build the two ladders; in fact, it was not proven that he built any of them.

The plumber that repaired the leaking pipe, in the rented house of Hauptman, long after the crime and the ransom money paid, testified that there was no board out of the floor at the time he fixed the pipe, then surely the board must have been removed afterward, most likely after the arrest of Hauptmann.

This disinterested witness's testimony is positive and proves no doubt, that the board was removed for a cause, after Hauptmann was arrested and his tools taken, by someone other than Hauptmann, to make a ladder, for other purposes than kidnapping the Lindberg baby.

The motive and purpose of removing the board from the floor after the arrest, and taking one of Hauptmann's planes that he had not used for years, picking one that had nicks in the bit and made marks on the wood, and using it on the board that was removed from the floor, to put a piece in the ladder after the fact in the case and the plane marks taken as expert evidence look very much like a transparent frame-up. A skilled carpenter would not use a plane with nicked or bruised bit to surface boards, especially when he has other planes that are sharp, smooth, and not nicked.

The matching of the boards is equally faulty, if you will carefully examine the matching, you will find that there are more growth on one side of the joint in one board than in the one on the other side, in the same distance, to the ordinary eye and inexperienced eye and mind the matching may seem reasonable, but to use it as positive evidence is too dangerous and doubtful. And Governor, do the opposite sides and the edges also all match? Unless there is a complete matching on all sides of both boards, as compared with the other, it cannot be a matched board. And even though the matching were genuine, what bearing could the matching have in the case, or the ladder, if the ladder was not made until after the ransom money was found, and likely the flooring board substituted and placed into the other ladder that was found on the premises after the fact, to bolster up evidence. This might give some light on the question of nail holes and marks appearing on the ladder after the expert's first examination of the ladder.

And unless it was proven that Hauptmann; bought the lumber, at the lumber yard, made the ladder, and used to kidnap the baby; what use is there in tracing the lumber? And it was not proven, that be bought the lumber, nor made the ladder, nor that he kidnaped the baby. A carpenter that was making a ladder to kidnap a baby, by climbing a ladder and take a baby out the window, certainly would not take a chance to build such a flimsy ladder and take chances in breaking the ladder and break an arm, leg, or his neck by falling from a broken ladder. Neither was it proven that Hauptmann, was ever on the ladder, or that the baby was taken out the window by way of the ladder.

Knot in The Board of the Ladder

The contention that an inch and a half was cut out of the board in the ladder, on account of a knot, or known hole, attempting to give some reason for the board not exactly matching, is very amusing. If the board had a bad knot or flaw, that needed cutting out, the carpenter that originally laid the floor, would most likely have had cut out all knots and flaws, it is an infallible rule of all carpenters when laying floors to cut out all such knots and flaws when the floor is originally laid, that the man making the ladder, or substituting a board into another ladder, would not have had any need, chance or cause to do so. But an inexperienced man making a ladder does not know the rule and therefore would advance such a bungle of ideas. It was stated that there were many other kinds of lumber used in making the ladder, and only a small portion of the flooring used, why? Then was it necessary only to use out of the flooring the part that seemed to match, this fact may lead to reasoning that the board was substituted into the other ladder. And again, an arch-criminal, so careful as to use gloves to hide his fingerprints in making a ladder, certainly would not be so stupid as to tear a flooring board out of the floor at such an open and conspicuous place that the very act would arouse suspicion when there were all kinds of other lumber in the garage to make it with.

New nail holes and marks in the ladder

When there are now nail holes and marks on the ladder that were not there when the expert examined the first view of the ladder, is again proof of a substitution, or alteration, or both. And 2500, or more fingerprints and marks on the ladder, and none of them being the prints of Hauptmann. And the witnesses who testified they saw Hauptmann, with a ladder on a truck, or wagon several days before, in the region of the crime, and none of them noticed him having gloves on, creates another impractical idea. If we assume that one would be so criminally careful as to use gloves in attempt to hide his fingerprints in making a ladder, he must have been equally criminal neglectful to haul a ladder around in daylight, on a truck, or wagon, handling the ladder and exposing his fingerprints to the wagon and ladder without gloves, for how could he have known that the wagon or truck would not be recognized and identified, and his fingerprints taken from them. It is not reasonable, and all the facts indicate that the board was taken out of the floor of the Hauptmann house after the plumber had made the repairs to the pipe, and even after Hauptmann's arrest and if a ladder was made out of this board, or a piece of the board substituted and put into the ladder that was supposed to be found on the premises shortly after the crime was committed. "Who dare say nay?" Everything seems to point to this fact, and the change of nail holes and marks and nail holes appearing on the board after the first examination of the expert, certainly indicate that such an alteration and substitution was likely.

The whole case centers around the question of the two ladders, "there was no other material evidence produced." With the exception of possession of part of the ransom money and he gave a reasonable accounting for having the money. Then the conviction and his guilt either stands or falls with the ladder story, and the whole of it does not seem conclusive, sufficient to convict. The whole case and ladder business seem a bundle of contradictions and a bungles mess. Which is, ever the case when part of a story is true, and the rest manufactured to suit and taken as evidence.

Dr. Condon's (Jafsie) story and Lindbergh Identification

Dr. Condon's story is full of crude impractical ambiguous assumed intellectual fiction, unintelligent in practice. Dr. Condon, after he and Lindberg, paid the ransom money at night, in the Cemetery to one John: Condon made a public statement to the effect that he made payment of the ransom money to a John, a man with a deep, bad, hollow cough, and to detain him and get more conversation he told this mad John, who got the ransom money, that he (John) had better do something for that cough. "It is positively known that Hauptmann, never had such a cough. But that Fisch had such a cough and died with it and had consumption. This throws out all of Dr. Condon's and Lindbergh's evidence as to identification, as too anxious to convict without consideration or regard for their own statements. It is facts that are material and not fancy that should convince. A statement of identification from Dr. Condon, and Lindy, in the Cemetery, at night, in the dark, "GET THAT" at night, in the dark, when neither saw or talked to this (John) before, a man with a deep hollow bad cough, and identify him as Hauptmann, who never had such a cough, and never saw him. Also, those that stated they saw Hauptmann in the vicinity of the crime several days before the crime was committed and never saw him before, "Should not be taken as evidence."

I am here giving a concrete case to consider. Identification

In 1906 I investigated a case of ED. N. Atkinson, of 1220, Wallace Street Philadelphia, PA. Who had committed Bigamy, left wife No 1, took his trunks to Hoboken, with wife No 2 and, by boat, shipped them to South Carolina? Later he and wife No 2 left by train for South Carolina, lifted their trunks there and went to St Augustine, Fla. The Bigamy was discovered, to avoid public scandal, he (Atkinson) was privately confronted, but he denied the charge. But left St. Augustine, and went to Savannah, Ga. I located him at Savannah, but upon my arrival there, the police had tipped him from Savanah, I raced him to Montgomery and Birmingham, Ala. At Birmingham, he very aptly covered his trail. Later I apprehended him at St Louis, Mo. and he admitted the charge. Now here is the strangest coincidence and should make every man extremely careful as to identifying any man under any circumstances, except long acquaintance, or a very special mark to identification.

While I was at Montgomery Ala, on the clue of Atkinson, I saw a man at the depot, that answered the exact description of the man Atkinson, I followed this man to the Hotel. I had

Atkinson's Photograph, three letters of his handwriting, and had met and talked with Atkinson, on two former occasions. I looked at the register of the Hotel and found the signature of this man to be identical with the writing of Atkinson, something seemed to make me cautious because of the actions of this man, I later accosted this man in the Hotel Lobby and had a talk with him and showed him the photograph, he at once admitted it was his picture, I took him to the register and compared the handwriting, he admitted it was his writing and picture but could not understand it, of course, I was convinced it was not my man Atkinson, and after carefully examining the man, the photograph of Atkinson, I discovered a slight difference in the lobes of the ears, I showed this to him. But the size, the weight, hair, eyes, teeth, complexion, mannerism, and voice were identical the same, and yet it was not my man Atkinson. A check-up later proved that Atkinson was at Memphis Tenn. When this other man and I were at Montgomery.

This positively shows that no one should identify a man unless they had previously well-known or have some special mark to identify one accused for a criminal offense. "It is criminally dangerous to identify anyone in criminal action unless being absolutely positive." "Unless recent contact."

The Court and Twelve Fallible Jurymen can be mistaken

People should not be so hasty as to say that one is guilty, where there is reasonable doubt. Just because a Jury of twelve inexperienced fallible, and often prejudiced and swayed by the biting words of a pleading lawyer, plea is often an error. Or to say that the dignity of the Court in question and should not be questioned or doubted no matter what has been done or found by a frail and weak-minded jury, of men and women, who are easily led and swayed by feelings other than justice.

Entirely too often, law procedure and jurisprudence has run afoul with truth and justice, for the very reasons herein stated. And by it out Courts are in bad repute. And it would be bad to have another case so extremely notorious, to go amiss by reason of disregarding all reasonable doubt, and heed possibly a prejudiced jury. Because a jury brought in a verdict of guilty, regardless of doubt, truth, and more reasonable facts, and contend that the Court cannot err and must not be questioned is not well taken or solidly founded.

Race Hatred, Prejudice, and Malice must be laid aside

Forgetting all prejudice, malice, hatred, and forgetting all vengeance. Would it not be infinitely more wise and prudent to let this man live and be given a chance to clear, or help to clear up the matter, whether it leads to guilt or innocence, instead of burning him which would, or many not hide the errors and mistakes thereby keeping undercover the actual criminal that is at large, especially since Hauptmann has repeatedly declared his innocence and volunteers to help to solve the mysteries in the case if given a chance, And since above all things punishment and the severity of punishment never has, and never will, lessen crime. If we can't reason criminality out of the human mind by better methods and more intellectual training higher ideals, we certainly cannot burn it into them by electric chairs and reason it into them by the threat of the hangman's rope and persecution.

Attorneys and Officers Duties

The position taken by Attorneys and officers, that it is their sole duty to convict, using all means fair, or unfair, to accomplish this end, and preventing the facts to be admitted by shrewd third practice, and objections sustained according to a fixed rule, and not according to sensible introduction to establish the facts, "is all wrong." It should be the duty of our Courts, The Commonwealth Attorneys, and Officers to use all means to establish the truth, regardless of whether the truth will or will not convict the accused.

Violet Sharp, Ladder, and Fingerprints

The public is convinced that Violet Sharp held the key to the whole situation, and by investigating here associates and the acquaintances immediately before the crime, the night of the crime, and immediately after, would likely involve someone closer home, and some man other than Hauptmann. If the ladder found on the premises does not contain Hauptmann's fingerprints, Then Whose Fingerprints are on the ladder? We all might be surprised to find whose fingerprints are on this ladder. If so, be the ladder was used to do the kidnaping job, are we certain the ladder was used or was the baby taken out by the door, and the ladder used as a hoax to divert the minds of the people and the officers. Can it be possible that the baby was taken out by way of the window, without disturbing the things on the windowsill, and taken down a ladder, without making more marks on the side of the house? If a ladder was placed against a house and a man climbed the ladder and then taking a baby in his arm down the ladder, the friction of the ladder, with the different weights on the ladder and against the sidewall of the house would being a long line well marked, by reason of the different weights up and down, and the ladder sinking in the sod or ground deeper as the weight was added.

Rumor afloat, And Motive for Slaying the Baby

Besides all the other doubts and possible errors, there never has been any motive advanced for slaying the baby, if so, be it was slain. Is it a fact that Dwight Morrow had made a will, giving the baby a portion of his wealth, in work? But maybe not meant in act and deed, that might have been intended for someone else, is this correct, or is it a weird tale? I do not like such insinuations, and if it is correct, it should be thoroughly investigated, and if not found correct, it should be silenced by the facts.

I hope this will be received by and possibly the board of pardons in the same impartial spirit as it is given. Above all am attempting to be fair and favoring none, especially I do not desire to favor the prisoner or a criminal any more that is due under the strange contradicting circumstances in the case.

Sincerely,

George C. Statler

Summary of Doubt

The most astounding thing in the whole proceedings that points to the gravest doubt as to the prisoner's guilt is that if Hauptmann had invented all of his alibis, accountings, precise statements, etc. and being subject, to hours, as he was, to the closest severe and cunning drillings on the witness stand, and did not entrap himself at some points in his testimony is, beyond all doubt a reasonable proof of his innocence, and positive proof of his truthfulness on his part, and should have great weight in the statement as to how he came in possession of part of the ransom money.

The law, and all criminal procedures and trials, especially provide for the prisoner to have the benefit of all reasonable doubt. And the people feel that Hauptmann has not had an impartial trial and given the benefit of reasonable doubt. But all the doubt seemed to have been taken as positive evidence against him, that unless he could positively prove himself clear, he must stand as convicted, and then was not permitted to have his evidence introduced, so to do, by reason of attorney's objections sustained.

It would be very bad to burn him, and someday baby Lindberg, found to be alive, or some other than Hauptmann, make confession of the crime, or evidence discovered involving some others as the arch criminals in the case, such things have happened and may again happen. The only man ever hung in Bedford Co, Pa, maintained and declared his innocence, nearly 200 years ago, later another on his death bed confessed the crime, and since then, there has been on one hung or electrocuted in that county, and there is less crime in that county than any other in the state.

Note: Ellis Parker wrote "Good Thoughts" in pencil on George Statler's front page in the upper left-hand corner. Since George mentions that he had done some investigation in another case, I think he was most likely a Detective or a Police officer, but I couldn't find any evidence of this.

George wrote that he was writing "as to the public's general feeling" about the Lindbergh case.

We (Andy Sahol & Russ Lloyd, the writers of this book) feel very strongly that those in charge of the Lindbergh case participated in hiding and falsifying evidence throughout the investigation and the prosecution of Bruno Richard Hauptman. The motive was simply their desire for fame. As George Statler states, the case against Hauptmann was full of manufactured, invented, and assumed evidence.

Why were there two ladders at the crime scene? Hauptmann was an experienced carpenter, and the ladders were of low quality. Why were there no boards missing from Hauptmann's floor when the plumber did his repair?

Why wasn't Isidor Fisch suspected of being the man in the Cemetery? He had a deep, bad, hollow cough. Hauptmann had no cough.

Why didn't the prosecution want Hauptmann to live and be given a chance to clear himself? Did he die to hide and cover up the errors and false evidence created by the prosecution?

Who did Violet Sharp take her own life? Of all the things discovered during the Lindbergh case, this is the single most unbelievable and mysterious occurrence unexplained. How can anyone not agree that Hauptmann should be spared from the electric chair after learning this?

Whose fingerprints were on the ladder if they were not Hauptmann's? Nobody but Ellis Parker took the time to question this. Detective Parker even attempted to have Isidor Fisch's body exhumed to obtain his fingerprints. Ellis was familiar with scientific methods that could capture prints off the ladders that could not be seen by the naked eye. Yet, the prosecution elected not to continue working on the prints' investigation to ensure that Hauptmann would remain the only suspect and that they had arrested the right man.

Were the ladders just a hoax to cover that the baby was taken out the front door? This book (written by Andy Sahol & Russ Lloyd) again wants to tell you that we believe that Ellis Parker solved the case and then was falsely imprisoned with manufactured evidence to silence him forever. The baby was handed out the door to Paul H. Wendel. Isidor Fisch was with Wendel. The person handing Wendel the baby was Charles Lindbergh himself.

Was there ever more reasonable doubt in any other case in history? Electrocuting Hauptmann was a wrong move, poor judgment, and was accomplished with manufactured evidence. If the Lindbergh baby was found alive later or if someone else confessed to the crime after Hauptmann's electrocution, David Wilentz would be ridiculed, and his reputation destroyed.

FROM THE ELLIS PARKER LOST FILES

NORTHWESTERN NATIONAL INSURANCE COMPANY
MILWAUKEE, WISCONSIN

WASHINGTON D.C. BRANCH
JAMES H. SHANNON, MANAGER
927 WOODWARD BUILDING
WASHINGTON D.C.

Sunday, Dec. 8, 1935

Gov. Harold G. Hoffman, Trenton, N.J.:
Hon. A Harry Moore, U.S. Senate, Wash. D.C. &
Ellis H. Parker, Burlington Co. Detective Chief, Trenton, N.J.

Gentlemen; --- I am mailing a triplicate copy of this letter to all three of the above, in the hope that at least one of the three will get it, and use their influence in securing a reprieve, an investigation, in this case, and avert a miscarriage of Justice, in the conviction of Bruno Richard Hauptmann, for the kidnapping and murder of the Lindbergh baby, on to my mind very flimsy circumstantial evidence; as the evidence of Dr. (Jafsie) Condon on the witness stand as I followed it in the newspapers at the time was very fantastic, silly, not having the sense or "ring of truth," and as much so that I was and am surprised that defense counsel did not note it and call attention to it, -----------for instance --------

1.) Dr. Condon met Hauptman at the cemetery IN THE NIGHT," "Hauptman was in the inside of the iron gate & Condon was on the outside; talking together thru the iron gate: the cemetery guard was over there a little way in plain sight (resting on his arms?): and did not do a thing or say a thing about it." "It was against the law for anyone to be in the cemetery in the middle of the night: did he holler to Hauptman TO GET OUT: did he run over and arrest him? Did he take a shot at Hauptman for trespass in a graveyard at midnight? .....No, he didn't do a thing: it was perfectly all right.......????????........... Don't sound like the truth.

2.) "That Hauptman jumped over the high iron fence onto the outside of the cemetery (where Condon was): then Hauptman ran away from Condon (like a child's play): then Condon ran after Hauptman (like a papa running after a bad boy): then Condon caught up with Hauptman and grabbed him by the shoulder (just imagine a hard-boiled criminal letting an old Geezer like Condon CACH HIM IN A FOOT RACE; grab him, etc. (why a desperate criminal would have killed Condon right then and there if necessary).....

3.) Then they (Condon & Hauptman) went over and set on a bench and talked it all over (like a couple of pals or old cronies) .... Just imagine such evidence......

3a.) And before setting on the bench to talk, Dr. (Jafsie) Condon walked around the shack to take a good look and see if there was anyone around-first-----(what did Condon have to be scared of) ----? Don't have "the ring of truth," OR THE RING OF COMMON SENSE. I think that the flimsy story was made up and that Dr. Condon (himself) should be more thoroughly looked into.

I do not believe that Hauptman is guilty of the charge. I kind of think that he knows something about it: he may have been one of the gangs that did it: he may have been just the go-between—hired—to get the ransom money.

It would be a terrible miscarriage of Justice and a shame to electrocute him on the evidence that has been produced, which, to say the least, has been very flimsy.

Too many times, the prosecutor is too anxious to get a conviction (right or wrong) as though he was running for a prize to the one that secured the most convictions.

I have no personal interest in the matter, whatever, and I am only following the dictates of my conscience in trying to secure your valuable assistance to this man to give him a fair chance, which may take a little time. And I do not care for any publicity.

Sincerely,

E. C. Bickford

Detective Ellis Parker responded to the above letter on 1-22-1936:

January 22, 1936

Mr. E. C. Bickford
c/o Northeastern National Insurance Company
Milwaukee, Wisconsin

Dear Sir,

A copy of your letter that was sent to Governor Hoffman has been received by me. In addition to the information submitted by you in the case in California. There was one in Rhode Island back in 1847 where a man was hanged, and afterward, it was discovered that he was innocent. Some years later, they passed a law abolishing capital punishment.

In this particular case, I am convinced that this man is innocent of what he has been found guilty. The kidnapping and the extortion are two separate and distinct propositions.

If you or I left one hundred thousand dollars, there would be one hundred thousand people to separate us from it.

To electrocute Bruno Hauptmann would not clear up this case in my judgment. I have no more interest in him than any other individual. The only interest I have is one of Justice.

Our Governor is a person of decision and courage. He is of the type of Teddy Roosevelt. He doesn't care what the public or the press says. If he thinks he is right, he stands by what he thinks. All the investigation that I have conducted in this case has been at my own expense. I could have commercialized and made hundreds of thousands of dollars. I am not interested in this case for publicity, as I said before, only for Justice.

I appreciate your writing to me, and I'm sure the Governor will read your communication as he is that type. No clerks around his office think for him, and I know as a matter of fact that he reads these communications, especially one like yours.

Thanking you for the Governor, and I am assuring you that I will do what I can to save this man's life as I am positive in my own mind that he is innocent. Any person with common sense and judgment can see that the evidence was manufactured to convict this man. Thank you for sending me a copy of this letter. I remain,

Very Truly Yours,

Detective Ellis H. Parker

Note: Imagine finding the thoughts of Ellis Parker so many years later. Well, we have them here. It is obvious Ellis is exceptionally close to N.J. Governor Harold Hoffman. In the letter, he explains why by comparing the Governor's character with that of Teddy Roosevelt. Ellis and Governor Hoffman share everything, particularly communications with the public about the Lindbergh case. Detective Parker tells us that he is concerned about Bruno Richard Hoffman's life by describing cases where guilt was doubted. Ellis explains that capital punishment was abolished in Rhode Island after establishing that a man convicted and then executed had been innocent. Ellis discloses that he worries that Bruno Hauptman will be executed even though he is an innocent man. Ellis tells us that the evidence used in the Hauptmann trial was manufactured. Who is responsible for that?

FROM THE ELLIS PARKER LOST FILES

P. O. ADDRESS MIDLAND AVE., (Near President St.) Garfield, N.J.

December 8, 1935

Dear Friend Mr. Parker:

As you may recall, our conversation of last year regarding the olden times of our Detective organization of which the late Bob Haggerty was at the head in Newark. Well, time does fly, and I'm glad you're feeling well and active as ever.

I cannot express in words how happy I feel to have noticed in the Papers, your opinion that Hauptmann is not guilty of kidnapping and murder. I fully agree with you, and you should be congratulated by all the fair-minded people of our Country for your courage in the interest of Justice and

Humanity. Don't let any group of individuals discourage you. Keep up your good work. I had the same feeling of inspiration, that's all a good investigator needs for success.

I had offered my services to the State, but it was turned down. The reason I extend my sympathy to Hauptmann is because the State was careless and unfair, spending many hundreds of thousands of dollars giving witnesses overpayment and good times at the expense of the taxpayers. This ridiculous condition and mystery were made possible by the insane methods of the officials in charge of this case. They ignored the motto over the dome of our Supreme Court in Washington, "Equal – Justice – Under – Law." They allowed influence and sympathy to supersede law and their oath of office by permitting Dr. Condon the tool for the criminals to spend over an hour while he payment of $50,000 was being made and no arrest made at the time. The officials responsible for this disgraceful condition became an accessory to the crime and are equally as guilty as the kidnappers. Our government should investigate the investigators. Laws should be enacted, making it a crime to pay over ransom money. This should stop the crime of kidnapping.

The above statement of criticism is made in the interest of Crime prevention. Should you be in need of any assistance, I will be glad to help. I remain,

Your sincere friend,

John Sistaro

Note: Letter writer John Sistaro was a highly regarded State Detective based in Saddle River, N.J. He was a bonded State detective in New Jersey for over 32 years. He was intelligent and resourceful. In one case, the Bergen County Record newspaper described his ruse to impersonate a Jewish man as "a clever disguise." It was done so that Detective Sistaro could enter a Jewish neighborhood to arrest a notorious criminal wanted for multiple crimes, found by his untiring labors. It was also reported that in his later years, Sistaro became active in the rehabilitation of criminals attempting to reenter society. A noble cause. It is apparent in his writing that John Sistaro considered Ellis Parker a respected peer.

FROM THE ELLIS PARKER LOST FILES

New York

December 9, 1935

Mr. Ellis H. Parker

Mt. Holly, N.J.

Dear Sir:

On March first, was it, when the news about the kidnapping of the Lindbergh baby was announced, at eleven A.M., I was passing through the main floor of the Mealpin Hotel, New York City, from 33rd Street to the 34th Street entrance. When I reached the front of the Hotel, I found my way blocked at the most Easterly front door by two men, both foreigners from their talk. I gave them scant notice until I heard the one facing the 33rd Street entrance, that is, his back was to the 34th Street door, say in German or another foreign language, "de baby is det (dead)." I was shocked, for there was only one baby in the world at that moment, and nobody believed he was dead at the time. The two men were without overcoats or hats, and I thought they were guests at the Hotel. Have you examined the register of the Hotel for this seemingly unimportant item? I ask this because I sent the word to Colonel Schwarzkopf. I am now waiting to see a photo or the man you suspect. The one who made the sad announcement was a tall, swarthy, smooth-faced German, whose hands looked well cared for, soft and white. He had dark brown or black eyes. I did not get a glimpse of the second man, my first impulse being to bring in the officer in front of the Hotel, but knowing that Colonel Lindbergh had demanded no publicity, I went on my way.

Anonymous.

Note: Detective Parker received countless letters from all over the world. The "Crime of the Century" was on everyone's mind. Many of them, just like this one, were leads or tips that the writer wanted Ellis or some authority to follow up on. Ellis would respond to every one of them regardless of what value he saw in the communication. Ellis Parker was a kind, understanding, and respectful man, aware of how much the most famous case of the era affected the public.

FROM THE ELLIS PARKER LOST FILES

December 9, 1935

St. Louis, Mo.

Mr. Ellis H. Parker, Burlington, New Jersey

Dear Sir,

I have 199 shares of Capital Stock of the "Allen Oil Company" (Batson Texas) incorporated 1906 entire outstanding stock – 300 shares. For $100, I wish to sell this security so if you will make arrangements for the sale of the same to some large Oil Co. or a New York Brokerage. I will pay you (Ellis Parker) 50 percent of sale, money to be used in your investigation of new evidence in the Bruno Richard Hauptmann case.

I will also pay a brokerage fee.

Very Truly Yours

Joseph Sudbeck

4132 a North Eleventh St., St. Louis, Mo.

P.S. Will send Certificates for 199 shares when you locate a buyer. Get busy, and let me hear from you by return mail.

Ellis Parker responded to Joseph Sudbeck's letter on 12-27-1935

December 27, 1935

Joseph Sudbeck

4132 a North 11th

St. Louis, Mo.

Dear Friend; -

I received your letter with your request and your offer of assistance financially. I am not working on this case, for publicity or financial gain. I am simply working on it to see that Justice may be done and that an innocent person should not be sacrificed.

I more than appreciate your communication, and I want to assure you that I don't care what comment is made or the criticism of me, I intend to do all I can, to save this man's life and to solve this case.

With best wishes, I remain, very truly yours,

Ellis H. Parker

Chief of Co. Detectives

Note: Above is an example of Ellis Parker's true character. It is a window into his soul. Ellis Parker was indeed a man to admire. Andrew Sahol, Ellis's Grandson, and I, Russell Lloyd, want him to be acknowledged as one of our nation's most significant Law Enforcement Officers of all time and for his reputation to be restored. That is the Justice we seek for him.

FROM THE ELLIS PARKER LOST FILES

American Legion Post 211
WILLIAM MACDONALD
1128 HARRIS STREET, PHILADELPHIA, PA

December 9, 1935.

Hon. Ellis Parker, Chief of Detectives, Mt. Holly, N.J.

My dear Mr. Parker:

Allow me to congratulate you on the splendid stand you have taken in the interests of justice in delving into the Hauptmann Case. Also, may I not state that your course is commended and upheld by all the people with whom I come into contact.

There is no question in my mind but that this man, Hauptmann, is entirely innocent of the kidnapping and murder of the child of our beloved fellow citizen, Colonel Lindbergh, and that his conviction was brought about in one, if not the most disgraceful trial that ever took place in an American courtroom.

Of course, my opinion about Hauptmann only applies to the murder and kidnapping trial, and not the question of his possession of the ransom money. That is something else, of which I cannot speak, and that connection, possession of the money, is an entirely different issue from the murder indictment and should never have been brought into the trial in the New Jersey Court.

My own opinion of the case of the little son of Colonel Lindbergh, and I studied the case carefully, is that the child was never kidnaped and murdered at all. I believe that the child met its death accidentally at the hands of someone in the Lindbergh home, one of the servants, very likely. When it was seen that the child was dead, this servant, or someone visiting a servant, took the body to the woods close by, where it was found, placed the ladder against the window, and proclaimed a kidnapping.

Again, commending you, and invoking the blessings of Providence upon your efforts, I am,

Respectfully,

Captain William Macdonald,

1128 Harrison Street

Philadelphia, PA

<u>Note</u>: Captain MacDonald is of one mind with Detective Parker on many points except who left the Lindbergh home with the baby. Ellis Parker was convinced it was Paul Wendel, the only person ever to sign a confession. Captain Macdonald believes it was a member of the Lindbergh household that had accidentally dropped the baby before arranging the scene to look like a kidnapping. We, Andy Sahol and Russell Lloyd agree with Detective Ellis H. Parker.

FROM THE ELLIS PARKER LOST FILES

12-10-1935

Mr. E. H. Ellis

Governor Hoffman

C. Lloyd Fischer

The Times

As a professional "analyst" who has followed with utter unprejudiced the entire "Lindbergh Case," I have been amazed that the one theory which almost miraculously brings the contradictory elements of the case into a convincing whole, was not advanced, and has not as yet been publicized.

The moment this theory is advanced, the innocence of Hauptmann becomes evident, and it also clears up the hitherto ridiculed defense in Re: Fisch.

Consider how extremely obvious becomes the case when the following theory is developed: Hauptmann is a German Dreyfus!

If the Jewish gang that "snatched" the baby realized to their shame what an uncomfortable prejudice would be leveled at their racial kin. (It is to be recalled that every individual, especially after the money was passed, secretly hoped that the perpetrators of the crime would not prove to be a member of his particular race), they have two alternatives-

A   Not pass the money, and so escape detection

B   Sell it, as the defense intimated was done

C   Find a suitable victim

Why? Consider what happened to Dreyfus.

Why not put a German on the spot? By doing so, this group could strike back at the deplorable, to them, movement occurring in Germany.

Talk about humiliation! And recall too, the delight Mr. Wilentz took in condemning the Teutons through the victim, Hauptmann.

Fisch was evidently the tool that shaped Hauptmann into the desired mold, and Hauptmann's escapades in Germany were very deftly used to bind him to his doom.

Signed, A. Man (Anonymous)

<u>Note</u>: The theory expressed here is that Bruno Richard Hauptmann was a German Dreyfus. Alfred Dreyfus (1859-1935) was a French artillery officer of Jewish ancestry convicted of treason in 1894. He was sentenced to life imprisonment for allegedly communicating French military secrets to the German embassy in Paris. Dreyfus was later exonerated of the crime. When discovered that much of the evidence against him had been forged, he was returned to his military life. The entire affair is now given credit for a passionate repudiation of antisemitism by the French.

The letter writer suggests that the Jewish gang responsible for kidnapping the Lindbergh child was worried about their race being identified as the crime perpetrators. Did they reason why not set up a German as the goat? That goat became Hauptmann, according to the letter's writer.

To fully understand the writer's comment: *"Talk about humiliation! And recall too, the delight Mr. Wilentz took in condemning the Teutons through the victim, Hauptmann"*. The "Teutons" were people that lived in Jutland in the 4th century BC and fought the Romans in France in the 2nd century BC. The term "Teutons" used in this manner can be considered derogatory by Germans.

One last observation to ponder. The writer stated that there were two alternatives and then listed three. Keep that in mind when considering the writer's theories in this letter.

FROM THE ELLIS PARKER LOST FILES

New York, December 10, 1935

Mr. Ellis H. Parker,
Mount Holly, N.J.

Dear Sir:

May I tell you that I am exceedingly glad to learn of the latest development in the Hauptmann case, for I believe it to be the most flagrantly unjust affair that could be imagined. I was especially pleased to read in the press what you had to say relative to the constant practice of calling this man "a German machine gunner." This I took to be one way of arousing the wrath of the unthinking, who would not pause to reflect that there were many American machine gunners as well, all sent out to slay by their respective Governments. It was not a case of holding a man innocent until he was proved guilty: but from the start, newspaper editors and, in fact, anyone who pleased, could talk about the arrest of "the kidnapper and murderer" of the Lindbergh baby. The most fantastic stories and articles were published, such for instance as one which appeared in

"To-Day," where its author described in detail the "facts" in the case. Indeed, so many wise people have found this man guilty that it would be a bitter pill for them to swallow to discover that they were wrong, to say nothing of those who found it expedient to have the case solved.

Dr. Condon recently stated, according to the press, that he considered it as further proof of Hauptmann's guilt that in dating a letter which the latter wrote him not long ago, he placed the month after the day, for in such manner the ransom notes were dated. I believe that the Germans always write the date so, just as the French do. In this connection, I might say that in considering the peculiarities of spelling and script, in my opinion, as expert familiar with the German should study the ransom notes.

The whole trial was a farce, where absolutely no evidence was presented - - according to newspaper accounts, - - that would convince a sensible, unprejudiced person that the arrest of this prisoner had solved the Lindbergh case.

I am writing this letter because I presume that you are receiving much mail on the case in question, and I believe it behooves everyone to express an opinion if he feels, as I very decidedly do, that Hauptmann never kidnapped the baby, whatever might be his guilt in connection with the ransom money.

ONE CITIZEN'S VIEW.

<u>Note</u>: An excellent letter, with good points from an anonymous writer. Yes, Ellis Parker was receiving "much mail" on the case. It was overwhelming him.

FROM THE ELLIS PARKER LOST FILES

<u>Note</u>: This series of letters are written to Detective Ellis H. Parker by Mrs. E. R. Just (who once signed as Minnie Just). They read like a flight of fantasy

that only she could create. I included it because I think it is an example of just how much "The Crime of the Century affected and fascinated the American people and because I had a great laugh over it.

The case dominated their thinking, personal communications, the arts, movie reels, the newspapers, and the radio. News reports reached everyone daily. I think all this was more than Mrs. E. R. Just could handle. She even suspected that her husband might be plotting to kill her. (These notes are continued at the end of this series of letters. It would be best if you didn't miss them.)

MEALS SERVED AT ALL HOURS
E. R. JUST RESTAURANT
2468 BLUE ISLAND AVE, CHICAGO, IL

December 11, 1935

Mr. Ellis Parker

Mt. Holly, N.J.

Dear Sir:

I've read in the papers that you don't believe Hauptmann did the kidnapping. You are right. The kidnapping was done by more people than one. The brains of the kidnapping was C. Matousek, who came to this country about 22 or 23 years ago with his widowed mother and little sister. He has a wife in Chicago and another one in New Jersey. His cousin runs the Circle Café at 3474 Blue Island Avenue. He did not kill the baby. That was done by someone else. A man living in Chicago, over 50 years old and Grandfather. He admitted it himself in front of a witness named Joe Nemec, a soda water salesman. Nemec was an agent for the Bon-Ton soda works and wanted to deliver the man to justice. He died in the year 1933 with a fractured skull. Mrs. Nemec could tell you that her husband was working on the case. She runs the soda business with her sons now. The kidnapper's name is Jim Svantner. He owned the house at 2450 Central Park Ave but sold it to his son-in-law W. Benesh.

He is one of the two sons-in-laws, the kidnapper I mean, of John Koocourek, Hazen Arkansaw. The other son-in-law is Holzendorf, Doc. Holzen-Gasto B. Means-Kren? —brother of Al Capone? Which, by the way, is not the right name. Capone has four brothers, all big shots. John Kocourek is my husband's uncle, being his mother's brother. His son-in-law's cause him much sorrow, especially Jim.

The kidnapping occurred soon after the funeral of Mrs. Anna Kocourek of Hazen Ark. It seems the two men made final arrangement. My husband knew something about it. He said to me: When Jim comes here, call the police, but he did not do that himself, why did he want me to do it? Was it maybe more becoming to me? Or did he want me to get killed?

Well, here it is. I can't stand by and let an innocent man suffer for someone else, especially when that person is not worthy of the sacrifice. It would not redeem them. They would only laugh and keep right on being just as bad as ever. Hauptmann was in Chicago on the date of the kidnapping. He was called there by a telegram, which was charged to telephone number Canal 5537.

Please keep his secret. My husband must not know about this. He does not care if Hauptmann goes to the chair.

Yours truly,

Mrs. E. R. Just
2709 Ridgeway Ave
Chicago, Ill

<u>Mrs. E. R. Just wrote to Ellis Parker again on 12-18-1935:</u>

December 18, 1935

Mr. Ellis H. Parker

Burlington County, NJ

Dear Sir,

Here is more information about this man C. MATOUSEK, who is supposed to be the brains of the kidnapping. He came from Czechoslovakia, vicinity of Budweis his cousin owns the Circle Tavern, his name is Henry Matousek, son of Joseph and Elizabeth Matousek, 2466 Blue Island Ave. They are friends of the "Capones" and know all the rest of them. Mr. "Dato" of Ken and Dato Real Estate firm is Jim Svantner's brother. Their real name is Condon, and they came from New York. I believe, Frank Nitti is their brother, also. Gana Walska is their sister, so is Fifi Stilman McCormik, represented by one of their sisters. One of the maids at the Lindbergh home is supposed to be the daughter of Holtzendorfs. When Al Capone offered to expose the kidnapper, Jim was mad. They are always double-crossing one another. When my husband told me to call certain phone numbers when Jim comes, he did not tell me which Jim and why, or who the other party was, but I've made sure by calling the number, and the answer was that it was the private home of Captain Mikes of Marquette police station on Damen Ave. To my question, why was I supposed to call him when Jim comes and Jim, who? The captain said he did not know.

Jim Svantner came to our store Wednesday, March 3, 1932, while Mr. Nemec, the soda man, was there and said, "I got him." I did not know what he was talking about, I did not read the paper yet that morning, and I thought Jim was fooling me. I did not know he was had, although I knew him since 1919 when they came to live in Chicago. I was too hot in Arkansas, they said, but I did not understand it at the time.

In the year of 1923, the Sheriff from Arkansas came to look for him after a tip from his father-in-law John Kocourek, but I did not think it was anything serious.

In the evening of March 2nd, 1932, I was in the store, our store, and reading the newspaper, Frank Mikulich came in and asked is there anything in the paper about the kidnapping? And I said, what kidnapping? And he told me I would not believe it, he said, that he is to get the child and as a proof pulled a whiskey bottle of milk from his hip pocket and said he was ready for the baby, but Jim did not bring it, he killed it and said so. Frank Mikulich hangs around Blue Island Ave. I hope I can be of some help to Mr. Hauptmann because I know he is innocent.

Yours Truly,

Mrs. E. R. Just
2709 S. Ridgeway Ave.

Mrs. E. R. Just wrote to Ellis Parker once again on 1-19-1936:

January 19, 1936
Mr. Ellis H. Parker, Mt. Holly, N.J.

Dear Sir:

Many thanks to you and Governor Hoffman for what you have done for Mr. Hauptmann. I am sure you will be glad someday when it is found out he really is innocent. I had found out about the kidnapping plot about a week before it happened. It was like this: My husband was talking with Mrs. Matousek of 2466 Blue Island Ave., our neighbor, in our restaurant. I was in the kitchen in the rear of the store. They spoke in whispers. I wondered what secret they had that I should not hear it. No one else was there, what was the idea of whispering? My husband was facing toward the kitchen, and I was trying to read his lips to find out what he was saying.

I am not good at lip-reading, but one word I've made out, and that was child in Bohemian language, we say, "dita." I also heard Mrs. Matousek say: In Mr. Putru's car, I came into the store and asked my husband whether he said the word "child," that I've read his lips. He looked at me angry and said nothing, but Mrs. Matousek opened her mouth at me as if I was a servant of hers and said, go in the kitchen and mind your stove. This was not the first time she spoke to me like this. My husband never took my part. They came into the kitchen then, but I've walked out. I was mad at them. I went out in front of the store. Mrs. Filips was out there. I told her about Mrs. Matousek, how mean she is, and how does she get that way? I told Betty Fillips that they talked about a child and wondered if she knew what it was all about. She knew and told me it was about kidnaping the Lindberg's child. Don't give me away, she warned me. I would not like to cause her any trouble, to Betty, I mean.

Mr. Petru is a real estate man. He is a good friend of Mr. Kocourek of Hazen Ark., my husband's uncle. He is more than a friend, he is related. That's what Mr. Hovorka told me. Mr. Hovorka lives at 2611 S. Ridgeway Ave. Chicago. Mr. Frank Petru's brother married Mr. Kocourek's daughter, Mr. Hovorka, said. Mr. Kocourek only has two daughters, Kristine is married to Jim Svantner, Anna married Holzendorf. Therefore, Holzendorf is Mr. Petru's brother, and Petru is his real name. There are five Petru brothers that I heard a long time ago. Al Capone is one of the Petru brothers. Frank Mikulich knows all of them, he knows their father also.

At the time of the Lindbergh kidnapping, Mr. Frank Petru was in Hot Springs and how surprised was he when he returned home to Chicago, and his car was standing in front of his office. The story was in the Bohemian newspaper Hlasatel. I believe that the child was kidnaped in Mr. Petru's car.

They put the blame on Mr. Hauptman after they tried to put the blame on two other victims unsuccessfully.

The first one was Jim Lakota, who at that time was boarding at our place, now he lives at his brother's house in the vicinity of Homan Ave. and 25th St. Chicago. It was mostly Mr. Nemeces' fault that Mr. Lakota was taken to the police head-quarters and came home with a swollen jaw and a black eye. Mr. Nemec thought that the man who came into our store that day and admitted the kidnapping was our border. I told Mr. Nemec that he is wrong, and Mr. Nemec would not let up. I believe that he was instigated by my husband and Jim Svantner himself, who by that time acted as a "G" man, and Mr. Nemec, who did not know him very well, was easily fooled.

Second victim was a stranger, an unemployed man who lived at the municipal lodging house and ate whenever he got anything. To this man, they gave a two-dollar bill of the ran-som money and told him to go and buy himself something to eat at our place. It was in the middle of the afternoon, so I made him some pork and beans and placed it on the counter. The stranger was in the lavatory. In comes Jim Svanter, behind him, Mr. Nemec and my husband. Jim was all dressed up in his Sunday clothes. The first time I saw him looking decent. I was surprised and said so. He looked at me coldly, like he never saw me before and wanted to know where the man was who ordered the meal. I knew right away that something was wrong and felt sorry for the stranger. I told Jim that no one ordered that meal, that it was for me that I brought it out. Jim said, "that's a lie, his hat is right here." Jim told me that I was under arrest for harboring kidnappers. He said, can you swear that the kidnaper is not at your house? Of course, I could not, not as long as Jim was there anyway. The dirty nerve of him.

I grabbed a hand full of those beans on the counter and hit Jim right in the face, next I hit him with a small dish, then I picked up the empty cup and saucer and while I was aiming at him with the saucer in my left hand, I held the cup in my right and hit him with the cup and knocked a revolver out of his hand. By that time, the stranger came out of the lavatory, and I told him to pick up that revolver, but he did not do it. Next, I grabbed the teapot, but Jim was going out, and I hit him in the back right between his shoulders. Well, you should have seen that suit of clothes. Just look at your apron said the stranger. What was wrong with it? Only a few holes. The fold of my wide sleeve was punctured, one bullet must have passed under my arm, there was a hole there, fold only on my hip was perforated, the hair on top of my head was singed. You see, I know how to dodge bullets already. He missed me by a hair. Mr. Hauptman was in Chicago at that time, and he saw the fight, and he came in and asked me: How is the "bean War"?

Then he said: Well, what have you to say: I said, tell him that he is lucky it was not my apron. It belongs to the Independent Linen Supply. After the fiver picked up the apron, he came back and said: Have you been shot? The apron is full of holes. I told him that the mice must have got into it. He said no, those were bullets holes. That's what I got for considering Jim. He would shoot me as well as not. That was the time Jim introduced himself as Condon, the son of Jafsie Condon.

Their real name is Konvalinka I've heard Mrs. Matousek call Jim by that name and spoke to her about it afterward, she said that was their name. I believe that Jafsie's wife was Miss Petru before her marriage, that is why Al Capone and Frank Nitti are cousins. There was another Nitti in Stickney Ill. Who was murdered by his wife, he too was Jim's brother? That Indian guide in Canadian woods of Fifi Stilman fame is also Jim's brother, and Fifi is his sister.

This Charles Matousek, one of the kidnappers, is a friend of my husband's uncle Mr. Kocourek, he has done some favor for Mr. Kocourek, he delivered something of value to Mr. Kocourek's brother Frank, in Mirotice, Czechoslovakia.

For that reason, Mrs. Matousek thinks that she can boss me as if it would do me any good. I mean the delivery of valuables I've never heard of before the Matouske's told me and would have never known it. My husband has many secrets that he keeps away from me. His secrets are mostly crimes, and I would never agree with him. I hope I don't tire you with my tales. It's the truth. About Isidor Fisch, he is well known to Matousek's. When he was in Chicago, he was stopping with Rudy Luczak on Blue Island Ave. Few doors away from our house. His father is in jail for murdering a little girl. He lived in Yorkville. I mean Fisch's father. Joe Jahelka, the sports promoter of Chicago, also knows the Fisch family. Joe Zajic, furrier, of Champaign Ill. knows both the Fisch's and he knows Mr. Hauptman, for whom he had high regard.

I don't believe that Fisch is dead because last winter, after the Hauptman trial, while I was aboard a streetcar, I saw a man on Blue Island Ave who looked just like Fisch. I saw him near Luczak's house.

Fisch's brother is the famous Netley Lucas. He also works as a shop steward. That is what he was doing aboard the

S.S. Rotterdam in the year of 1928 when I was going to Europe to visit my mother. His wife was in the first-class cabin. His sister Minni was a maid to her Ladyship, her sister-in-law. Please excuse this long letter.

Yours truly,

Minnie Just

Note: (continued) This is the only time she signed as "Minnie Just. I could not identify Minnie's names (or Mrs. E. R. Just) mentioned (except for Frank Nitti & Al Capone) in her letters. I could not find any mention of the restaurant either during my research. Interestingly, many of those mentioned had ties to the Restaurant. I suspect the Soda family. Isn't it strange that Mrs. E. R. Just suspected the owner of a competing tavern, Circle Tavern, as the brains of the Lindbergh kidnapping. It may be that Ellis kept these letters for reference in case any of these names appeared in his investigations. The writer did a great job convincing us that the city of Chicago was full of suspects and that her elevator didn't go to the second floor.

One last thought. Isn't it strange how many of the Lindbergh case suspects ate at the E. R. Just Restaurant?

FROM THE ELLIS PARKER LOST FILES

228 North Rhode Island, Atlantic City, N.J.

Dec 11th, 1935

Ellis Parker, Burlington County, N.J.

Dear Parker.

Have given the Hauptmann case intensive study and believe Hauptmann innocent of kidnapping for the following reason.

I cannot conceive any man negotiating for ransom money for a famous child and sitting in a Cemetery talking to an intermediary for over an hour if he possessed the knowledge that the child was already dead.

If he was the kidnapper, he certainly knew the child was dead, and naturally, he would be the last man in the world to attempt to negotiate alone in a Cemetery with the possibility of being arrested for murder. Give this thought your intensive study, and I believe you will that it has more weight behind it than you can see at first glance.

If he wasn't the kidnapper, I can readily understand the meeting in the Cemetery, not knowing the child was dead, and if caught, the worst that could happen would be a prison sentence for extortion.

I shall be glad to hear from you at your convenience.

Truly Yours,

Jack Laird

PS: I challenge Dr. Condon and Colonel Lindbergh to a test of Germans who speak the same dialect from the same section of Germany to pick out Hauptmann's voice on the word "Doktor."

Laird, written by an Irishman.

Ellis Parker responded to Jack Laird's letter on 12-14-1935:

December 14, 1935.

Jack Laird

228 No. Rhode Island Ave.

Atlantic City, N.J.

Dear Friend: -

I received your letter of December 11th, and there is more common sense in your letter than most anything I have received in this case.

All the thoughts you have expressed in writing have been considered by me in this case. I have never felt right about this thing from its inception, but I am being quoted in the press, which, of course, I can't help, as I have only two short statements.

The whole state has known from the first that I didn't think Hauptmann had a thing to do with the actual kidnapping and murder – if there was a murder; I meant by that, the child might have died after it was kidnapped, and I have always contended that the two things were entirely separate. The kidnapping was one, and the extortion was the other.

There are so many facts to prove the above, and any sensible thinking person can see it, and it would be a shame if his life is taken when there is such a grave doubt about his guilt and what he is convicted with; although, it would be unethical for me to give out anything at this time.

I certainly thank you for your communication and assure you your views coincide with mine 100%.

Very truly yours,

Ellis H. Parker

Chief of Detectives

Note: Jack Laird addressed the envelope he used to write Ellis Parker "Detective Extraordinary." That is a sample of how much the general public believed in his character and reputation. Ellis had earned the title with unparalleled excellence at his chosen occupation over many years. He was a remarkable intellect and "Extraordinary" Law Enforcement Officer.

FROM THE ELLIS PARKER LOST FILES

Hotel Briggs
West Adams Avenue at Grand Circus Park, Detroit

Note: *the enveloped was postmarked 12-12-1935*

Governor Hoffman,

The fact is that the nurse who killed herself is the person who suggested the kidnapping to a Detroit man. The man is right here in Detroit now, and he told a woman the nurse dropped the baby by accident when she went to the window to pass the baby to him. That's the reason the dog did not bark because the dog knew her. No stranger could have went in the room and picked up the child. She passed it out and let it slip from her hands and fall.

Hauptmann was used by this man to build the ladder, but he did not know it was used for. That man is here, and he told this woman Hauptmann stole the money from him as he knew where this man buried the money after he paid Hauptmann for making the ladder. This man belongs to the Purple Gang here, and he and that nurse are the two responsible. After the thing was done, this man was afraid Hauptmann would tell of building the ladder and went east once to kill Hauptmann so to be sure of his never telling.

Hauptmann is a stoical German, and he has lied about the ladder, and now he is afraid to change his story. He had no hand in the kidnapping, and it is sure that he does not know right now exactly what did transpire. I think this man got him to write the notes, but I do not know this for sure. If the appeal court will hold Hauptmann for a life sentence, the thing will come out clear within a year or so as this woman has Tuberculosis and cannot live over a year or two, and she is going to tell all she knows on her death bed. She is afraid of her life if she tells anything now as he would exterminate her. She drove down to New York with this man when he had first received a letter from the woman who killed herself, she says Hauptmann does not even know the man's correct name as he used the wrong name there. Of course, people who get mixed in it will get exterminated sure, and I am sure I cannot lay myself and my family open to this Purple Mob here.

If the Appeal Court holds it open, it will eventually all come out. I think Hauptmann has told so many lies about it he now just does not know where to start to straighten himself out. He is not the kidnapper, that much is certain. It is an awful web of circumstances Hauptmann is in. And his record in Germany hurts him too. Keep him alive as he did not do it. If he was released, these people here would probably kill him, and of course, he could not be released until the matter is definitely cleared up. She will tell it and prove it on her death bed, and that will not be very long. You will be vindicated in time if you keep him alive.

Anonymous

Note: The critical thing to know is that the FBI suspected that the Purple Gang was initially the Prime suspects in the Crime of The Century. They had a reputation for kidnapping and for snatching up other gangsters for ransom. The Purple Gang became the dominant criminal gang in Detroit during the 1920s until 1932. The mob's activities included murder, extortion, theft, armed robbery, kidnapping, gambling, hijacking, and bootlegging. The members were predominantly Jewish, which makes me wonder if Isidor Fisch was connected to them. The gang leaders had moved to Detroit from New York City and then formed a relationship with Al Capone of Chicago. Capone was known to have associated with Paul Wendel and had offered to recover the baby in exchange for release from prison. Paul Wendel had also reported to Ellis Parker that he had contacted the Purple Gang (see Lost File report in this manuscript). The FBI wanted Harry Fleisher and Eddie Fletcher of the gang for questioning. Fletcher was eventually brought into the FBI's Detroit office for questioning in April of 1932. Fletcher was killed in 1933. He was still a suspect in the famous St. Valentine's Massacre in Chicago. Another connection is that Charles Lindbergh was born in Detroit, and his mother was a popular teacher in the Detroit school system. Betty Gow, the baby's nurse and the nanny was the last person to see the Lindbergh baby alive. Gow's brother, Scotty Gow, was a high-standing Purple Gang associate. Charles

Lindbergh himself suspected the Purple Gang and Bruno Hauptmann used the Purple Gang theory in his defense. At the trial, Betty Gow fainted on the witness stand when Hauptmann's lawyer accused her of allowing her brother access to the nursery.

(Note was compiled with the help of Wikipedia and gangsterreport. com)

FROM THE ELLIS PARKER LOST FILES

Vincentown, N.J.

Dec. 9th, 1935

Dear Mr. Parker: -

Whatever your motives might be, or are, in the Hauptmann matter. I feel the many hundreds of people who feel his guilt was not proven should thank you for your efforts in his behalf. I do. Also, does my husband.

The prosecution did their job as well as anyone could, but they did not have the evidence to convict him. The attorney generals' clowns were ridiculous, and the judge in charge was highly prejudiced.

Dr. Condon's tale was impossible to believe, in my opinion. Condon is either mixed up in the case or not in his right mind.

In regard to Lindbergh's testimony, I believe he committed perjury when he stated that after two years had gone by, he could now state under oath that he recognized it was Hauptmann's voice he had heard in the Cemetery. He was under extreme verbal strain to only hear one sentence at some distance off. He swore off a man's life that way. I was disgusted! His statement could not be true.

We did not rely only on the papers. We took pains to listen to it all on the radio, including Prosecutor David Wilentz's final charge (where he contradicted himself entirely) and the utterly disgraceful scenes when the jury came in. A blot upon the whole state!

My sister was in England at the time. She says her English friends asked her, "Is that the way murder trials are conducted in your country"? They were surprised and disgusted! So was almost everyone I know! Hauptmann may be guilty, but he certainly was not proved to be, and most surely, he should not have been executed.

Your enemies may say what they please. I thank you for your efforts and trust you will continue them. You are doing right, that I know. It seemed strange to me that the expressed opinion of the National Bar Association had no weight with the Court of Pardons, but of course, they wanted to be polite and show respect to the Justices.

These are all simply personal opinions.

Detective Ellis Parker responded on 12-12-1935:

December 12, 1935

Mrs. Florence H. Haines,

P.O. Box 167

Vincentown, N.J.

My dear Mrs. Haines: -

The thoughts expressed in your letter; I coincide with 100%. My only interest, in this case, is to see that justice was done. I cannot see it if this man's life is destroyed, which I trust will not occur. In my own judgment, the kidnapping is one part of it, and the extortion is another.

As you will note by some press articles, they have said I was the only one who had that opinion. It is far from being the truth, as I find that nine out of ten people that I have met during that time and since have asked me the questions, "What do you think of the case?" Which shows conclusively there is a doubt in their minds.

Of course, I have refrained from discussing it as much as possible, but your letter recalls to my mind what Will Rogers himself said, "It was the greatest three-ring circus I ever saw," and you will also recall that our President's wife said she didn't think Hauptmann was guilty. She had a right to express that opinion because she was in a position to get information from the Department of Justice, which would show a different set of facts.

The Governor of the State has been criticized for going down to the cell and talking to him. This has been done before and is, in my judgment, the only humane thing to do, and I know if I had to sit in judgment where a person's life was at stake, I would certainly like to know from the person's own lips, his expressions and attitude. It is the only humane thing to do, as the Court of Pardons is a Court of Mercy.

I wish to say, in conclusion, that I more than appreciate a letter from one of my own people, such as you have sent.

Again, thanking you and assuring you and your husband I am 100% in my thought on this matter.

Very truly yours,

Ellis H. Parker
Chief of Detectives.

FROM THE ELLIS PARKER LOST FILES

December 12, 1935

Note: *In a letter, a local woman (Mrs. Florence H. Haines) praised Ellis Parker and his efforts to save Bruno Richard Hauptmann. Ellis wrote back as follows:*

Mrs. Florence H. Haynes, PO Box 167, Vincentown, NJ

My Dear Mrs. Haynes,

The thoughts expressed in your letter; I coincide with hundred percent.

My only interest, in this case, is to see that justice was done. I cannot see it if this man's life is destroyed, which I trust will not occur. In my own judgment, the kidnapping is one part of it, and the extortion is another.

As you will note by some press articles, they have said I was the only one who had that opinion. It is far from being the truth, as I find that nine out of 10 people I have met during that time and since have asked me the question, "What do you think of the case?" Which shows conclusively there is a doubt in their mind.

Of course, I have refrained from discussing it as much as possible, but your letter recalls to my mind what will Rogers himself said "It was the greatest three-ring circus I ever saw" and you will also recall that our President's wife said she didn't think Hauptmann was guilty. She had a right to express that opinion because she was in a position to get information from the Department of Justice, which would show a different set of facts.

The Governor of the state has been criticized for going down to the cell and talking to him. This has been done before and is, in my judgment, the only humane thing to do, and I know if I had to sit in judgment where a person's life was at stake, I would certainly like to know from the person's own lips, his expression and attitude. It is the only humane thing to do, as the Court of Pardons is a Court of Mercy.

I wish to say, in conclusion, that I more than appreciate a letter from one of my own people, such as you have sent.

Again, thanking you and assuring you and your husband I am 100% in my thought on this matter.

Very truly yours,

Ellis H. Parker, Chief of Detectives

FROM THE ELLIS PARKER LOST FILES

12-13-1935

Mr. Ellis Parker,

Sir.

You may be a Corn Cob detective to the Press, but after reading the too few statements made by you in the papers, I have an idea that you may have solved the Lindbergh case, if you would have been given the case.

Will you please read every word on this sheet before you throw it in the wastebasket? It may give you a new slant to work on.

Col. Lindbergh made a statement at the time of the crime, "that he did not have an enemy to his knowledge."

For a year before the crime, the Radio programs were flooded by a lot of fakirs, such as crystal gazers, mental telepathists, and horoscope drawers. One, in particular, was on the air four times a day selling horoscopes to silly housewives at a dollar apiece. She even went so far as to read a supposed horoscope of the Lindbergh baby, when it was born, four times a day, to help advertise herself. The Col. resented this unwanted publicity, and he and his father-in-law, Mr. Morrow, who was alive at the time, managed to have a bill passed at Washington, that none of these fakirs are permitted to peddle their rotten tripe on the airwaves. Perhaps you have noticed their absence.

One party lost an income of over $200,000 a year because of Col. Lindbergh's activity. Do you think that so great a loss would make a person feel kindly toward the one who caused the loss?

The Lindbergh's go to Maine. THIS PERSON ALSO WENT TO MAINE. She rode around the different back roads. She found a BABY FARM. Red Johnson's aunt ran it. A deal was made. Red flirted with the maids to get inside information. Followed the Morrows and Lindbergh back to their Jersey home. The week before the crime, Red kept dates with Betty Gow, Thursday, Friday, Saturday, and Sunday Nights. There were two dogs on the estate. The vicious one was poisoned on Sunday, if you remember what the Press said at the time. Red Johnson never failed to keep an engagement with Betty Gow, but on the night of the kidnapping, has a date with her and gave her a stand-up. Was that date made perhaps as an alibi in the event that he was caught prowling about the grounds? The baby was killed and half-buried, and that was the finish of that job.

Then the Press very kindly printed a very complete description of the sleeping suit, blanket pins, etc. So complete that anyone could have gone to Best & Co. and purchased the duplicate. Then the wise ones got the idea of picking up some easy money. Enter a very kindly old gentleman, who, for no other reason than his love of humanity, offers $1000 of his personal money to help solve the mystery. Incidentally, he also is a student of the stars, and the symbols on the ransom notes have a connection with ancient astrology. You carry on from here.

I sincerely hope that I haven't confused your own ideas of the case, but I have had these thoughts since the night that the extra came out and just had to annoy someone. I told my last employer my idea before the baby's body was found, and she insisted that I write (on her stationary) to Schwarzkopf. Naturally, I thought it best to mind my own business. But something has been telling me that I should write to you since Mr. Hauptmann has been given such a raw deal. We all realize that the police have had a hard time explaining why the mystery was not cleared up after all this time; we also feel that the person who could do kidnapping or murder of an infant in cold blood should be made to pay and pay plenty, BUT don't forget that it could have you or I that was framed, as easily as the man who now is in jail.

Hoping that you are able to make these wiseacres who have dubbed you the corn-cob detective, admit that they don't know it all as yet, by solving this case properly,

I am, with every respect for your ability,

Signed, ONE WHO READS VOX POP EVERY DAY, IN THE NEW YORK DAILY NEWS.

Note: Ellis Parker not only didn't throw this letter in the wastebasket; it has survived 85 years!

The author of the above letter reviews some theories we have heard before, but he does it very interestingly. Sitting here in 2020, I find it fascinating how large a following and fascination the public had with astrology, horoscopes, and fakirs. Was this because there was no TV? Interestingly Dwight Morrow had a bill passed in Washington to outlaw the "Fakirs" advertisements on the radio. Radio being the era's TV. The loss of the advertising revenue is mentioned as a motivation to dislike Lindbergh. Enough to punish him.

The writer has labeled Detective Parker as "The Corn Cob detective," but he goes on to state that he believes Ellis is the one who should have been given the case. Andy Sahol and I agree!

FROM THE ELLIS PARKER LOST FILES

12-13-1935

Dear Mr. Parker:

Excuse me for being so forward, but a life is in the balance, and many things can be overlooked concerning formality. Please consider me as one believing that Bruno Hauptmann is guilty of the kidnapping charge.

Approve of the stand you have taken in this case and hope you are able by some means of proving to those thick-skulled people that Hauptmann did not kidnap the baby.

If Hauptmann is electrocuted, then all of us are in danger if someone having more power wants us out of the way, and perhaps to cover some inane person's blunderings.

Honestly, do you think the child is dead? Have talked to many people about the case, and intelligent people have their doubts whether it is dead. Explain this, the baby disappeared in cold weather, and when the body was found, it was badly decomposed, and the funeral services were held as soon as possible and don't know whether an autopsy was held over it or not, but the remains were quickly disposed of.

Another thing damning to Hauptmann was the thumb shield. It was lost until Hauptmann was put on the stand, and then it was found. After laying in the elements for a year, it was produced and almost as good as new. Perhaps the weather wouldn't affect that. Have found Indian relics of stone, and they had lain for at least a hundred years, and they were practically in good condition, so the thumb guard must have been made of stone, as other materials would have shown traces of the weather. But never found any tomahawks with intact wooden handles, so the thumb guard must have been made of stone.

The evidence to me seemed flimsy all the way thru, am afraid many of the witnesses were just publicity seekers. Tell me, would such a fuss be made over my child or someone else's in peer circumstances? Oh, what is the use we did not fly over the ocean. Perhaps if the baby had been of an ordinary family, all this publicity would have been avoided.

Now tell me, would a sane person have carried a ladder on private grounds and put it to the right window? If so, he must have been a fortune teller sublime. Another thing, would you have left a baby as young as that in a room by itself with a nurse just coming in. Don't know but feel the nurse should have slept in the same room with a baby that age, perhaps the nurse had halitosis, or some other disease and the parents didn't want their offspring to catch it.

And then there was a dog in the child's room. It was certainly a good dog not to bark at a stranger, and probably it was so scared it lost its voice then again it may have lacked the qualities of a dog, then again it may have been a toy. Would you carry a ladder and raise it to the right window and crawl in and kidnap a baby? This evidence of the case seems to me so foolish that anyone accepting it is either silly or has an ax to grind.

Another thing that seems peculiar to me is, the experts in the case against Hauptmann were so "cocksure," there wasn't any it "might have been," but IT WAS. Please tell me, can any crime be the same as another? And can one event be just like another? That is foolish. The experts acted like some kids drilled in a school recitation, just what to say and at the right time.

Well, I will close now, as feel am just consuming your valuable time, hoping God will help Hauptmann out of this "frame-up." Have I said anything could be sent to the electric chair for, well and good? Know some would like to do it because I am siding with one, I think guiltless of the kidnapping, but think the trial should have been held for extortion. If the truth is ever known, maybe some prominent people will be implicated, think that is why Hauptmann is remaining silent. In my way of thinking, he is just a "game guy," shielding someone "higher up." Well anyway, hope he escapes the electric chair, and if he gets free, think he has learned his lesson. Well hoping he gets free and commending you on your stand, I remain as ever your well-wisher.

Sincerely,

P. Folwell Lock

Note: The writer, P. Folwell Lock, theorized that the Lindbergh baby was still alive. He had a hard time with the story that the thumb shield was found a year after the crime. He took the time to satirize the story, comparing it to stone Indian relics. He sets Hauptmann in a "frame-up" with him shielding someone higher up. He felt if the truth were ever known, some prominent people would be implicated. The writers of this book think that the most likely well-known person would be Charles Lindbergh.

FROM THE ELLIS PARKER LOST FILES

Dec 14, 1935

Ellis Parker, Esq.

Mount Holly, N.J.

When I saw in the papers that the Democrats are going to investigate Governor Hoffman, I intended to write him, but supposing that he has a lot of Catholics in the State office, I decided to write you instead; It may give you a clue in the Hauptmann case.

There is and have been a conspiracy against Col. Lindbergh ever since the favored Mr. Hoover, for President, in place of Al Smith, and against his father-in-law, the late Mr. Morrow, ambassador to Mexico, for writing the Mexican Constitution, which took all the power away from the Catholics in that country.

I am positive that Hauptmann did not kill Lindbergh's child, if it is killed, someone else has done it, and some catholic priest could enlighten the world on that subject, Condon-Jafsie included.

There was a catholic priest that called on the maid in the Morrow's house for weeks before the kidnapping took place, then he disappeared, the maid was poisoned. Suicide-rot-the catholic priest could tell. And why was not the catholic priest called to the witness stand, simply because all Catholics are Democrats and the Democrats controlled the case, that is why they are squealing now when the Governor is taking up the case.

The first thing that catholic Farly did when he came to power was to cancel all air contracts, so as to hit Lindbergh company: he could not take L. alone, so he took them all so that there would be no suspicion.

Put that Catholic priest and Jafsie through the third degree, or better still, put them in a hospital for a few days and give them a few treatments of Dcopolamine Hyddrobromide Solution then they will answer all questions put to them in regard to the case: That is all that they know.

The priest will tell you that the maid carried the child out and down the front stairs and that he poisoned her after he got the nearby orphanage; Jafsie will tell what did off the $10,000 that Smith gave him for putting it on Hauptmann.

Signed,

A friend to Justice

Note: At first, this anonymous letter writer's spelling and typing skills caused me to doubt his opinions. Like many of us today, he sees people in either a Democrat or Republican light, separate and waring with each other and obsessed with religion. However, he makes some good points and the motivations for the individual actions of some.

The concern for the upcoming elections, the participation of Dwight Morrow in them, and the possibility that Charles Lindbergh had political ambitions cannot be overlooked. Much of what occurred in the "Crime of the Century" could have been designed to cover up what Charles feared would become common knowledge and ruin any thought of a political carrier. I don't think Charles Lindbergh's motivations have ever been given the importance they should have in investigating the death of his child. We know he was decidedly pro-Hitler and pro-Germany. The Fuhrer himself may have shared Lindbergh's desire to see him successfully enter into Presidential politics. Hitler knew America was a sleeping giant and that the powerful country could bring failure to his world domination plans. What could be better for him than a neutral United State with a German American leaning President that was loyal to him?

If you are wondering what "Dcopolamine Hyddrobromide Solution" is, you are not alone. I spent an hour attempting to make sense of these words to no avail. The closest I came is to a drug used for Nausea or seasickness. I suspected truth serum but found no evidence of it. It has since dawned on me that it was used in torture, much like waterboarding, to eliminate the subject's will to keep secrets.

FROM THE ELLIS PARKER LOST FILES

Dec. 14, 1935

Florence E. Cobb

506 Key Building

Wewoka, Okla.

Hon. Harold H. Hoffman

Governor of the State of New Jersey, Trenton, New Jersey.

Dear Sir:

Please accept my appreciation, as a member of the American public, of your action in visiting Bruno Richard Hauptmann in his cell, for the purpose of ascertaining whether his was a case in which executive clemency should be exerted. My own opinion, and, I think, the opinion of a considerable section of the American public, is that the sentence of Mr. Hauptmann should be reduced to imprisonment for life, and the reason for this is as follows:

The evidence on which Hauptmann was convicted was purely circumstantial. Direct proof of his commission of the crime is, unless the newspaper reports are incorrect, lacking, and the influences operating for conviction, amounting to popular hysteria, were such as could not have failed to produce an effect upon a jury.

The tragedy of the Lindbergh baby kidnapping and murder is one of the most horrible that have occurred in the United States in recent years, and the murderer ought to be found, tried, and executed, but that fact does not warrant the legal killing of a human being unless the fact that he did the deed is legitimately and adequately proved.

The trial of Bruno Hauptmann in the Court House at Flemington, New Jersey, for the kidnapping and murder of the Lindbergh infant was one of the most shocking examples of public hysteria which have ever occurred in American courts of justice. Sob sisters and brothers compared the allegedly still, composed, heroic face of Colonel Lindbergh as he sat throughout the trial with the contained but tense expression of Hauptmann, a few feet away from whom he had his position, and commented in the newspapers which they represented, with the deduction that such coolness as that displayed by Hauptmann indicated that he was a capable and self-reliant murderer. Little wooden ladders sold as models of the one on which Hauptmann was supposed to have climbed to the window of the Lindbergh home from which the baby was stolen were worn upon coat lapels and as shoulder adornments by dozens of attendants at the trial, if the newspaper reports are correct.

Northerners and Easterners regard with anger and contempt and charges that justice has been violated the lynching's of the Southern states. Let them reflect that the execution of Hauptmann, in view of the circumstances of his trial and the evidence adduced at it, may in the light of future events and information turn out to be a lynching in New Jersey.

In the spirit of justice and fair play, of the protection of human life and liberty involved in the "beyond a reasonable doubt" requirement of proof in capital offenses which our distant forbears wrenched from King John upon the Field of the Cloth of Gold so many centuries ago, this human life should not be taken without more definite proof than has yet been given that it is legitimately forfeit to the State.

I have no connection of any kind with the Hauptmann case or the Hauptmann's and am writing the above merely because it seems to me that a sense of justice demands such action. You may use this letter in any way you wish.

Yours truly,

Florence E. Cobb

Note: Florence E. Cobb's intent in his letter is clear: Bruno Richard Hauptmann's guilt was not proven "Beyond a reasonable doubt" at the "Hysteria" in Flemington. "Beyond a reasonable doubt" is a requirement in Capital offenses.

FROM THE ELLIS PARKER LOST FILES

Gary, Indiana

Dec. 15, 1935

Mr. Ellis H. Parker

Burlington County Detective Bureau,

Trenton, NJ

Dear Sir:

Regarding the Lindbergh case, the writer is neither convinced that Hauptmann is or is not the guilty party. If he is, I feel he should pay the penalty, if not, every effort should be made to stay the execution.

I am sending you this note on the one out of a hundred possibilities that it may have any connection. At the time of search being made for the baby, a Mr. Curtis claimed to be in touch with the kidnappers, although later he said it was all a hoax. However, the coincidence that names he gave as parties he contacted, John, Neal, and Sam, as published in the papers here, should be the same as those of three of the men connected with robbing freight cars and selling to a man by the name of Goodman who ran a large department store in this town, is something I think might be investigated. I believe this case was up about 8 or 9 years ago and these men sentenced to Leavenworth for terms of 2 years. Evidence is enclosed that one of these parties was a hijacker, rum runner, and generally rotten.

I have no intention of getting into trouble anyone not connected with the case but appreciate that you are in position to conduct investigation, if you think there is anything to the above, without these parties ever being bothered, except you should find evidence to show they have had connection with it. In as much as they took all fingerprints obtainable from the letters, ladder, etc., these could be compared with fingerprints of parties mentioned, which would be on file at the penitentiary.

Anonymous

Note: John Hughes Curtis told Charles Lindbergh that he knew his sons' location soon after he went missing. Curtis told Colonel Lindbergh of a Norfolk, Virginia sailor who was holding his son. Ships and airplanes were dispatched to search for the vessel with the baby aboard. They failed to find him. The names of the accomplices listed above do not match those mentioned by Curtis. When the supposed body of the Lindbergh baby was discovered on May 12, 1932, Curtis was considered a fraud and his story a hoax.

FROM THE ELLIS PARKER LOST FILES

Whitewood – South Dakota

December 15th, 1935

His Excellency

Gov. Harold G. Hoffmann, Trenton, N.J.

Dear Sir: -

This is Not an appeal for Hauptmann's life but decidedly one for JUSTICE and Fair Play for the rank and file of American citizens when opposed in the Courts of Justice of this land by the "over-rich" and the politicians.

As did every other red-blooded American, I guess, I followed the Hauptmann case thru from the beginning to the end and early saw the divers' motives that prompted the different participants to follow the courses they have. At least I think I did and have come to the conclusion that this is a case of a rich man dreading the rattling of the skeletons in his closet to become public property; of personal revenge on the part of jilted moron female; perhaps the more vicious revenge of the sympathetic brother; similar fear of rattling skeletons on the part of a lascivious schoolmaster and finally the eagerness of the political machine to serve the rich even at the cost of innocent life.

Here is a resume of rather interesting facts (?) I have gleaned from different papers at different times, and not entirely forgotten, that certainly would clear ANY man, but the really guilty one.

1. "Slim" Anderson and "Slim" Lindbergh became pals while in training before the war and were known as the "two slims"; they went overseas together but became separated there, and it was sometime over here before they met again.

2. When they did, it was for Anderson to introduce Lindbergh to his finance, one Elizabeth Morrow.

3. Lindbergh fell for Elizabeth and showed his first yellow streak when he stole Anderson's sweetheart from him and became engaged to Elizabeth himself.

4. With the year he met his wife-to-be, Anna, on her return from her overseas schooling and – as promptly Lindbergh fell for her, engaged himself to her and ditched his fiancé, Elizabeth. (Elizabeth was then teaching in California, I believe.)

5. The losing of a landing wheel in midair in Mexico City while taking Anna "for a ride" is the first unexplained "incident" in the one-two-three order of fatalistic events that lead to an end. (Could Elizabeth explain?)

6. When Elizabeth visited the Lindbergh's in their new home, Lindbergh got wise to a planned kidnapping of his wife Anna and counter planned to put Elizabeth in the car on that trip and nab the kidnappers. The plan failed because no kidnappers showed up! (Could Elizabeth explain?)

7. There are many things about the actual kidnapping that the general public (myself included) is far from satisfied with and which just as clearly point to a smothering of Actual facts and a Distortion of others which naturally enough reasonably permit the public to assume that the incidents of which it has learned MUST be true for they are certainly disparaging enough to any man's character that he should wish to keep them hid. (Could Elizabeth tell?)

8. When it is considered that the Morrows have a moron son, the taint may well be expected to be found in the blood of all of the descendants, and as usual, manifest itself in savagery.

9. Any man that will steal a pals sweetheart, then ditch her for her sister, will also sell out an over-enthusiastic public that have

boosted him high on the pedestal of public worship, and if crowded, will likewise sacrifice an innocent man, any old time!

10. Why did the little nurse commit suicide? Why did her lover run away, and why wasn't he extradited? Why wasn't the house-keeper and her husband grilled, and WHY wasn't Hauptmann (?) nabbed when Jafsie and Lindbergh (of all men) handed over the money at the cemetery? These are very pertinent questions, "Main Street" up and down the continent have been asking! If it were me in Lindbergh's place, I'd GOTTEN that fellow!

It is not alone an innocent man that I am pleading for, it is Justice in the Courts of the land to whom we Must appeal for final judgment. Such a judge Must consider every appeal with due solemnly and consider that each contender should feel that it was their own judgment that was at fault and not the Judges.

That trial was not a "three-ringed circus," it was a dis-grace to the State wherein it was held for it clearly showed all who would cherish our form of American liberty that "you cannot hang anything on the rich."

That ladder testimony: that thumbstall testimony and that old reprobate of a Jafsie all point towards the whole deal being loaded – framed.

The fact that you have injected yourself into this case at this last moment, clearly indicates to all the world that you yourself are not satisfied with what has taken place and that you mean to "do what is right." For this, you are receiving many fine words in commendation for by no stretch of the imagination is "public opinion" with Lindbergh any longer.

Hauptmann's pictures certainly do not portray a hard-ened criminal, and his side of the presentation certainly looks a whole lot cleaner than does the governments with its phony boards and choked-off testimony. Such stuff shakes our confidence in the Justice of our courts, – and of which I have had my own share of experience.

Very respectfully yours,

Chas. C. Haas.

Note: Charles C. Haas (1872-1959) was born in Schleswig-Holstein, Germany. He emigrated to Whitewood, South Dakota, at the age of 25. Whitewood was approximately 12 miles from the iconic and historic Deadwood, South Dakota. He was considered one of the early settlers of the area. He married twice and sired ten children. Charles became a farmer specializing in the crops of Alfalfa. He wrote an Alfalfa seed catalog (1915) that is still referenced to this day. When South Dakota began a program to name your farm, Charles purchased the name "Glenheim" for $1. He was invited to write for the South Dakota Federal Writes Program organized to ensure the State's history was preserved. He continued writing for the South Dakota History Society Press and the notable "Memoirs of The State."

As you would expect, after reviewing Charles's life of writing, the letter he composed to Ellis Parker is exceptional, although he rehashes some popular theories.

FROM THE ELLIS PARKER LOST FILES

Claude De Haven

193 Ellison St., Paterson N.J.

December 15, 1935

Mr. Ellis Parker, Mt. Holly N.J.

Dear Mr. Parker,

I have some information that might help you in the Hauptmann case, one thing I ask of you, and that is to keep my name out of the papers as I do not want any publicity or any money whatsoever. As I am giving you this information because I do not believe Hauptmann guilty. However, this information may not be worth the paper it's written on. I will relate the happenings as I remember it.

During March of 1932 I was stationed at the U-Drive It Co, 128 N. Warren St. In Trenton, N.J. (The company I worked for 9 Years before we were forced to close due to business conditions,) Our business was the renting of cars to people who drove them themselves. Around the last of March 1932, a man and woman came in to rent a car with a driver. There were times when we could get someone to drive. However, on this day, no one was around, and I took it on myself to drive this party rather than to lose the trip. I drove this party to the Lindbergh estate. The woman did most of the talking, and the man with her tried to keep her still. On the way, she told me she had an appointment with Mrs. Morrow at the Lindbergh Estate and that she called Mrs. Morrow on the unlisted phone and made the appointment for 4 P.M.

When we arrived at the gates of the Estate the N.J. State Police refused to let this woman go into the house. There were words between her and the Police, she then told the Police that she would go back to N.Y. and keep her mouth shut as to who did the job. She also told the Police that the baby was dead and within five miles of where she was standing. (This was at the gate leading to the estate) The Police then took her into the house and put questions to her that she told me she refused to answer.

I tried to get her name on the way back, but she wouldn't tell me, she did say that she was the past President of the D.A.R. That would be in 1931 and that she lives (at that time) in West Chester N.Y. and that she was an Official of the West Chester Police that is the West Chester County Police.

Mrs. Morrow was (at the time she was President of the D.A.R.) a charter member, and that being the means of her meeting Mrs. Morrow.

She told me and the N.J. State Police that she knew who kidnaped the baby, but she would not tell anyone unless she was permitted to see Mrs. Morrow, On the way back to Trenton, she told me that Mrs. Morrow's own son planned the job, with the aid of some others and that she also knew just where the guilty one could be picked up.

After we returned to Trenton, she paid her bill and I drove them to the Pennsylvania Station, where she was going to get a train for New York.

The man with her did not talk only to keep her still.

One thing I can never understand is why the Police let her get away from them like they did. Maybe you can make something out of this and get a lead to work on and help to free a man that a lot of people think not guilty.

I will be at the above address every night except Mondays and Thursdays if you or someone of your staff care to go over this with me.

This information was given to Reilly and Fischer. That is, it was mailed to them some time ago. So far, nothing has happened as I know of, if they traced the woman or not.

Very truly yours,
Claude De Haven

Note: Ellis Parker must have done an excellent job because I couldn't find anything on Claude DeHaven of Patterson, NJ, in the papers. In his well-typed letter, Claude tells an interesting and believable story. It could be that Mrs. Morrow had changed her mind about seeing her visitor. If Dwight Morrow Jr was the baby's kidnapper and evidence was presented, it might have been painful for her to hear it, or someone may have had time to talk her out of it. Rumors were that her son, Dwight Morrow Jr, was illegitimate, fathered by her husband with a mistress. It was also thought that Dwight Jr was angry when cut out of his father's will with his son-in-law Charles Lindbergh being gifted in it. Claude's letter also details another example of the NJ State Police's poor performance and the investigation team of Norman Schwarzkopf that Ellis Parker spoke of on many occasions when they let her drive away.

FROM THE ELLIS PARKER LOST FILES

884 North 21st Street, Philadelphia, Pa.,

Dec. 16th, 1935

Mr. Ellis Parker.

Dear Sir.

This is just one more of many letters that you must be receiving in reference to the Hauptmann case. Though I have never met you I have followed your work for years and admire your ability. As a detective you have no equal. I wish you success in your efforts to prove Hauptmann's innocence. There are millions that feel the same as you do in regard to this case.

A theory of mine is that Hauptmann's friend Isidore Fisch got the ransom money through the commission of a robbery, either by his own or someone else's efforts. As soon as he learned that it was the ransom money, he decided to wish it on Hauptmann until things cooled down and in the meantime he died.

I feel that Dr Condon knows a lot more about this case than he has told. He is avoiding the truth. I feel that he is in a position to clear up the mystery and in doing so it will liberate Hauptmann.

With all the success possible I sincerely hope that you are able to fine evidence that will prove Hauptmann's innocence and bring the guilty to Justice.

Very Respectfully

Byron Charlesworth

Ellis Parker responded on the same day:

December 16, 1935.

Byron Charlesworth,

884 No. 21st Street,

Philadelphia, Pa.

Dear Sir: -

Your letter of the 16th received, and I wish to thank you for same. Your thoughts are very interesting, and I will give them my consideration.

Again, thanking you for your interest, I remain,

Very truly yours,

Ellis H. Parker

Chief of Detectives

Note: Another writer suggests Isidor Fisch is one of the main conspirators in the Lindbergh baby abduction. We, Ellis Parker, his Grandson Andy Sahol and I, Russell Lloyd, believe that the baby was handed to Paul Wendel and Isidor Fisch out the front door.

FROM THE ELLIS PARKER LOST FILES

The following is exerted from Detective Dick Nugent's letter to Ellis Parker, written on 12-16-1935. Nugent of the Tate Detective Agency was then a County Detective at Carney's Point, NJ. He had met Ellis 20 years before he wrote the letter. At that time, he was working on an arson case.

"My real purpose in writing you is relative to the Lindbergh case. I think I have some important facts and theories or leads that might break this case wide open. I spent considerable time and money trying to crack this problem but was always discouraged by Schwarzkopf's 'Secretive' attitude towards outsiders. I had the correct lead on the case 4 days after it occurred but ignored it like you. If I had known you would devote your efforts independently, I certainly would have contacted you then.

The solution to this case in New Jersey does not suit me or the rest of the world. I'm glad to see a courageous governor and a real old fashioned conscientious Detective step in and try to prevent what later proved to be a "World Miscarriage of Justice." It would have been a blemish on that age-old tradition of "Jersey Justice" because, in this case, "doubt" is a possibility, regardless of the experts. Handwritings and wood grains should not be considered conclusive evidence of a man's guilt in murder. Fingerprints? None? Alibi's 50-50? Identification flaws? Not absolute or positive? Evidence of murder? None whatsoever?

If there were absolute proof, I would be willing to turn on the current in this case. I've got two notches in that chair, and I am responsible for several guests up at the 'Big House.' One of them for 80 years. So, I am not chickenhearted, but I will not stand by and see this chap burned so that the case can be officially marked closed.

Dick Nugent signed the Above letter on 12-16-1935.

FROM THE ELLIS PARKER LOST FILES

December 16th, 1935.

Governor Harold G. Hoffman,

Executive Mansion, State Capitol, Trenton, N.J.

Dear Governor: -

As a Republican who voted for my personal friend, William L. Dill, at the last gubernatorial election, I want to commend you for the interest you have taken in the fate of Bruno Hauptman. It is at least one of your good acts, and you were justified in everything you did.

No doubt you have received many letters favorable and unfavorable, but feel it my duty to express a personal opinion on the celebrated case, as follows: -

First - The trial was like a three-ring circus and would have done credit to a P. T. Barnum.

Second – The district Attorney Wilentz was vulgar, bitter, and vindictive, and a Jew.

Third – The judges' charge to the jury was decidedly unfair and prejudiced.

Fourth – The evidence was largely circumstantial, and I believe some of it was faked.

Fifth – Colonel Schwarzkopf and State Police muddled up the case at the start and had to convict someone to save their faces.

Sixth – 25 years would have been a fair verdict until the real culprit was found, as do not think that Hauptman was ever in the vicinity of Hopewell.

I have confidence in you as a man to believe that justice will be done this unfortunate man.

Very respectfully yours,

Stuart Beaver Rote

11 Monroe Avenue, East Orange, N.J.

Note: Stuart Beaver Rote was 55 years old when he composed this letter. It is an excellent list of opinions except for the Second one. I don't think much of Wilentz or how he gathered evidence for Bruno Hauptmann's trial, but Wilentz's race, ethnicity, or religion has nothing to do with it. The "Jew" comment in the Second opinion only reflects poorly on the author of this letter. I do, however, agree that fake evidence was presented during the trial to convict Hauptmann.

FROM THE ELLIS PARKER LOST FILES

Dec. 17th, 1935

Mr. Ellis H. Parker, Chief of Detectives, Mount Holly, New Jersey

Dear Sir: -

I wish to tell you of my own appreciation of your interest in the Hauptmann case, and more, to tell you that I appreciate your spirit of fair play and justice and add my own words of commendation of your courage in facing out such almost unsurmountable opposition. You are a Worthy American! And I am glad to know there are still a few who are not the serfs of the rich, - which includes Gov. Hoffmann.

I am enclosing you a carbon of my letter to Gov. Hoffman that may be of interest to you, not that it is prima facie evidence in itself, but to me, and many others here - this stuff should not lead you up a "blind alley."

We have had plenty of occasion to learn to know Lindbergh to the "quick" since he broke into the limelight, and these ten suggestions reflect the understanding his public life gives us of him, hence any prove of value to you, which I hope to God they will.

While I do not have the original clippings of these news items, when this kidnapping began to cover the front pages, these references to his earlier life came to mind and appeared more and more to fit in with the vagaries of moron minds and as a solution to this perplexing (?) problem. Lindbergh's behavior throughout is but the natural sequence of his type and of his martial position.

Jafsie's interest appears to be a very personal one judging by the bitterness he displays, although he professes to be an outsider. My own interest is purely for the reasons stated as "Hauptmann's" name was entirely strange to me in the beginning. For that reason, I sincerely hope that YOU <u>win</u> and with such a fair-minded man as your governor to help you. I feel confident that you <u>Will</u>. I wish you luck.

Yours very truly,

Chas. C. Haas, Whitewood-S.D.

<u>Note</u>: At first, I thought that Whitewood must be a misspelling, but it turns out that there is a Whitewood and a Whitewood in the state. Fascination with the Lindbergh case swept the country. People were very familiar with the main characters and knowledgeable about them. The writer mentions Jafsie, Lindbergh, Hauptmann, and New Jersey Governor Harold Hoffman, whom he also wrote. Men that the case had brought much fame. The writer commented that he wanted Detective Parker to "win" as if it was a contest. Detective Parker did not win and eventually was unjustly imprisoned.

FROM THE ELLIS PARKER LOST FILES

December 17th, 1935

1106 Lindley Ave., Philadelphia, Pa.

Mr. Ellis Parker,

Chief – Burlington County Detectives

Do you recall that the papers printed an account of a man and woman having stopped at a Drug store in Hopewell, N. J. at about 10 o'clock on the night the Lindbergh baby was kidnapped and purchased some ether? The papers of March 2nd or 3rd 1932 carried his statement. Has this ever been investigated?

Jafsie said the man he spoke to in the Cemetery (whom he claimed was Hauptmann) had a tubercular cough. Hauptmann was a healthy man – while Isidor Fisch, who was connected with the case, died of Tuberculosis. According to Jafsie's statement, he might have been talking to Fisch. The first time he met Hauptmann after Hauptmann's arrest, he (Jafsie) did not seem to be sure that he was the man he had met in the Cemetery; he wanted to see him again. Why did he feel sure later that he was the man?

In view of the sudden death of Mr. Whately and the suicide of Violet Sharpe – are you in your own mind, convinced that this was not an inside job?

With reference to the above-mentioned ether – my theory is that the ether was bought to put the baby out of its misery in a humane way – after it was injured through the breaking of the ladder – and as it could not be produced to secure the ransom it was quickly buried.

If Hauptmann is guilty, I have no sympathy for him; but as no direct evidence has been produced to connect him with the death of the baby, I feel there is not enough evidence to send him to the electric chair.

Very truly yours,

Mrs. J. T. Lerch

Ellis Parker responded to Mrs. T. J. Lerch on 12-19-1935:

Mrs. J. T. Lerch

1106 Lindley Ave, Phila. Pa.

Dear Madam,

I received your letter, and I appreciate your thoughts and expressions. They co-inside with mine to a large degree.

I have no interest in this case, only that of Justice. My investigation has been along that line. I know there is a different story than that which has been told. To have Hauptmann's life sacrificed, in my judgment, would be a mistake.

Thanking you for your interest in this matter, and assuring you that I more than appreciate it, I remain,

Very truly yours,

Ellis H. Parker
Chief of Detectives

Mrs. J. T. Lerch responded to Ellis Parker's return letter on 2-10-1936:

1106 Lindley Ave., Philadelphia, Pa.
February 10th, 1936

Dear Sir:

I want to thank you for your reply to my letter of December 17th last.

At the risk of making myself tiresome but in the interest of a man who may be innocent, I want again to call your attention to the cemetery meeting "Jafsie" had with a man who had a tubercular cough. Hauptmann, according to newspaper accounts, was employed on March 1st, 1932. It seems to me it should be easy to get in touch with the man for whom worked that day as well as with some of his fellow workers and find out for certain whether or not Hauptmann had such a cough at that time. By that time, I mean, of course, not March 1st but of the evening "Jafsie" talked with the same man in the Cemetery.

I bring the matter to your attention for what it is worth.

Very truly yours,
Mrs. J. T. Lerch

<u>Note</u>: Mrs. Lerch has focused on an issue that many others have. Who did Jafsie meet in the Cemetery? The suspects are Hauptmann, Fisch, and years later, John Knoll (see the book Cemetery John written by Robert Zorn). Hauptmann didn't cough, and Fisch had Tuberculosis and did cough, which makes him the #1 suspect in my mind. Mrs. Lerch also brings up the possibility that Ellis could determine if Bruno Hauptmann was coughing the day of his appearance in the Cemetery by interviewing people at his employment place. It was tried during the initial investigation to determine if he was working on the day of the Lindbergh kidnapping. Mysteriously, the records for that day were missing.

The purchase of the chemical ether the night of kidnapping (10 am) is interesting information. The possible sinister reason for the purchase is disturbing.

Last, Mrs. Lerch brings up the deaths of Mr. Whately and Violet Sharpe. In other letters, we read that they had a relationship. These deaths are very suspicious.

FROM THE ELLIS PARKER LOST FILES

Stacy Trent

NY Office, Murray Hill 2-0831

December 18, 1935

Dear Mr. Parker,

Re: our conversation:

My work on the Fisch angle of the Hauptmann case began so soon after Hauptmann's arrest that I was able to get first-hand information before it became clouded, and before any wall of lies could have been built up, in my opinion.

Outstanding was the indication that Fisch was a forger, and that he posed as a handwriting expert. In this, he might have been acting for Uhlig, whom I could never get to see, and who was Fisch's closest friend. Uhlig, for instance, told Henkle he had seen Fisch with a large sum of money after the ransom was paid, and that Fisch had tried to dispose of it. Uhlig may have the key to the entire mystery, or be it, many things indicate.

Mrs. Kohl, whom Fisch defrauded of $5,000, and several others whose names I know but have not with me; also a young woman who wrote letters for Fisch charged that he committed the crime of forgery by using letterheads of a defunct fur firm and forging signatures to show he had fur there. Fisch, as you know, was good with the pen. I don't know about Uhlig, who spent much time in England and speaks well, and who is supposed to be part Jew.

Here is the best anecdote about Fisch and handwriting. It is based on what I was told by Mrs. Hauptmann, by Mrs. Henkle, by Henkle, and by Kloppenburg, separately, without and disagreement among them, and in my opinion, truthfully:

Hauptmann's baby was to be named Manfred. Only Fisch and the Henkle couple knew it, besides Hauptmann and Mrs. Hauptmann. On his first birthday, a letter, written on Hotel Pennsylvania stationary, came to the Hauptmann's house. It was addressed to Manfred Von Hauptmann. The Von is high-toned, and pleased Mrs. Hauptmann; yet it was ironic, too, and disturbed her. But she was pleased to have a letter come on distinguished stationery.

She was troubled however, only Fisch, the Henkle's, and her husband, outside herself, knew the child's name was to be Manfred. Of course, Fisch might have told Uhlig. The Henkle's told no one.

Mrs. Hauptmann opened the letter. It contained a lot of writing in GERMAN, which called the baby a thief and said various things in dirty language about the child. Fisch, inci-dentally, had always been "jealous" of the baby.

Mrs. Hauptmann said she did not dare tell Hauptmann about the letter, knowing it would distress him, said that he would be angry at whoever sent it. Fisch came around---this was a week or two before he sailed for Europe---and she decided to show him the letter. She did. He read it and laughed at it. He said it was not meant for the baby, but Bruno Hauptmann, and that it probably was a joke.

"Let me have it," Fisch said. "I know about handwriting, and I can tell who wrote it." "How?" asked Mrs. Hauptmann. "I will get samples of the writing of the Henkle's and compare it. I can tell."

Fisch went to the Henkle's there is no doubt about this, and without speaking about the letter got them to do some writing for him. He took the samples of their writing away with him. Just before he sailed for Europe, he told Mrs. Hauptmann:

"I have compared the writing, and it is the writing of Mrs. Henkle."

Mrs. Henkle convinced me that was not true, and that all she knew of it was that she had done some writing for Fisch, on his pretense that he could not write English well, and that he took the sample with him.

Now, Uhlig told Henkle about the dirty letter, however, Uhlig said he had seen it, and that Fisch had kept it.

When Fisch sailed, Mrs. Hauptmann asked him about the letter, and he said he had turned it over to Uhlig, who wanted to send it to some friends in Germany as a joke.

Now, out of this, it is clear, that Fisch posed as a hand-writing expert, and that he did get copies of two persons' handwriting under that pretense. That is about all it proves.

But I am sure the Henkle's were not lying, and that Hauptmann had not persuaded them to thus lay a ground-work about Fisch, for it wasn't laid on thick enough. I was sure the incident occurred.

At the least, that makes Fisch an interesting person---or Uhlig, whose work he might have done---since handwriting was to figure so importantly in the case. A forger might thus have obtained Hauptmann's handwriting.

The other angle I was interested in regards the Faulkner bank deposit. We are still obtaining information of this angle, and it may prove valuable. It leads toward the Condon family. Uhlig, by the way, made toys for children out of fur. He is unmarried. He's a fur worker. But he is the least interviewed man in the whole case.

LOU WEDEMAR

I expect to be in Trenton for a few more days.

Note: Lou Wedemar was a reporter, author, and even a comic book creator. In my opinion, he is believable. Lou was talented and well regarded while making a living like everyone else. He was also very political. His letter to Ellis Parker is interesting and pointing in the right direction. That Fisch was a forger has been suggested in many articles. It is widely suspected that Fisch participated in the creation of the ransom notes. Uhlig is Harry Uhlig, a close friend of Isidor Fisch. The Henkle's owned or operated the apartment building where Fisch resided. Why Fisch was jealous of the baby was beyond me. Maybe it was because he knew he was terminal. That knowledge can change a man.

J.J. Faulkner is mentioned in this letter. Faulkner was never identified or proven to exist. It is apparent it was an alias. J.J. Faulkner, or someone posing as him/her, had deposited $2980 of the ransom money in the New York Federal Reserve Bank. The address on the deposit slip led police to the residence of J. Faulkner. It turned out the initial J. stood for Jane Faulkner. Jane Faulkner had married and moved to Larchmont, NY. It turned out that she had no connection to the money or the deposit.

FROM THE ELLIS PARKER LOST FILES

THE BERGEN EVENING RECORD
HACKENSACK, N. J., THURSDAY DECEMBER 19, 1935, Member of Associated Press

TEANECK MAN CLAIMS NEW EVIDENCE IN LINDY PROBE,
Saw Violet Sharpe at Princeton with Man, Salesman Says, Got
Car Number,
Traced To Ex-Morrow Employee Here, He Declares

Violet Sharpe, the English-born maid in the household of Mrs. Dwight W. Morrow, who committed suicide at the height of the Lindbergh kidnapping investigation, and a mysterious slouch-hatted man were dragged today into the shifting spotlight of the revived kidnap-murder on the testimony of a Teaneck resident.

Roscoe La Rue, 50, of 271 Van Buren Avenue, Teaneck, salesman, publicly revealed today for the first-time evidence which he charged police had refused to investigate.

SAW MAID NEAR SCENE

According to La Rue, he saw Violet Sharpe and her mysterious companion, several times on Route 27 near Princeton early in the morning of March 1, 1932, in a car with the back seat piled with bedding.

The license number of the car, given by La Rue to police of Springfield, N. J., where La Rue at the time resided, was checked with Bergen County Police and found to bear the initial and number issued to a former employee of Dwight D. Morrow, La Rue asserted.

Notified by the Springfield Police of La Rue's information, prosecuting officials failed to check the information with La Rue, the salesman said.

He said that in a final attempt to see justice done, he had sent registered letters containing the information to Charles A. Lindbergh, Attorney General David Wilentz, and Superintendent of State Police H. Norman Schwarzkopf. The letter was sent on January 12, 1935, shortly after the beginning of the trial of Bruno Richard Hauptmann. He received no reply, La Rue said.

La Rue was reached at his Teaneck residence, where he has lived there and a half years, early this morning. He told his story to two reporters as he finished dressing to go to work.

HOPES FOR JUSTICE

A tall man, quietly dressed, La Rue appeared a typical commuter. He explained that until now, he assiduously avoided publicity, fearing retaliation against his wife and children in the event his information was made public. His motive for finally revealing his information was simply a desire to see justice done, he said.

Asked whom he saw in the car on Route 27 on the morning of March 1, 1032, La Rue answered without recitation that he had seen Violet Sharpe. He said that he recognized her afterward from her pictures in the newspapers.

He first saw the car, with a man and a woman in the front seat, parked at the side of the road on Route 27 near the main intersection road from Princeton and Hopewell. The actions of the car were strange, La Rue reported.

As he approached, the car started up and quickly picked up speed, not permitting La Rue to pass it. It repeated this performance at four different intersecting roads, slowing up and the getting up speed as La Rue approached, although La Rue did not blow his horn.

Finally, after the car had crossed the Reading Railroad tracks in Trenton, La Rue said, the car was stopped by a traffic officer at an intersection. La Rue, going in the same direction, drew up beside it and also stopped, getting a perfect view of the occupants and the interior of the car. "In the back of the car was a pile of something – apparently bedding," La Rue said.

GOT LICENSE NUMBER

La Rue noted the license number, which he reported verbally to Springfield Police Chief Runyan, Sergeant Sorge, and Patrolmen Day and Phillips. The car bore a Bergen plate. La Rue reported the number to the police on March 3, 1932.

On March 7, La Rue said, the Sergeant had come to his home in Springfield to report informally on the checkup resulting from the lead given by La Rue

La Rue said that the Sergeant had reported the car number had been referred to the Bergen County police, and that the report came back to the Springfield police from Bergen that the license had been issued to a car of a totally different description as to kind, model and color, than the car on which the license had been seen by La Rue.

The report showed that the correct car was in the owner's garage, La Rue said, but maintained that the report did not continue to say what had become of the license plates on the car in the garage.

La Rue said that the Springfield police added that the strange thing about the license number reported was that it had been issued to a former employee of Mr. Morrow. La Rue did not know the name of the man.

At this point, La Rue severed his connection with the case, stating that he wished to avoid publicity for fear of retaliation on his family.

He felt called upon to investigate last fall, however, upon the arrest of Hauptmann, who, he said, was definitely not the man in the car with Violet Sharpe. He then asked that his information on the case be given a thorough investigation.

He found from the Springfield police, he said, an order to them from the State police to return all information the State police, which closed out the Springfield cops.

On Jan. 12, 1935, determined to get some action on the information he had furnished, La Rue wrote registered letters to Lindbergh, Wilentz, and Schwarzkopf, none of whom replied. In desperation. He wrote a similar letter to Lloyd Fischer, Hauptmann's attorney. Fischer assigned an investigator to work on La Rue's story, but the investigator got nowhere.

Two weeks ago, La Rue wrote to Fischer notifying him that unless he got some action from the evidence which La Rue had furnished him, he would personally turn over his information either to Hauptmann or J. Edgar Hoover, Director of the Bureau of Investigation of the Department of Justice at Washington.

DESCRIBES OCCUPANT OF CAR

La Rue described the man in the car with Violet Sharpe as short, heavy-set with unusually broad shoulders, about five feet six inches tall, of a ruddy complexion, and wearing a slouch hat. He drove slumped forward in the car, as though trying to conceal his appearance, La Rue said. La Rue said he saw the car shortly after daylight, at about 6:30 a.m. on the day of the kidnapping.

La Rue then made routine calls at Philadelphia and Camden, talked over his experience with his wife, and on March 3, 1932, decided that it was his duty to notify police.

La Rue claimed that he had affidavits of his second conversation with Springfield police, when Sergeant Sorge came to tell him the result of the police checkup of the license on March 7. 1932.

Note: The alarming thing about this newspaper account is that Roscoe La Ru points explicitly to the prosecution officials as failing to check his information. The criticism of the prosecution's diligence is troubling. It is apparent that Wilentz was willing to remove or cover up anything that would hinder a guilty verdict in the Hauptmann prosecution, even if it proved Hauptmann's absolute innocence. I don't believe that is the way American justice is supposed to work.

Once again, Violet Sharpe's suicide is prominent in the case. There has never been a believable explanation of her actions. This alone is reasonable doubt. Hauptmann should have been given a jail sentence, not an execution. Yet the prosecution, led by David Wilentz, wanted him silenced forever. No wonder they buried so much evidence.

One last thought. The man described in the car sounds very much how a description of Paul Wendel would be written.

FROM THE ELLIS PARKER LOST FILES

NORTHERN CALIFORNIA DETECTIVE BUREAU

15,000 Criminal and Forger Print Records

829 Orange Street, Yuba City, California.

Phone Marysville 537-J

A Genuine Secret Service, Licensed and Bonded

Sacramento Valley Since 1898, Efficient Operatives

Wanted: Descriptive Circulars, Photographs and Fingerprint Cards of All Fugitives

Affiliate of National Co-operative Detective Service

12-19-1935

Mr. Ellis Parker, Mt. Holly, N.J.

SIR:

We approve Governor Hoffman's position. The writer – thirty-five years in Police Work and Investigations – does not believe the LINDBERGH'S kidnapping a One-man Job.

I love children and hate criminals. Hauptmann did not bring the baby down that ladder. Had he gone to the Sourland Estate that night, his wife would have accompanied him. Too many unsolved elements of mystery. Where, for instance, is J.J. FAULKNER? And VIOLET SHARPE'S ex-husband. Who was to keep the child quiet as the Kidnapper passed the police? What of the car described by Conover's with the very bright lights? Where is the "Rest of the money" Why never a FINGER-PRINT of Hauptmann anywhere? Why did the little DOG not bark? How did he know Lindbergh's were remaining over at the Sourland home that night? I do not know if he is innocent, but what evidence we've read does NOT justify his execution.

M.A. CARPENTER.

<u>Ellis Parker responded to M. A. Carpenter on 12-19-1935:</u>

Dec. 19, 1935

M.A. Carpenter, Principal,
Yuba City, California.

Dear Friend,

I received your letter and appreciated your thoughts. This affair is two distinct acts. One is the kidnapping, and one is the Extortion.

In my opinion, Hauptmann is not connected with either one but was a victim. This would be hard to explain to the public, and I refrain from attempting it, but my object in this matter is only one of Justice as I know he had nothing whatever to do with the kidnapping or so-called Murder.

A lot of your thoughts contained in your communications coincide with facts that I have discovered.

Again, thanking you, I remain, very truly yours,

Ellis H. Parker
Chief of County Detectives

<u>Ellis wrote one last letter after the received a card from M. A. Carpenter:</u>

January 20, 1936

Northern California Detective Bureau, 829 Orange Street, Yuba City, California

Attention Mr. M. A. Carpenter

Dear Sir:

I acknowledge receipt of your card, and I want to thank you for your thoughtfulness and interest in this matter.

Very truly yours,

Ellis H. Parker

Chief of Detectives

<u>Same day Ellis Parker addressed another letter to M. A. Carpenter:</u>

January 20, 1936

Northern California Detective Bureau

829 Orange Street

Yuba City, California

Attention: Mr. M. A. Carpenter

Dear Sir:

I acknowledge receipt of your card and want to thank you for your thoughtfulness and interest in this matter. A woman named J. Faulkner once did live in the

Very truly yours,

Ellis H. Parker

Chief of County Detectives

<u>Note:</u> There never was a J. J. Falkner. The name was used to hide the identity of the person using the deposit slips. The address was traced to a New York City address. A woman named J. Faulkner (J = Jane) once did live at the address. She was found now living in Larchmont, New York. The investigation determined that she was not connected to the deposits.

The Conover family mentioned in M. A. Carpenter's note saw a vehicle on Featherbed Lane the night of the Lindbergh kidnapping near their home. Charles Lindbergh planned to build an airstrip behind his residence along Featherbed. The driver turned out his headlights when he noticed a light was turned on inside the Conover home. Henry Conover saw the vehicle when he was sharpening a pencil by a window.

Violet Sharpe's name appears here. She is by far the most suspicious and unexplained character of the Lindbergh case. Did you know that her sister, Emily (Edna), was a dead ringer for her? Is it possible she exchanged places with her frequently? Violet poisoned herself when the police returned to the Lindbergh home to question her. What did she know, and what was she hiding? What could be severe enough for her to take her own life? Was Violet a member of the kidnap gang? Did she help them escape detection and successfully get away that night? Violet lies in an unmarked Englewood grave for the rest of eternity.

FROM THE ELLIS PARKER LOST FILES

December 19, 1935

Hon Harold G. Hoffman, Trenton, N.J.

Your Excellency: -

I have profound regards to the manner and method that the Hauptmann matter is handled, and every person who mentions the matter agrees with you, and this is the old home locality of Col. Lindbergh.

I presume letters are received from all sorts of cranks at these times, however I do not feel that I am such, for I am now and for 27 years last past have been the prosecuting attorney of this county.

A.C. Aderman owns a half section of land some few miles from this village, but he lives at or near Waterloo, Iowa. During the threshing season, Mrs. A.C. Aderman came up to look after the farm interests, and had occasion to call at my office, and while here told me a story that may be worth tracing. Her neighbor at or near Waterloo, Iowa, is a German woman who receives letters from Germany about every month. In many of these letters she would be advised to return to Germany for all they heard of the United States over there was the bank robberies, kidnappings, and gang murders, and among other things stated that one of their neighbors, Isador Fisch, had recently returned from America, and died, but before his death told two boyhood friends that the Lindbergh baby was killed by accident, that the baby cried and was hit to make him keep still, and was hit too hard, and thus killed by accident.

This Mrs. Aderman told me that such a letter was received by this friend of hers, and I can see no reason in the world for her stating such a thing unless it was true, and since you have a doubt, and rightly so, and all other humans have, it might be worth investigating.

After Lindbergh's testimony, in that case, he has fallen from the ranks of heroes in his original home state.

I am enclosing a carbon copy which I trust might be forwarded to the Detective, Mr. Parker.

Yours truly,
R.J. Stromme – County Detective
Elbow Lake, Minnesota

FROM THE ELLIS PARKER LOST FILES

Dec 20, 1935

Carneys Point, N.J.

Mr. Parker,

I am writing to you to express my opinions of the Lindbergh case. First of all, I firmly believe Mr. Hauptmann is innocent of the murder of the baby. I firmly believe that the greater part of the evidence that the State produced was planted evidence. The finding of the baby's body by those two men after the State Police and others had trampled every foot of that ground over thoroughly searching it and did not find it, but Mr. Parker, one thing that I have tried to find out was this, during this entire time something that you know Mr. Parker, that if he body of a human being or animal had lain there that length of time, that the Turkey Buzzards would have been on the job, but as near as I could find out from people who were acquainted in that vicinity they were never seen there, convincing me that it was a plant.

Then the ladder, the State contends throughout the trial the ladder was the main piece of evidence, and then in answer to Mr. Riley's questions, Mr. Wilentz in his summation to the jury he made the statement that the baby was strangled to death in its crib, thereby proving that the State did not or could not prove that the baby was dead. Mr. Parker, I firmly believe the baby is not dead. There are a lot of other things I do not feel sure of. Namely, Dr. Condon's connection with it; I feel sure he knows more than what he has revealed.

Mr. Parker, I hope that in these few simple remarks, I have expressed my honest and sincere opinion and hope that something that I have said may be of help to free, in my opinion, an innocent man. I would appreciate very much to hear from you if you are not busy.

I remain yours truly for a quick solution of this crime.

Stanley Simmerman

367 Ave H, Carneys Point, NJ

<u>Ellis Parker responded to Stanley Simmerman on 12-27-1935:</u>

Dec. 27, 1935

Mr. Stanley Simmerman

367 Ave. H

Carneys Point, N.J.

Dear Friend; -

I received your communication, and I agree with your thoughts. In my judgment, this man is not guilty of the crime od which he has been convicted.

It is a fact that no buzzards hovered over this district, neither were there any maggots around the body when found. The body was found on May 12th, at a time of the year when there should have been.

I appreciate your writing me, and I wish you a happy New Year, and with best wishes, I am, very truly yours,

Ellis H. Parker

Chief o Co. Detectives

<u>Note</u>: Stanley Simmerman's s letter is full of common sense. A large number of the U.S. population felt the same as him. The evidence presented at Hauptmann's trial was fraudulent and planted by individuals that had a lot to lose if he was acquitted. Dr. Condon was a participant in the plot, paid for his participation to ensure that the real criminals remained unidentified.

I live on the outskirts of the New Jersey Pine Barrens. Even in this era (2020), Turkey Buzzards find roadkill almost immediately after an accident. I cannot believe that the Lindbergh baby could have remained intact for that length of time. As for the rest, Stanley Simmerman echoed what many had already suspected, no maggots, then the baby's body was planted there, and it was doubtful that it was the body of Charles Lindbergh's child.

FROM THE ELLIS PARKER LOST FILES

December 21, 1935.

TO WHOM IT MAY CONCERN:

My Dear Sir:

As far as the name Bruno Hauptmann is concerned, I want to say that I have no personal interest in him. – I have never seen him but the feeling for justice dictates the following:

Everybody likes to see that terrible crime cleared up.

But is Hauptmann really the kidnaper of Colonel Lindbergh's Baby? I doubt it. That the jury has said so is no proof. I know of many jury cases where the verdict was positively unjust or wrong.

I am convinced that many of the witnesses committed perjury for publicity reasons! To point out Hauptmann in the courtroom was easy after his picture had appeared in the press so often. Very, very few people do recognize a face, seen once only, after two years. It would be different if Hauptmann's face would show special outstanding characteristics different from an everyday face. There have been 80 or more who claim to be able to identify him. Ridiculous!

Of course, any witness on the prosecutor's side were welcome. That side had the money to spend.

Take the defense side: Short of funds, and when a new witness showed willingness to testify, he was immediately investigated, etc. Until the prospective witness was scared. etc. Or rather stayed away.

This happens to a party by the name Muller at that time. At 3026-29 St. Astoria, L.I., N.Y. They got scared and moved immediately without leaving their address. At that time while the public was aroused, it took courage to testify for Hauptmann.

Take Condon, the Star witness. I think he is a publicity seeker first class. He wanted to appear as being willing to spend a fortune for solving the case. According to press reports, at one time he was so stingy he would not pay for a telephone call to Mr. Lindbergh, so he used somebody else's phone.

Lately he claimed, according to the press, that he was offered up to $250, 000 dollars if he would change his testimony in favor of Hauptmann. WHO IS THE PARTY WHO MADE THAT OFFER? THAT WOULD BE A GREAT LEAD.

The whole case was very badly handled. It was the jealousy and the desire of certain Individuals to gain glory for having the problem solved with the help of the press and publicity seekers that were responsible. They were desperate to have the job had to be pinned on somebody!

One remark. Try to climb out of a window and hold onto a ladder that is a few feet short of the window while still carrying the baby! Some difficulty!

There was inside help? That SUICIDE!

Now I want to give you two rumors, I have been, they are true, or assured they are true. I now give them to you.

No.1: During the time Mrs. Lindbergh was pregnant she was taken along on an air trip by her celebrated husband. After coming back, she was taken to a hospital (some claim for a premature birth). After that she went on another air trip with her husband to Hartford, Connecticut. She was seen by several aviators who positively claimed she was no more pregnant. Shortly after that Lindbergh Jr. was born. Adopted or what?

My question is: What is the truth?

Did the family want to avoid the reproach from the public of being guilty of the premature birth due to the long air trip?

When the baby was found dead, did Mrs. Lindberg go and see it?

If not, why not? As a mother?

No.2: Is it correct that Mrs. Lindbergh had a stepbrother or an adopted brother-who is now in an INSANE ASYLUM in FRANCE?

This brother is said to have made the remark during an unfriendly discussion: I WILL GET EVEN WITH ANN!

How much is the truth of these two rumors?

I have misplaced the address of the party who gave me the information. Otherwise, I would gladly Let you have it.

Hoping this case will be satisfactorily solved, so that the kidnaper gets its punishment he deserves

I am very,

Truly yours,

To Whom It May Concern

Note: An outstanding letter! Great points. The complexity of the Lindbergh case always amazes me. No wonder that after 90 years, the controversy survives.

FROM THE ELLIS PARKER LOST FILES

FRANK J. LORE AND ELLIS H. PARKER EXCHANGE LETTERS, ELLIS EXPLAINS HIS PARTICIPATION IN THE LINDBERGH CASE.

Note: Ellis H. Parker never expressed his feelings and thoughts about his conduct during the Lindbergh case, better than he did in his letter to Frank

J. Lore (Judge of The Municipal Court) on 12-23-1935. Ellis was prompted by Lore's 12-20-1935 letter.

When I reflect on Ellis Parker's 3rd paragraph (italicized and in bold below), it is hard for me to also ignore the injustice and ambition afflicted on Bruno Richard Hauptman by ruthless, self-serving individuals in powerful jobs.

Frank J. Lore's letter:

City Of Bridgeton, New Jersey

Bridgeton on Dec. 20th, 1935

Mr. Ellis H. Parker, Chief of Detectives, Burlington County, NJ

Dear Ellis, When the old bald eagle sits up in his nest and sees another eagle doing business, it makes him feel good. I consider you the Detective genius of the age, I am 68 years old, and I hope before I have to go, I will see you and shake your hand, as probably the main boss will have us looking around to find a good fishing pond, as that is both of our hobbies. I can think a lot in regard to cases that arise. Keep on. An honest man cannot be wrong after a great many years' experience.

Merry Christmas to you and all your family.

Yours Truly,

Frank J. Lore

Ellis H. Parker's response written on 12-23, 1935:

Frank J. Lore, Esq.,

Bridgeton, N. J.

Dear Judge: -

I received your letter, and I was awful glad to hear from you. One day when I was in Bridgeton, last summer, I stopped down at your home, which no doubt, you know about, and they told me you were out fishing. I would dearly love to have seen you. At the time, I was trying to locate a woman in

Bridgeton, which I did, who was the "Moll" of James Cappazzi, who had just been returned from Texas, for sticking up a job in Mercer County. It was through watching this women's mail that we located him. The women's mother lives in Bridgeton, and she lives and puts up in a bawdy house in Trenton.

I was awfully glad to get your letter and to know that some of the old birds, who know the game, still have confidence in me.

In this particular case, I took into consideration every element, and after a full study of all facts, I am thoroughly convinced that there were two separate and distinct things, in this case. One was the kidnapping, and the other was extortion.

I feel morally certain in my mind that the man now convicted was not guilty of kidnapping or murder, and therefore to stand by having the knowledge that I have and allow a man's life to be sacrificed. Perhaps later, this case shows an entirely different aspect, I realize if this should take place, it would do more to break down justice, in the world, than anything that could happen, and that is the reason I have taken the stand which I have: in the name of Justice.

I am not interested in this individual- in any way. Neither am I employed in any way. All the investigation which I have done has been done at my own expense.

I want to thank you for writing to me, and I want to be remembered to your folks, and the first time I am down that way, I will stop in and give you a call.

With best wishes for a Merry Christmas and Happy New Year, I am,

Very truly yours,

Ellis H. Parker, Chief of Co. Detectives

FROM THE ELLIS PARKER LOST FILES

<u>Note</u>: What is this? The fingering of a perfect suspect or someone upset with the service performed at R & M Chevrolet? The letter, grammar, composition, and spelling are copied exactly as written by "An Up-to-Date Dresser." Ellis Parker wrote "Anonymous" on the back of the envelope. Maybe wishful thinking? The writer certainly had great difficulty with the Caps key on his typewriter.

Dec 20, 1935

New York City

Mr. Ellis Parker, Mt. Holly, N.J.,

Dear Sir,

In the records of the early arrest of Bruno Hauptmann was it proven he had a lookout man at St, Raymands, was it brought that he Spent Some three months or so in a hideout place in the Tennessee river if so how did Hauptmann know of such a place without someone connected with the crime sending him there the hide out place being near Nashville this in my mind connects Bruno with Al Hill Formally of that city hill who was employed by R & M Chevrolet Co, Sa Repair Manager, on West Farms Road, Bronx, N, Y, this man fits in the case Serval Ways, Also traveled For Dodge Bros' In Previous years, Hill became very Prospers al of a student about the time the ransom was paid married a beautiful girl bought a new auburn car which did not suit him turned it in for a new Chrysler imperial eighty of which his position did not warrant for 4500 dollars.

When Hauptmann Was first arrested in the Bronx as I remember it was mentioned it was mentioned the lookout man at St. Raymonds was about 5 ft' 4-6, in height slightly drooped shoulders sinuous of the head, walked with a shuffle, this description fits, Hill perfectly, on two occasions when called at The Repair shop Hill Was Down town and I waited for him because he was an expert at his job he returned to look at my car and seemed verry nervous and one of the times it was necessary to take a ride in my car to find the trouble so seeing he was a bit upset I said what's the trouble he said something about the dam changing of money that was the last two days of changing the gold money, Mr., Hill was seen in a Bronx restaurant with a man resembling Hauptmann three days before the arrest at lunch time and seemed verry much concerned the both of them on the day of Hauptmann's Arrest without the slightest inclination this man dropped from sight or sound leaving his wife home position clothing and has not been heard from since This Man Is A very shroud Article And might be of some benefit worth mentioning.

I have thought of this for so long and it remains in my mind that I have to write perhaps every little bit helps in case of this kind, there is a figure in the back ground somewhere, Hill is Irish, Wait 135-40, Black Curly Hair, Age. 38-40, Height, 5-4-6 Clean Shaved. Shallow Face, WALK WITH SHUFFLE'

Signed,

an Up-to-Date Dresser

Note (2): This was the worst letter written in the Lost Files. It is hard to believe any of this, but it is plausible that the writer stumbled upon a connection to Bruno Hauptmann with this Al Hill individual he writes of, but I doubt it. An Al Hill was born in New York City that became a very successful movie actor. He appeared in over 320 films. Maybe he was confused?

Bruno Richard Hauptmann very well could have been disposing of some of the ransom cash. After all, it is certain that Hauptmann played a large part in the extortion plot.

FROM THE ELLIS PARKER LOST FILES

<u>Note</u>: It is a shame that this writer's grammar is so poor. However, it is possible to make sense out of most of the letter.

Postmarked Chicago, December 23, 1935

Ellis Parker

Burlington County, N.J.

Try and find out if Lindbergh made out a check to himself or someone before stealing to give to someone to keep the baby, as I heard from some that flew with Lindbergh that the baby had a club foot due to syphilis and was deaf and dumb.

That Mrs. Lindbergh's brother is in an insane asylum.

Take up some of the dirt where the baby was found and see if it contains some of the embalming fluid and if they found some in the Lindbergh baby and if the body of the baby was the same Lindbergh baby did not have and the length of the baby was not the same, also why did Lindbergh hide the baby 3 times in a closet and shut the door to scare Mrs. Lindbergh has bullied Mrs. Until she dares not say a word and why was the nurse given such protection by Lindbergh also this boyfriend of hers. Why did he take the case out of the hands of the Governor and where is the cast of the foot that was sent to Washington, did it match too closely to Lindbergh's?

Why doesn't his mother appear as a character witness and tell he was thrown out of Wis. U. and nearly out of the Mail service because he was so damn brutal, and why did he start suit to collect clippings from his mother, out of papers. Why didn't Lindbergh hear all that went on, out in the country where it is quiet, and he is sitting near the window. Why didn't the dog bark as he always did, and why was the hair found on the butler's coat where he held it to keep the dog quiet and was the butler's body examined for poison.

Why the special box made for the money and why didn't Condom go to the door alone and not have police there to get the messenger, and if it was by a gang and they knew the baby was dead, why not grab off the 50 grand, and Lindbergh kept 20 G.

I bet the Lindbergh kid is alive and kept by someone.

You never heard of nor saw a man go into the bush – has off the road to take a leak 300 feet, right on the road, and you know it, push them.

I am not saying who is wrong, but these things and a hundred of other fishy things should be pressed hard.

News of more dope would not startle America if a gangster was found or a group of men or some on the case, and who would make such a stir in America? Says the Governor.

And the thumb guard found on the front walk after hundreds had walked there a week before.

Anonymous

Note: The Anonymous writer of this letter has loaded it with many plausible theories reported in the era's newspapers. Many of the requests make sense and should have been investigated by the New Jersey State Police or Ellis Parker after being invited into Governor Harold Hoffman's case. However, once they arrested Hauptmann, the authorities and the prosecution declined to consider any other suspects. They were only concerned with building a tighter case around Hauptmann for a conviction.

FROM THE ELLIS PARKER LOST FILES

December 23, 1935

Law offices of Herr & Fisher, Flemington, N.J.

Phones 180-181

Ryman Herr

Lloyd Fisher

Mr. Ellis H. Parker

Mt. Holly, N.J.

My dear Chief:

I had a representative see the Arnold boy who formerly lived in Hopewell. I finally located him at Trenton, N.J. working for a doctor. He is employed by Dr. Seely, at 942 West State Street, Trenton, N.J. and the office address is 1129 Hamilton Avenue, and the telephone number is 9841. Arnold chauffeurs for this Doctor. He says that he never had any information in reference to the child's body being embalmed, although he was present when the body was removed. He stated to my investigator there was one or two things he would like to speak to me about, but that he really knew nothing of any importance. He also stated that the reporters have been after him a number of times for some sort of a story.

The Princeton baby angle I have as yet been unable to run down. I sent an investigator over there yesterday, and he hasn't as yet reported back to me, although I told him just how important this was. I had him over there two or three other days, but everyone seems very reticent about giving any information. My own thought is that this body was not found by a member of the Whited family, but I do not have this information definite as yet.

In connection with the German family living near Flemington, the name of whom was given to us the other evening by the young lady we saw, which name she gave as Fred and Paula Blasch or Plasch. There is no family living on the Frederich farm by that name. We also checked through Post offices other than Flemington by people of this name but were unable to locate anybody. We did locate half a dozen people of similar name, but in no instance did they know anything about the Hauptmann case.

I also had the Frederich farm angle looked up, and I believe there is something here with accounts for this information we are getting, but I can't see that it is of any value to us. The Frederich farm is located between Frenchtown and Flemington on the main road. Frederich was a former cabinet maker, but he died a year or so ago, and his widow still lives on the farm. She stated that both she and her husband were acquainted with Condon and that Condon visited their home a number of times, always, however, prior to his connection with the Lindbergh case. She says she has not seen Dr. Condon either at her place or in New York since his activity in this case; that she never was called to the Flemington Jail to look at anybody and knows nothing whatever about that story. I am sure these two stories dove-tail and are of no value to us.

In connection with the chisel information which Ellis, Jr. wanted me to get, I beg to advise as follows: Hauptmann had a set of five high-class Stanley chisels, ranging in size from ½ x one-quarter inch to one and a half inches. They were bought new and were very expensive, and they were kept rolled in a cloth or imitation leather roll. He also had three or four cheaper chisels, bought one at a time, and not at all uniform. These had been used considerably. Hauptmann states these old chisels ranged from 1/4''' to 1". He states that the ¼" chisel among his old chisels looks very much like the three-quarter-inch chisel in the Stanley set – that is, the handle and the physical features of it. He states that the three-quarter-inch chisel produced by the state as the one that was found near Hopewell looks very much like the one-quarter inch chisel from his old set, which was at his house at the time the authorities made their search.

He states that this old quarter-inch chisel was purchased from a hardware store on the East side of Second Avenue, and he thinks between 76th and 77th Street.

I will let you know further on the Princeton angle just as soon as I hear.

Sincerely yours,

Lloyd Fisher

Note: We learn here just how thorough an investigator Detective Ellis Parker was. He was interested in looking at anything that could be relevant to the investigation. Every lead was followed. If he did not have the time or resources to do it himself, Ellis reached out to his professional contacts, like Herr & Fisher's Law Offices. The questions raised about the Hauptmann chisel are interesting. Hauptmann states that the chisel produced at his trial was in his house when it was searched.

FROM THE ELLIS PARKER LOST FILES

Oakland, California.

December 24, 1935

Mr. Ellis Parker

Dear Sir: -

I was very glad to get your letter. There was court Proceedings in San Francisco on December 23, 1935, pertaining to the Al Capone angle there. His men beat up that barber who told on John H. not Hauptmann, the real Lindbergh kidnaper, the John of the cemetery, who told the barber on February 3, 1932, that he was going East to snatch the Lindbergh baby to help free Al Capone who was in jail in Chicago at the time.

My detective, who has my angle here also as it fits in with the Al Capone angle in San Francisco, says he told plenty at the trial and who the gang was. It will come up again on January 2, 1936. He will tell of my angle then.

Now I can prove Bruno Hauptmann did not come into the case until later in 1932. He stated in his story in The San Francisco Chronicle he did not meet the Henkel family until the summer of 1932. This was when he went to Hunters Island after his wife had gone to Germany.

Well, Greta Henkel was the woman I had seen here with the disguised Lindbergh baby. She is a blond, German woman, with beautiful eyes, using mascara (mascara was found on the Ransom notes). She had a small mouth, plump figure (Liberty Magazine stated).

My proof it was her was that John Curtis, the Norfolk boat builder said when he testified in court in 1932, a blond German woman by the name of (Gretchen) Greta for short was one of the kidnappers she sat in the back seat of the kidnap car, and a cradle was stretched across one corner for the kidnaped Lindbergh baby.

Now when Lloyd Fisher was out here, he sent for my detective and I and he had me describe Greta Henkel, but he said she had dark hair. (She could easily have dyed it.)

She and that elderly course, straight, haired elderly, brother-in-law of New Jersey, helped her bring the child out here. This Evelyn here has been married three times, and a True Detective Magazine of 1932 stated she was the Estranged wife of Edward B. Mclean, the Washington D.C. Publisher, who entered the case because she had lost a son in an automobile accident.

She has a thirteen-year-old son by another marriage (not by Mclean), and a son was born to her and her third husband, (A Portuguese carpenter), July 13, 1931, but he was killed in an automobile accident, and the Lindbergh child kidnaped to take his place. They have named him Lockwood.

This house where he is now a private home, but before the kidnapping, it was a Private Sanitarium managed by Evelyn's husband's large, violet-eyed mother. She runs it for Al Capone, and John H. was the tall thin, Swedish, Chinese eyed cook. The John the barber told on. Also, the child took me for Betty Gow on March 18, 1933. He called me Beggie. He Lisps and sucks his thumb.

Detectives say he is still there but closely guarded. Never let out of the house. He is sometimes bundled up and taken out for a ride in their dark green Sedan.

How can Lloyd Fisher say I am on the wrong track? I offered to take him to see the child, but he wouldn't come along. One look at the child would have convinced him I was right. The woman, Evelyn, called my detective one day and wanted to know who I was. He wouldn't tell her. She only knows what Greta Henkel told her about me coming to the house to ask if they had seen my landlady's bullpup in the neighborhood.

Also, another proof. In the Call Bulletin from San Francisco in 1932, it stated one meaning of the Symbol was. "A Surviving child has within himself a germ to a new family."

I think this is all. Please let me hear from you, I am,

Mrs. Amy Mayhew

138 Grand Ave., Oakland, California

Note: The fantastic plot described by Mrs. Amy Mayhew is not so farfetched. It was reported many times that Al Capone used the Lindbergh case to barter his way out of prison. The deal was he would deliver the baby for his freedom. After the baby's body was found, he offered up his help to bring in the killer. Is it hard to believe that the Lindbergh child, who many believe was retarded and deformed, ended up in a sanitarium? Isn't that the same thing the Kennedy family did some years later?

The Henkel family was Carl Henkel and Greta Henkel. Along with Henry Uhlig, they were all Bruno Richard Hauptman's acquaintances and lived in the Bronx. All three testified on Hauptmann's behalf at the Flemington "Crime of the Century" trial.

FROM THE ELLIS PARKER LOST FILES

Note: Mrs. Mayfair tells a sensational story in her letter to Ellis Parker.

Oakland California

December 24, 1935

Mr. Ellis Parker

Dear Sir:

I was very glad to get your letter. There were court proceedings in San Francisco on December 23, 1935, about the Al Capone angle. His men beat up that barber, told on John, not Hauptman, the real Lindbergh kidnapper, this was the John of the cemetery who told the barber on February 3, 1932, that he was going East to snatch the Lindbergh baby to help free Al Capone who was in jail in Chicago. My detective, who has my angle here also, as it fits in with the out Capone angle in San Francisco, says he told plenty at the trial and who the gang was. It will come up again on January 2, 1936. He will also tell of my angle then.

Now I can prove Bruno Hauptmann did not come into the case until late 1932. He stated in his story, in the San Francisco Chronicle, he did not meet the Henkel family until the summer of 1932, this was when he went to Hunter's Island and after his wife had gone to Germany.

Well, Greta Henkel was the woman I seen here with the disguised Lindbergh baby. She is a blonde, German woman, with beautiful eyes, using mascara (mascara was found on the ransom notes) she had a small mouth and a plump figure as stated in Liberty Magazine.

My proof it was her, was that John Curtis, the Norfolk, VA. Boatbuilder had said, when he testified in court in 1932, a blonde German woman by the name of Greta (Greta is short for Gretchen) was one of the kidnappers. She sat in the back seat of the kidnap bar, and the cradle was stretched across one corner for the kidnapped Lindbergh baby. Now when Lloyd Fisher was out here, he sent for my detective and me, he described Greta Henkel, but he said she had dark hair, but she could easily have died her hair.

She and that elderly, course, straight-haired, brother-in-law from New Jersey helped her bring the child out here. This Evelyn has been married three times. Detective magazine of 1932 stated she was the estranged wife of Edward B. McClean (Washington DC publisher) who entered the case because she had lost a son in an automobile accident. She has a 13-year-old son by another marriage (not fathered by McClean) and a son fathered by her third husband, a Portuguese carpenter. But he was killed in an automobile accident, and the Lindbergh child was kidnapped to take his place. They have named him Lockwood. This house where he is held now is a private home, but before the kidnapping, it was a private Sanitarian closely guarded by Evelyn's husband's, large, Violet eyed mother. She runs it for Al Capone, and John H. He is a tall, thin, Swedish, Chinese eyed cook that John the barber told on. The child took me for Betty Gow on March 18, 1938; he called me "Beggie." He lisps and sucks his thumb.

Detectives say he is still there, but closely guarded and never let out of the house. He is sometimes bundled up and taken out for a ride in their dark green sedan. How can Lloyd Fisher say I am on the wrong track? I offered to take him to see the child, but he wouldn't come along. One look at the child would've convinced him I was right. The woman, Evelyn, called my detective one day and wanted to know who I was. He wouldn't tell her. She only knows what Greta Henkel told her about me coming to the house to ask if they had seen my landlady's bullpup in the neighborhood.

Another proof was in the California Bulletin (San Francisco, 1932). It stated the meaning of the symbol was, "A surviving child has within himself a germ to a new family." I think this is all. Please let me hear from you.

I am,

Mrs. Amy Mayhew

138 Grand Ave.

Oakland, CA

FROM THE ELLIS PARKER LOST FILES

December 29th, 1935

Post Office, Budd Lake, N. J.

Mr. Ellis Parker, Chief of County Detectives, Burlington County, N.J.

Dear Mr. Parker: -

By tonight's paper, I see that you will probably be called before the Board of Pardons in regard to the Hauptmann case. While it is absolutely none of my business, I have always been curious, relative to the bungling job that was made of the fingerprint evidence at the trial. Perhaps my little knowledge of this type of evidence might give you a lead if Attorney Wilentz jumps you.

It has been the contention of Dr. Hudson, I believe that latent fingerprints can be developed by the silver nitrate methods over periods of time extending from a few hours to months. Dr. Hudson developed fingerprints on the ladder, from the newspaper accounts, hundreds were developed. Why were these fingerprints not checked and produced as evidence in court? What happened to the fingerprints after they were developed? Were they photographed or not? If, as Doctor Hudson claimed through Reilly that there were 500 impressions developed, why did not Wilentz demand their introduction as evidence? Also, in my experience, a latent impression developed by the use of silver nitrate and properly fixed does not disappear or smudge with time. Enclosed, you will some that have been developed by me over a year ago. They are just as good today as the day I developed them. Were they clear impressions developed, or were they just plain smudges? Who saw these impressions developed? I think that this item itself is one of which a great deal could have hinged. If a number of impressions were developed on the ladder and none of the were Hauptmann's, I can't see for the life of me how they could pin it on him. For if Dr. Hudson could develop impressions from a few hours old to several months old, he surely had a chance to find the fingerprints of Hauptmann as well as the others. The idea that he wore gloves in handling the ladder is in my mind bunk, for he certainly had no knowledge that fingerprints could be developed from raw wood by the silver nitrate process, and surely you can give him credit in knowing that they could not develop the fingerprints by the powder method. So therefor he would have no use for gloves.

In regard to your case, I wrote you some time ago for further instructions, but up to date I have not heard from you. If you care to have me do anything further on the case, I will the information I requested in my last letter at least a week before the case came to trial.

With very kindest regards and a Happy New Year, I am, Sincerely, William W. Hill

Note: First, let me tell you that after 85 years, there was an intact sample of the silver nitrate process attached to this letter. The fingerprint is visible and preserved. It exceeds my expectations. How could the fingerprints not be important when the life of Bruno Hauptmann hung in the balance? Why was this evidence hidden from the defense, public, and the media? The only reason could have been that the prosecution feared that it would prove that Hauptmann wasn't there that night, and someone else was, destroying their case against him. 500 impressions? Hard to believe that he was convicted with this much evidence being hidden or altered. As writer Anthony Scaduto called it, Bruno Richard Hauptman was a Scapegoat and maybe a patsy as well.

FROM THE ELLIS PARKER LOST FILES

Jasper, Indiana

December 31, 1935

Dear Mr. Parker:

I have been reading your True Crime Stories in the Evansville Press for the last two weeks. I haven't missed a story. I am keeping them for future reference. I think they are swell and hope they will be continued for some time yet.

I am 22 years old and have been married for 3 months. I live here in Jasper, the county seat of Dubois County. Jasper has a population of about 5 thousand.

I have a steady job as an upholsterer in a local furniture factory. I have always been interested in reading True Detective or crime stories.

I would like to do Detective work. There is no detective within a radius of 5 miles, which is Evansville. Have I a chance? I have answers from different correspondence courses that sell their training for as low as $10.00. What have you got to say about them?

Mr. Parker, would you please suggest to me the best preparation to make in order to become a successful detective?

Thanking you in advance, I am, Yours truly,

Hugo Collignon

Jasper, Ind.

Ellis Parker responded to Hugo on January 22, 1936:

January 22, 1936

Mr. Hugo J. Collignon

Leopold Street, Jasper, Indiana

Dear Friend:

I received your letter, and so far as the correspondence school of learning this business, that's all wet. The only way that you can learn is when anything occurs, try to get the facts as near as you can and then study them, and from the facts, theorize, and when the case is closed, see whether or not it fits your theories. There are no schools that I know of that are any good concerning this class of work. All that is needed is common sense.

If you happen to be where you might be around some officer who has a general idea of this class of work, confer with him on cases, and in that way, you can soon educate yourself.

Very truly yours,

Ellis H. Parker

Chief of Detectives Burlington County

Note: This is an excellent example of the type of man Ellis Parker was. The Hauptmann case and his investigation of Paul Wendel were very demanding of his time when he received this request. Yet, Ellis made the time to respond to this newly married young man with advice and words of experience. Ellis Parker was a remarkable man of character.

I found that Hugo was born in 1913 and lived until March 24, 1969. He was found dead in his home. He had probably been dead for a day. Hugo had been forced to give up his job about six months before his death because of crippling arthritis in his hands. Hugo was still working at the Furniture store he had told Ellis Parker about in his letter of 33 years earlier. He was survived by a son, three daughters, and 11 grandchildren. There was no mention of his wife in the obituary, but I learned he had married Lucille Flora Klier Collignon in 1935.

FROM THE ELLIS PARKER LOST FILES

FOLLOWING SERIES OF 7 LETTERS. Notes can be read on Letter # 3, Letter # 5

LETTER # 1:

SMITHSONIAN INSTITUTION, WASHINGTON D. C.
BUREAU OF AMERICAN ETHNOLOGY

December 31, 1935

Dear Mr. Parker:

I am enclosing herewith a letter which I have just this moment written to Mr. C. Lloyd Fisher concerning the Hauptmann case. Please give this letter and the copy of the letter I sent you December 22nd, your earnest attention, and immediate study.

Very sincerely yours,

John P. Harrington, Ethnologist.

LETTER # 2: This is the letter that was enclosed

December 31, 1935

C. Lloyd Fisher, Esq., Attorney-at-Law, Flemington, N.J.

Dear Mr. Fisher:

A few days ago, I wrote Governor Hoffman concerning the Hauptmann case. I sent you a carbon copy of my letter to the Governor. In this letter, I expressed my conviction that many things point to Fisch as having been involved fundamentally in the case and stated that from the first, I have believed implicitly Hauptmann's statement that he obtained the money from Fisch.

For twenty years, I have been Ethnologist in the Smithsonian Institution, doing work among the Indian tribes for the government, which was closely akin to high-class detective work, making a special study of handwriting, dialectology, speech mixture, and the like. When I was a young man, I spent a couple of years in Germany, most of the time as a student at Leipzig University, in the city from which Hauptman and Fisch came. I have been associated with Germans and German Jews all my life.

I am writing this letter in order to state to you that it is entirely possible to determine whether or not Hauptmann wrote the ransom letters without taking into consideration the handwriting at all. I would be able to ascertain with absolute surety whether he wrote these letters by making a study of the DICTION only. To do this, I would obtain on aluminum discs an adequate amount of his German and of his broken English, working unknown to him on every expression and peculiarity contained in the ransom letters. By making a comparative study of his DICTION, I could prove if he is the author of the ransom letter. Since this authorship is a matter of moot and not settled in the mind of any earnest student of the case, it is a matter of great importance that the authorship be determined by scientific method as suggested above. As an expert in the German and English languages, I could demonstrate with little expense and with scientific accuracy the authorship of these letters. IN A CASE OF BROKEN ENGLISH LIKE THIS, THERE IS A SUPER KEY TO AUTHORSHIP THAN THROUGH HANDWRITING. THAT KEY HAS NOT YET BEEN USED IN THE PRESENT CASE. In my opinion, Hauptmann is not the author of these ransom letters. A thorough study would doubtless furnish proof for this opinion.

Another gaping crevice in the case is the ack of Fisch's fingerprints. How do we know that the kidnap ladder may not be full of Fisch's fingerprints? It would be inexpensive to have Fisch disinterred at Leipzig and his fingerprints taken, and scientific, through study absolutely requires that this be done.

For Fisch's coughing in the cemetery and other points, see the copy of the letter to Governor Hoffman that I filed with you under the date of December 22nd.

I believe it would be a black stain on the history of the United States forever if Hauptmann is executed without having a further scientific investigation of this case. I stand ready to help in any way.

Very sincerely yours,

John P. Harrington, Ethnologist.

LETTER # 3: Ellis Parker's response to John Harrington on 1-6-1935

January 6, 1935

Doctor John F. Harrington

Smithsonian Institution, Bureau of American Ethnology, Washington, DC

My dear Doctor:

I received a copy of the letter that you sent to the Governor, and I am very much interested. I agree with you 100% concerning the handwriting experts, as I know they didn't testify to the facts.

I am no professional myself in that line, but I know that the person who wrote the first note did not write the notes that followed, and I do know that Hauptmann did not write the first note, as he writes the Palmer system, and the first note was of the Spencerian type - a much older person.

At this particular time, there cannot be very much done, only to pray that the board of pardons will commute the sentence of Hauptmann to that of life imprisonment. After that is done, I intend to continue the investigation of this case as I have been doing recently. I am not seeking any publicity, neither am I trying to commercialize on the matter. I am just interested the same as your letter shows me you are.

I appreciate more than words can express receiving a copy of the letter you sent to the Governor, and I agree with you that if Hauptmann is executed and later develops that it was wrong, it would do more to breakdown justice in this world than anything that has ever happened, and that is one thing that I have held uppermost before me and am willing to accept any criticism the critics and cranks or the press might give me, as I know I am right and therefore, I'm going to stick.

Later on, if this man's life is saved, or if it isn't, I will be pleased to get in touch with you and have a talk with you.

With best wishes for the new year, I remain, very truly yours,

Ellis H. Parker
Chief of Detectives

Note: This is another letter written by Ellis Parker to John Harrington just three months before Bruno Hauptmann's execution. Again, Ellis states his opinion of the ransom notes. He is adamant that he does not believe that Hauptmann wrote the first note. Thus, it seems less likely that Hauptmann was at the Lindbergh estate the night of the kidnapping. Ellis also states very clearly that if Hauptmann is executed, he will continue his investigation. David Wilentz, Hauptmann prosecutor, if learning of this, would not feel very secure in his victory.

LETTER # 4: This is the letter written by Harrington to the Leipzig police on 1-8-1935

SMITHSONIAN INSTITUTION, WASHINGTON D. C.
BUREAU OF AMERICAN ETHNOLOGY

January 8, 1935

To: Police Department, Leipzig, Germany:

I (we, or name of the law firm) request the immediate disinterment of the late Isidor Fisch, known in the Lindbergh case, merely for the purpose of taking his fingerprints, in case his condition on disinterment is found to be such that the prints still can be taken. We make this request for the purpose of securing evidence, in order to prevent the execution of a prisoner condemned according to our opinion through false witnesses and circumstantial and loose evidence, and for showing his innocence.

We ask further if his fingerprints are (1) in possession of the Leipzig police, (2) in possession of the German army, (3) in possession of the hospital in which the departed died, (4) in possession of the immigration bureaus in Hamburg or Bremen, or (5) in other possession as a result of having been taken in earlier times or perhaps on the occasion of his emigration to the United States.

We beg of you most kindly and urgently for an early answer, in interest of the execution of an apparently innocent man which has been set for the 14th of this month.

Most respectfully (if sent as a letter or merely Respectfully, if cabled, Name & Address here)

LETTER # 5: Following is Ellis Parker's response to John Harrington on 1-2-1936

January 2, 1936

SMITHSONIAN INSTITUTION, WASHINGTON D. C.
BUREAU OF AMERICAN ETHNOLOGY

Mr. Ellis H. Parker, Chief of Detectives
Office of Prosecutor of the Pleas of Burlington County
County Detectives Office, Mount Holly, N. J.

My dear Mr. Parker:

Your letter of December 31st is this moment received, and I am delighted that you and I see the case through the same eyes. Your letter is a source of great satisfaction to me, and if sentence is commuted, I shall be glad to go ahead, as you intend to, with the scientific investigation of the case, which is anything but settled.

What would you think of you and I immediately, even before the meeting of the Board of Pardons, starting a movement to have Fisch disinterred in Leipzig, Germany, for the purpose of taking his fingerprints, and thereby being able to check these with the fingerprints on the kidnap ladder? I believe that this will be an important move to attract the attention of the Board of Pardons, and to bring home to them the fact that the case is not closed to any open-minded investigator. You will know better than I do whom to write at Leipzig. Would you address the chief of police department pf the city of Leipzig? By getting in touch with German lawyers or with the German consul in New York. The German officials, since Fisch was a Jew, will, if anything, favor this move, and will loyally assist us to have the work done and the fingerprints taken. Could you immediately on receipt of this letter, write a letter to the Leipzig officials, using my name if it will help the matter along, and send a copy of copies of your letter to the Governor and others who may be able to use it immediately. You will know better than I how to arrange the expense of disinterment, and it is possible that the German officials themselves out of sheer interest in the case and desire to clear Hauptmann will bear the expense. Hauptmann is a pure German, while Fisch is a Jew, and the Leipzig officials will be delighted to have a chance to clear a German against a Jew. Please launch a letter at once, and if the matter of expense cannot be immediately settled, write the German officials asking them to bear the expense, and explain why you ask this. The main thing is to get copies of this letter which you write to German officials into the hands of the Governor and others without an hour's delay. I can think of nothing which will help Hauptmann as much as this immediate writing by you to the Chief of Police, Leipzig, Germany. You do not even need to write the letter in German, since they have expert translators at the Police headquarters there.

Very Sincerely Yours,

John P. Harrington, Ethnologist

Note: According to Wikipedia, John Peabody Harrington (1884-1961) was an Author, American Linguist, Ethnologist, and Anthropologist. His massive writings were so extensive that much of his reputed 700 feet of shelved manuscripts remain unpublished. Harrington attended Stanford, University of California, Berkley, and the University of Leipzig. His stay at Leipzig was instrumental in his opinions on the Lindbergh case and Isidor Fisch. He was a knowledgeable man. Harrington was appointed an Ethnologist at the Smithsonian Institute in Washington, D. C., where he held the position for over 40 years, documenting over 50 languages during his life specializing in American native peoples.

Why Harrington was interested in the Lindbergh case and determined to save Hauptmann from the Electric Chair is unknown. Maybe it was just vanity, or his disgust of the way Hauptmann was railroaded to a death sentence. His passion was evident during the letters exchanged with Ellis Parker. Especially in his attempts to push for the disinterment of Isidor Fisch to obtain his fingerprints.

The frequency of the letters between John Harrington, New Jersey Governor Harold Hoffman, and Detective Ellis Parker indicates that they all understood that identifying Fisch's prints on the kidnap ladder would shock the world. It would also ignite a demand for Hauptmann to be saved from the electric chair. I cannot help thinking that the Hauptmann prosecution led by David Wilentz was aware of this threat, and the stakes were high. Wilentz eventually triumphed when Ellis Parker was sentenced to prison, which became a death sentence after Ellis's health deteriorated during his incarceration.

Detective Parker did want to obtain the Fisch fingerprints for comparison to those lifted from the kidnapping ladder. He even consulted experts to gauge whether they felt that Fisch's fingers would be preserved enough to compare after his body was taken out of the ground. Ellis thought that experts doubted that a final match could be made as the prints taken from the ladder were of low quality to start.

The pressure was mounting on Ellis. He had written many times that it was difficult to finance his investigations, and he was shortly to produce Paul Wendel's confession. Then, needing to defend himself from the accusations that he had kidnapped and tortured Wendel for the confession, he simply ran out of time and resources to defend himself. I believe the disinterment of Fisch was placed on the back burner. That was precisely what David Wilentz wanted.

After reading Harrington's letters, I wondered at first if he was anti-Semitic. After reflection, I do not believe he was. He was just brilliantly sarcastic—his German vs. Jew comments were a product of the times. The conflict was beginning to be seen and understood in America as well as in Germany. History later showed us just how horrible and destructive anti-Semitism could become.

LETTER # 6: On January 6, 1936, Ellis Parker responded to the above letter

John P. Harrington

Smithsonian Institution, Bureau of American Ethnology, Washington, D. C.

My Dear Friend: -

I received your letter of January 2nd, wherein you mention having the body of Fisch disinterred for the purpose of taking fingerprints.

I don't think this would do any good, as in my mind, I feel positive that the kidnapping was one proposition, and the extortion was another. Whether Fisch was in on the extortion, or whether he purchased or stole it, I do not know, but I would rather think he purchased it; however, your suggestion is a good one if it could be done. After talking with the undertaker here, who has some considerable experience in taking up bodies and removing them to other cemeteries, the time has passed when it would be possible to obtain any fingerprints from Fisch.

Again, thanking you, I remain, very truly yours,

Ellis H. Parker, Chief of Detectives

LETTER # 7: Ellis Parker's letter to John Harrington on 1-9-1936

SMITHSONIAN INSTITUTION, WASHINGTON D. C.
BUREAU OF AMERICAN ETHNOLOGY

January 9, 1936

Mr. Ellis H. Parker,
Chief of Detectives, Mt. Holly, N.J.

My dear Friend:

Enclosed herewith is a second and better-worded letter to the Leipzig Police Department asking for fingerprints of Fisch through various possible channels, either from records already taken or through disinterment. Just as I am sending this your telegram is received, I hope that you can get one or both of these letters off to Germany through the counsel in the case or direct without the slightest delay since it will be a good point to bring up at the Saturday meeting that this movement is underway. It would be a most startling discovery if it could be shown that Fisch's fingerprints are on the ladder. No matter what develops, it can do no harm to have this fingerprint move underway.

Most sincerely,

John P. Harrington, Ethnologist

FROM THE ELLIS PARKER LOST FILES

Introduction: I found three pages of scribbled notes (on both sides) in The Ellis Parker's Lost Files. I am not a handwriting expert, but it looks to me that the notes are all in the same handwriting. In my opinion, it is Ellis Parker's handwriting. Most of the notes are completely legible. However, the writing is in script, making it difficult to read. These notes are Ellis's observations and thoughts on the case. I can't think of anyone else that could have come to these conclusions, and there are too many instances where they mirror the themes or statements Ellis has made in his letters of the Lost Files. Ellis wrote these notes down to help him contemplate his next steps in the investigation. I believe that these jotted-down notes are the work of a brilliant mind, Detective Ellis H. Parker, at work. "Fische" is the spelling used by Ellis Parker for 'Isidor Fisch."

Date: Unknown

Addressed to: Unknown

"I think Fisch got in company with big bootleggers. Handed hot money to Hauptmann. Now to discover the real culprit, you need to hunt up the leading Bootleggers at that time. Hunt up Fisch's companions at that time."

Note: Could this be the key to the whole Lindbergh case? It certainly makes sense to me. Bootlegging was the number 1 criminal activity during this era, and Fisch was experienced in laundering money. Paul Wendel knew Fisch and Fisch had worked with Hauptmann. The connection is there.

If contemplating a criminal act in this era, you would think of Bootlegging gangs first. These gangs are where criminals went to socialize with other criminals and join to pursue easy profits. Fisch, Hauptmann, and Paul Wendel all had access to contacts within these gangs, and all three of them wanted to make easy money without caring if it was legal.

Ellis Parker was well aware of the bootlegging activity in New Jersey as a Law Enforcement Officer. Much of the illegal liquor was transported on the Rancocas Creek that ran through his hometown of Mt. Holly, New Jersey. The creek eventually flowed into the Delaware River with easy access to New York and Philadelphia. Ellis often led raids on sites within Mt. Holly to seize the illegal spirits and arrest those involved.

I can attest to this because, ironically, at the time, my Great Grandfather owned the Mill Street Hotel that was just across the creek from the Rancocas. He was raided several times by the Mt. Holly Police. I am reasonably sure that Ellis Parker must have led these raids. Once, even my Great Grandfather's home was raided. It was located just a few blocks away from the Hotel. My father, then a 2-year-old, was asleep in the attic.

"Bootleggers" were everywhere in America during Prohibition. The Prohibition act was a joke to most Americans. They never stopped drinking. They just went to the same seller in a different location. Whatever you wanted to call them, Underworld, mob, organized criminals, they were ready to pour you a drink or sell you a bottle of illegal spirits. The act of Prohibition increased the demand for alcohol in America. Everyone wanted to go to the party to see what they were missing. Prohibition was only a problem for law enforcement. The majority of Americans could have cared less. The government wanted the laws enforced, but the citizens looked the other way, making the enforcement difficult. The workload and pressure on men like Detective Ellis Parker were intense. If you looked within those distributing alcohol, you would find men willing to take any job. Jobs much worse than that of transporting and distributing liquor. You might even find Isadore Fisch's companions like Richard Hauptmann and Paul Wendel hanging there.

"A prediction that the kidnapped baby could have died on the night of March 1, 1932, because the stars and moon were not aligned correctly, but it was not a good night for babies. Astrology readings of little Lindy's kidnapping. The birthday of little Lindy, June 22, PM, 1930. A martial open enemy is pictured. Mars controls bootlegging and violence and super activity. Hauptmann is Venus. Venus stands high and in good relation here. The child stands near the top. Was in danger of the bootleggers. Hot flaming killer. Not Fisch."

Note: Isn't it probable the baby died on that night or someday proceeding the arranged kidnapping? I will never top that line, "but it was not a good night for babies."

"Well, now what became of Violet Sharpe's sister who was right there working at the McCabe Apartments in Englewood, New Jersey? No doubt in easy communication with Violet."

Note: It was well known that Violet was very close to her sister. She probably knew much more than she ever told. Violet's part in the Lindbergh case was never defined. She will remain a suspect forever because her reason for suicide is a mystery.

"Lindbergh would not allow his servants to be questioned. They were English and very loyal."

Note: Ellis explains why the servants remained silent. I think it was more like the English, very well paid and terrified of Charles Lindbergh. Charles had much to hide.

"And Lindy wants to have Hauptmann killed."

Note: Why would Charles Lindbergh's main objective be to have Hauptmann killed? Wouldn't a father want the actual killer of his son caught and proven that he was the killer beyond a shadow of a doubt? Was Charles Lindbergh hiding the real motive? During the investigation, his behavior is reason to suspect that he had reasons to draw the investigation away from the truth.

"But the New Jersey Police has to have a victim. And the Attorney General Wilentz must win."

Note: This is self-explanatory. Norman Schwarzkopf was leading the New Jersey State Police. Schwarzkopf was taking orders from his hero, Charles Lindbergh. David Wilentz, Schwarzkopf, and Lindbergh all wanted the same thing. To convict Richard Hauptmann of the Crime of the Century at any cost, with using any evidence discovered or created, for the reward of everlasting fame and fortune.

"I am 30 years an artist. I know that the handwriting here was alike except the very first."

Note: Ellis Parker expressed his opinion of this in many letters. He felt that the first ransom note was written by one man and the rest by someone else.

"You didn't run all your clues down."

Note: This could be a criticism of the investigation team being led by Norman Schwarzkopf and David Wilentz. Ellis had issues with how the investigation was conducted, especially on the night of the crime.

"Hauptmann, according to his horoscope, is super-domestic. Very much affectionate of his wife and baby. Jersey well knows how Mrs. Hauptmann could be protected in case a big, millionaire Bootlegger was brought into the spot. Bootleggers will do anything. Hauptmann may or may not know who did the crime. But, if his wife is in danger, he won't tell. You might make him tell! The Whole USA Government couldn't keep Mrs. Hauptmann or the son alive. If Hauptmann really knows and really tells!"

Note: Ellis plainly explains why Hauptmann went to his death without telling what he knew about the Lindbergh crime.

"Hauptmann was speculating at that time. Fisch, I believe, used this tendency in him and the fact that Hauptmann loved money."

Note: Yes, he did. But as Ellis Parker wrote many times. The kidnapping and the extortion were two separate crimes. Ellis did not believe that Hauptmann was at the Lindbergh mansion the night of the abduction. He did think he was guilty of extortion.

"That it wouldn't have cost much to keep Hauptmann in jail for another year instead of executing him while there were still doubts. The electrocution of Hauptmann-you cut off every clue to the real killer. I don't care who you kill, but this is an extraordinary case, and it would not cost much more to hold that man in jail for another year."

Note: History would have been changed had Hauptmann lived. I do not think he would have ever squealed on anyone. He feared for the life of his son and his wife. He had dangerous enemies that would have retaliated. It is more likely that Ellis Parker and others would have broken the case despite him.

"That the Bootleggers warned Richard Hauptmann that his wife and baby would die if he told the real story."

Note: See what I mean?

"Jersey justice has become a fake."

<u>Note</u>: I believe this is a statement of Ellis's frustration. At first, Ellis only wanted to see the baby returned and reunited with his family. He was passionate about it. Later after it was thought the baby was dead, Ellis believed that Hauptmann was an innocent man, guilty of only extortion. Ellis did not want to see him electrocuted to satisfy a vengeful public and an ambitious prosecution team.

<u>One last thought</u>: This is my favorite discovery from the Lost Files. To have this opportunity to see Detective Ellis Parker at work like this is fantastic!

FROM THE ELLIS PARKER LOST FILES

Date: No Date

Mr. Ellis Parker

Dear Sir,

Dr. Mitchell testified at the Hauptmann trial concerning blood clots on the brain of the child. He said that the soft parts of the face were intact, and the face recognizable. During the Wendel publicity, he said that there was no trace of viscera and no male organ. Putrefaction could not have gone on so unevenly.

In the public library are many accounts of child mutilation in middle Europe. The most famous one is called the Mendel Bayles case because he was accused unjustly of the crime. He had the support of Jews all over the world and was cleared through the Czar attended his trial and believed him guilty. He died in New York a few years ago.

The child, in this case, was taken on the first of March. The body was found in a cave. One leg and arm were missing, as was the viscera and the male organ.

If a leg, arm, and viscera were removed from the Lindbergh baby before it was placed in the woods, that may partly account for the lack of odor, which was not sufficient to attract attention to the body while it was being searched for.

Peasants of middle Europe have strong ideas about the many bathtub murders of women in New York in the Spring. The date always falls within certain limits. Their hands are always tied behind them, and they are of childbearing age, they are never Jews. Two of them occurred on March 15, though then years apart. The crime is always unsolved, or someone is framed for it, and when framing is done, it is worked out to a fine point of nicety, as is being done in the Titterton case. The public does not notice in this case that the bit of string made a belated appearance. The paint on the bedspread suddenly ceased to be.

My best wishes to you, J.D.K.

Note: There is not a way to identify J.D.K. His letter is confusing. I certainly cannot value the information he supplied about the bathtub murders. I also doubt that because they were Jewish is essential. The information provided by J.K.D. is useless and has no bearing on the Lindbergh case. Was J.K.D. trying to impress us? It did not work. He should find another cause. The part about the child mutilation in middle Europe he found in the library. Are you kidding me? I have a library in my town. This is total crap! That the Czar attended the trial of Mendel Bayles? J.D.K. is wasting our time, and he is a complete fake.

The last thing to consider is J.D.K's mention of the Titterton case. Nancy Titterton was raped, strangled, and murdered in her New York City home on April 10, 1936. She was a novelist and wife of Lewis Titterton, an N.B.C. executive. The only clues found were a foot-long piece of cord used to tie her hands and a single horsehair found on her bedspread. That cord was all that was needed to solve the crime, and it was traced to the point of purchase.

There, an employee was found with a questionable criminal record. Case closed. What this case had to do with the Lindbergh kidnapping is beyond me. I don't think J.D.K.'s elevator went to the upper floors.

FROM THE ELLIS PARKER LOST FILES

The following letter, signed by the writer C.R., is reproduced in its entirety. Detective Ellis Parker had written anonymous in pencil at the top of the typewritten letter.

TO WHOM IT MAY CONCERN:

I have been following the developments and treatment of the Hauptmann case, and at the same time, I have been trying to understand or rather unfathomed the deep mysteries enveloping the case. Mr. Walter Winchell, in his very zealous way, mentioned in one of his columns that Mr. Ellis Parker has no new evidence or clues on which to work. I'd like to submit some deductions I have made on the case, possibly they might suggest something to help bring the rightfully guilty parties to judgment and spare an innocent man. I hope you will pardon the liberty I am taking in sending this to you, but I feel you will welcome any well-meaning expressions of interest from a member of the public who can offer a studied account of his opinions. Well, here goes. Please read it through.

LET'S START WITH MOTIVES

Two people have a motive: Dr. Condon and Elizabeth Morrow

Condon's motive is an obsession; hero-worship of Lindbergh, wanting to be near him if only just once, and to bask intimately in the sunlight of the flier's glory. Mr. or rather Dr. Condon is rather well known as being shall we say an eccentric. Miss Morrow's motive is that of revenge. She had an idea of revenge for what she considered a keen hurt. Wasn't

Lindy married by Anne, her sister, when he was supposed to have been her own future husband, or at least her family had thought he would be.

She was interested in children and so as the child was the nearest thing to both Anne and Lindy, and as she would naturally think of children, she decided to kidnap the child and make them suffer through the loss of the thing they loved as she had suffered because of what she thought was a lost love or stolen love.

Dr. Condon was admittedly, always interesting himself in other people's troubles so when he met Elizabeth at the upper N.Y.C. college, he welcomed the opportunity when he was presented with it, to appease two desires—to champion somebody in trouble and to get close to Lindbergh.

KIDNAPPING WAS THE MOTIVE FOR EMOTIONAL REASONS, NOT FINANCIAL.

THE AGENTS

Elizabeth Morrow enlisted the aid of Violet Sharpe and Whately to aid her in getting the child kidnapped, and Codon enlisted the aid of Fisch in order to carry out his part of the scheme. Of course, the accident of death caused a great change in the procedure of the crime from what was first intended.

Condon thought in order to direct authorities away from the real culprits, he would include the ransom element, so he enlisted the services of Fisch.

I believe Condon has been a kind of adviser all along to these ambitious young men (Fisch and Hauptmann) who were speculating in stocks as he was educated and well informed while they hadn't the higher training to make them particularly fitted to follow successfully the financial dealings in wall street affairs.

Condon has often showed signs of having a very high regard for physical development and strength. He even measured himself in court with a court official. He was always attended by an ex-pugilist who used to keep him (Condon) in trim physical condition.

Well, if you notice the pictures of Hauptmann, you will notice that they almost invariably show him off to a physical advantage. I think Condon was acquainted with Hauptmann's physical development prior to the time of the case during the time he was advising Hauptmann and Fisch in their business enterprises. This is a fact, I believe, that Hauptmann doesn't wish to admit because of his wife and family and because all the world is not ready or willing to accept and understand what we might call irregular emotional experiences. He, like many other young men who have wanted to get somewhere in life, consented to allow certain privileges to persons who had these peculiar interests, in return for educational and sometimes financial help. A lot was learned in this direction by the young men who were forced to spend those many years in restricted army service through the World War. It wasn't their fault that the experiences were theirs, it is the fault of the corrupt society that allows such things as war to rob healthy young men of the opportunity to normally live their lives and gratify their normal emotional desires. I believe the Lindbergh and Morrow families and others in who they have confided, know of the implication of the Morrow girl.

OTHER EXTENUATING CIRCUMSTANCES

Fisch went in the affair for the money, and Bruno helped with the receiving the money. Condon, their wise man, having told them that they would be safe.

Immediately after the affair the Morrow girl begun to ail. She eventually married a young man the Morrow family raised to a position of importance in a business in Great Britain. The two of them went there to live.

Anne started to be very daring in her flying habits; daring as if she were tempting fate to help her solve a problem in which she did not want to take the initiative.

When Anne and Lindy went to England, he wouldn't visit Elizabeth and Anne did so only for a short time, I believe I read for 15 minutes.

When too, Mrs. Morrow, the mother, began to break physically. Soon it was reported that Elizabeth was in California and Mexico recuperating from and illness. Nothing had been said in the interim about her mysterious comings and goings. Then she finally died, after suffering a strange and lingering sickness; such a sickness as often accompanies mental disorders. It can be noticed that the Lindbergh's always seemed to try to block direct investigation.

There are other facts that I have neither time nor space to include here, such as particular words uttered by Condon on the stand and other details concerning the family that have been printed but ignored. However, I feel I have included enough facts to offer another clue which Mr. Parker and all the other unbiased and justice-minded citizens can work from.

I am sending copies of this to several key men in the case hoping that one of them at least, will find it worthy of his attention. I plan to send copies to Gov. Hoffman, Ellis Parker and Walter Winchell, the last named because so many people read his column in the Daily Mirror, and he seems to be so definitely willing to accuse Mr. Hauptmann and to write everything he can to throw public opinion against him I hope I have been able to give Mr. Winchell a new vision on the matter.

As my work brings me before the public, and not wishing to gain any unnecessary publicity, I refrain from signing my full name. However, I will sign my initials so that if ever needed, if you will ask for me through the papers, I will be very willing to confer with you and explain anything I have already written or the rest of the things I haven't included because of lack of space and time. I do feel Mr. Hauptmann is going to get the consideration due him.

Sincerely yours,

CR

Note: As we have previously told you, the writers of this book, Russell Lloyd & Andy Sahol, believe that the Lindbergh case was solved when Detective Ellis Parker presented the only signed confession to the baby kidnapping. Paul H. Wendel signed that confession. The letter above brings several theories forward. One, in particular, is shocking. Is this theory plausible? You have to decide. I warn you that what I am about to point out is controversial. Of the hundreds of theories, this is far and away the most outlandish, and there have been some unbelievable ones. The suspicions revealed may have been correct. In this instance, I lean towards the improbable.

It starts in paragraph 5 of the above letter, where the writer tells us that Condon knew Hauptmann and Fisch before Hauptmann was arrested and jailed. He wrote:

Condon thought in order to direct authorities away from the real culprits, he would include the ransom element, so he enlisted the services of Fisch.

Note: This line suggests that Condon sought out Fisch to lead the police on a wild goose chase.

I believe Condon has been a kind of adviser all along to these ambitious young men (Fisch and Hauptmann) who were speculating in stocks as he was educated and well informed while they hadn't the higher training to make them particularly fitted to follow successfully the financial dealings in wall street affairs.

Note: This line suggests that Condon became a mentor to Fisch and Hauptmann.

Condon has often showed signs of having a very high regard for physical development and strength. He even measured himself in court with a court official. He was always attended by an ex-pugilist who used to keep him (Condon) in trim physical condition.

Note: These lines suggest Condon, a teacher, was attracted to a particular type of man. He points out that Condon was always in the company of an ex-fighter. Something that the Newspapers had reported as peculiar. That fighter was Al Reich, a former professional boxer and professional basketball player. Al lost a heavyweight championship bout in 1924 and once knocked Jack Dempsey out of their boxing ring. Unfortunately for Al, Jack Dempsey was able to return to the ring and win the fight. Al Reich was married to Agnes Sweeney, a schoolteacher, at the time of his death in 1963. There have been many questions raised about John Condon and Al Riech's relationship on the internet. However, nothing other than a friendship that started with a mutual interest in sports and boxing are for sure.

John F. Condon was also known as "Jafsie" during the Lindbergh case. He loved children and loved teaching them. He felt that children should be physically fit and able to defend themselves. The school board agreed with him.

Well, if you notice the pictures of Hauptmann, you will notice that they almost invariably show him off to a physical advantage. I think Condon was acquainted with Hauptmann's physical development prior to the time of the case during the time he was advising Hauptmann and Fisch in their business enterprises. This is a fact, I believe, that Hauptmann doesn't wish to admit because of his wife and family and because all the world is not ready or willing to accept and understand what we might call irregular emotional experiences.

Note: The above paragraph is where the writer comes to the point. The writer is suggesting that Hauptmann was in a physical relationship with Condon. Then the writer concludes that Hauptmann did not want to embarrass his wife and family by confessing the relationship to a world not ready to accept it.

He, like many other young men who have wanted to get somewhere in life, consented to allow certain privileges to persons who had these peculiar interests, in return for educational and sometimes financial help. A lot was learned in this direction by the young men who were forced to spend those many years in restricted army service through the World War. It wasn't their fault that the experiences were theirs, it is the fault of the corrupt society that allows such things as war to rob healthy young men of the opportunity to normally live their lives and gratify their normal emotional desires.

Note: in this final paragraph, the writer mentions that Hauptmann was selling "these peculiar interests" for educational and financial help. Then for some reason, the writer goes off to tell us that it was the fault of the war.

Conclusion: I don't value this letter or this information. I wonder about the writer of it. I think he may be the one with emotional problems. I have looked at the same newspaper pictures he probably did. I don't see it.

Final Note: There were problems in the staff and the families of both the Morrow family and the Lindbergh family. Deep, disturbing issues. The baby was removed for either financial gain or to hide something that the culprits did not want the public to know. We believe that Paul Wendel and Isidor Fisch carried the baby from the Lindbergh home on March 1st, 1932, but the people inside knew more than they ever told.

FROM THE ELLIS PARKER LOST FILES

On February 13, 1935, **THE NEW YORK TIMES** reported that the Reverend Vincent G. Burns of Palisades, N. J. interrupted the Bruno Hauptmann trial near to its close. He threw the Flemington, NJ, crowded

Courthouse room into tumult with his outburst in an attempt to announce Hauptmann was not guilty of the murder of Charles A. Lindbergh Jr.

On February 8, 1936, W. J. Reimer, Chief of Police, Allendale, NJ, wrote to Detective Ellis Parker about this incident. In his letter, he told Ellis Parker that he didn't know if the Reverend Burns had been allowed to substantiate his claims. The publication of a lengthy interview given by Reverend Burns in the magazine 'Real Detective' had raised his suspicions. Police Chief Reimer enclosed a copy of the Burn's article in his letter to Detective Parker.

On February 12, 1936, Detective Ellis Parker responded to Chief Reimer:

> "In one of the statements given by Condon to the Government, and also the State Police, on the night the ransom money was paid over Condon said the man was in a stooped position, and he, Condon, said to him, "How do I know you are the right man?" and Condon said, "You can take my body and keep it for hostage for the money," and the person he was talking to said, "No, my father wouldn't let me." This statement made at the time was contrary to testimony given later by Condon at the trial. The description of the man that night was entirely different from the description of the man he met in the park. Whether the Reverend Burns contacted the actual kidnapper, I do not know. I would like to talk personally to Reverend Burns sometimes if I get the opportunity."

The following information was taken from the 'Real Detective' magazine story:

> During his summation at the Crime of The Century trial in Flemington, NJ, Hauptmann Prosecutor David Wilentz stood waving a bible shouting, "Here is our law, an eye for an eye, a tooth for a tooth, a life for a life." He finished his summation calling Bruno Richard Hauptmann "not a man, but an animal." Unable to control himself, Reverend Burns suddenly

leaped to his feet, shouting to the Judge, "your honor, a man, not Hauptmann, confessed this crime to me in my church."

The Reverend Burns was then dragged from the courtroom by NJ State Troopers with their hands over his mouth. Shouts of "You've disgraced yourself!", You will be sentenced to contempt of court!", "You damned publicity seeker, you've almost caused a mistrial" were heard. Prosecutor Wilentz called out, "I think you are a faker."

Reverend Burns was a respected and admired clergyman in charge of a prominent church located just 3 miles from the Morrow home in Englewood, NJ. He was acquainted with the son in law of John F. (Jafsie) Condon and to NJ Governor A. Harry Moore. He presented a sworn affidavit to the 'Real Detective' writers of the article. The Reverend couldn't live with his conscience after he had heard the confession, but he knew that he must keep his promise not to disclose any information about the identity of the man. At first, Reverend Burns hoped to convince his contact to return the baby. Then, after the baby's body was discovered, he became concerned with Hauptmann's guilt and the possibility that the confessor was the man Condon had met in the cemetery.

In the article, Burns describes the things told him that convinced him that the confession was real. The man confessed that the crime he committed was, "A second-story job, not a burglary." Most damning of all was, "It was a kidnapping." Burns added, "He did not ever mention the words "Lindbergh or Baby."

Reverend Burns disclosed that after three years, he recovered a letter had been written to him by the confessor three days after his outcry in Flemington.

Here is a transcript of the letter that was written in pencil:

Dear Rev. Burns,

When I heard the verdict over the radio last night, something in me seemed to snap. My conscience is beginning to bother me so that I can't sleep or eat, and I'm afraid I'm going insane. When you made that outcry in Flemington, I had to force myself not to tell what I know. I'm the man that came to you to confess, and I don't know what to do. I assure you I never got a penny of the money. Two of my friends are dead, and one is safe. When I read the paper about Hauptmann and a dear lady like Mrs. Morrow committing perjury all on account of us, I feel like doing away with it all.

PLEASE DESTROY THIS LETTER

MAY GOD FORGIVE ME

FROM THE ELLIS PARKER LOST FILES

January 2, 1936

Mr. Dennis J. Walsh

45-47 43rd Street, Long Island City, N.Y.

Dear Friend:

I received your letter together with the report of the occurrence that happened at that time. This is a true picture of the procedure and the way the State Police conducted the investigation. It wasn't only you, but myself and hundreds of others who offered information and was really made fun of.

There is a report going around that I want to be head of the State Police, I would not have it if it was handed to me on a silver platter. It is only another one of their stories handed out to justify themselves.

Whether the matter that you spoke of had any significance or whether it didn't, it should have been gone into because it was in the close proximity of the crime.

I know of a fellow who was taken to Captain Lane, who actually saw the kidnapper's car with the ladder in it. It was between 5:30 and 6:00 P.M. on the night of the kidnapping, and he said to the fellow, "did you get the license number?", the fellow said, "No," "Well," he said, "I'll send for you when we want you." "This shows conclusively that they are not fit to conduct any investigation.

I wish that you would write to Governor Harold Hoffman and send him a copy of this same communication that you sent me, but don't let on that I suggested it. I feel that he should have a slant on just what was going on.

Again, thanking you and trusting that someday I will have the opportunity to talk to you in person, I remain, Your Friend,

Ellis H. Parker

Chief of Detectives

Note: Although the communication written by Dennis J. Walsh has not been found, at least we know that Ellis Parker knew a car with a ladder was seen the evening of the kidnapping in the vicinity of the Lindbergh home. Ellis criticizes the State Police for not following up on the lead and their ability to lead a case and again states that he has no interest in running the New Jersey State Police.

FROM THE ELLIS PARKER LOST FILES

Following is a Telegram received by Detective Ellis H. Parker January 1, 1936

WESTERN UNION

PAM83 53/58 NL 5 EXTRA COLLECT = SPRINGFIELD MASS 31 VIA

TRENTON NJ JAN 1

DETECTIVE ELLIS PARKER =

INVESTIGATOR OF HAUPTMANN CASE OY=

DEAR SIR, A MAN NOW HERE LIVING IN LUDLOW MASS COMING FROM TRENTON ABOUT 1932 WHO BROUGHT AN ISOLATED HOME FROM A LAWYER PAYING NINE HUNDRED

DOLLARS FOR SAME IN GOLD CERTIFICATES IF YOU ARE
INTERESTED COULD ARRANGE INTERVIEW REGARDING
THIS MATTER AT YOUR CONVENIENCE
WIRE TRANSFER BY WESTERN UNION=

J P Martin

Ellis Parker responded as follows:

January 2, 1936

J. P. Martin

c/o Western Union

Springfield, Mass

AM INTERESTED. WILL SEND REPRESENTATIVE>
ADVISE TIME AND PLACE BY WIRE AT MY EXPENSE.

Ellis H. Parker

Chief of Detectives

Note: Unsure of the outcome of this investigation or if Ellis did arrange
to send a representative. This wire represents how Ellis was able to run an
investigation in other states. He had relationships with other Detectives, Law
Enforcement Officers, Lawyers, Politicians, and many other contacts in all
walks of life. He was relentless and thorough when on a case.

FROM THE ELLIS PARKER LOST FILES

January 4, 1936

Mr. Ellis H. Parker

Trenton, NJ

c/o Governor Harold G. Hoffman

Mr. Parker,

The baby Charles Lindbergh Jr. belonged to Elizabeth
Morrow, it was her and Lindy's. There is a doctor in Englewood
who was well paid to say nothing. Ann, the sister, took it and

passed it off as her child to save scandal. Like the same as her mother, Mrs. Dwight Morrow, who took the boy named Dwight Morrow Jr., who belonged to another woman but was the son of Dwight Morrow Sr. Look up the birth certificate of Charles Jr. It is a rotten family mess.

And fear, nothing else is making the Morrow's and the Lindbergh's leave their native land. Surely, you can do something to save an innocent man. Jafsie was a friend of Lindy's of long-standing. What man would let a complete stranger handle $5000 to hand over a fence to a strange man? Would you or anyone that is sane? The Sharp girl was to take that child to England but got cold feet when going to be quizzed again by the State Police and was given a dose, so was the Butler. Then when Elizabeth heard of Hauptmann, fear made her take a dose too, not knowing what might come up. One who knows and not a fortune teller.

Anonymous (written by Ellis Parker on the back of the envelope)

Note: It has been alleged that Charles Lindbergh had dated Elizabeth Morrow before his relationship with her younger sister and future wife, Anne Morrow. Many have suspected that Elizabeth was insanely jealous and angry over losing Charles' affection. It has also been alleged that Elizabeth Cutter Morrow killed the family dog before killing Charles Lindbergh Jr. in a jealous rage. Charles Lindbergh then had to stage an elaborate coverup that is now known as "The Trail of the Century" to avoid a scandal that would have destroyed the Lindbergh and the Morrow family's reputation, and possibly Charles Lindbergh's political ambitions.

The writer also suggests that Charles Lindbergh may have mimicked his Father-In-Law's (Dwight Morrow Sr.) solution to a similar problem when he had impregnated his mistress. Morrow Sr. brought the baby into his home and named him Dwight Morrow Jr. to avoid a scandal.

The writer of the letter believes that Doctor John F. Condon (aka Jafsie) was a long-time friend of Charles Lindbergh and that handling of the ransom money over a fence to a complete stranger was staged.

The writer also believed that Violet Sharp was supposed to take the baby to England for hiding, but she got cold feet when she faced continued questioning by the NJ State Police. She swallowed the same poison that the Butler Oliver Whatley did a short time later when it was reported he died suddenly. The same letter also alleged that Elizabeth, the oldest of the Morrow children, died at the age of 30 after taking a dose of the same poison because she was afraid of what might come up at the Hauptmann trial.

FROM THE ELLIS PARKER LOST FILES

January 4, 1936

From: Anonymous

To: Mr. Ellis Parker

Mt. Holly, Burlington County, New Jersey

Marked Personal

Dear Mr. Parker:

I am wondering if certain leaves from my book of memories would be of interest to you – perhaps connecting links with other data. Bootlegging data.

Early in the summer of 1928, my son, a lad of 18 years, went with an auto load of young people to spend a Saturday night in a bungalow on the Mt. Holly branch of the Rancocas Creek. We were close pals, my boy and I, and upon his return, I received a detailed account of that night's adventures. I was quick to see that a mature man, a Jew named "Abe," was the ringleader of this summer colony of young boys and girls, and a menacing influence to good morals. Quite frankly, he was a bootlegger. About this time, my son left this section of the country, but as a mother, I felt a certain duty toward other mothers' nice boys and girls and wondered if I ought to notify the authorities. I really intended to do so, but my own private troubles and worries crowded the matter from my mind.

Then in the summer of 1929, as I left the office one Saturday afternoon, I encountered an auto load of young friends, boys, and girls of 25 or so, who insisted upon my joining them for a weekend up the Rancocas, the Mt. Holly Branch. I went. While canoeing someone requested us to take a message up to "Abe's bungalow," we did. "Abe's bunga-low" stood on the highest point of the left bank of the creek – going upstream. His appearance verified my impression of him, acquired thru conversation with my son. Furthermore, the 24-year-old boy with me apologized for introducing me by my first name. – said he: "I thought you wouldn't want him to know your last name, and I couldn't avoid the introduction."

In 1930 while in Atlantic City, I noticed on a drugstore window, the name "Fred Beck" and old school mate of mine. Impulsively I went in. He was alone, and we were renewing childhood memories when two men came in—evidently old customers, flashy Jews, the fresh type that force themselves upon women. I sipped my soda and avoided their gaze while Fred walked quickly away to avoid an introduction. But to no avail, for they deliberately asked for one, and reluctantly he introduced us. I immediately recognized one as the "Abe" of the Rancocas Creek summer colony. He did not remem-ber me however, as my Atlantic City costume was so different from my canoeing appearance. After they left, I learned that the men were brothers, well know bootleggers, lived at The Breakers Hotel just back of the drugstore, and probably had an interest in that Hotel.

I had forgotten these incidents until tonight. Now I am wondering if they didn't constitute a chain from Atlantic City to Adams Wharf on the Rancocas, the lonely bungalow near Mt. Holly, and is this the same "Abie" who is so notorious in Newark – as I see by the papers. I could find no evidence that he was involved in the Rancocas Creek bootlegging operations.

The lonely bungalow, in March, would have been a swell place to hide the Lindbergh child, then taken it by motorboat down the creek, the bay, to sea.

As I said before, Dan had been a railroad brakeman. Did those three strange ransom symbols, by any chance, resemble railroad light signals?

I am not signing my name as you both know whom this letter is from.

Copy to Lloyd Fisher, Esq.

Note: The Lloyd Fisher that was sent a copy of this letter was C. Lloyd Fisher (1896-1960), one of Bruno Richard Hauptmann's defense attorneys. After the trial, he became a Hunterdon County Prosecutor. He is buried in Flemington, New Jersey. His gravestone reads, "GREAT ACHIEVEMENTS RAISE A MONUMENT WHICH SHALL ENDURE UNTIL THE SUN GROWS COLD."

The "Abie" referenced in this letter could likely have been Abie Bain, the Jewish boxer from Newark. Bain was a Middleweight before moving on to the Light Heavyweight Division. He fought 108 professional fights, winning 66 of them. After retiring from Boxing, Bain relocated to Hollywood to become an actor. He was cast into a few movies and hired as a technical advisor for the movie "Requiem for A Heavyweight." Star Anthony Quinn said that he had modeled his character in the film after Abie Bain.

Bootlegging was a flourishing business on the Rancocas Creek during Prohibition. It was commonly known that liquor and beer could be found at the Mill Street Hotel (Mt. Holly), located just across the street from the creek. Hack's Canoe Rental was close by, which is probably why Anonymous mentioned canoeing. The Hotel and the owner's home were frequently raided by law enforcement.

FROM THE ELLIS PARKER LOST FILES

Almake
Stove Sheet Metal & Tank Works
Manufacturers and Jobbers

14-16 East 8th St., Victor 6933, Kansas City, Missouri

1/9/36

Mr. Ellis Parker.

Mount Holly, New Jersey.

Dear Mr. Parker,

I take the liberty of addressing you at this time as I have seen your name in the print several times and especially the last time I saw your name, and your way of thinking is the same as mine especially in the Hauptman case. I and lots of others think as you do, it was a poor three-ring circus.

What I want to ask you is what you think about – starting a fingerprint school, and giving a course in secret service intelligence along with the F P, there is several of us getting ready to open up a personal instruction school for fingerprint work and was figuring on adding the intelligence with it and was wondering if you might be willing to give us some advice along this line or possibly become an advisor on the advisory board, this, of course, would carry a salary with it but the amount will have to be determined later.

Wishing you would express yourself freely to us just how and the best way to start and conduct a first-class school and your feelings toward a school of this nature, and you can be assured your advice will be highly appreciated.

Thanking you in advance for your time and trouble for an answer to the above, and I want to beg to remain.

Yours Very Truly,

Per B. J. Hicks

Proprietor of Above

Ellis Parker responded to B. J. Hicks on 1-13-1936:

January 13, 1936

B.J. Hicks

814-16 East 8th St., Kansas City, Mo.

Dear Friend,

I received your letter, and I think it would be a fine thing, in fact, I think if you would try in every school in your State, to get them fingerprinted, or to adopt it, other states would follow; it would be a wonderful thing. In later life, if a person's mind goes blank or a child may drift away, or he was left some estate, it would be no trouble to identify them.

Another thing, it would have a tendency to keep people on the right path.

My time is so taken that I could not be an Advisor, but I wish you success in your venture.

I remain,

Your friend,

Ellis H. Parker

Chief of County Detectives

Note: Ellis Parker was first and foremost a Detective but always interested in advancing and applying modern scientific procedures to Law Enforcement. His brilliant mind and use of scientific deductions resulted in many successful arrests and prosecutions. If this request hadn't come during his final days of the Hauptmann investigation, I would like to think he would have participated in the child fingerprinting program. Hauptmann was executed a little under three months after Hick's letter was written. Ellis always cared about children, his, and others.

FROM THE ELLIS PARKER LOST FILES

January 9, 1936

Mr. Ellis Parker,

Dear Sir,

If you are really trying to help clear Mr. Hauptmann, why not look at the coat the police found on the grave of the dead baby, that coat if properly studied will tell you who was the man who really did the crime.

If you try the coat on Bruno, I am sure you will find that it does not fit him, and the gloves can aid too, if you notice when looking at the gloves can aid too. If you notice when looking at the gloves, the left-hand shows more wear than the right hand, meaning the owner of the gloves is left-handed, now put the coat & gloves together, and you could guess the size of the man and if still curious show them to a tailor and have him measure them for the size suit the man wears, and the height can be obtained by an old medical trick, place the garment across a large table measure across from shoulder to shoulder then measure the arm stretched out as the coat has only one arm you can multiply the inches got on the one arm twice and then add the inches of shoulder to the arm, then measure the gloves. You then have the height of the owner of the coat. You think he's left-handed, he sent a post-card from Newark to the Lindbergh's after the crime, it would be a good place to look as people in trouble don't visit strange places.

Yours Truly.

<u>Note</u>: Ellis Parker did not make any comments on this letter. His mail was overwhelming during the years of the Lindbergh-Hauptman investigations. I do think that the unsigned letter writer had some plausible ideas that would have been interesting if acted investigated. As usual, the people that wrote Ellis were well-spoken.

FROM THE ELLIS PARKER LOST FILES

Mrs. Ellis Parker

Mt. Holly, New Jersey

Dear Sir,

If you went up to Beacon, N.Y. and saw Holkum you will find Mr. Morrow (brother-in-law of Charles Lindbergh) was just there 3 months after the Charles Lindbergh Jr. was stolen and he Morrow told in Beacon, he took the baby from the house, in one of the garages in Beacon he told this, his father's will say he got nothing but C. Lindbergh did making him mad.

Look into Condon fast maybe he was the one who sold the ransom money at $40 per $1000. Get Condon to go to Trenton to face Hauptmann. There is something between them.

If you want to do anything, you can now. I wrote to two of Hauptmann's lawyers last Feb. 1935, but as yet, they did nothing for him.

Signed, A Stranger to All

<u>Note</u>: This poorly handwritten letter, resulting in some uncertainty, was addressed to Mrs. Ellis Parker in Burlington, NJ. Someone has corrected the address to Mt. Holly. It was postmarked on Jan 9, 1936, in Philadelphia, PA. I know that Ellis Parker knew his mail was being scrutinized and that the Hauptmann prosecution tapped his phones. It would be logical to think that addressing this letter to Mrs. Parker was a ruse to avoid being intercepted.

The writer has speculated that Charles Lindbergh's brother-in-law was upset that he had been left nothing in his father's (Dwight Morrow) will. It was reported that Charles Lindbergh had been remembered sustainably by his father-in-law. In this letter, it is suspected that Morrow's son (Dwight Morrow Jr.) took the Lindbergh baby from the Lindbergh home in retaliation. Could it have been for revenge, or could it have been to get the funds he felt were due him?

These are interesting theories but hard to verify. I was unable to find any breakdown of the beneficiaries of Dwight Morrow's estate. The family patriot died in 1931 at the age of 58. In today's value, the estate would total approximately 10 million dollars. The brother-in-law mentioned was indeed Dwight Morrow Jr., his only son. In a letter also found in Ellis Parker's files (dated 1-4-1936), the writer suspected that Dwight Morrow Jr. was an illegitimate child born out of wedlock. His father gave him his name to keep it private as he was a highly respected figure in politics and finance. Rumors circulated that Charles Lindbergh may have done the same thing by fathering a child with his sister-in-law Elizabeth, whom he had dated before marrying his wife, Ann. Lindbergh named his baby Charles Lindbergh Jr.! Deja Vue?

FROM THE ELLIS PARKER LOST FILES

Date: 1-10-1936

Postmarked: Punta Gorda, FL

Writer: D. P. Deegan Jr., Headmaster

The writer of this letter is very suspicious of Dr. Condon. But even more suspicious of Dr. Condoms, bodyguard, Al Roth, who could be the "John" in the cemetery. The writer doesn't trust the character of Charles Lindbergh's wife Anne, complaining that she was too reserved when confronted with the awful crime of her missing son. The whereabouts of Al Roth is questioned, where has he been since the ransom was paid?

<u>Ellis Parker responded on 1-20-1936:</u>

Dear Sir:

I received your letter, and I was to thank you for your kind words and assure you that I am interested in this case only for justice, although I have been criticized and called a publicity seeker and everything under the sun, but anybody with good sense knows there is something wrong with this case.

FROM THE ELLIS PARKER LOST FILES

BEN BOTKISS ---- LEONARD TRIMPOL
1424 WIDNER BUILDING
PHILADELPHIA, PA.

JANUARY 10, 1936

Dear Mr. Parker:

If you would consider doing some commercial radio broadcasting in the near future and having the writer act as your exclusive agent in arranging such engagements, I should be very glad to discuss the matter further with you, any time you suggest.

Sincerely yours,

Ben Botkiss

<u>Ellis Parker responded to Ben Botkiss on 1-13-1936:</u>

Jan. 13, 1936

Ben Botkiss

1424 Widener Building, Phila. Pa.

Dear Friend; -

I am not interested in Broad Casting. I thank you for the invitation.

Very truly yours,

Ellis H. Parker

Chief of County Detectives

Ben Botkiss did not give up easily. This is his response of 1-10-1936:

BEN BOTKISS ---- LEONARD TRIMPOL
1424 WIDNER BUILDING, PHILADELPHIA, PA.

January 14, 1936

Mr. Ellis H. Parker,

County Detectives Office, Mt. Holly, N, J.

Dear Mr. Parker:

I have your letter of January 13th. I can readily understand that you do not care to make any public utterance on any angle of the case that is now occupying so much front-page space, and for that reason, you declined radio work. That is a commendable, ethical viewpoint.

By way of explanation what I did have in mind was this: acting as your agent for radio work that would have you recounting some of your previous and old experiences, something along the line you wrote in collaboration with Mr. Fletcher Pratt. Such radio work would not necessarily have to be "personal"; it could be in the nature of radio recordings or transcriptions, made at your leisure.

I hope this explains my purpose satisfactorily, and that you will reconsider the matter.

Naturally, I shall be glad to see you wherever and whenever you suggest, to discuss the matter further.

Sincerely yours,

Ben Botkiss

P.S. – I shall appreciate it very much if you will advise me who controls the radio and motion-picture rights to the stories you wrote in collaboration with Mr. Pratt.

<u>Ellis Parker responded to Ben Botkiss on 12-22-1936:</u>

Mr. Ben Botkiss

1424 Widener Building

Philadelphia, Pa.

Dear Friend:

Your letter received. Cannot in any way interest myself in moving picture or radio work, at this time it would be suicidal. I only interest myself in this case for justice. I have had plenty of opportunities to raise enormous sums of money both from radio and motion pictures, and through other sources. One person offered to heat the mike and collect me one hundred thousand dollars a week, and I could receive the collection. Another offered me eighty-four thousand dollars' worth of good stock that I could take fifty percent of.

I am not interested in finances in this matter neither am I in it for politics or publicity as I said before, only am I interested in this for justice. It wouldn't matter if you were my worst enemy, and I knew you were convicted wrongfully. I would go to your rescue.

Trusting you will see my position in this matter, I remain,

Very truly yours,

Ellis H. Parker

Chief of Detectives

<u>Ben Botkiss ended the exchange of letters on 1-24-1936:</u>

BEN BOTKISS ---- LEONARD TRIMPOL

1424 WIDNER BUILDING

PHILADELPHIA, PA.

January 24, 1936

Mr. Ellis H. Parker,

County Detectives Office,

Mt. Holly, N, J.

Dear Mr. Parker:

I have read with considerable interest your letter dated January 22nd.

All I can say is that your attitude is highly commendable and that if we had more men like yourself in public office – well, it would be a grander United States.

My sincerest thanks for the consideration you gave my suggestion, and my earnest hope that you will bear me in mind for future reference as a possible representative when you see your way clear to doing some radio and motion picture work. I hope that time won't be too long or distant.

Sincerely yours,

Ben Botkiss

Note: Agent Ben Botkiss knew that Ellis Parker's fame had risen to a high level and that it could be very profitable. He was aware that the book "The Cunning Mulatto" was very successful and had been serialized in newspapers across the country along with daily updates covering Ellis's work on the Lindbergh case.

Ellis's reply confirms what his family, Grandson Andy Sahol, in particular, has said for many years. Ellis Parker was not an ambitious man. He did not want to be wealthy, the head of the FBI, or harbored grand political ambitions. His heart, kindness, and character were solid and pure. Ellis Parker just wanted to be the best law-enforcement officer he could be, work for justice and then come home to his family in Mount Holly every night. That is precisely who Ellis Parker was.

FROM THE ELLIS PARKER LOST FILES

Date: 1-14-1936

Postmarked: strangely, no postmark on the envelope. Marked "Quick delivery" in the writer's script.

The letter was addressed to Gov. Hoffman in Trenton, New Jersey. The letter is anonymous. Anonymous is written on the envelope in what seems to be Ellis Parker's handwriting. The grammar is poor.

The writer claims to have seen a motor vehicle on the road ahead with a man in the road. The man plopped down his car and asked for a pump that he needed to repair a flat tire. He gave the man upon, and while he was helping to fix the flat, he looked in the car. A woman sat in the front seat, and he noticed a man in the back seat who was wearing a big hat. He had a blanket covering him on his neck down over a very large stomach. It looked as if he was holding something under the blanket. After the tire was fixed, the man thanked him and went on his way. We drove all night and came to a town and an eating place. The customers were talking about the Lindbergh baby kidnapping. He now suspected that the passengers in the car were Violet Sharp and maybe Isidor Fisch, along with someone else.

FROM THE ELLIS PARKER LOST FILES

ELLIS PARKER'S LETTER TO HENRY G. KRESS ON 2-1-1936 RE MEETING WITH UNIDENTIFIED MEMBER

On 2-1-1936, Ellis Parker wrote to Henry G. Kress concerning the newspaper stories reporting that the Governor had ordered the State Police Superintendent to conduct further investigations into the Hauptmann case. Ellis theorized that the Governor wanted to know why no effort was made to ascertain who was present during a meeting that included Condon, Charles Lindbergh, and others.

Note: This shows that Ellis Parker was concerned that the ongoing Lindbergh-Hauptmann investigation was controlled to deny others from gaining knowledge of their progress. You have to wonder what they were hiding and why they were suspicious of others joining the investigation.

FROM THE ELLIS PARKER LOST FILES

Date: 4-18-1936

From: Marceline-MO

Written by: Cy Fischer

Mr. Fischer wrote to Governor Hoffman to tell that Paul H. Wendel was seen in the states of Iowa, Minnesota, Kansas, and Marceline, Missouri, about 4 or 5 months after the Lindbergh baby kidnapping. He also wanted to know if Paul H. Wendel was seen on or about March 1, 1932, driving with a man in a Hudson 8 Sedan or a red 1932 Chevy Sedan or in the company of a strange woman that was driving a Model A Ford Coach. Fischer speculated that Paul Wendel was the guide that drove the kidnapper to the Lindbergh home on the night of the kidnapping. He also thinks that the baby was killed by a door handle in the car Wendel was driving.

FROM THE ELLIS PARKER LOST FILES

Date: 4-6-1936

From: Philadelphia-PA

Written by: Mrs. Bertha Trusdell

Mrs. Truesdell claims to have seen Bruno Richard Hauptmann buying some ransom money from a Mr. Salus (actually Paul Wendel) and Mr. J. T. Broslowski (actually Paul Wendel Jr.) in Pleasant Hill on July 21, 1932. Hauptmann purchase $1200 worth of ransom bills for $800 cash. They planned to meet in the Magnolia Cemetery. Paul Jr. said that it was an inside job. Elsie carried baby Charles down the stairs, and the butler carried the ladder.

FROM THE ELLIS PARKER LOST FILES

Macon City Iowa

December 25, 1936

WE HAVE THE LINDBERGH BABY ALIVE. WE HAVE BEEN HIDING IN THE OZARK MOUNTAINS WITH HIM. ISADOR FISCH AND US GOT THE KID. MY WIFE WANTS TO KEEP HIM. SOMETIMES SHE WANTS TO SEND HIM TO LINDBERGH. I AM AFRAID SHE WILL SQUEEL. I TOLD HER IF SHE DID SQUEEL THEY WOULD CATCH HER AND HANG HER. SO, WE CAN NOT SEND LINDBERGH BABY UNTIL HE IS 20.

WE PUT THE CLOTHES OF THE LINDBERGH BABY ON OUR DEAD BABY WHICH DIED AND BUT HIM IN THE BUSHES. AND PUT OUR BABYS CLOTHES ON THE LINDBERGH BABY. NOW THE LINDBERGH'S WOULD NOT KNOW HIM.

ISODOR FISH GOT THE MONEY SOME WAY. HE GAVE US SOME OF IT AND PROMISED US MORE. WE NEVER GOT IT.

WE NEVER SAW HAUPTMANN AND HE NEVER SEEN US SO MR. FISSH MUST HAVE LEFT THE MONEY WITHIN HAUPTMANN'S HOUSE SO HAUPTMANN GOT THE MONEY FISH PROMISED US.

WE ARE ON OUR WAY TO CANADA. WE WILL LEAVE THIS LETTER IN OUR ROOM READY TO MAIL AND WJHEN THE BOSS COMES HOME IN JAN AFTER VACATION WE THINK THEY WILL MAIL IT BY THE TIME WE WILL BE FAR AWAY.

Note: The envelope this letter was mailed in was addressed to Mrs. Anna Hauptmann, Trenton, NJ. It was postmarked January 10, 1936, from Saint Paul, Minnesota, 55 days before her husband's electrocution. Someone, probably in the post office, crossed out the Trenton address and hand wrote 2501 Lorillard Pl, Bronx, NYC. Hauptmann's home was actually at 1279 East 222 Street, approximately 4 miles away). Who gave it to Detective Parker is unknown, but we know that Anna Hauptmann kept in contact with Ellis after her husband's arrest. The letter was typed in all caps except for the address and the date in the heading. The grammar and spelling are poor.

Knowing Detective Parker as we do, makes us confident that he investigated this claim as well as he could. The world still wondered if the Lindbergh baby could be alive. Sightings of the child were widely reported. The writer's attempt to implicate Isidor Fisch is interesting because Detective Parker believed he was a part of the plot to kidnap the baby along with Paul Wendel. Could the Lindbergh baby have made it to Canada safely? There are hundreds of websites where you can debate that.

FROM THE ELLIS PARKER LOST FILES

January 13, 1936

39 Highland Terrace, Brockton, Massachusetts

OPEN LETTER TO

Defense Counsel,

c/o C. Lloyd Fisher,

Flemington, N.J.

SUBJECT: Hauptmann Case.

Gentlemen:

Do you choose to avail yourselves of the following further, i.e., new evidence in the Hauptmann case?

Irrefutably tending to show that the ladder put in evidence at Flemington was a forgery. A manufactured object. A

Falsified monument of the evidence. But now reposing vicariously as an "accredited" monument of the evidence in the record of the trial.

Proving conclusively that by unveiling but this single monument of the evidence in the case that your client must be acquitted of the charge laid against him. And by no more elaborate procedure than a motion for a new trial upon the grounds of fraud and a directed verdict of not guilty in the circumstances; and a solid, prima facie case for the motion.

Details, of course, are only for counsel – if desired. But as for the actual importance, existence, and availability of such new evidence, the public is entitled to know of it at the same time that you are.

Unlike some, I am under no maudlin restraint not to go the full distance in believing Hauptmann innocent of any participation in the crime at all.

The single purpose has been to give you and Jake Public ample notice of the new issue. If it gets no farther, I am "square with my conscience" and leave others to look after their own.

Very truly yours,

Hugh Orr

Copy to: Mr. Ellis H. Parker

Mark: f8 + m

Telephone: 4905

Note: "The ladder put in evidence at Flemington was a forgery." When evidence is tainted or proven as being manipulated, it should result in a mistrial or a not guilty verdict, certainly not a judgment of execution. This is not the first time we have learned of multiple ladders. We have no proof of their existence, who made them, why they were made, or any record of their movement. There was even one seen in Detective Ellis Parker's office in Mount Holly, according to his Grandson Andy Sahol. I have often read that the ladder is what convicted Bruno Richard Hauptmann of the crime because it was proved that he constructed it. That seems like very flimsy evidence now that I have read this letter. There have been countless pages written about the ladder. It almost has a personality of its own. Toy replicas were sold outside the Flemington courthouse while the Hauptman trial was in session. Entire books have been published about it and the supposed wood that matches it in the Hauptmann attic. Which ladder was that?

FROM THE ELLIS PARKER LOST FILES

Jan 13, 1936

Dear Ellis,

Something I don't think anyone investigated and is that note of J.J. Faulkner that was deposited in the Federal Reserve bank with the handwriting of Dr. John F. Condon and how much money he put into the bank in the last 5 years. Ellis, you better look at the ransom notes and his handwriting. You know he seen the one that was left at the house when the baby was stolen.

Yours truly,

John W. Higham

5202 Tulip St., Phila., Pa.

PS. Ellis, I am a Philadelphia Patrolman # 1505

Ellis Parker responded on 1-10-1936:

Jan 10, 1936

Mr. John E. Higham (Patrolman # 1505)

5202 Tulip St., Phila. Pa.

Dear Friend: -

Your letter received. I appreciate your writing to me. The man convicted of this crime is positively innocent of any connection whatever, in my judgment, and is a victim of circumstances. When they have such witnesses to put a man's life away as Dr. Condon, Hocksmith, and Whitehead, who are all crazy, it is just too bad.

If this poor fellow has to pay with his life, it will be a smudge on the star representing the State of New Jersey in the American Flag.

I have no interest personally in the man. The only interest I entertain is one of Justice.

This poor Devil never had a china man's chance at the trial. Again, thanking you for writing to me, I remain,

Very truly yours,

Ellis H. Parker

Chief of County Detectives

Note: On May 2, 1933, the Federal Reserve Bank of New York found 296 ten-dollar gold certificates and one twenty-dollar gold certificate totaling 2980 dollars. They were all ransom certificates. The deposit slips showed J. J. Falkner of 537 West 149th Street had deposited the money. A woman named J. Falkner once had lived at the address. After an investigation, it turned out the J.J. Falkner was Jane Falkner. She was located and then cleared after giving handwriting samples. It has never been determined who made the deposit and what connection they may have had with Jane Falkner.

FROM THE ELLIS PARKER LOST FILES

January 14, 1936

New York

Dear Sir:

It was with interest that I read in the newspapers that you expressed the wish that you could overhear the conversation between Condon and a questioner, for I believe many citizens believe that the man was mainly instrumental in having Hauptmann convicted of kidnapping and murder of the Lindbergh child is not reliable. The New York Post, after stating in its news columns that it was not surprising that the articles which Condon has written for Liberty Magazine should contain several statements at variance with testimony at the Hauptmann trial, goes on to explain:

"Newspapermen working on the Lindbergh case have been wholly familiar, since he first appeared in the case April 1932, of the erratic nature of the aged Bronx schoolteacher. Sometimes with the deliberate intent of throwing reporters and the public off the track, sometimes because of slips in memory, he made dozens and dozens of conflicting statements."

There was no name or signature on this note.

Note: How could the public believe the information they were being fed? Or that Condon was anything other than an opportunist or a member of the kidnap gang? Could a more questionable character have been found? Condon was an actor very likely chosen by the kidnap gang because he was able to run a con on everyone. No doubt, he was selected because of his loyalty. It was an opportunity for fame and fortune for him. How much do you think Liberty Magazine paid him? Why did the media believe him? Was it just because he gave them a good copy? Remember, it was Charles Lindbergh that choose him as the mediator.

FROM THE ELLIS PARKER LOST FILES

Mr. E. Parker, Mt. Holly N.J.

Dear Sir,

I am just wondering if it wouldn't help Hauptman to investigate the rumor going around that young Morrow had something to do in the case. The guards in Mattawan where he was at the time of kidnapping say that he was absent from the place when Lindbergh's son was taken, they say why don't they get a hold of him, but after the kid was gone, the Morrows brought him over to England where the whole click went. Lindbergh sure didn't feel safe anymore, not in fear of another kidnapping but the outcome of your investigation. It got too hot for him. Also, Jafsie's disappearance showed that they had to fear something coming, and they just didn't know how much is known. And Hauptman, the poor sucker, has to pay for someone who really did it. Is that fair? I hope the Governor gives Hauptmann a reprieve, and as long there is life, there is hope. It would be a terrible crime of the State, to kill that man, who was made the goat just to please Wilentz and all the others who know and don't talk.

During the trial, the evening Journal showed large headlines saying Inspector Walsh of Jersey City will aid Bruno. He promised to tell how Lindbergh interfered in all their investigation. It was a long article. I was glad when I read that, but what he told on the witness stand was altogether different. Schwarzkopf knows all of it too, why aren't they man enough, to be honest, and fair? And they talk about crime prevention when the heads of them are so crooked. Thought there would be some new light through Henry Uhlig, who was a close friend of Fisch, he paid his fair fare to Germany, but the State got a good hold of him, and the chances for Hauptman was gone again, I am sure he knows more than he told at the trial. First, he had no money to go to Flemington, and after Wilentz got a hand in it, he had plenty, and for what? Can't you question him? IT MIGHT HELP A LITTLE.

Signed, One for the truth and fairness. Postmarked on 1-15-1936, Brooklyn, N.Y.2

<u>Note</u>: Dwight Whitney Morrow Jr. (1908-1976) was considered a suspect in the Lindbergh case by many after his brother, Charles Lindbergh Jr, went

missing. Dwight was married twice and fathered one son, Stephen Dwight Morrow. There were speculation and rumors that Dwight Jr. was an illegitimate child of his father with a woman that was not his wife and that he was angry at his father for not leaving him a proper inheritance after his death. It was reported that Dwight Jr. was upset that Charles Lindbergh was left a significant portion of his father's, Dwight Whitney Morrow (1873-1931) estate. Some years later, Elizabeth Cutter Morrow, his mother, acknowledge the difficulties of managing his care as he supposedly struggled with mental illness. This knowledge is countered because Dwight Jr. graduated from Amherst College and received a P.H.D. from Harvard. Hardly the record of a man with mental illness. The writer makes some good points in this letter. His allegation that Charles Lindbergh interfered with the investigations has been suspected by many.

FROM THE ELLIS PARKER LOST FILES

ANONYMOUS LETTER OF 1-18-1936 KEPT BY ELLIS PARKER IN HIS PERSONAL FILES

Ellis Parker received an interesting letter, postmarked 1-18-1936. Ellis wrote "anonymous" on the back of the envelope. It is well written by someone with superior knowledge of the Lindbergh-Hauptmann case. The contents are indicative of the public's fascination with the case at the time and with their confidence in Ellis Parker. Ordinary people studied the case relentlessly. The letter, found in Ellis Parker's personal files follows:

"Pardon the privilege I am taking in addressing these lines to you. I am told you will not pay any attention to this letter, be that as it may. I am writing it anyway, hoping it will be of some help, and because I believe as you do. When a life is at stake, we should go to the authorities with any bit of information we obtain. So here it is. I sat behind 2 ladies on a streetcar a few days ago. They were discussing the Lindbergh baby kidnapping case. One said, do you think Jafsie really had anything to do with the kidnapping of the Lindbergh baby? The other replied, well, I don't know. He seems to know a lot about it. He changed his story again, just before sailing. He says now that the baby was killed in his crib, that takes the suspicion from the nursemaid (Betty Gow) and places it squarely on Whately. He was the man that took the baby from its crib and carried it out to an automobile where Isidor Fisch and Violet Sharpe were waiting. Violet had a shawl on her arm she had brought to wrap around the baby. Who was Isidor Fisch? The woman that was doing most of the talking said: he was the man with the cough, the man that Jafsie handed the money to over the shrubbery in the cemetery. Remember: Poor Fisch was left holding the bag when things went haywire. He was to have left only a few thousand dollars with his friend Hauptmann, that was so he wouldn't get wise. Hauptmann was not to be let in on it. There was a long pause. One that seemed to be inquiring of the other asked: What about the ladder? They convicted this man Hauptmann on the ladder testimony. The other said: That ladder was just planted on the side of the house. For the same reason, the note was pinned on the windowsill. To throw them off. The other said: There was a bard nailed on the ladder from the upper part of the house where the Hauptmann's lived. She replied: Oh! That was ripped off the floor when they were searching through Hauptmann's house, and it was nailed to the ladder. The other said: Oh, how could they do that? Money will do anything, the other replied. That's all. They left the car. Please tell Governor Hoffman that the people of California are unanimous in their expression of praise and admiration for him, because of the firm stand he has taken in the cause of justice. That includes Detective Ellis H. Parker of Mt. Holly, NJ. God be with you.

PS: Pardon my writing with a pencil, and this stationery is all they have on hand out here in the country where I am visiting.

FROM THE ELLIS PARKER LOST FILES

Note: This first letter from Fred Shanbacker was not dated. Fred did some great investigation work for Ellis Parker over many years. From time to time, Ellis would hire Fred Shanbacker to investigate for him. There is a history of him providing information to Detective Parker on the Lindbergh case.

Date – Unknown

Hotel Bristol

129 West 48th Street New York City, N.Y.

Phone: Bryant 9-8400, Ext. 1143

Ellis H. Parker Esq., Chief Burlington County Detectives, Mt. Holly, N.J.

Dear Ellis: -

I enclose a rare and late photograph of one, Ludwig Schmidt, as well as the Post Office flier of his fingerprints. When you have copied it or otherwise used it, will you send it to me as soon as possible in the self-addressed envelope?

I likewise enclose five specimens of handwriting admittedly and unquestionable all by the same man. In these five, taking into consideration that some were written as early as 1933, you will undoubtedly see resemblances in the Faulkner letter. I have taken the liberty of calling your attention to some of them. The writer of these specimens I have located in New Jersey. He is a German American and a house painter. He is presently unemployed. He has been talked to but not in any way about the case in point. He was involved in a civil litigation in 1932 or 1933, and I believe a judgment stands against him and William Krippen Dorf, whose signature appears on one of the checks.

The handwriting is that of Ernest Grueter, who speaks English with a marked German accent. He is fair complexioned, blue-eyed, powerfully built, and of medium height. His hair is brown. The attorney who turned over these documents to me describes him as extraordinarily dunning and quite capable of committing any offense.

These handwriting specimens MUST positively be returned to me. They are not mine. They form part of the legal procedure.

The printing on the card which I enclose is perhaps not that of Grueter. I have no way of finding out.

To return to the gentleman, Ludwig Schmidt, who so much interests me. Several times his name has come in my investigation. The last time, only several days ago. I decided to look into his career and learned from the Department of Justice and the Chief Postal Inspector that:

He is known under the aliases of Louis Schmidt, Dutch Louie, Fred Schmidt, and Dutch Schmidt. In 1934 he was 40 years old, 5'8 7/8" tall, weighed 158, has blue eyes, medium-dark chestnut hair, a fair complexion, now turning sallow and tuberculosis. This ailment developed about 1924. He has an American and a German flag tattooed between the thumb and index finger of one hand, which one I don't know. He is semi-literate and speaks with a marked accent.

His fingerprint classification is <u>17 13 U 00</u>

5 U 00 14

His Bertillon is: 75.5:80.0:93.0;19.5:15.5:14.4;7.4:26.1:1 1.7:

Mr. Schmidt was a gentleman who shot and was, in turn, shot with impunity. He first enters the picture back in 1920 for infractions of some sort of the Post Office Department. Shortly thereafter, he was sent to a government prison camp suffering with T.B. He tunneled his way to freedom, was captured, and returned to Atlanta Penitentiary. From this institution, he escaped with Dutch Anderson, nine months after the Gerald Chapman departure. Anderson was shot to death in Minneapolis or Milwaukee. Chapman was hanged in Connecticut for a new Britain murder.

In 1924, April 24, Mr. Schmidt appeared in fashionable Tuxedo, N.Y., where he was shot by detectives for breaking into an Erie freight train. He was taken to the Tuxedo Hospital, where he was fingerprinted. The flags of which I earlier spoke proved his undoing. He admitted his identity and was returned to Atlanta.

On Oct. 10, 1931, he was released from Atlanta and was immediately slapped with a deportation warrant. Apparently, he posted a head tax before a United States Commissioner and then jumped the bond because he turned up in Knoxville, Tenn. On June 11, 1932, where he was shot for reasons unknown to me. Apparently, he served a short sentence and was paroled. Then on Nov. 15, 1933, with three companions, he turned off a mail job to the tune of $105,000. He was tried, convicted, and sentenced to thirty-two years on Alcatraz Island, San Francisco Bay. He was one of the ringleaders of the last January revolt at the prison.

Mr. Schmidt was a member of the notorious Roger Touhy mob. He was sought in the Jake Factor, Mamm, and Urschel kidnapping. He was never tried in those cases because he was not apprehended until the mail job in Charlotte, N.C.

The fact that Mr. Schmidt seems quite able to adjust himself to any crime, particularly the "snatch" racket, and the fact that no one seems to know just what his activities were between Oct. 10, 1931, and June 11, 1932, aroused my suspicions.

That I am not entirely flat on one side of the head and that my suspicions of Mr. Schmidt seem justifiable are borne out by a conversation I had only two days ago with Inspector Doran, Agent in charge of the New York District for the Post Office. Doran is a friend of mine. He told me I was not the first to question the possibility of Schmidt's participation in the Lindbergh matter. He said that the day following the purported meeting of Condon and the man in the cemetery, one of his old and most trusted operatives had written him a long memorandum saying that "it looks like Dutch Louie is in this case." Doran, in all fairness, informed me that he was skeptical about Schmidt's possible complicity. Nevertheless, further inquiry failed to show me that Schmidt was ever questioned about the New Jersey affair. It seems reasonable to believe Schmidt was not in prison from Oct. 1931 to June 1932, or else the agent would not have written about him to Doran.

You will notice that in the flier sent out by the Post Office Department in 1933 and in the data I give you concerning Schmidt, there are apparent discrepancies. This is explainable by the fact that my figures are later (1934), whereas the ones in the flier are from his police folder of a much earlier date. Then too, he is losing weight because of tuberculosis.

One other item concerning Schmidt. It may be significant. He has always been extremely cagey about his fingerprints. When he was taken to the Tuxedo Hospital, he said he could not open his thumb and index finger because of paralysis. The prints that were taken of the remaining fingers indicated his identity when they were shipped to New York. Detectives there went to the hospital and forced open the thumb and index finger and found the two flags.

Now, if you recall early in the case, Condon and another man, whose description fits precisely Schmidt's, went to an apartment house, and there attempted to leave a bundle wrapped in newspapers. This bundle was supposed to have contained part of the ransom, if not all, of it. The janitor refused to store the bundle. He afterward positively identified Condon as one of the men who had called on him. This Condon emphatically denied. But Reilly very definitely is supposed to have taken an affidavit from the janitor. The man was never called to the stand. This potential witness described the man whom he identified as Condon, as being accompanied by a man with a "stiff hand."

Of course, the whole value of the Schmidt information resolves itself into where the man was during those nine months in 1931 and 1932. My inquiries have brought unsatisfactory results, though I expect to have definite info from the D of J. in Washington within the next 48 hours. Perhaps you can put the bite on.

There is another matter at this time I would like to broach because it has caused me considerable distress and embarrassment. It concerns the part being played by a publication edited by Paul G. Clancy, known as "American Astrology,"

Clancy has offered me what appears to be rather a fat job with his star-spangled magazine. I have flatly refused to have anything to do with his so-called plan financed by the Washington lady. He, learning that I had known you for a long time, asked that I write you and tell you that he would pay for any investigation you would conduct. I advised him that I would do nothing of the sort and that if he chose, he could make his proposal directly to you or the Governor. I told him further that I was morally obliged to you for many past favors and that I was not a liberty to divulge information that you sent me unless I had an unconditional release from you. In seventeen years of working on crime investigations, I have done pretty well without having a horoscopes case or personally consulting the conjunctions of the zodiac. When the time comes that I must resort to the heavenly bodies for revelation, it is time that I am shot, stuffed, mounted, and preserved for posterity.

You would do me a great favor if you would let me know, not what dealings you are having with Clancy or his subaltern, Toby, Dr. Hudson, and Lieut. Hicks, but whether or not you are having any dealings with these worthies. I shall regard this information as inviolate. Specifically, I want to know if I may work with them, and if you feel they can be trusted.

The stories that have appeared in the New York American have set back my work by about two months. It seems to be that Governor Hoffman is surrounded by political legacies and those forced on him by associates. It might be well if he glanced about his so-called intimate friends. For Hoffman, I have nothing but the utmost regard. I believe he is honest and courageous.

Will you please note my change of address and telephone number?

My kindest regards to young Ellis and Anna.

I ask you please to view all the forgoing matter in complete confidence.

With very best wishes, I am, as ever,
Fred Shanbacker

Note: Ludwig Schmidt (AKA Dutch Schmidt) was a member of the Chicago-based Touhy Mob known for a famous mail robbery that they were convicted of. The Mob fought a long battle in Chicago over beer and liquor distribution. Legendary Al Capone had decided he wanted a piece of this action. Letter writer Fred Shanbacker may have suspected Duch Schmidt because of the Touhy mob's reputation of participating in kidnapping plots. The FBI eventually took the gang down in a bloody raid.

This is a Copy of note sent by Fred Shanbacker on 12-23-1935 that referenced investigating Hauptmann, Wilentz, Leborric, Condon, and Fisch:

> Please don't tear up this letter before you read it. If you want to learn something, you go to the Morgan building in New York City. There you will find out about two shyster lawyers who went there at the beginning of the Hauptmann trial and left after the trial was finished. They spoke to Wilentz to keep Fisch's name out of the whole thing at one time, and it seems to me that I am Leborric saws the go-between of the shyster's and Wilentz's people. If you are afraid to say something for fear of embarrassment as you talk to Leborric over the telephone and see him undercover and see what information, he gave Wilentz. If you remember, it was Leborric who said over the radio that Lindbergh could pick out Hauptmann by his voice. He said five names must be kept out after, and if Hauptmann burns when you see the evidence left – too often, he also said we got him where we want him now that we got that old fellow on our side and I think he meant Condon. That old Hocksmith don't see at all if you put him to it you can make something out after he also said he remembered the name.

Note: This note is reproduced exactly as it was found. The grammar can be confusing. Fred Shanbacker often worked for Ellis Parker, and we know the Isidor Fisch was a main suspect of his. Why did these lawyers want to keep Fisch's name out of the trial?

<u>The following letter was addressed to Fred Shanbacker by Ellis Parker on 1-19-1936:</u>

September 19, 1936

Mr. Fred Shanbacker

129 West 40th Street

Room 1144

New York City

Dear Freddie:

It's been sometime since we corresponded, and many things have happened. The reason I haven't contacted you is because I didn't want you in any way, to become embarrassed by anything that was going on, and I know that all my lines have been tapped. I would like to have a talk to you and Henry sometime later, perhaps after a month or so.

A person has asked me to find out who occupied room 221, second floor, in the Hotel Pennsylvania, New York City, on September 4,5,6, and 7, 1936. I do not know what they want this information for, I didn't ask them, but would you see, if possible, who was registered on these dates, and advise me.

Remember me to Henry, and rest assured that I am ever your friend.

Very truly yours,

Ellis H. Parker

Chief of County Detectives

<u>Note:</u> Even though Ellis Parker hadn't been in touch with Fred Shanbacker for some time, he still valued his investigating ability. I wonder why Ellis needed to know who occupied room 221? I suspect it had to do with Paul Wendel. There was a lot of pressure being placed on Ellis in 1936. Bruno Richard Hauptmann had been executed just six months before this communication. Ellis was now fighting for not only his very life but also for the professional

reputation that he had spent many productive years building. The enemy was aggressive, they had tapped his phones, and he knew it.

In the lost files, we found a letter dated January 24, 1936, written by Ellis Parker to Fred Shanbacker. It describes a task that Detective Parker wanted to be handled by Fred. Note that again Ellis has an interest in the actions of Isidor Fisch:

January 24, 1936

Fred Shanbacker
104 W. 49th Street, New York City

Dear Friend Fred,

You can go to the German Consulate, and if you can obtain any information from him concerning the sums of money that Isidor Fisch sent from this country to Leipzig, Germany, the amounts and dates, I will appreciate it.

Very Truly Yours,
Ellis H. Parker
Chief Of Detectives

Fred Shanbacker wrote to Ellis Parker on 1-26-1936:

January 26, 1936

Ellis H. Parker
Chief Burlington County Detectives
Mt., Holly, N.J.

Dear Ellis:

I received your letter yesterday. I am enclosing a joint statement by Mr. and Mrs. Gustave Mancke of the Bronx. This statement is self-explanatory excepting that on its face, it may seem a little too pat. The fact is, it could have run into thirty or so pages, but I made a digest, in fact, several of them in order to condense what they had said. All these digests I read to them before making a final draft which each read and then signed. The condensed one I forward with their signatures.

The man is a high Mason, and his wife is chairman of her chapter of the Daughters Eastern Star. The only thing I have found which could possibly militate against them is that they lost their store in New Rochelle in bankruptcy. This, they freely admit. They had that store for seven years.

I am also enclosing a receipt from the Western Union dated January 8 for cables to the Kriminal Police of Leipsig. Here there appears to have been some misunderstanding. The Kriminal Police replied to our message direct to the German Consul, who, in turn, relayed it to a Mr. Legree in Trenton. I am not sure of the spelling of the name. The Consul, very busy on last Saturday, said the message contained the information about Fisch that you wanted. He has promised me a copy of this cable along with a copy of a cable sent from the Consuls by one Harold Keyes. My info is that Fisch sent two money orders, one for $25 and another for $50 to Pincus Fisch. Where they were sent from, I do not know, nor am I sure of the transaction being a fact. Within the next twenty-four hours, however, I should have the complete details. As soon as I get them, I shall send them to you pronto.

For your information, Mrs. Thieben, whose statement you already have, has tentatively identified the picture of Morris Rosner as the man who came to that hotel about 1 p.m. daily while she worked there. I will show her other pictures of him along with pictures of certain suspects we (Kress) have in mind. These pictures I must get from the Police Department's gallery, and I expect to encounter difficulty in obtaining them.

Kress and I have just learned of a woman stowaway who followed her lover to Germany shortly after his departure for that country. The man, Kress, is convinced, is the one who approached Trost and introduced him to Fisch, whom he already knew. Trost's statement you have.

I end this note with a bill for that advertisement in the Brooklyn Eagle. I am in no hurry to be reimbursed. But the cable receipt should prove to you that we have not laid down on the job here. I sincerely hope we may be of service to you and that your success in solving the current matter will be swift and glorious.

Sincerely yours,

Fred Shanbacker

The following statement was included in the letter of 1-26-1936:

January 19, 1936

My name is Gustave Mancke. I reside with my wife, Sophie, at 2474 Tiebout Avenue, The Bronx, New York City, N.Y.

I make this statement voluntarily and under no duress believing that it may serve the ends of justice.

In January and February of 1932, a man whom I identify as Dr. John F. Condon came to my ice cream store at 583 Mail Street, New Rochelle, N.Y. A customer told me he was a professor at the New Rochelle College for Girls at New Rochelle, N.Y.

This man was accompanied by a dark, pretty girl with bobbed hair, perhaps of Italian type. She was about eighteen to twenty-three years old. The man wore a derby and a dark overcoat. He was tall, heavyset, and carried a cane with a silver knob and a briefcase. He wore a white scarf. He invariably ordered maple walnut or tutti-frutti ice cream. They always sat at one table behind a partition. They whispered and held hands. They came to my place together at least once a week, generally about 3:30 p.m. I think it was on Thursdays.

During these eight weeks and I believe usually on Sundays about 9 p.m., or later a man and woman whom I identify absolutely from photographs as Ollie Whatley and Violet Sharpe came to my place four or five times to eat. On three or four occasions, they were accompanied by a short, thin, dark man who looked like Eddie Cantor only with much larger ears. He coughed badly, and I slapped him on the back, saying, "You resemble Eddie Cantor." His friend said, "No, his name is Fisch." I said, "Why not herring?" They laughed and went out. The man who coughed always spoke to me in German, I positively identify this man as Isadore Fisch.

The man whom I identify as Whately wore a gray suit, an oxford gray overcoat, and a dark gray slouch hat. He limped slightly and had blond hair thinning at the temples.

The woman whom I identify as Violet Sharpe always ordered tea and sandwiches. She was hard to please and was nearly always disagreeable.

The whispering of these people attracted my attention and the attention of my wife.

The man, Fisch, never came to my place alone. He was there with Violet Sharpe and Whatley about three or four times.

None of these people whom I have mentioned above ever came back to my ice cream parlor after March 1, 1932.

On a Monday either in May or June, while I was in Sheepshead Bay, N.Y. with Albert Waitsziger, 15 Fir Place, New Rochelle, N.Y. to go fishing, I saw the man who had come to my place with the young woman.

I introduced myself to this man calling him Professor Condon. He acknowledged the introduction and said he did not recall my name? I told him I remembered his coming to my place with a young woman. He said, "Oh, yes. Oh, yes." The man with him jerked him away when I invited him to go fishing with us. I do not know who the man was that was with Dr. Condon.

My wife and I lived in New Rochelle, N.Y. from December 10, 1927, to November 6, 1933, during which time my wife owned the store at 583 Main Street, New Rochelle, N.Y. I was the manager of the store during this entire period. Since then, we have lived continuously at 2474 Tiebout Avenue, The Bronx, New York City, N.Y.

Signed: Gustave Mancke

Witnessed: John Schwiebert & Sophie W. Mancke

To all that part of the above set forth statement given by my husband, Gustave Mancke, relatively to what he said or observed, I subscribe excepting that part pertaining to his meeting with Dr. Condon at Sheepshead Bay, N.Y. I was not with him when he went fishing.

Signed: Sophie W. Mancke

Witnessed: John Schwiebert & Gustave Mancke

Note: Again, we see additional evidence that Isadore Fisch and Violet Shape had a personal relationship. We previously saw a letter that stated that they once lived together as man and wife. Gustave Mancke has written and signed a statement that Ollie Whatley and Violet Shape visited his Ice Cream Store in New Rochelle numerous times. On three or four occasions, they were joined by Isadore Fisch. Before and during this period (January and February 1932), John F. Condon had patronized the store with a young woman. Condon was a professor at a nearby college.

This information establishes a relationship that existed between Violet Sharpe, Ollie Whatley, Isadore Fisch, and John Condon weeks before the Lindbergh baby was taken from his home.

Ellis Parker responds to Fred Shanbacker on 1-27-1936:

January 27, 1936

Fred Shanbacker

104 w. 49th Street

New York City

Dear Friend Fred:

Enclosed is a check for the expenditures. Seems to me all I have been doing ever since I got into this mess is to hand out money. The damn thing now cost me over $3,000 out of my own pocket, and I have never received anything from anyone for anything I have done; in fact, I don't expect it. I am only interested as far as justice is concerned.

On January 13th, you sent me a telegram, asking me about a gaming place. Inquiry was made of the party, and he said that Fisch once pointed to a gambling place which he thought was around 40th Street, but I couldn't tell just where it was. This is all the information I could get.

Remember me to Kress.

Many thanks for your assistance to date.

Very truly yours,

Ellis H. Parker

Chief of Detectives

Note: This letter was written by Detective Parker to his frequent investigative partner, Fred Shanbacker, confirms what we have discovered many times. Detective Ellis Parker's motives were pure. He spent his own money investigating the Hauptmann case because he and Governor Harold Hoffman, his close friend, did not believe there was enough evidence to send him to death. He continued working until he produced the only man to confess to the Crime of the Century, Paul H. Wendel.

Fred Shanbacker writes to Ellis Parker on 3-11-1936:

> March 11, 1936
>
> Dear Ellis: -
>
> This note is setting forth in some detail of the occurrences on the Massachusetts argosy. It seems to me both a bitter and a thundering anti-climax to my conversation with Anna today.
>
> Trost emphatically denied that the man we pointed to him was the Fritz Karge with whom he talked in 1934 several days before Karge sailed for Germany.
>
> Equally, emphatic is Trost that Fritz Karge is the right name of the man with whom he talked.
>
> The story of the Massachusetts Karge and Trost's Karge has many striking parallels. The substantial differences in the two Karge's is their ages and their physical formations.
>
> But let me explain where and how I got my information about the Chelsea man:
>
> There is in New York City at 295 Madison Ave, the Lithographers National Association. A Miss Cantwell is a secretary. A Mr. Saunders, I believe, is the president. This organization is in almost constant communication with all the prominent lithographing companies in the country. It acts as a clearinghouse for lithographers seeking work and companies seeking lithographers.
>
> The Forbes Lithograph Mfg. Co. outside Boston has obtained a number of employees from the National Association among them, one, Fritz Karge. It was from the inquiries of the Forbes Co. and the ensuing correspondence

between that concern and the Association that I got most of my information.

Neither Mr. William S. Forbes, President, nor his son, J. Stuart Forbes, Vice-President, were at the plant the day we called. Instead, we talked with a Mr. Arthur R. Hitchings, an executive of lower rank, but officially able to answer our questions. From these aforementioned sources, then, we learned that:

The Fritz Karge of Forbes is a naturalized American who came to this country from Germany in 1923. Shortly after his arrival here, he was employed by the lithographing concern of Edwards & Deutsch in Chicago. He remained there for about ten years, but at the height of the depression was released. He went to the National Printing and Engraving Co. of Niles, Michigan. How long he worked there, I have not found out.

A letter of reference from the Association to Forbes said that he had worked for about seven months with the Erie Lithographing Co. of Erie, Pa.

He was employed by the Forbes company on Dec. 17, 1934, and has worked there continuously since. He is now and was, apparently, at all the other places of his employment, a poster artist earning between $40 and $50 weekly. He says he is married and that when he was hired by Forbes, living at 33 Ellis Avenue, Irvington, N.J. now lives at 134 Clark Ave., Chelsea, Mass.

Mr. Hitchings, we found both pleasant and quite willing to cooperate with us.

While Trost remained outside the plant in the car, Hitchings took Kress and me to Karge's department. We had ample opportunity to see him. He is about 5'4", possibly a trifle taller; weighs about 140, and has his age as 45. He now looks to be about 42. He is smooth shaved, wears horned rimmed spectacles both while working and at leisure, and possesses no characteristic, observable marks to classify him. His features are regular, his nose slightly upturned. He is compactly built.

This is the man Hitchings pointed out to us. But since he was unfamiliar with all the men in Karge's department, he confirmed his identification with someone out of earshot.

Karge finished work at 4:35 p.m. and apparently went directly to his home in Clark Ave. We had hoped for this move and had taken up our positions near his house.

Trost and I stood inconspicuously behind a tree. Kress remained in the car, which commanded a side view to the entrance to the house.

The house is a brown clapboard one standing on a corner. It is old, poorly constructed, and similar to all the others in the neighborhood.

As Karge approached his home up a steep hill, a girl child about 8 years old ran to greet him. They embraced, talked together for several seconds, and then walked up the steps into the house. The two passed within fifteen or eighteen feet of us, and we saw their faces distinctly.

Unfalteringly. Trost declared that the man was not the Karge with whom he had talked in 1934. He said his Karge today would be about 33 years old, was less solidly built, and had a semi-Hebraic nose.

While we waited for Karge to return, a woman came to the window of the Karge house and shook out a dust cloth. In our fleeting glance, she appeared to be a blond. Apparently, this was Mrs. Karge, for Karge stated in his application for work that he was married. I mention her blondness because the woman who is supposed to have followed Karge to Hamburg is a brunette of the Latin type.

I regret that I haven't more pleasant news for you. I sincerely wish that I had. The trip was a backbreaker but well worthwhile taking to clinch the identification.

Today I hope to see Miss Cantwell at the Madison Ave. address and learn something more about the Chelsea man… perhaps a picture.

I had taken with me some old and seldom printed pictures of Dr. C. hoping to show them to Mrs. Lillian Collings in Stamford, but we passed through there so early in the morning, and so late at night, I thought it unwise to disturb her.

Kindest Regards to all,

Fred Shanbacker

Ellis Parker responded on 3-12-1936:

March 12, 1936

Mr. Fred Shanbacker

129 W. 48th Street

New York City

Dear Freddy:

I received your report. There is no doubt in my mind, but what the man that lived at 33 Ellis Avenue, Irvington, N.J., is the man that you saw up at Chelsea, Mass. I was talking to his wife's sister, whose name is Zimmerman, and she lives on the third-floor apartment of this same house. After I talked with her and her daughter, when I had located her, I felt that this might not be the man, but there is only one way to satisfy yourself, and that is to run it out.

I had the records of the Fishers there in Irvington searched, and this man did not go to Europe in any part of '32.

The Fritz Karge that Trost says he knows his right name, and that he saw with Isidor Fisch, is the man we want to locate. I have written a letter to the German Counsel General's office in New York City, and asked them to check on the Hamburg Line and others to try and find if any Fritz Karge or Karge's went over from this Country to Germany in 1932 and to furnish me with the addresses that he had in this Country, and all other information possible. As soon as I receive a reply, I will immediately forward it to you, as I think this would be a most important discovery. If Trost is correct, this man would know how Fisch came in possession of that money and might be in a position to assist us, and no doubt would if we could locate him.

Remember me to Kress, and I will advise you as soon as I hear something.

Yours very truly,

Ellis H. Parker

Chief of County Detectives

Following is Ellis Parker's letter of 4-9-1938:

Note: Detective Ellis Parker wrote to Fred Shanbacker, asking him to meet with Attorney Peter Baumer and Chief Thomas Dixon. On April 16, 1936, Ellis received the following report:

Dear Ellis,

I talked with Chief Thomas Dixon and with Peter Baumer, attorney. Dixon is a full-blooded Cherokee Indian, 53 years old, the son of the famous Black Hawk. He has a long but undistinguished record as a sergeant in the U.S. Army in the State of Washington, Mexico, and in France. I fear he is a bit of a theorist and given to vague romancing.

Mr. Baumer, I found courteous, somewhat exciting, and slightly drunk. He says he knows the Governor intimately and you very well. He's a bald man about 58, speaks with what appears brogue, and desires to enter the case, though in what manner he didn't make clear to me. Baumer wants no money: Dixon wants his expenses and to work alone in the case. He wishes to meet you.

The stories of these two gentlemen, combined and separately, left me unimpressed. But perhaps there is some significance to them. Only you can tell. Dixon's story follows:

After the Armistice, he remained in Paris, where he opened a private detective agency. During the treaty negotiations between the several warring nations, he was employed by the Secret Service in counter-espionage work. While in Mexico, he was employed by the Army Intelligence Service as was he also while in the State of Washington. He seemed to have some difficulty in distinguishing the two branches of the service. In his Army discharge papers, his character is marked excellent.

In the Fall of 1932, he said his duties brought him in touch with a man known to him only as "John the Wop." This man showed him a letter purportedly to have been written by Fisch. The contents of the letter he does not remember. But it made enough impression on him to impart its significance to the Vice Consul at Bordeaux, France. He signed himself merely, "49".

He describes "John the Wop" as having a defect in one eye and being a flashy dresser of Italian American birth. This "John" was known as a racketeer and cardsharper, dealer in narcotics, and given to sundry arts of swindling. His accomplices were a woman, he thinks to be either Swiss or German, name unknown to him, and Sol, last name unknown to him, a Russian Jew, wanted in Canada for murder.

These 3 persons he is sure made the Jersey "snatch." All three are living in Europe, "John" seeming to be a commuter between Paris and Berlin.

During the Governor's campaign, Dixon declares that he went to the Robert Treat Hotel and there gave the mentioned information to the Governor's campaign manager. The letter, according to Dixon, said that for the present, it could not be very well investigated.

When Hauptmann was arrested, he sent the same information to Colonel Breckenridge and Colonel Schwarzkopf. Neither of these worthies, he continues, replied to his communications.

Mr. Dixon adds that as recently as six months ago, $10,000 of the ransom money was in New York. All my efforts to relieve him of how he knew it, where in New York it was and who had it, he stubbornly resisted. To digress, he stated that 10 days after his report to the Vice Consul at Bordeaux, the Paris Tribune reported that some of the ransom money had been passed in Switzerland.

"John the Wop," whom he further described as being swarthy, weighing about 180 and speaking English with an accent, explained his possession of some of the ransom money as having been part of the loot taken during an American bank robbery. The Swiss woman, whom he thinks is John's sweetheart, was in this country a year and a half ago.

According to Baumer, Dixon was wounded and gassed overseas, receives compensation from the Government, and is incapable of further production. For the last two years, Dixon says he has been devoting himself to perfecting inventions.

Mr. Baumer's contribution to the interview consisted in several coy references to one Nick Montana, a Sylvian Ortlieb, and a New York lawyer named Marder.

The implication was that these men might know something about the case. It seems that back in 1913 or thereabouts, they conspired and succeeded in ruining him financially because he refused them permission in Providence, R.I., to use his yacht to transport narcotics. He implied further, and with some heat that Wilentz and Ortlieb some years ago were interested in the girl racquet among New Jersey roadhouses.

For your information, Nick Montana was recently convicted and is now serving a long sentence for forcing girls into prosecution. I know nothing off-hand about Ortlieb.

In no sense do I want you to draw from what I have said that these two men are fools. They are not. But I do not believe they are in any way familiar with the case.

I sincerely hope your health stands up under the political battering. It has been getting the last few weeks, and that you will eventually glory in a solution of this case. My kindest regards to Junior and Ana.

FBS (Fred Shanbacker)

Note: This is a fantastic letter. The author (Fred Shanbacker), who signed as FBS, can tell a story. I learned online that Fred worked at one time for the New York Evening Post. His report reads like one of the era's true crime magazines. He tells us that Chief Thomas Dixon is a full-blooded Cherokee Indian and the famous Blackhawk son. The famous Blackhawk was a Sauk Indian who died in 1838. Chief Dixon was born in 1883. It does not add up. Fred also drops the names "Wilentz" and "Ortlieb" into a girl running and prosecution racquet. I am not a fan of N.J. Attorney General David Wilentz if that is who he means, but it is improbable that it was David Wilentz, in my opinion. The only thing of interest is his claim that Dixon was shown a letter written by Fisch by a man known only as "49". It sounds like the kind of alias that Paul Wendel was fond of using. I hope that Ellis didn't pay much for this report. Maybe Fred was just writing down what he heard at the meeting as a reporter should.

FROM THE ELLIS PARKER LOST FILES

New York

Jan. 19, 1936

Mr. Ellis Parker,

Mount Holly, N.J.

Dear Sir,

You can take the following for what it is worth, but may not the kidnapping of the Lindbergh baby be in some way connected with the Morrow family? And if so, there is no reason why just because they are socially prominent, an innocent man should be condemned to death to avoid a public scandal. Of course, I do not give much credence to the rumor, and what I am about to say may be idle gossip, you are the best judge of that, however, in either the New York Herald Tribune or World Telegraph of March 28, 1932, before the police came to the Lindbergh home and when Colonel Lindbergh received the first note before it was opened, he Colonel said he feared the kidnapping might be the work of a maniac or deranged woman, some person likely to do the infant harm, but when the note was opened they became convinced it was written by a person perfectly sane. The rumor that there was an illegitimate son whose mother had been a maid in the Morrow house and had from time to time written threatening letters and was placed in an institute at Skillman where she is now supposed to give rise to the thought that the kidnapping may have been the work of the boy in question, or someone connected with it.

Whether this is true or not, the fact remains that the Morrow's and Lindbergh's seem to have balked investigation of their homes all along the line, and there is no reason why they should not have the skeleton dragged from their own closets if it is to save an innocent man. This angle of the case warrants the strictest investigation, for why should the poor pay for the rich where a matter of justice is concerned? The words of Colonel Lindbergh to his wife just after the discovery that the child was missing, "Anne, they have stolen our baby," is somewhat significant, for they presuppose a threat.

Very truly,

Mary Douglas

Note: If you are a student of "The Crime of the Century" and have been reading "From The Lost Files of Ellis Parker," the theories of the Lindbergh family (including the Morrow family) being involved in the crime are overwhelming. Can you even contemplate that only one man, Bruno Richard Hauptmann, was guilty of the crime? Aren't we only supposed to convict if it is proved beyond a reasonable doubt that a man is guilty? With all this doubt, Hauptmann was not only convicted. He was executed. We, America, did not gain from this. Who did benefit, I ask? Simple, those that found fame and fortune organizing his conviction by any means necessary.

FROM THE ELLIS PARKER LOST FILES

Jan 20, 1936

Mr. Ellis Parker

Burlington County, N.J.

Dear Sir,

As a post-office man of 22 years' experience, I think I have learned a bit about handwriting and being of German-born parents, I know something of a German writing in

English. That is, I know that he can't help getting his German letters into his English letters.

Thus, I want to state that insofar as I could see from the sample enclosed, I am positive that the original and one of the subsequent notes were written by a different man. The first letter in my estimation was not written by a German at all, and I have noted the one word "gute," which is German for Good, and the word "signature." If several men whose parents and grandparents were born here, but had no education to speak of, were asked to spell signature, I think a few signatures would result.

Now to take up the second letter. It is full of German letters and is written by someone who has no doubt written many letters, in other words, a letter-writer. In line 5, the k is a German one used in that script. In line 6, the t is German script, as are the others. The use of the word as for than is just caused by (line 5) a faulty translation, "as and than" being translated into German by the same word "als." The p s are distinctly German. In line 6 there is an – over the u in amount which is used in German and is called an "umlaut." This does not appear in "public" in the original note, nor in "gute." Note the "K" at the end of the word mark in line 9. Americans don't make an a such as in "any" in line 9 nor an as in one in line 10. The word nommer for number is easily understood as the German translation has no b in it.

In line 13, they use to for do because the German word is tuen.

In conclusion, I wish to state that I am certain that 6 people familiar with the writing of a German not here very long will unanimously pick the second note as written by a German, and the same 6 will at least disagree on the first one.

Why not try it? Please don't take this as a crank letter, but I was just wondering if it were possible that experts declared both notes written by the same man.

Very truly yours,

Edward P. Graeser, College Point, NY

23-21, W 124th Street W.

College Point, NY

Detective Ellis Parker responded to Edward P. Graeser on January 22, 1936:

January 22, 1936

Mr. Edward P. Graeser

23-21 124th Street

College Point, New York

Dear Sir:

Your letter received, and it is very interesting.

The handwriting experts all testified that all of the notes were written by the same person at the trial, since the trial some of them have changed their minds. Any person that has seen the first note, and the others, they could see that they were positively different. The first note was undoubtedly written by the kidnapper, the others were tracings or attempted tracings, which were used by the extortionists.

I agree with what you say in your communication, and I want to thank you for writing me.

I am returning your clippings as I have photostatic copies of the original notes.

Very truly yours,

Ellis H. Parker

Chief of Detectives

Note: The writer's full name to Ellis Parker was Edward Peter Graeser (1893-1957). He married, served in WWI, and had two sons during his lifetime.

The conversation between Edward Graeser and Ellis Parker confirmed what Detective Parker had theorized all along. One person wrote the first ransom note, the others by someone else. Graeser told Ellis that he did not believe the same person wrote all the ransom notes. Graeser also stated that the first note and a subsequent note were not written by a German, in his opinion.

At the Hauptmann trial, the experts testified that they were all written by the same person. The David Wilentz-led prosecution wanted to convince the public that Hauptmann was the lone kidnapper and killer of the baby. The plan was successful. Hauptman was found guilty in a flawed trial and then executed for the crime.

The words of Ellis Parker in his response are significant. First of all, remember that Hauptmann was German and that Graeser's opinion was that a German could not have written the first note. Without convincing the Hauptmann jury that Bruno Richard Hauptman had written all the ransom notes himself, I doubt the jury would have sentenced him to death. The mere suspicion of other individuals being involved in the kidnapping plot should have been enough to save Hauptmann's life. Even with Hauptmann jailed for life, the case could have then been fully solved. Who had the most to lose if Hauptmann lived?

FROM THE ELLIS PARKER LOST FILES

January 20, 1936

Mignon Writtenhouse

583 West 215 Street

New York City

Dear Sir,

I received your communication dated January 14, and it was very, very interesting. It is typical of Condon, and when you said that Condon wrote all the ransom notes except the first, in my judgment, you are correct. The first note was written invariably by the kidnapper, the other notes were written by different parties entirely. There is one significant thing about the first note and the others. It stands out like Gibraltar to me and shows conclusively that the kidnapper and the extortionists are two different and distinct persons.

The deductions in your communication concerning Condon picturing this case are true characteristics of him. Condon is a type of person exactly as expressed by you.

Again, I want to thank you for writing me and assure you that I appreciate the thoughts behind this because you are the class of person whom I have the highest regard for a person who steps deep into every angle.

My only interest, in this case, is one of justice, and I feel that I would be laying down if I did not stand up for what I feel is right. The kidnapper is one thing, and the extortionist is another. Condon is by no means eliminated by me concerning the extortion.

Again, thanking you, I remain,

Very truly yours,

Detective Ellis H. Parker

Note: Thanks to discovering the lost letters, we can learn directly from Ellis Parker his opinions on the Lindbergh case. His investigated conclusions are definite in this letter. Ellis believes that the kidnapper wrote the ransom letter left on the night of the kidnapping and that the rest of the ransom letters were written by someone else. Ellis Parker explained in a previous letter (his letter to John Harrington on 12-31, 1935) that Bruno Hauptmann could not have written it and explained why he believed so. In this letter and others, Ellis has stated that kidnapping and extortion are separate crimes.

Ellis also informed Mignon Writtenhouse that he was still very suspicious of Condon's (Jafsie) role in the crime.

Magnon Rittenhouse wrote to Ellis Parker on many occasions. She later became famous for writing the book 'The Amazing Nellie Bly' in 1956.

Magnon Rittenhouse wrote again on 5-31-1936:

> Ellis H. Parker
>
> Chief of Detectives
>
> Mount Holly, NJ,
>
> Dear Ellis,
>
> Don't let that damn Condon get away with it. WNEW reports that he was out in the garden this afternoon (Tuesday, the afternoon Hauptmann was scheduled to die) digging in his garden. Does this not confirm what I said? God bless you and Governor Hoffman for your decent hearts. May you win.
>
> Sincerely,
>
> Magnon Rittenhouse

FROM THE ELLIS PARKER LOST FILES

January 20th, 1936

City of Wilmington Delaware
Department of Public Safety

Directors of Public Safety

George L. Coppage, President

William M. Mask, Jr.

Dr. Joseph P. Wales

George Black, Superintendent of Public Safety

Howard L. Boyd, Chief of Police

Mr. Ellis H. Parker,

Chief of County Detectives,

Burlington County, Mount Holly, N.J.

Dear Sir; -

Recently a resident of this city, gave some information, that may have a bearing on the Lindbergh case, early in 1934, he was employed on a Fishing Trawler, the Captain of the Trawler while sober was a very close-mouthed man, but when under the influence of liquor, was very talkative and loud in making threats, about a certain man who double-crossed him.

At one time, while under the influence of liquor, he showed the informer a check for the sum of $14,500.00, that he claimed was given to him by a man, the informer claimed that the name of John Curtis was signed on the check.

The captain several years ago, had a boat that had formerly been a Sub chaser and converted it into a fishing boat, this boat was supposed to have caught fire, burnt and sunk at sea, the captain, his wife, and the crew took to the boat dories, and were later picked up by the crew of another boat.

Also, while under the influence of liquor, he told the informer that he would tell who got the baby, the captain in question is a resident of this city and is still engaged in Trawler fishing.

If you think this might be of any value to you, you can get in touch with the party who gave the information, by coming to Police Headquarters, this City.

Kindly keep the above information confidential, as we wish to be kept out of the matter.

Very Truly yours,

George Black

Superintendent of Public Safety

Note: It is possible that the John Curtis John Hughes Curtis was the same John Curtis that Chief George Black was writing to Ellis Parker about. John Hughes Curtis was a bankrupt shipbuilder from Norfolk, Virginia, who had convinced Charles Lindbergh that he was in actual contact with his son's kidnappers. He eventually confessed to the hoax, but not before leading Lindbergh on a wild goose chase from Cape May, New Jersey, to Virginia's coast.

Many of those that had a relationship with Detective Ellis Parker or wrote to him were successful and exceptional. George A. Black, the author of this letter to Ellis Parker, was born in 1968 in Delaware. George Black joined the Wilmington Police Department as a patrol officer in 1891. By 1896 he had risen to Sergeant before being promoted to Chief in 1902. He commanded a force of 166. Chief Black wrote Ellis Parker on stationary titled "City of Wilmington, Department of Public safety." The title "Superintendent of Safety was typed beneath his signature. The title of "Superintendent of Safety" was added in 1921 when Wilmington merged police and fire administrations. The fact that Howard L. Boyd is listed as Chief of Police in this letter is puzzling since George Black didn't resign until December 1936 unless he held both titles simultaneously.

Chief George Black worked hard to control gambling in Wilmington. He was also credited with making the town free of crime. He was working to end the vice trade, speakeasies, and houses of prosecution, like the well-known house controlled by Madam Edna Powell.

In 1903 a teenage daughter of a school superintendent was murdered by a black farmhand named George White. A crowd of 2000 gathered to execute White for the crime. They marched to the prison where he was held. Chief Black blocked the door, shouting out that anyone coming closer would be shot, but the mob could still force their way into the prison. White was forced from there to a nearby field. He was bound, set on a pile of straw and fence rails. He was then burned to death.

The story made the National news. President Theodore Roosevelt condemned the actions of the crowd. Later in life (1936), Chief Black was praised by J. Edgar Hoover.

Chief Black and his son (a Captain on the force) had 16 charges entered against them on 12-1-1936. The Chief was accused of allowing the Police Department to be on the take and being an out-of-control Superintendent. The charges included willful disobedience to orders and neglect of duty.

The newspapers portrayed him as dishonorable and bullying while shaking down bookies & bootleggers and selling police protection to the bawdy houses. Thirty other officers were named by Edna Powell and her associates in affidavits for participation in the scheme.

Chief Black put up no defense at his trial. He denied each and every one of the charges. He decided to resign, but the Board refused his resignation and dismissed him from his positions. The Board then revised their decision. Chief Black was allowed to resign but was denied any pension benefits.

It later was said that there was no direct evidence concerning the receipt of money by Chief Black. Further investigation concluded that Chief Black was not a crook. He did not take money directly.

Those that served with Black often praised him and respected him for doing an excellent job under trying circumstances. Chief Black had faced the day's social problems that included gambling, bookmaking, and prostitution head-on.

If you want to learn more about the reign of Chief George Black in Wilmington, I recommend you read the 6-part series written by Kevin McGonegal titled "Bookies, Bawdy Houses, and Chief Black," which can be found on the internet. Much of my writings here were based on it. I strongly recommend you seek it out if you are intrigued by this case. It is an impressive piece of historical reporting.

Ellis Parker responded to George Black:

> January 23, 1936
>
> George Black, Superintendent of Police
>
> Wilmington, Delaware
>
> Dear Friend George:

I received your letter. As soon as I get a chance, I will either come or send my son down to talk to you personally.

I wish to thank you for writing me. Remember me to your son, and anytime I can be of service to you or your department, please command me.

Very truly yours,

Ellis H. Parker

Chief of Detectives

FROM THE ELLIS PARKER LOST FILES

1816 Holmes Avenue

Racine, Wisconsin

January 20, 1936

Dear Sir:

I read in Liberty of January 25 That Dr. Condon (Jafsie) makes a statement that sign OO found on one of the ransom notes was the distinguishing mark of the German machine-gun attachments. That statement is entirely false.

I have been through the last war as a Machine gunner in the German army, but I never heard of any such sign or symbol.

To verify my statement, I simply refer you to the German War Department.

Very truly yours,

V. Walter Becker

1816 Holmes Ave., Racine, Wisconsin

Detective Ellis H. Parker responded to V. Walter Becker on 1-23-1936:

January 23, 1936

Mr. V. Walter Becker

1816 Holmes Avenue, Racine, Wisconsin

Dear Friend:

Your letter received. Just such witnesses as Jafsie, who is crazy and untruthful, is what convicted Hauptmann. The more Jafsie talks, the more the public will get on him.

They branded Hauptmann a machine gunner so as to poison the people against him. This, in my judgment, is wrong.

I want to thank you for writing me, I remain, very truly yours,

Ellis H. Parker
Chief of Detectives

Note: The media picked up on portraying Hauptmann as the German machine gunner. I believe that the Prosecution was a party to this with the hope of influencing the American public to hate him. I also think that they called him Bruno Hauptmann rather than Richard Hauptman for the same reason. Bruno is much more threatening than Richard, a typical American name.

FROM THE ELLIS PARKER LOST FILES

45-47 43rd Street, Long Island City, N.Y.

January 21, 1936

Ellis H. Parker
Chief of Detectives
Burlington County, Mt. Holly, New Jersey

Dear Chief Parker,

I received your letter of December 12, 1935, but refrained from acknowledging it because I did not want to bother you with any unnecessary correspondence, realizing that you must be very busy.

My reason for writing to you at this time follows: In a recent issue of the New York Evening Journal, I noticed that a house occupied at the time of the Lindbergh kidnapping by one Ernest Wend, former German Army Officer, is said to be under investigation by your men, This recalls to my mind an incident which occurred during the early phases of the investigation. I do not recall the exact date, but it was within ten days or two weeks after the commission of the crime. At the time, I was connected with the Prosecutor's office in New Brunswick, and I received a telephone call from the late Sergeant George Kozusko of Perth Amboy Police, whom I had known since my childhood. Sergeant Kozusko informed me that his brother, John, who is a well-known businessman of Perth Amboy, that is, in the house furnishing business, and well known to me, had some information which he thought should be called to the attention of the Lindbergh investigators.

Upon meeting Mr. John Kozusko, he informed me that a housemaid in his employ had a cousin by the name of Habina who had married one Vincent Vasquez who has on a number of occasions, had trouble with the police and has been an inmate of the Middlesex workhouse.

Shortly after the marriage, Vasquez, who is as you may have surmised, a "Spick", either Spanish or Portuguese, moved with his wife to a more or less run-down farm about two miles from the Lindbergh estate. There they just existed, Vasquez not being very ambitious, made no effort to farm the place.

On several occasions, Mr. Kozusko' s maid visited them, they are bringing her to and from Perth Amboy in their Dodge touring car. In order to reach their place, they had to pass the Lindbergh estate, and invariably Vasquez would make some remark about Lindbergh's wealth and what a haul one might get from the place, etc.

At the time, I was, on instructions of the Prosecutor, act-ing as a sort of a Liaison man between our office and the State Police at Hopewell.

Upon hearing Mr. Kozusko's story, I telephoned the State Police at Hopewell and spoke to one of the superior offi-cers in charge, i.e., Captain Lamb, told him the story and that I thought Vasquez was worth checking up on, in as much as I had known my informant for many years, that he was a repu-table businessman, and not a person seeking publicity, etc. The suggestion was not received very favorably. I was more or less curtly informed that every place and its occupants "For miles around" had been investigated.

Presuming on my acquaintance, I more or less argued with the captain, and the wind-up was a request for me to per-sonally investigate despite the fact that it was outside of my jurisdiction and approximately twenty-some miles from my headquarters and only two or three miles from theirs. I might add that this was not an unusual request as at the time, I was not very long off the State Department, and some of the offi-cers took advantage of good nature in requesting that I handle obvious "Crank" leads.

Accompanied by Mr. Kozusko, we located the prem-ises and found them vacant. Interviewed the nearest neighbor whose name I do not recall but who was obviously a high type of American farm wife. Before I had an opportunity to identify myself and state my mission, this woman wanted to know if I was an officer, that she had heard over her radio that officers were checking the entire neighborhood, that none as yet had called on her, and she immediately started to tell me about her recent neighbor, Vasquez. She said that since he had moved into the adjoining place, she had reasons to suspect him of various petty thefts, that the night following the Lindbergh kidnapping, they had moved away very suddenly, that she was so suspicious of their seemingly hurried departure in the night she had noted the name of the truck that moved their household furnishings. All the foregoing information was supplied without any prompting whatsoever on my part.

Obtaining the trucker's name, I went to the Lindbergh place and gave Captain Lamb all the data I had. For some inexplicable reason, there was no enthusiasm over the possibility of Vasquez having any knowledge of the crime. After some argument, I informed the officers present that I was policemen enough to at least check up with the trucker who came from Manville, Somerset County, and proceeded to do so. There I learned that Vasquez had left most of his belongings in storage and went to some small town in the coal-mining region of West Virginia by car. I telephoned the information to Hopewell and later submitted a written report covering the entire investigation.

Returning to New Brunswick, I took the matter up with Prosecutor Hicks, who could not see why our office should bear the expense, etc., of continuing the investigation. The Prosecutor did consent to my wiring the sheriff of the County in West Virginia requesting an investigation, etc., of Vasquez. After a delay of several days, I received a return wire advising that the town mentioned was some fifteen miles away and not within my correspondent's jurisdiction. I thereupon wired the sheriff of the adjoining County and, after a delay of several more days, received a very brief wire to the effect that Vasquez did not have the Lindbergh baby with him. I mention these details in order that you may readily see just how intelligent the investigation on that end must have been. To the best of my knowledge, nothing further was ever done on this.

Unfortunately, I am very hazy as to some of the details, etc., but I am sure that all of the necessary information can be obtained should you deem it necessary.

I am forwarding you this long drawn out and rather rambling epistle with the thought in mind that the information herein contained might possibly be of use to you if you are conducting a check-up of the Lindbergh neighborhood. Should the information be of any use whatsoever and you wish me to contact Mr. Kozusko, I shall be very glad to do so, or in the event you wish to have someone else do so, you will find him at Hall Avenue and Catherine Streets, Perth Amboy, New Jersey where he has a large furniture store. Incidentally, I am of the opinion that the housemaid mentioned is still in the employ of Mr. Kozusko.

In closing, may I congratulate you on the fact that the Governor saw fit to grant Hauptmann a reprieve? There is no doubt in my mind but that the reprieve can be taken as an expression of the Governor's confidence in you, and I sincerely trust that it is but the first step in an ultimate victory over those who obviously are anxious to mark the case closed with the execution of Hauptmann and thus cover up their own bungling methods.

In your letter, you mentioned being criticized and rebuked. Please don't let that deter you. I assure you that in my travels about the Metropolitan area, I have heard much favorable comment on both yourself and the Governor.

Trusting that you will not hesitate to call upon me if I can be of service and with the kindest personal regards, I am, Yours very truly,

Dennis J. Walsh

Note: I researched every name in this letter without any results. In his letter, Daniel J. Walsh tells us that he was an investigator for the Prosecutor in New Brunswick, N.J. Later he tells us it was Prosecutor Hicks, and he was acting as a sort of liaison man between his office and the State Police in Hopewell, N.J. I think Walsh's own story was a little vague, but his case story did warrant investigation since it was such a high-profile one. I learned from this letter that individual policing or investigation forces were very cost-conscious. They would push the investigation costs off on one another if possible. Somehow, I get a feeling that Walsh may have been fishing for employment.

FROM THE ELLIS PARKER LOST FILES

Vineland New Jersey

January 21st, 1936.

Ellis H. Parker. Esq.
Chief of County Detectives.
Burlington County, N.J., Mount Holly, N.J.

Dear Sir-:

Please allow me thru the medium of the mail to write your office a few lines with regards as to the Lindberg case. I presume that you daily receive many missives of a nature such as the one which I am now writing. I feel as many others that if the man Hauptmann is to be killed, let him be at least given a fair and impartial trial, and not just wipe him out of existence just because someone must be electrocuted to appease the desires of the Schwarzkopf forces. Please do not misunderstand me in my intentions. Schwarzkopf never will be able to confront a situation such as the Lindbergh case as he has never known how to conduct an investigation.

Before I get into the main reasons for writing your office, I hope you will allow me to state that if Lieutenant Allen L. Smith had anything to do with the prosecution in this case. I will say he is the Frame-Up man in the State Police for Schwarzkopf, he is the one who tried to plant a gun on me at the Court House in Mount Holly at the Rancocas Trial. Captain Schoeffel is the one who went to Germany for evidence. He in the early days of the State Police and ran away with another man's wife to Florida.

I have read in the press that Governor Hoffman is about to can the Kaiser Schwarzkopf in July, that should have been done years ago, in fact, he should have never been appointed to that office. I have been fighting the State Police for a pension due to me since April 1st, 1926, and the Kaiser has always engineered it, so I have not received notice of a hearing in my case.

I have been looking over some rulings on cases such as this one, and I will give you that ruling in the hope that in my small way, I have come to the assistance of the man Hauptmann. As I have been framed several times and you have to be framed yourself to best understand how this man feels, and it is my belief that he likewise has been framed and having been tried by the Hunterdon County Jury is just another reason one would agree that he was framed.

This is the question in law that I wish you to investigate and If it fits the case, I respectfully request that it be applied.

AMERICAN BILL of RIGHTS, - Due Process of Law, - Arrest without Warrant. - Trial by Jury. - This right of immunity from illegal restraint was brought to the American shores by our forefathers and became a part of the common law of this country. Subsequently, it was incorporated into the American Bill of Rights - as embraced in the first ten amendments to the Constitution of the United States - by the adoption of the fifth amendment, which provides that no person shall be deprived of his liberty without due process of law. And a similar provision exists in all the State constitutions.

Due process of law means that whatever the legal proceeding may be, it must be enforced by public authority, whether sanctioned by age or custom, or newly devised in the discretion of the legislative power, the furtherance of the general public good, which regards and preserves the principles of liberty and justice. It means that neither life, liberty, nor property can be taken, nor the enjoyment thereof impaired except in the course of the regular administration of the law in the established tribunals. Therefore, an arrest without a warrant, where one is required by law, is not due process of law. But if there is likely to be a failure of justice for want of a magistrate to issue a warrant, an officer may arrest without a warrant. And an arrest without a warrant, where one necessary may be waived by the defendant pleading guilty to the complaint contained in a subsequently issued warrant. Where a warrant is required by existing laws and authority to arrest without a warrant cannot be implied from a general grant to the municipality of power to arrest.

Please take note this is the one paragraph which is very important and should be carefully studied.

Relating to the higher crimes, due process of law is said to denote a lawful indictment or presentment of good and lawful men, and a public trial by jury, before a court of competent jurisdiction.

THEREFORE, WHERE THE COURT AT THE TRIAL OF ONE CHARGED WITH MURDER, DIRECTED AN OFFICER TO STAND AT THE DOOR OF THE COURT-ROOM "AND SEE THAT THE ROOM IS NOT OVERCROWDED, BUT THAT ALL RESPECTABLE CITIZENS BE ADMITTED,

AND HAVE AN OPPORTUNITY TO GET IN WHEN THEY SHALL APPLY," IT WAS HELD THAT THE RIGHT OF THE ACCUSED TO A PUBLIC TRIAL, GUARANTEED TO HIM BY THE CONSTITUTION, HAD BEEN VIOLATED.

Following this is the remarks as to CONSTITUTIONAL RIGHTS CANNOT BE WAIVED.

Following are the cases which are recorded relative to the points which I have tried to help by bringing them to your attention.

1.) Ex parte Virginia, 100 U.S. 366,65 L.ed.686. Read carefully this one.
2.) Muscoe v Com., 86 Va.443,10 S.E.534, State v James, 78 N.C.455; Trustees v Schroeder, 58 Ill.353.

I hope I have not bored you with this letter, and as I realize that it is up to all lovers of justice to see that everyone has the rights that which they are entitled to by their birthright, whether others believe in that way of thinking or not.

I have always said that the Lindberg baby was alive, and I will never believe otherwise. And when some men in the N.J. State Police say a man or woman is guilty. I always have my doubts. I know a man who is serving from 10-12 years in State Prison for a crime he did not commit, and one State Trooper had a hand in framing him in Millville N.J. his last name is Brady, for hold-up of a Bond Store.

Charging admission into the Hunterdon County Court House was a flagrant Moving Picture Violation of Hauptmann's rights if this were done during the entire trial.

Please let me hear from you not when you do take over the State Police, which I hope comes true. But write to me now, and I will promise not to divulge the contents. I will always be ready to assist when humanely possible, like in this case.

Enclosed is a news clipping in which the Lindberg boy and Bobby Dolfen does it not appear to you that the significant features depicted in the Dolfen boy are the same as of the Charles Lindberg Sr. and ask to give some concern to the wearing of the Aviators hat on the part of the Dolfen boy.

Very Respectfully submitted.

WILLIAM H. O'DONNELL SR.

239 Plum Street. Vineland New Jersey

Ellis Parker responded on 1-22-1936:

January 22, 1936

Mr. William H. O'Donnell, Sr.

239 Plum Street, Vineland, New Jersey

My Dear Friend:

I received your letter with enclosure, and I appreciate very much you're writing me what you believe concerning the rights of each individual, which was certainly abused.

The American Bar Association that met in California denounced the procedure in his case as being an insult to American Justice, and they were right.

The trial at Flemington was the greatest three-ring circus ever pulled off, and Hauptmann never had a chainman's chance. This case was a blot on the State Police for two and a half years. The fact of him having the money, being in the country illegally, made a wonderful subject. As far as Hauptmann having anything to do with the kidnapping and murder, it was not proven, the kidnapping and the extortion were two separate and distinct propositions. Hauptmann was never allowed to prove what he said was true, how he came in possession of the money. The letters that he received from Fisch from Germany, as they were in the same handwriting on the notes, might contain information that showed what Hauptmann said was true. That would have been the most valuable piece of evidence the state could have produced, but as a matter of fact, the state did not produce those letters of evidence, which shows that they robbed him of his rights. If they would do that in one thing, they wouldn't stop in any other thing.

My only interest, in this case, is one of justice. I didn't get in this for publicity or financial gain. All the investigation I have conducted has been at my own expense.

I wouldn't be the Superintendent of the New Jersey State Police under any consideration. They couldn't give me the job on a silver platter. I feel that the man that should be the head of the State Police should be a real Policeman. Schwarzkopf is a military man and an organizer. No one is capable of directing men in investigations unless he has had the experience himself. A man not knowing the job, the men under him can take advantage of him.

He puts me in the mind of the tired old man who was elected to be Justice of the Peace. His friends said to him, "You are going to take out your commission, aren't you?" he replied, "They elected me, didn't they?" and his friend said, "You don't know enough to be Justice of the Peace," the tired old man replied, "The people think I do," his friend again said, "Well suppose a person was brought in front of you charged with arson what would you do?" and the tired old man said, "I think I would make him support the children."

I don't care how much criticism I get in this case I know I am right, and I know what you have stated in your letter is a fact concerning the department. It would seem to me the bigger rat you are, the better you can get along in the kind of department.

Thank you for writing to me. I remain, Your friend,

Ellis H. Parker

Chief of Detectives

Note: In his letter, Ellis Parker calls the Hauptmann trial "an insult to American Justice." He also wrote that as far as Hauptmann having anything to do with the kidnapping and murder, "it was not proven."

Ellis wrote that "Hauptmann was never allowed to prove what he said was true, how he came in possession of the money. The letters that he received from Fisch from Germany, as they were in the handwriting the same as on the notes, might contain information that showed what Hauptmann said was true. That would have been the most valuable piece of evidence the state could have produced, but as a matter of fact, the state did not produce those letters of evidence, which shows that they robbed him of his rights."

What Ellis Parker wrote next is what Andy Sahol and I (Russell Lloyd) have been saying for some time about the Hauptmann prosecution team led by David Wilentz, "*If they would do that in one thing, they wouldn't stop in any other thing.*" A grave charge from Detective Ellis Parker, a man of such intense integrity. This evidence alone might have spared Hauptmann from the death penalty or have led to his being found innocent.

FROM THE ELLIS PARKER LOST FILES

Note: Pastor J. Matthiesen wrote to Major Frank Pease (1879-1959) on January 21, 1936. Wikipedia lists Pease's occupation as an Anti-Communist propagandist. He identified himself as a retired Army "Major," but he held no such rank. Pease served as a private until he was discharged in 1902. Pastor J. Matthiesen was aware of Frank Pease's book "The Hole in The Hauptmann Case," which he released in 1936. This was probably the reason the Pastor elected to write Major Frank Pease. The book alleged that Richard Hauptmann was framed for the Lindbergh kidnapping.

I counted 35 letters that Major Frank Pease wrote to Detective Ellis Parker beginning in December 1935, running out through August of 1936. All were after Governor Harold Hoffman suggested that Pease should write to the Detective. The majority of Pease's letters were mailed in March when the Lindbergh trial was at its peak. Ellis Parker did respond to most of them. I suspect that Pease was looking for information to fill up his book. After his book-writing career had fizzled out, Frank Pease turned his attention on Hollywood. He identified himself as a screenwriter, but there is no evidence that he ever wrote one or received screen credit.

Ellis Parker kept in touch with many individuals during his career. Usually by mail. He considered them as informants or what was commonly called stool pigeons in the law enforcement field. He was very tactful and kind in his replies to not endanger the relationship as he might need them in the future.

Frank Pease was one such contact. Frank Pease called himself Major Frank Pease, although it is doubted that he ever earned the Major's title. Wikipedia lists his occupation as "Anti-Communist propagandist" and noted that Pease was best known for his opposition to a Russian filmmaker that he felt contaminated his films with communist propaganda. Wikipedia documented Pease's work as a fascist and anti-Semitic pamphleteer. Wikipedia also noted that Pease had no organized following and was often dismissed as a crank.

Ellis kept a letter from Mr. Pease, his reply, and two pamphlets written by Pease in his file. The flyers were titled: What I learned in Nazi Germany & Campfires of Ghenghiz.

Frank Pease pressed Ellis to "SPILL THE WORKS" in his letter, referring to what he knew about the Lindbergh case. Pease's letter was filled with opinions and suggestions about the kidnapping case. In Ellis's reply, he advises, *"Nothing that I have done in my life has ever worried me. It is the things that I have been charged with that I didn't do that is annoying".*

Pease wrote to Ellis, saying: *"perhaps an Ellis H. Parker and Frank Pease to tell the story properly."*

Frank Pease also wrote, *"for much the same reason you are working for Hauptmann, namely, to tell the people the truth."*

Here is Pastor J. Matthiesen letter of 1-21-1936:

TRINITY LUTHERAN CHURCH
Trenton, N.J.
J. Matthiesen, Pastor

JANUARY 21, 1936

International Legion Against Communism
Major Frank Pease

Dear Sir: -

Received your brilliant exposition regarding the Lindbergh-Hauptmann case a few days ago. Thank you. There is no doubt a great deal of truth in what you say. However, your appraisal of Bruno Richard Hauptmann is absolutely wrong.

Hauptmann had nothing to do whatsoever with the case. He is not the Master Mind of the gang or a lone wolf, but he is an easygoing, unsuspecting, and credulous fellow who considers other people to be just as honest as himself.

This conclusion, I came to not only by learning to know him personally but also by studying his former life and business transactions with Mr. Isidor Fisch. I have read his extensive correspondence with the Fisch family, which was carried on after the Fisch's departure.

Since you are very interested in the case, let me sum up my findings.

His credulous and unsuspecting mind did not forewarn him in his association with Fisch. It did not tell him that he had to secure a good lawyer for his defense (in Germany, the

State-Attorney takes the case of the defense as well as that of the prosecution). He did not ask for a much-needed interpreter. If ever anybody was framed, it was Mr. Hauptmann.

Hauptmann is a sincere Christian man and speaks the truth even to his own hurt.

And now take the side of the prosecution.

It is a well-known fact that the best witnesses for the defense were intimidated by the prosecution Attorney. These witnesses were foreigners, and they are being constantly threatened with prosecution for perjury, were scared stiff, and remained away.

And what kind of evidence did the prosecution produce and with what cost? I understand the cost reaches the 2 million mark. And what did they get? The handwriting experts' very dubious findings have long since been proven to be contradictory to his own analysis regarding prevalent systems of penmanship. And the wood expert is not at all sure about his case since he is now asserting that he was never asked to examine the ladder itself but only that little piece which supposedly came out of Hauptmann's attic. And even that piece of wood was 4 inches too short and had to be planed off so that the grain of the wood would fit into the grain of the other wood from which it was supposedly taken. And the witness that placed Hauptmann in the vicinity of Hopewell, old blind Hochmuth and that Crook-Lier and thief Whithed. And the one that most famous of all, Jafsie, who would not and could not identify Hauptmann at first-but after having had a strong prompting by the prosecution, was ready to identify Hauptmann in Flemington. I am not trying to criticize Colonel Lindbergh. I have my greatest sympathy for him. Hauptmann has no ill-feeling against him. But to identify a voice in the manner in which Lindbergh identified Hauptmann's is preposterous, to say the least.

Now my dear Major, let me tell you this; among all the witnesses that the prosecution offered, there were only three that a degree of decency could be cross-examined, and these were Jafsie, Hochmuth, and Whited; all three made a sorry spectacle. Decency forbade a thorough cross-examination of the Lindbergh family—if that had been done by the defense-who knows-perhaps many things would have come to light. A cross-examination of experts is well-nigh impossible-but what the payment of $7000 and $15,000 included we do not know. In the meantime, the fate of the innocent Hauptmann hangs in the balance. May God save him.

Signed,

J. Matthiesen, Pastor

On 2-5-1936, Detective Ellis Parker wrote to Pastor J. Matthiesen:

February 5, 1936

J. Matthiesen, Pastor

259 Mercer Street, Trenton, N. J.

Dear Friend:

I received your letter and enclosures and wish to thank you for sending them to me. I have studied them carefully, and there is a possibility that there might be something there that would fit this case, however, I always feel that when a person takes a personal interest in a thing like Dr. Schwartz, he does not do it with the idea to deceive, but to assist, and I always consider any information sent to me confidential and give it every consideration.

I have spent more time and worked harder on this case on the side of Justice only, than any case I ever had in my life.

I am trusting and praying to God I will be able to bring it through. I remain, very truly yours,

Ellis H. Parker

Chief OF County Detectives

Note: Col. Mark O. Kimberling (warden of the New Jersey State Penitentiary in Trenton) wrote to Reverend John Matthiesen (Pastor of the Trinity Lutheran Church), who spoke German, to tell him that Bruno Richardson Hauptman requested that he visit him as a spiritual advisor on November 22, 1935. Anthony Scaduto (Scapegoat) describes Reverend John Matthiesen as praying with Hauptmann 5 minutes before his execution on April 3, 1936. Suddenly Hauptmann started speaking in German. When asked what he had said, the Reverend replied, "That he is absolutely innocent of the crime that has been laid at his door." After saying he was at peace with God, Hauptmann told Matthiesen in German to help his wife and child, fight to clear his name, and then said, "You may now open the door." That door led to the execution chamber.

We are suspicious because both Bruno Richard Hauptmann and Paul Wendel had a connection with the Reverend Matthiesen. Supposedly Wendel had been booted out of the Church for embezzling at an earlier date. There were also claims that the wood in the Church's basement matched that of the Lindbergh case's ladder. Hauptmann was a member of the Church and was ministered by Pastor Matthiesen before he was arrested. During the Hauptmann investigation, the floor of the Church was dug up. It was believed that the Lindbergh ransom money was buried there.

Isidor Fisch's connection to Hauptmann (their fur business) and the connection of Isidor Fisch to Paul Wendel (Wendel represented Fisch before he was disbarred) is too convenient to ignore.

FROM THE ELLIS PARKER LOST FILES

January 22, 1936

Mr. Frank Pearl

1873 Loring Place, Bronx, New York City

Dear Sir:

I received your letter. I wish to thank you for the thoughts, and I agree with you concerning this three-ring circus they had at Flemington, but I doubt whether anybody could ever get him cleared by that jury as he was guilty when he was arrested, and the money was found on him.

The part that Dr. Condon played on the case is that of a crazy individual, another one of the peculiar types that seem to fit into this case all the way through. To have a man sent to his death on such testimony is beyond conception. It looks to me as though if Hauptmann isn't executed pretty soon all the people involved in the case will be in Europe or some other place as they are taking to the woods. I can stay on for a while anyhow. I realize I am being criticized, but I don't mind. If I didn't get criticized, I would feel I was slipping.

Again, thanking you for writing me, I remain,

Very truly yours,

Ellis H. Parker

Chief of Detectives

Note: It is nice to see that even at this late date, approximately two months before the execution of Hauptmann, Ellis Parker still had a sense of humor. To come for Ellis was the Paul Wendel confession and Ellis's trial for kidnapping.

FROM THE ELLIS PARKER LOST FILES

January 22, 1936

Mrs. Marie N. Rhodes

333 North 12th Street, Philadelphia, Pa

Dear Friend:

Your letter addressed to Mr. Kimberling was shown to me today, and I feel as you do, it would be a sin to electrocute an innocent person. The kidnapping was one proposition, and the extortion was another. Hauptmann is a victim of circumstances, but there seem to be a lot of people who have a lust for blood, and they want to satisfy that lust in sacrificing this man's life.

I entered this case not to seek anybody's blood but for justice only. I feel that anyone that has information should tell it. In my judgment, this baby was never murdered but died of natural causes. It was undoubtedly kidnapped but was sick at the time and died.

I want to thank you for writing Mr. Kimberling as he feels as I do. There is something wrong here.

I remain, very truly yours,

Ellis H. Parker

Chief of Detectives

Note: This is a significant letter. Ellis Parker expresses his feelings on the Lindbergh case clearly in it. Ellis talks of the "lust for blood." The crime was horrible, first the kidnapping of an innocent child and then the child's violent death, the child of an American hero. Next was the discovery of the baby's mutilated corpse lying in the woods like some discarded trash.

When Hauptmann was arrested, he was already guilty in the public's mind. They wanted revenge, satisfaction and lusted for his blood. Those that caught Hauptmann tried to give the public blood. Hauptmann was tried in the press. Never had so many words been written about an American crime. Hauptmann was pronounced guilty and sentenced to death before he ever entered that courtroom. Ellis Parker and Governor Hoffman tried to save him. They were not successful. Ellis tried to impress on everyone that kidnapping, and extortion were separate crimes. He also consistently expressed his opinion that the baby died of natural causes and was not murdered. Ellis also believed that the baby was sick at the time of the kidnapping. Ellis even produced a signed confession from Paul Wendel that stated he was the real killer just before Hauptmann's execution was scheduled. Indeed, there was enough doubt to save Hauptmann from the chair. The Police and the Prosecution gave Hauptmann's blood to the public with manufactured evidence. Their reward was fame and wealth.

Ellis Parker was right. There was something wrong here.

FROM THE ELLIS PARKER LOST FILES

January 23, 1936

Thomas J. Pancoast

Miami Beach, Florida

Dear Friend,

I received your letter and should have written to you before but have been very busy. I appreciate the nice things that you said. I have none of the books you speak of, but the publishers of that book are Smith, Hass, and Smith, of New York City.

Now, as to the Lindbergh case, the only thing that they could actually prove was the fact that Hauptmann had the money. In my honest judgment, the kidnapping was one proposition, and the extortion was another. The Witnesses that were produced to identify him in or around Flemington were ridiculous. Hochmuth, who claimed he lived in New Jersey for the last ten years, I find that he was living in New York City in 1932 and received compensation for being blind. This man is actually crazy. Now as for Dr. Condon, anyone who reads the articles in the Literary Digest published under his signature and read the testimony given at the trial, also read the statements given to the State Police by him, and the statements given to the Department of Justice by him know that it wasn't Hauptmann that he met and dealt with. A person can only imagine what made him identify this man the fact that he had been taken for such a ride by these buncoed thieves and extortionists and placed him in a position where he might have been indicted for extortion in New York State might have a tendency to make him identify Hauptmann to save his own skin.

The handwriting experts have testified at the trial of Hauptmann went against every book that they have ever written. The handwriting on the original note and those that saw it could see that it was not the handwriting of Bruno Richard Hauptmann. Since I challenged them, they have started to sidestep.

The only interest I have in this case is one of justice, and I am glad the Governor of our state has enough courage in the face of the Yellow Journal's criticism, to stand up for what he knows is right. I certainly take my hat off to him.

If I'm ever down in Florida, which I hope to be someday, I will make it my business to give you a call. Again, thanking you for writing, I remain,

Your friend,

Ellis H. Parker

Chief of Detectives

Note: Ellis Parker's letter was addressed to the very wealthy Thomas J. Pancoast of Miami Beach. I learned on the internet that he was a city council member before being elected the mayor in 1918. He only lived for four more years after receiving Ellis Parker's letter. Pancoast was considered one of the most prominent men who had developed Miami and Miami Beach's City. He moved to the area after growing up in Moorestown, NJ.

Ellis points out again that Hochmuth was not a believable witness. He had stated that he had lived in New Jersey for ten years. Ellis Parker says that he found that Hochmuth was living in New York City in 1932 and that he had been collecting compensation for the blind. This was the same man who had testified in court that he recognized Bruno Hauptmann from across the street on the kidnapping night. Ellis calls him "actually crazy."

Ellis also questions Dr. John Condon's integrity. He opinioned that he might have identified Hauptmann to save his own skin from extortion charges. Ellis did not believe that it was Hauptmann that Condon dealt with in the Cemetery.

FROM THE ELLIS PARKER LOST FILES

January 24, 1936
P.O. Box 34, Elmira, N.Y.

Mr. Ellis H. Parker
Mt. Holly Court House, Mount Holly, N.J.

Dear Mr. Parker:

I am in receipt of your letter to-day. You can rest assured that I will be glad to give you my help at any time. I am particularly interested in all the work you handle. I am wishing you success in your present job.

Very truly yours,
Stanley L. Arndt

Stanley L. Arndt again writes to Ellis Parker on 3-18-1936:

March 18, 1936
P.O. Box 34, Elmira, N.Y.

Mr. Ellis Parker, Mount Holly, N.J.

Dear Mr. Parker:

I have read all of Jafsie's stories published in the "Liberty" magazine. Also, the last story of "New Evidence" from the interview, Jafsie, and a Liberty editor, was supposed to have had in Panama.

I hope I am not indecent or interfering with your duties. I assume that you are working with Governor Hoffman. I have great confidence in you both. I am here making a personal suggestion to you. Hoping it does not sound "dry" and "out of the question."

Why not, somehow, someway, you or a person could get together all of Jafsie's stories, take them into Hauptmann, let him have a piece of paper and pencil, and give him plenty of time to read and write, there in the cell alone. I think that after he learned what Jafsie has said, that the outcome of it would be a story from the cell. Or maybe I guess wrong. Of course, reading in the cell may be forbidden. You or the Governor might be able to do it. I hope you understand me and the point of view I have taken, only from reading.

I am one, and there are many others that are not satisfied with Jafsie's stories. We all have our own opinions, you know. Mr. Parker, will you please keep this very confidential. After all, it is just a suggestion. Thank you.

As I read on, I just cannot believe all of it, and I, the same as a lot of others, are wondering why Hauptmann does not give some kind of a story. I guess pretty near everything has already been tried.

However, in whatever turns up, I am wishing you both the best of luck and success.

Very truly yours,

Stanley L. Arndt

Ellis Parker writes to Stanley Arndt again on 3-23-1936:

March 23, 1936

Mr. Stanley Arndt

P.O. Box 34, Elmire, New York

Dear Friend Stanley:

Your letter received, and what you suggest is all right in a way, but Hauptmann could not answer anything that Jafsie puts in the paper, because if you will follow the articles, they are more or less haywire. When you try to outguess a person, who's mind rambles like his, it can't be done.

Condon is the kind of man who likes to be in the limelight, and he would sacrifice anything in the world to accomplish that want. That is my belief, however, we should not judge people too harshly, but when there is a life at stake, everyone should be on the level and not try to magnify such things.

Again, thanking you for writing to me, I remain,

Very truly yours,

Ellis H. Parker

Chief of County Detectives

Note: There is not much love here for Dr. Condon (Jafsie) in these letters. "Jafsie" is a troubling character in the Lindbergh crime story. I think more people believe he was part of the crime, meaning part of the Kidnap gang that abducted the baby rather than a sympathetic man who volunteered to be a State Police tool. That left Schwarzkopf and Charles Lindbergh to negotiate with the kidnappers and recover the child.

FROM THE ELLIS PARKER LOST FILES

"Western Trout"

January 24, 1936

Gov. Harold G. Hoffman,

Mr. Ellis H. Parker

World Importance

Gentleman,

The Lindbergh baby kidnapping case should be brought to a speedy conclusion by action on the part of officials of the

State of New Jersey, which will result in the destruction of the roots of all the kinds of hell on Earth. A scientific possibility.

This section on the part of officials of the State of New Jersey will eliminate nearly all kinds of crime from all parts of the world, a great scientific fact.

When Colonel Lindbergh learns the kidnapping of his baby resulted in abolition of crime from all parts of the world, he will, in a measure, feel repaid for the loss of his baby.

Read Carefully. God's lone ranger was born August 28, 1882, in Van Buren County, Iowa. This makes me the same age as that of the blind man now occupying the White House.

From my boyhood days on the farm, I have devoted all of my spare time to research work.

I am now in possession of a great scientific message for the people of America and other parts of the world, which is, at least, 1,000,000 times of greater importance to mankind that anything Abraham Lincoln ever said.

It is my ambition, if permitted to do so, to bring this message to the people of the world by means of radio broadcast from the State Capital building at Trenton, N.J.

Read Carefully. If I am permitted to broadcast this great scientific message to the people of the world from the Stare Capital Building at Trenton, N.J. one of the results will be the formation of a United States of the World. Trenton, New Jersey will become the capital city of the world.

Washington, D.C. will soon become a permanent monument to social affairs, ignorance, and waste in government.

If the State of New Jersey fails to assist me in getting my great scientific message to the people of the world, the last two stages of the destruction of the savage flesh-eating nations of the world will be another great World War and a great world famine. This is a scientific fact.

Read Carefully. The kidnapping and murder of the Lindbergh baby and nearly all other crimes committed in America for many years' past were only minor incidents in the destruction of the people of the world by fire, indirectly.

Please Read Carefully. The World War of 1914-18 was a major incident in the destruction of the people of the world by fire, directly and indirectly.

The destruction of the people of the world by fire, directly or indirectly, centers around the scientific fact that the savage hell-producing slaughterhouses can operate only through the insane use of fire.

Savage mankind does not eat, except in rare cases, the raw flesh of its invaluable animal and bird friends. Ask any cook about this.

Read Carefully. The hell producing slaughterhouse business conducted by the institute of meatpackers began as a sausage and insane religious rite, which consisted in the beginning of animals and birds as a sacrifice to a pagan god.

Read Carefully. Read the history of the beginning of modern savagery, the prevalence of all kinds of crime everywhere, the World War and the world depression in your bible, the latter part of the 8th chapter of Genesis, and the 1st part of the 9th chapter. Noah burned animals and birds as a sacrifice to a pagan God. No greater of true God would be pleased with such an insane act.

This insane use of fire started the production of all kinds of hell on Earth. Satan has been laughing heartily for many years' past.

Read Carefully. It was the institution of the greater and true God that man, as the agent of God, should exercise intelligent and just "dominion over" the many wonderful, invaluable, and beautiful creations of God in nature (natural resources). This stands to reason.

If the State of New Jersey can find $100 for my railroad fare and hotel expenses, I will come to Trenton at once and bring to a dramatic conclusion the Lindbergh baby kidnapping case.

Yours for swift action,

James R. Clark
God's Lone Ranger,
President World Recovery Administration
624 North Parkside Ave. Chicago, ILL

Confidential Postscript: - J. Edgar Hoover knows as much about the prevention and elimination of crime as does a newborn mouse, born dead.

Note: You might have guessed this. James R. Clark, calling himself God's Lone Ranger, wrote "Very Important" outside the envelope. Of course, he underlined it. I am reasonably sure that Ellis Parker did not send him the $100 traveling expense asked. Although, it seemed like a bargain when he threw in solving the Lindbergh crime. All I can add is that he was great at underlining.

FROM THE ELLIS PARKER LOST FILES

People's Store
Ladies and Men's Clothing
631 McKean Avenue
Charleroi, PA.,

January 26, 1936
Mr. Ellis Parker,
Burlington Co., Trenton, N.J.

Dear Sir:

I am writing this letter, which I hope may be of some assistance in your investigation of the Lindbergh case. I have studied the case very closely right from the beginning. I have versed my opinion in a letter addressed to the investigating force c/o Lindbergh, in which I stated that I thought the kidnapping was the work of an amateur and that I believed it was done by one or more of the household personal and I suggested the butler Whatley whom I suspected.

I based my theory on the grounds that some jealousy may have entered against that lover of Betty Gow, whose name I believe was described as Johnson. I thought it would be reasonable to believe that some act of vengeance may have been done against Betty Gow to make her lose her job so as to avenge her lover Johnson and suggested that they search the premises beginning right at the building and for a few miles around that the baby may be found. My common sense dictated to me that an amateur in the act of vengeance wouldn't carry the baby very far from the place of abduction.

I didn't believe it was the act of an experience underworld organization, for they would have made more specific and prompt negotiations. My theory seemed to prove correct.

I don't believe that Hauptmann is the actual kidnaper of the baby. I do believe that he was the recipient of the ransom and that the ransom was engineered by his able tutor, Jafsie, who was the actual brains of the extortion plot that was developed later as a result of the kidnapping.

I also believe that Jafsie was the writer of the notes and copied these notes from the handwriting of Hauptmann very identical. He could have made these exact imitations of Hauptmann's handwriting, which was the logical disguise he would use. When Jafsie visited Hauptmann in his cell, he demonstrated some of the circles or whatever symbols were used in writing notes.

I believe a close check up on Jafsie's handwriting by directing him to rewrite these notes as those supposed to have been written by Hauptmann, would reveal this fact.

I would suggest that you make Jafsie write similar notes and make similar circles with subdivisions. This writing should be under close watch by psychologists and handwriting experts, watch his reaction while writing and how much he is trying to avoid exact imitations. I am firm in my belief that Jafsie and Hauptmann are simply the ransom extortionists but to prove it is another angle. The specimens of Jafsie's handwriting through expert examination will throw you on the right track, and once you have the drop on Jafsie, the rest will be easy.

It is also possible that the story of extortion and the plot was originated by Hauptmann in this fashion; Hauptmann taking advantage of the kidnapping act, could have confronted Jafsie whom he probably knew, telling him that he knew or has in his possession the Lindbergh baby, and all he needs is some brainy man like Jafsie to act as the main negotiator about the ransom. Jafsie not knowing that the baby was dead, nor did Hauptmann know that the baby was not alive, and they took a chance in an extortion plot that netted them the sum which was paid. This, of course, had been done by either party with no murderous intentions, and when it was discovered that the baby was murdered, Jafsie for one stepped out of the game. He probably didn't want any blood money. Hauptmann was more greedy for money, and he didn't care of the outcome but hoped to enrich himself and held on to the loot.

At the trial, Jafsie called Hauptmann, a ransom snatcher. He was mad at him because Hauptmann deceived him that the baby was alive. I firmly believe that from every indication, one of these theories is correct or at least nearly correct and that nothing could sway me from believing that Jafsie had a finger in the pie and that he is the man you want to examine with close scrutiny.

How an efficient police force and investigators can regard Hauptmann as the lone wolf in the case, is beyond my conception. The authorities on crime have regarded Hauptmann as a cunning criminal, and they have attributed this to his offenses committed in Germany. This sort of offenses can be portrayed to a jury to effect a conviction, but for analyzing the degree of a criminal, a killer and a kidnapper such as in the Lindbergh case, this sort of minor offenses would hold no water in determining the degree of a criminal engaged in kidnapping.

The check-up on Hauptmann shows that he in company of another man, snatched a purse from a woman. This offense is a very serious one in Germany, and many persons by a repetition of such crimes have served from 10 to 20 years. In this country, we have them into the thousands walking the streets as respectable politicians, and some have even held and are now holding jobs as high officials in public life. What I mean to point out that his past activities have no bearing upon a kidnapping and murder case.

In checking up his record in the United States, we find his illegal entry. This has no bearing upon criminal tendencies. It merely shows that this man had no means of immigration from a country of starvation to a better land, which is regarded on the outside as the land of milk and honey.

There is further indications that he engaged in an honest hard working occupation as a carpenter. It shows that he was not a trained carpenter. I can answer this from experience from foreign schools which I have personally attended, that every pupil engages in some manual training which they freely designate as a trade upon arriving in this country and most of them make a good bluff at it until they become proficient. However, it shows that he was working steadily in honest occupations and that he was very thrifty, in fact, he was a miser, very greedy for money. From this, we may draw our conclusion that he would be the person that would willingly engage in an extortion plot with a view of getting rich quick.

Hauptmann is not an educated person, but as a German who traveled extensively, he would understand well enough that it takes a better-trained person in the American language and the knowledge of negotiating with authorities than a person like himself. He is equipped with enough knowledge and common sense to know that he himself is not big enough to secure $50,000 of extortion money from a person like Lindberg who has the whole world of police protection and backing, and it is logical to believe that he sold his idea to a man with brains and ability such as this Gentlemen Jafsie.

I am not interested in saving Hauptmann. I believe that if he is only guilty of extortion or even of obstruction of justice, he should ride. One criminal less in this county will do some good, but I believe two criminals in the plot would do still better.

If I had the funds and would be permitted to enter into the investigation, I shall concentrate on the theories above outlined.

Very truly yours,
Emil Huttner

<u>Note</u>: The writer of this letter addressed to Ellis Parker was Emil Huttner. Emil was born in Germany in 1891. He was 45 years of age when he wrote this letter. He became a naturalized American citizen in 1915. Emil married Ella Huttner, and the union produced at least two sons. Emil was the proprietor of the People's store in Charleroi, Pa.

Emil's logic was sound. He called the kidnapping amateurish. I agree with him. The entire case, the kidnapping, the investigation, the arrest, the extortion, and especially the conduct of the Prosecution and the Defense was amateurish. We should all be very ashamed of America's criminal justice system's performance during the Lindbergh case.

<u>Of all the letters found in the Ellis Parker Lost Files, the following was in the worst condition. However, I can reconstruct most of it as follows:</u>

January 29, 1936

Emil Huttner

631 Mcken Avenue, Charleroi, Pa.

Dear Friend,

I like yourself are interested only in Justice. When this thing occurred, being in the business I am in naturally attracted me, and I started to study from every angle of it from March 1, 1932 and have continued up to the present day. I am positively satisfied in my own mind that Bruno Hauptmann had nothing to do whatever with the kidnapping, as the kidnapping was one thing and the extortion another. There is a great possibility that he was a victim as far as the money is concerned with positive facts I have gained. If I thought for one minute that he was guilty of taking money from someone who had their child stolen, I would say "hang the son-of-a-bitch," but that would not clear up the case. Jafsie, who had speaking engagements ahead, all of a sudden, took a trip to South America. He is just one of those individuals that, by taking a chance, could gain fame and him being that kind of individual that could easily be picked by extortionists as an instrument to further their plan.

I personally know the statements Jafsie gave the State Police and the statements he gave to the government, and the magazine articles he has written, and the testimony he gave at the trial, that everyone is different, showing that the man has hallucinations, and therefore a man's life being taken on such testimony is ridiculous.

As to Hocksmith, he swore that he lived in this state for ten years, as a matter of fact, in 1932, he made application for help in New York City. It was investigated and discovered that he had cataracts on both eyes, was going blind, and received a compensation from New York City. I have affidavits from the Health Bureau of New York. The strange thing happened in the court when they led Hocksmith down from the stand to identify an individual. The lights went out, apparently at the correct time, and when the officer stopped in front of Hauptmann the lights again went on again, it was then that Hocksmith pointed Hauptmann out, a most peculiar dramatic scene enacted in a court of Justice.

Very truly yours,

Ellis H. Parker

Chief of Detectives

Note: Ellis Parker's letter indicates that he felt John Condon (aka Jafsie) was not a credible man. When Ellis tells of Jafsie suddenly taking a trip to South America, he alluded to individuals that were seeking fame. Jafsie left on the eve of the hearing called by the New Jersey Court of Pardons to decide upon Hauptmann's plea for a commutation of the death sentence he was facing.

Hocksmith referred to in this letter is most likely Amandus Hochmuth, as reported in the newspapers of the time. I think that the confusion over his name was caused by inadequate translation from German at some point.

According to Hauptmann Defense Attorney Ed Reilly, Hochmuth was an 84-year-old man with a bad memory, poor eyesight and was once in an asylum. Hochmuth loved to sit and watch an intersection near the Lindbergh home. He claims to have seen a vehicle brake suddenly to avoid the ditch at the intersection at about noon. At the Hauptmann trial, he pointed his finger at Bruno Hauptmann to indicate that Hauptmann was the Green Sedan driver that had stalled that day. As the driver attempted to restart the vehicle, he saw a ladder in the car. In the courtroom, Hochmuth pointed his finger at Hauptmann when asked who the man he saw with the ladder was. Ellis Parker tells of how that was pre-arranged in his letter to Emil Huttner to ensure that the elderly, nearly blind man pointed at the right man.

Emil Huttner's letter to Ellis Parker on 1-30-1936:

> Charleroi, Pa.
>
> January 30, 1936
>
> Mr. Ellis H. Parker
>
> Chief of Detectives, Mount Holly, N.J.
>
> Dear Mr. Parker:
>
> I hasten to answer your letter of January 29, for I can see how well you have analyzed the Hauptmann case in which I hope you will be able to show the world the true facts in the matter.
>
> Unfortunately, you do not seem to have the support of your state. Your District Attorney's Office and your State Police seem to have a firm opinion in the case. I gather this information from our Pittsburgh Press, who are very much in favor of your investigation, and the investigation which has been instituted by Governor Hoffman.
>
> I feel sure that in honest and sincere thinking, everyone connected with that case or anyone who had a keen interest in this Lindbergh case, believes that Jafsie is the main link in the extortion. I personally cannot see it in any other way.

Your time in this investigation is limited, and you must begin some real action at once and finish the first real act before the curtain drops on Hauptmann. It will require the cooperation of your state executives, to give you every available means of support.

Your case must begin with a base of determination of the implicitly of the party whom you suspect as the main link in the extortion plot. You are not interested at this instance in the kidnapping. You will leave this for later.

Curtain: Jafsie, the engineer of the extortion plot, the intermediary, takes advantage of the kidnapping, and gets an idea of how to secure easy money from a grief-stricken family. Another person who is in need of money is enlisted in the case. It may have been Fisch or someone else. I would think it was Fisch because of the connection with Hauptmann.

History of Fisch shows that he was a real concealed petty business crook and lived by his wits from using other people's capital in his business. Fisch was no fool and although not very educated so as to be able to engineer a crime or serve as a contact man, he was shrewd enough to be a recipient of the ransom, or still smarter he used this close friend of his, for the mere little job to receive the money for Jafsie.

P.S. I will appreciate your further comment on the case, and I shall be glad to answer any question that may be of assistance in the case I am interested in the solution of the crime, which I believe has not been solved to this writing.

I would prefer to believe that there was more than just Condon and Hauptmann on that Cemetery to take the money. In fact, Mr. Lindbergh affirms the third party with a handkerchief as the probable lookout man.

It is probable that Fish being a fur peddler must have visited Jafsie home before and formed an acquaintance, and it may be possible that Hauptmann came as the third party and met Jafsie at the Cemetery from which the ransom was paid. I am therefore convinced that there were three in the party, including Jafsie, Fisch, and Hauptmann.

It is probable that Hauptmann was enlisted by Fisch to act as the distributor of the hot money. Fisch or Jafsie were too shrewd to take the chance not only because it was marked ransom money but mainly because it was gold certificates as well.

Hauptmann, in the act of interchanging the money, may have betrayed his engineer by playing it freely on the stock market and not sharing as agreed. Bruno having no fear of being the murderer, and the actual kidnaper played a little more freely with the blood money that as actual killer and kidnapper would.

Fisch knowing that he had no chance to live much longer and that if stays here much longer he would die away from his people; he went out of the picture.

We have no knowledge whether he took his share with him or what was done with the third parties share, for nothing definite has been disclosed from the evidence thus so far presented.

The third act is the act which you must play the main part, and here is what you must do in order to prove to the world that there was more than one party in the game.

You have conflicting stories given by Jafsie in his publications that differ from the evidence which convicted Bruno Hauptmann. This, in my opinion, should warrant further questioning or probable detention. If so, do it at once. Bring this gentleman before the most competent experts you can

ANDREW SAHOL & RUSSELL LLYOD

secure for the state and have him write notes and symbols, the very kind that were presented at the trial. I believe these notes were imitated by him personally, and that they used Hauptmann for the patsy to take the rap in the event they are caught. The first click of evidence you have let the world know through the press, and the eyes of the world will see the rest and your case will be a cinch. Make up your mind that justice has not completed its real task and use the very best there is in you. Show your state and your people as well as the whole world that mistakes in administering justice are possible. We are not trying to save Hauptmann. We want the brain trust in the plot, and you are on the right trail. Request your governor to give his support in every respect and to get Jafsie back before the curtain drops.

Wishing you success, I am, sincerely yours,

Emil Huttner

Note: Emil Huttner began this letter stating his opinion that the New Jersey District Attorney and the New Jersey State Police were not supporting Detective Parker's efforts to bring forward the Hauptmann case's actual facts. We know it was more than just not supporting Ellis's efforts from the information we have found in THE ELLIS PARKER LOST FILES. Ellis was seen as an adversary to their investigation and, in their desperate attempt to prove Bruno Hauptmann was guilty. Ellis knew that they had his phone tapped and were reading his mail. They were extremely powerful, had more tools and more personnel than Ellis to accomplish their goal of executing Bruno Hauptmann. Revise that, not their goal of execution, their goal of fame and fortune for themselves.

Emil Huttner describes the steps Detective Ellis Parker would need to prove who the guilty parties are. They are very well presented. The only problem is that these moves would need the support of the very people that were blocking his every step.

FROM THE ELLIS PARKER LOST FILES

January 29, 1936

Col. Mark O. Kimberling

Prison Warden, Trenton, N.J.

My dear sir:

The reason of writing to you instead of Gov. Hoffman, which I've bombarded so often with some of my statements which I found important enough to remark. I've decided to let you know a few things in regard to Fisch, the man in quest in the Lindbergh case. You see, I am the party you probably read of at the beginning when I gave a statement to the press as my reports three years ago, about a gang of men in a hotel I live, was the noted members of the crime. In return I was jailed and called anything short a criminal myself until Washington stepped in and sort of apologized, I was mostly taking the place of the manager in his absence and had to watch comers and goers so Fisch passed me often in the hall so that I could not help noticing his frequent cough also being dressed in a brown overcoat and hat. His lower face was resembling Hauptmann's. Most of lean and pointy. You will remember that Condon particularly mentioned the cold on John. He. Met. I didn't mention that for Hauptmann's sake but correct the independence on the general mind by the defense of state, although I repeated that two places. Schwarzkopf called at the hotel managers as I asked him, he did not care to interview me, but the local police had me jailed and tried to bribe me. Most of my mail is confiscated since.

Miss H. Kinch to Nurse

1606 Pacific Ave., Atlantic City, N. J.

Note: The Colonel Miss H. Kinch wrote to was 2nd Colonel Mark O. Kimberling (1886-1964), who later replaced Colonel H. Norman

Schwarzkopf on the orders of then-Governor Harold Hoffman soon after Richard Hauptmann was executed on April 3, 1936. Hauptmann was 36 years old. Colonel Kimberling served in the NJ State Police from 6-17-1936 until 9/22/1941. According to a 1977 New York Times article, a long-suppressed 5000-word letter was found after his death.

The poignant letter was written to his mother by Richard Bruno Hauptmann shortly before his execution on April 3, 1936. In his letter, Hauptmann detailed his claim of innocence in the 1932 kidnapping of the Lindbergh baby. Sadly, his mother, Pauline, living in Kamenz, Germany, never received the letter from her condemned son. The letter was found in the papers left by Colonel Kimberling, the warden of Trenton State Prison at the time of Hauptmann's execution. In a note Kimberling left attached to then-Governor Harold G. Hoffman, Kimberling wrote: "I am of the opinion that it might receive some press comment over in Germany, which might result in some unfavorable reaction, or, at least in placing us in an embarrassing position for having released it from state prison."

Colonel Kimberling retained the letter in Hauptmann's German script with a translation made by his prison staff in his personal files until he died in 1964. Then his wife kept it until she died. It was finally disclosed in the March 28, 1977, edition of the New York Times.

Isidor Fisch again turns up as a suspect in Miss H. Kinch's letter, repeating an assertion made many times of Isidor Fisch's bad cough. She describes Colonel Schwarzkopf as not caring to interview her. Alarmingly, Miss Kinch contends that the local police jailed her and tried to bribe her. She ends her letter to Colonel Kimberling, claiming that her mail was being confiscated since.

Ironically, Ellis Parker was being watched at this time as well. Ellis's phones were being tapped, and his mail was being intercepted during his investigation of the Lindbergh case.

FROM THE ELLIS PARKER LOST FILES

663 West 178th. Street, New York City

Jan. 31st. 1936

Mr. Ellis Parker,

Mount Holly, New Jersey,

Dear Sir:

May I call your attention to what I consider a very important angle in the Lindbergh Kidnaping case of 1932?

It has been stated that Col. Lindbergh was not convinced of being in contact with the actual kidnaper by the presentation of the "sleeping suit," nor by the fact that Dr. Condon had a note bearing the same symbol, "a poor imitation" (Condon) as the one found on the windowsill in the nursery. But Dr. Condon told him that the kidnaper said he had left a note in the crib. On March 6th, one of the papers recalled this note left in the crib.

On May 13th, the first issue of the Bronx "Home News" stated that the original ransom note bore a "code" (1-2-3-4) (According to Dr. Condon's letters of 1933-1934- (Money-kidnaper-John-Baby) No newspaper picked this out of the skies!

If Col. Lindbergh took this note out of the crib and kept its contents secret, then he knew Dr. Condon was dealing with the right party. Dr. Codon must have known the kidnaper before the crime was committed. His knowledge of the code bears this out by the fact that he used it in 1933-34, and, it must have been he, (Condon) who inadvertently spilled the "beans" to the "Home News" in May 1932.

Very truly yours,

Margaret Levett

<u>Note</u>: Even today, Dr. John F "Jafsie" Condon (1860-1945) is one of the most suspicious characters in the Lindbergh case. The retired 72-year-old New York City schoolteacher, learning of the kidnapping, decided to directly contact the criminals through his hometown newspaper, "The Bronx Home News." He had contributed to the letters section of the paper for many years. Condon later nicknamed "Jafsie," had advertised in the newspaper to become an intermediary between the Lindbergh family and the kidnappers. Condon used "Jafsie" as a code name to be known to the kidnappers.

Condon received a letter from the kidnappers the very next evening. His proposal was accepted quickly, making him, after Charles Lindbergh's approval, a key figure in the ongoing investigation. Condon delivered the $50,000 ransom to the kidnappers. He was a key witness at the Hauptmann trial identifying the accused man as "Cemetery John." Without his testimony identifying Hauptmann, it is doubtful that Hauptman would have been convicted. At first, Condon did not recognize Hauptmann as the man he spent an hour with on the Cemetery bench. Condon later changed his mind after counseling with the Hauptmann prosecution. He claimed he could not be confident since a man's life was in the balance. Dr. Condon authored "Jafsie Tells All" a few years after Bruno Hauptmann was electrocuted, telling his side of the "Crime of the Century."

FROM THE ELLIS PARKER LOST FILES

February 1, 1936

Mr. Frank Ryan

Camden Courier, Camden, NJ

Dear Friend:

I enclose you a letter that you should have investigated from your record office, as it says on the back of the envelope J.J. David Stern, Philadelphia, Record, Philadelphia, Pa. If Davy Stern is going up in the district as he says in the communication, I think t ought to be looked into. Frank, if one of your men from the record office lives up that way get him to see who this guy is, and what it is all about, tell him I sent him. I tried to locate this person and haven't been able to do it.

Very truly yours,

Ellis H. Parker

Chief of County Detective

We found the following letter in Ellis Parker's files addressed to Frank Ryan 8-21-1936

COURIER POST NEWSPAPERS

EVENING COURIER --- MORNING POST
THE COURIER CO.
COVER HALF A STATE
Camden, N.J.

Aug. 21, 1936

Ellis H. Parker

Chief of County Detectives, Mt. Holly, N.J.

Dear Ellis:

I certainly was pleased to get your letter this week, but at the same time, it made me feel somewhat like a heel. I surely don't want my friends in the Parker office EVER to feel that I have deserted them, of that my friendship is anyway less sincere than it has always been. I am still 100% for Ellis Parker and everything he does. I still agree with him in the Hauptmann matter, and I still believe I am going to live long enough to see Ellis Parker's judgment in that case validated.

I know how badly you and Anna feel over the tragic windup of the Wendel matter. It surely was a miserable break after all the hours you folks gave to the case. And it was just as miserable, if not more so, for you folks to have such a rotten batch of criticism leveled at you – as a reward for your efforts in trying to clear up the Lindbergh case. No one knows of your sincerity in the matter anymore than I do. I had enough personal contacts, in that case, to know that you were doing what you thought right and just. But it is just one of those breaks that come to all of us once in a while.

I am terribly sorry I haven't had the opportunity to get up to see everybody for several months. Naturally, I have been quite busy trying to get a home furnished and take care of my job here, too. Running two newspapers, particularly in these exciting news days, is no mean job. It takes a lot of personal attention to keep things moving properly, and I'm just that conscientious that I try to keep in close contact with everything that I believe to be important.

I can appreciate how upset you and Anna, and young Ellis, have been. I know it was time when "a feller needs a friend," and I also realize that it is such times that a man or woman likes to find their friends at their elbows once in a while, at least. I also know that I certainly did not measure up to the standard of a real friend in that respect during the tough days. However, I'm hoping I will be forgiven and that everything will turn out in such a manner that we can have that celebration we planned so many times.

I have felt badly over some of the editorials we have carried in the Courier-Post on the Hauptmann matter, but it was something I could not control. That's only how some of the editorial writers felt. And none of them are the fellows who know you. But it will be all the sweeter if things turn out the right way some of these days.

My kindest regards to everybody with the hope that I will be seeing you soon.

Sincerely,

Frank (Frank Ryan)

<u>Note</u>: The first letter, written by Ellis Parker, was dated 2-1-1936. Bruno Richard Hauptmann was executed on April 3, 1936, approximately two months later. Only days before the execution, the Paul Wendel signed confession was presented to the Hauptmann prosecution. Frank Ryan wrote the second letter (above) on 8-21-1936.

In the February letter, Ellis asked Frank Ryan to investigate a lead he was concerned about that was somehow connected to a publication named "The Philadelphia Record." Unfortunately, we are not sure of the outcome. Ellis's relationships with the press and other newspapers have been well documented. The Courier-Post was located in the bordering Camden County. Ellis was the Chief of Detectives in Burlington County; however, his investigations often led to many of the Counties surrounding him. Much of Ellis's fame was earned by the newspaper coverage of papers like the Courier-Post. Ellis was known to have a warm relationship with many reporters and publishers. It is apparent he had that with Frank Ryan until his employer overruled him.

When Ellis Parker was accused of kidnapping Paul Wendel, he was forced to defend himself vigorously against David Wilentz and his prosecuting team. Ellis had been financing his work on the Lindbergh case and the Wendel case. His investigation led to Wendel's signed confession that he soon rescinded after speaking with Wilentz. Times were hard for Ellis. He was sadly forced into selling some of his properties to finance himself. The media was fickle, and Ellis wasn't always being portrayed as an innocent man. Still, we, Andrew Sahol and Russ Lloyd, believe Ellis Parker innocent of the Wendel kidnapping and the Paul Wendel confession true.

There is a possibility that the J.J. David Stern referenced by Ellis Parker is Julius David Stern (1886-1971). He was a reporter for the Philadelphia Public Ledger, who purchased the *New Brunswick Times* newspaper that then launched him into a life of newspaper ownership. Stern was best known as the liberal Democratic publisher of the *Philadelphia Record* from 1928 to 1939. In 1919 he had acquired the *Camden New Jersey Morning Courier*. Again in 1926, Stern acquired the *Camden Morning Post* and then combined them to create the *Courier-Post*. The paper is still publishing to this day. Of note is Stern's purchase of the *New York Evening Post*, which he owned from 1933 to 1939. Stern shortened the name of the paper to the iconic *New York Post*. There are too many coincidences not to suspect that Julius David Stern was not the man Ellis Parker was seeking in his letter of 2-1-1936.

FROM THE ELLIS PARKER LOST FILES

February 1, 1936

M.A. Carpenter

829 Orange Street, Yuba City, California

Dear Friend:

I received your letter and found your other communication. I want to thank you for the thoughts you express. Unfortunately, our State Police are run by two or three men who have no police or detective experience, and the thing that appeals to them more than anything else is strong-arm methods. They waited for someone to call them on the phone to tell them where it was, bring it in, and have medals pinned on them. It wouldn't matter how many suggestions made to them or how good they were, if they wouldn't strike their fancy, they would class you or anyone else in the line of cranks. In the early history of this case, communications were often referred to as cranks, which closed the door from any person for writing their thoughts or assisting with information.

The establishing of police headquarters at the Lindbergh home was a great mistake, as it shut off any possible contact that might afford to get the baby back alive, which in my thought is and was the best thing to be done as no mother or father would sacrifice their own child to satisfy some law on the statute book.

Again, thanking you for writing me, I remain, very truly yours,

Ellis H. Parker

Chief of County Detectives

<u>Note</u>: The method of refusing to consider any outside suggestions, leads, or other possible motives continued up to the Hauptmann execution. Establishing the police headquarters at the Lindbergh home was also wrong because Charles Lindbergh now had complete control of the investigation.

FROM THE ELLIS PARKER LOST FILES

February 1, 1936

Miss Margaret Levitt
663 West 178th Street, New York City

Dear Friend,

Your letter received, and I want to thank you for your thoughts, they are very good. Dr. Condon's part played in the particular extortion proposition is far from being explained. He visited the home of Col. Lindbergh and knew all about the note and was just a tool in the hands of the extortionists. He was the right kind of a subject for a bunch of slickers to work on to make a damn fool of, and humiliated before the world, as was done, and it is possible his identification of Hauptmann was to square himself with the public, but he knows down in his heart the identification was false.

Thank you for writing to me, and assure you that I appreciate letters from people of thoughts like yours, I remain,

Very truly yours,

Ellis H. Parker
Chief of County Detectives

<u>Note</u>: It is apparent that Ellis Parker wasn't a Dr. Condon fan. Ellis went on in this letter to question Condon's identification of Hauptmann and his motive for making it. Ellis Parker's comments on the ransom note are interesting. It should be remembered that Ellis believed that only the first note was genuine.

The ones following were questionable, in his opinion. He believed different people created them.

FROM THE ELLIS PARKER LOST FILES

SAMUEL A. KANTER
ATTORNEY AND COUNSELOR
Suite 1103-11 S. LaSalle St., Chicago
Telephone Central 6044

February 4, 1936

Ellis H. Parker, Esq.

Detective, Mount Holly, New Jersey

Dear Mr. Parker:

I am enclosing herewith a copy of a letter mailed to the Honorable Governor, Harold G. Hoffman, on this date. The contents of the same are self-exoplanetary.

I would appreciate an early reply from you.

Very truly yours,

Samuel A. Kanter

Following is the letter that was promised to Ellis Parker:

February 4th, 1936

Hon. Harold G. Hoffman

Governor of the State of New Jersey

Trenton, New Jersey

RE: BRUNO HAUPTMANN

Honorable Sir:

You no doubt are aware of the fact that I am the attorney who, on Wednesday, January the 8th, 1936, submitted to Your Excellency and to the other members of the Court of Pardons many pages of Depositions, Affidavits, Statements and Exhibits pertaining to the above. Among those submitted was the Deposition of Frank L. Davis; the other Depositions, Affidavits, and Statements were from other individuals and were of a nature lending to corroborate the statements of Frank L. Davis, whom I did, and still, represent. From that date until the present day, I have not communicated with Your Excellency, inasmuch as I was of the opinion that Your Excellency would give the matter the proper consideration, and if the same would warrant an investigation that Your Excellency would have the same investigated. I further felt that Your Excellency was extremely busy with the Hauptmann investigation, and for that reason, I reluctantly hesitated to disturb you with any unnecessary communication.

I had, and still have, every confidence that you, as a citizen and as the Governor of the State of New Jersey, are doing everything possible to bring out any and all facts surrounding the Lindbergh matter.

My reason for writing this letter is explained as follows: This afternoon, Frank L. Davis again visited me at my office. He informed me that he has additional information that he did not previously disclose and that he is anxious to convey any and all information that he possesses if any, to Your Excellency only in person, in the presence of myself as his counsel. He showed me certain Affidavits, four of them; one of these Affidavits is signed by himself bearing the date of April 28, 1932, in which Affidavit, among other things and names, he includes the name of Isadore Fisch, Cecil Snyder, and others, as being implicated in the Lindbergh matter. Another Affidavit signed by Mabel E. A. Davis and bearing the date of April 28, 1932, corroborates somewhat the Affidavit of Frank E. Davis. The third Affidavit bearing date of May 5, 1932, and signed by Rose Murfin, is of the same nature.

The Fourth Affidavit, signed by Frank L. Davis again bearing the date of June 2, 1934, is somewhat of a similar nature. All these Affidavits contain the name E. J. Cunningham, Notary Public, and have the Notary Public Impression or seal containing the name Edward J. Cunningham, Notary Public, Cook County. I have not gone into the genuineness of these Affidavits; however, superficially, they appear as being Affidavits.

These Affidavits were not disclosed to me before today, and that is the reason they were not mentioned in the previous Depositions that I submitted to Your Excellency on January 8th, 1936.

I am also of the opinion that Frank L. Davis has his own ideas and theories on the solution of the Lindbergh matter, and it is my further opinion that some of the ideas and theories are of an assumable nature, and for that reason, I am inclined to disregard them. However, the significance of Mr. Davis' statements is that he reasonably believes that he knew of the name of Isadore Fisch some two and a half years before Hauptmann was apprehended. The name of Isadore Fisch was not mentioned and does not become significant until the Fall of 1934 when Hauptmann was arrested and tried. Furthermore, an absolute fact which cannot be contradicted is that Frank L. Davis was visited at his home by one Cecil Snyder, a man with a criminal record. Lieutenant Cusack, a Chicago police officer, admits that Cecil Snyder was brought to the house of Frank L. Davis. Frank L. Davis at all times has insisted that he received his information from Cecil Snyder in April 1932, and he goes on further to state that Isadore Fisch saw him, Frank L. Davis, at Davis' home in April of 1932 subsequent to the visit of Snyder. Whether or not Isadore Fisch did visit Frank L. Davis is something that I cannot determine.

I assume that Your Excellency, or someone under the direction of Your Excellency, has studied the documents that I submitted several weeks ago. In order to understand the contents of this letter, it is necessary that the said documents be read and studied carefully.

In view of the fact that Frank L. Davis now insists that he has further information which he refuses to divulge only to Your Excellency in my presence. I am of the opinion that Your Excellency should send for Frank L. Davis and for myself, if you so see fit, so that Mr. Davis may be given the opportunity to tell anything and everything that he knows. I do not know of this additional information, if any, that he mentions, otherwise I would submit the same to you in writing. However, Mr. Davis insists that he has additional information which he deems of importance, and he informs me that he will only convey this information to you in person in my presence. With this in mind, I write this letter to you and take the liberty of stating that, in my opinion, we should be sent for. This is only my suggestion, as I know that Your Excellency knows what to do. By getting any and all information from Frank L. Davis, Your Excellency could determine what credit should be given to the story of Mr. Davis and whether or not it is worthwhile going into any further.

Should you decide to send for Mr. Davis and myself, or for Mr. Davis alone, what he or we would expect is that railroad fare be paid plus our expenses such as hotel and meals. The railroad fare to Trenton, New Jersey, I believe, is $46.00 a round trip plus $8.35 for berth each way. I believe that our total expenses, including everything, would not exceed more than $175.00 or $200.00.

I want Mr. Davis to tell everything that he knows regardless of what it may amount to, and I believe that the only way of getting all of this information from him is to send for him or both of us.

I will appreciate an early reply, and assuring you that I am willing to offer any cooperation that Your Excellency may desire,

I remain, very respectfully yours,

Samuel A. Kanter

PS: I am mailing a copy of this to Ellis Parker.

The story continues in Samuel Kanter's letter of 2-12-1936:

February 12th, 1936

2149 Warren Boulevard, Chicago, Illinois

Hon. Harold G. Hoffman

Governor of State of New Jersey

Trenton, N.J.

Honorable Sir: -

I have here before me a copy of the letter submitted to your Excellency "by Mr. Samuel A. Kanter, Attorney" of the 4th of this month. Is it true that Mr. Kanter forwarded the depositions as stated, but this was because of certain papers were interested in the proposition. I became acquainted with Mr. Kanter in April 1934 and gave him certain information, which proved to him later that I knew something about the Lindbergh kidnapping.

Yet, if I venture to open with some other information, which I have in my possession, he immediately suggests, as his letter states, that I have certain ideas and theories of my own, concerning this matter, whereas the truth is, everything which we have, has been in our possession since April 1932.

The only reliable evidence or information that has come to us in all these nearly four years has come from Mr. B. M. Finnigan and from California. Therefore, I consider it a lack of ability for anyone to pass and opinion on my information and disinterestedness, except for publicity purposes, which I detest.

In all my endeavors and correspondence, I have never asked for any compensation, and I certainly will not beg for expenses, and I don't like the nature of communications.

In respect to opinions, it is not necessary for anyone to throw cold water on reliable, truthful evidence. Since we are not interested in publicity or compensation, I see no need to co-operate with anyone who cannot investigate the honesty of a client.

At the present time, we are only interested in justice, if this is the object, we will do our very best to bring the guilty to justice. It is no question but that we have the authentic facts.

We cannot give out all our information because of so many opinions, it is strange in this particular case, everybody has to have their own ideas, and that's the way, such a mess has been made since 1932.

I offered Col. Lindbergh to return his baby positively in three days, in May 1932, two or three times, so how could that have been the Lindbergh baby that was found on the estate?

I am afraid the real truth is going to surprise many people, and when all the different angles of this case are explained and investigated, someone will get the credit, and I sincerely hope it will be your Excellency.

Very respectfully yours,

Frank L. Davis, Mus. Bac.

Member of Brotherhood Lodge No. 986 A.F. and A.M. was a K of P. also an I.O.O.R A member of the Musicians Union for 14 years. A resident of Chicago for 25 years. No criminal record. A family of 4 children. Known and respected by the leading men of Chicago, references furnished by request. Etc.

P.S. Copies mailed to Mr. Ellis Parker and others.

The only true authentic facts are in our possession. Detective Kane was here today from the office of Governor Horner, and Mr. Bernard M. Finnegan, Attorney. It appears to me that Mr. Finnegan will eventually take care of my information.

Frank L. Davis, Mus. Bac
Chicago, Ill.

Detective Ellis H. Parker replied to the above letter on 2-15-1936:

February 15, 1936

Frank L. Davis, M.B.,
2149 Warren Blvd., Chicago, Ill.

My dear Friend: -

I received a copy of a letter which you sent to the Governor. It is most interesting. The Governor, at this time, is in the hospital, having just undergone a nasal operation, which was considerably more serious than was first thought of. The hospital has refused to allow him to go out, owing to weather conditions, etc.

I will endeavor to confer with him in the next few days on this matter.

If I were in a position to pay your expenses or to come to Chicago, I would certainly do it, as I always feel that everything should be given the fullest consideration. In all investigations which I have conducted, I have been forced to pay all my expenses myself, and I know that your interest, in this case, is only one of justice and fairness from the tons of your communication, which would indicate it conclusively to me.

I want to thank you for keeping me advised, and as soon as I get the opportunity to confer with the Governor, I will write to you again.

Ellis H. Parker

Chief of Detectives

Note: I get a feeling that none of these parties wanted to incur the cost of investigating the Frank L. Davis information. His story may have been plausible. Attorney Kanter is very anxious to get his client in front of an investigator but not at any personal cost. The questions raised by these letters deserved further listening and investigation. Unfortunately, it looks like that never occurred.

I thought it was strange that I could find nothing about Attorney Samuel A. Kanter or Frank L. Davis on the internet. I did find some interesting information on Attorney Bernard M Finnigan on Michael Melsky's excellent website, The Lindbergh Kidnapping Discussion Board.

Mike is the author of 3 excellent books on the Lindbergh case, The Dark Corners of the Lindbergh Kidnapping Volume 1, Volume 2, and Volume 3. We (Andy Sahol & Russell Lloyd) endorse and recommend that you read Mike's books.

On the website, Finnigan is described as a young Chicago lawyer that was working with Governor Harold Hoffman on the Hauptmann case. According to a Syracuse Herold newspaper article (4/20/1936), Lawyer Finnigan claimed that $5000 in ransom money had been found, and a solution to the case was only hours away. Finnigan also alleged that Governor Hoffman now has evidence showing that Bruno Richard Hauptmann was "a positively innocent man."

FROM THE ELLIS PARKER LOST FILES

February 7, 1936

Mr. George E. Fleming

Attorney at Law

P.O. Box 27, Grand Central Station, New York City, N.Y.

My Dear Friend Mr. Fleming:

I have received your letter with enclosures, and I want to thank you for writing to me. Your letter expresses what I have always contended. How can six members of the highest court we have in our state, Court of Errors and Appeals, set in judgment as a board of pardons when they have already passed upon the case? It is the most ridiculous thing that I have ever seen. How in the world could you expect them to reverse themselves? Our court of pardons is supposed to be a court of mercy, and the way they terminate it is that a man has to admit his guilt, and then ask for mercy. If he denies his guilt, he gets no consideration. Now, if a man is not guilty, and he asks for clemency, shouldn't the Governor be allowed to take into consideration all the existing circumstances and be given the right to commute to life imprisonment when there is a doubt in his mind as to the actual guilt.

I sincerely thank you for writing me, and I am going to submit your thoughts to a very learned lawyer, a friend of mine who was connected with the Attorney General's office of this state for a long time, and he happens to be a Democrat, but he is backing the stand of the Governor in this matter. The Governor has already received your communication, and I have discussed it with him. The Governor of New Jersey is not playing politics for one minute. He is sincere in what he says and does. He doesn't care anything about his future when he thinks he is right. There is no power on earth that is going to jar him from it. I have known him from a boy, and I want to say his stand, in this case, is one hundred percent right.

The kidnapping is one thing, and the extortion is another, although the kidnaper might have acted as an intermediary with the extortionists. This I could prove to you in five minutes if I was in your presence, of what I have that is significant and outstanding proof.

You speak in your communication about Petrosio. I imagine the man you speak of is Felix DeMartini. I know Felix very well and have the highest regard for his judgment, and I consider him a man of exceptional ability.

Again, I want to thank you for writing to me and will be pleased to receive any thoughts that you might want to send me.

Very truly yours,

Ellis H. Parker

Chief of Detectives

Note: Ellis pointed out the Court of Errors' hypocrisy here and that they would never reverse themselves. There wasn't much time left because Bruno Hauptmann was executed on April 3, 1936.

I wish we knew more about the issue with Felix DeMartini. Felix was a Police Detective on the New York City Police Department and later a renowned private Detective that solved some of New York City's most challenging cases. He was so well-liked that the New York City Police Department would call on him to help with complex cases even after he had left the force for his private practice.

FROM THE ELLIS PARKER LOST FILES

Feb. 10, 1936

Mr. Ellis Parker, Mount Holly, N. J.

Dear Mr. Parker:

I have received assignment from the Country Press to write a series of stories on your true experiences and wish your permission to use your name as I intend to write these in the first person.

Also, should you have on file accounts of your cases, I would like very much to have these as a reference. In anticipation of a reply at your convenience and thanking you Courtesies, I am,

Very truly yours,

E. Newman Eveslade, 24 Stanislaus St., Buffalo, NY

Ellis Parker responded to E. Newman Eveslade on 2- 12-1936:

February 12, 1936

Mr. E. Norman Eveslade
24 Stanislaus St., Buffalo, N. Y.

Dear Mr. Eveslade:

Your letter is received, and I wish to thank you for writing to me. I am not interested at this time in writing any stories whatever, in fact, I do not even have time to think about past cases. Within the last year, I have assisted sixteen of the twenty-one prosecutors in this state on major crimes, and at the present time, I am assisting four prosecutors on murder cases, besides other work. Sometimes maybe if I should retire, I might decide to write up a lot of past experiences, but at this time, it would be out of the question.

Very truly yours,

Ellis H. Parker

Chief of County Detectives

Note: This is one of many instances we found of requests for Ellis Parker's assistance on media

FROM THE ELLIS PARKER LOST FILES

February 10, 1936

Mrs. Grace E. Mall

128 North Monroe Street, Hinsdale, Illinois

Dear Mrs. Hall

I received your letter this morning and was glad to hear from you. Now, as Bruno Hauptmann, he was more or less a victim in this affair. The kidnapping was one proposition, and the extortion was another. It might have been that the kidnapper acted as an intermediary with the extortionists, this I do not know. Fisch undoubtedly was one of the extortionists, as there was money traced to him long before Hauptmann ever spent any of his. Hauptmann said Fisch left the money in a package in his place, which I believe is the truth, and if it is the truth, Hauptmann would not tell one bit more than he has told. It is an honest to God fact that Fisch borrowed money from Hauptmann, whether he used this money to purchase the money that he left there I don't know. I also know that he borrowed four thousand dollars from another source, which would kind of indicate that Fisch brought hot money and was afraid to take it out of the country. Fisch spent over one thousand dollars of the Lindbergh money with the steamship company when he bought tickets for himself and Henry Uhlig to go to Germany. Had the steamship company been notified, Fisch would have been arrested before he got out of this country. This was neglect on someone's part.

I want to thank you for writing to me and assure you I appreciate the interest you have manifested in this particular case. As for myself, I am only interested in Justice.

Very truly yours,

Ellis H. Parker

Chief of County Detectives

Note: Apparently, Detective Parker was highly knowledgeable about the Hauptmann case and mainly the money trail left by Isidor Fisch. Ellis received a great deal of correspondence after the night of the kidnapping right through the Hauptmann execution. Ellis felt that it was his duty as a law enforcement officer to respond to the countless letters he received each week. He not only acknowledged them but made sure he answered every question asked in detail, just as he has done in the above letter. Ellis Parker was a man of great character, and he should be remembered for that.

FROM THE ELLIS PARKER LOST FILES

Note: There are six letters in this series between Mrs. Dulah Llan Evans and Detective Ellis Parker. A strong bond had developed between them. Mrs. Evans's thoughts are exceptional and enlightening. Her theory is one of the most plausible ones we have read.

February 14th, 1936

Mrs. Dulah Llan Evans, Studio Place Park Ridge, Illinois

THE LINDBERGH KIDNAPING CASE IS NOT SOLVED

Mr. Ellis Parker,

Chief of Detectives

Mount Holly, N.J.

Dear Mr. Parker:

I want you to know that we, all of us, were impressed with your sincerity in regard to the Lindbergh kidnapping case; and that it has never occurred to us to ever think of you as wishing publicity from any contact with this case. As far as publicity is concerned, you do not need any for you have accomplished enough in your work as a detective to place you in a position of importance without ever again having any publicity.

No detective of your ability and of your knowledge of life and of crime could be satisfied with the controversial conclusion that has taken place in the Lindbergh kidnapping case. The American Bar Association has already taken up this case and has been inspired by the "circus" that existed in that trial to try to formulate rules that will make such a trial for all time impossible. Mr. Newton D. Baer will have the chairmanship of a special committee to formulate rules.

I believe that no person would wish to be executed on the testimony of Amandus Hochmuth or of Millard Whitehead. And as far as the ladder is concerned, it was taken apart more than once, and this afforded an opportunity for some person interested in securing a close to this case, to insert a board from Hauptmann's attic. I don't know who did it, but I firmly believe that it was done. Hauptman has shown himself as too canny to do so dangerous a thing as to take a board from his attic for a ladder and then leave the ladder at the spot of the kidnapping. WHERE do you suppose the rest of the boards came from? I believe that these boards either came from the Skillman Epileptic Village, or they were boards left from the Lindbergh house that were gathered up by some person in that vicinity.

I cannot believe that Hauptmann came from the Bronx and stole the Lindbergh baby for a paltry $50,000. Any person playing the stock market as he was shown to have done for some years previous to the Lindbergh crime would have a larger idea of money, and his experiences in life would have given him some knowledge of the danger he was to undertake. Nobody can make me believe that Hauptmann would take that dead baby through Hopewell and leave it where it was left. Nobody can make me think that he would have made such a fragile ladder. All carpenters, painters, etc. that I know are terribly afraid of ladders that are not strong. I know for I have hired scores of them on property I own.

In the beginning, all authorities connected with this case insisted that the crime was committed by some person who had knowledge of the activities of the Lindbergh family; and of their habits of living; and of the plan of their house. You know how hard it is to find your way about those roads about the Lindbergh estate unless you are familiar with the place. Violet Sharpe was harassed to death by Inspector Walsh and others because they thought she might know something about the case. It was said that Verne Sankey out in the Dakotas had a copy of the NURSERY RANSOM NOTE in one of his hide-outs out West, and he committed suicide in Jail. That nursery ransom note, having gotten into the hands of Rosner, Spitale, and Bitz, was no longer a precious note. EXTORTIONISTS could have used it.

Hauptmann may or may not have been connected with the extortion plot, but he was certainly NOT connected with the kidnapping. Personally, I suspect that he bought "hot" money; or Fisch left the money, and Hauptmann kept it. I do not believe that Hauptmann was the man with whom Dr. Condon talked for over an hour. That is NOT in keeping with his character.

It is my personal belief that this is a crime of RETALIATION; and that it was committed by young Japanese patriots in the Lindbergh district. It certainly accomplished its purpose, for there was nothing more heard of the AMERICAN BOYCOTT ASSOCIATION that had been announced on that day of March 1, 1932, formed for the purpose of BOYCOTTING JAPAN in order to promote arbitration in the Sino-Japanese crisis.

Japan was able to go on with her plans for economic and territorial expansion without being molested in any way by our country. Having found that they could steal the Lindbergh baby without being detected, they now have become arrogant. I am glad that larger defenses are being planned for this country. Unless you have investigated Isamu Yamashito, George Yamata, "Berry Nagie," and S. Ben Lupica, they have not to my knowledge been investigated in connection with the kidnapping of the Lindbergh baby.

Colonel H. Norman Schwarzkopf stated to our party that he had not and could not investigate this Japanese butler, Isamu Yamashito, who KILLED the groom on the estate where he worked; shot and wounded his employer, and then committed suicide by shooting himself in the LEFT cheek. This murder and suicide occurred six miles from the Lindbergh's Hopewell house on May 7th, 1932, FIVE days before the finding of the body of the baby less than 3 miles from the Boice estate. Colonel Schwarzkopf gave as his reason for not investigating this Japanese, that Mrs. Boice, who employed him, was a fine woman and a friend of his wife's, and that she played BRIDGE in the same club with his wife!

Mrs. Boice stated to my party that she had thought of this Japanese butler in connection with the crime; that he was away the night of the kidnapping; that he had been acting strangely for some time; that he had been in some automobile wrecks, and that she had ascribed his queer actions to that cause; that he had been morose and that she had had to talk with him several times about his actions; that he was a good workman; that he had NOT been investigated in connection with the Lindbergh kidnapping; and that her estate had NOT been searched to find if wood or tools used in making the ladder were there.

There can be no doubt but that the SYMBOLE at the bottom of the nursery ransom note is more racial in design to Japan than to any other country. As an artist, I recognized that immediately upon reading the description of the <u>symbol</u> in the CHICAGO DAILY TIMES on March 2, 1932, when I saw the nursery ransom note CORRECTLY PRINTED with the description of the SYMBOL!

I have always believed, and still do believe, that Rosner or somebody gave out information in regard to the baby's sleeping suit. Or it may have been some trooper. There are a few things that have not yet come to light.

I am not certain that it is to the advantage of Hauptmann to have this new lawyer, Leibowitz, who may be a Jew. The Jews, from Rabbi Stephen Wise on down, are all glad to have this horrible crime attached to a <u>GERMAN</u>. I have no doubt but that the further persecutions of the Jews in Germany have been actuated by the activity of the Jews in this case. The lawyer, Reilly, injured Hauptmann's cause; and his other lawyers have not done so very well by him. Probably they could not. They have been placed in difficult positions because of the antagonism against Hauptmann. The Newspapers have acted as propagandists trying to convict him and keep him convicted and on the way to execution.

I hope that both you and Governor Hoffman will come out of this in good shape, for the two of you have been among the few who have been right-minded and fearless about this case. I have written hundreds of letters to Senators, etc. in regard to this case. I feel that there is no doubt but that some of them have had their effect. I feel certain that some of them have waked to the Japanese menace.

If you will take a look at that menacing letter that Governor Hoffman received after the Hauptmann trial, with a peculiar skull at the top, and signed 8-26, you will note the peculiar wording. That 8-26 could have referred to August, the 8th month, and the 26 to the 26th day of August. Colonel and Mrs. Lindbergh were received in Japan on August 26, 1931. Japanese are great about remembering DAYS, and that would be a great day with Japanese. The peculiar skull was the sort of a design for a skull that a Japanese would use and is familiar to me as a Japanese design. They are great about USING SYMBOLS; There was a dagger in that letter also.

I have been studying Japanese racial customs and have kept books on their activities both before and since the kidnapping. I have a large file on this case. I hope that you and your son are keeping a file for this is an important case, and the execution of Hauptmann, if it takes place, will not close this case in the hearts and minds of our American people.

I hope that Governor Hoffman will refuse to permit him to be executed. Colonel Schwarzkopf ought to be hauled over hot coals, for I believe that he KNOWS a lot about this case. He KNOWS WHY HE did NOT use those three trained bloodhounds that were kept at Wilburtha barracks. I was told that they were trained by a Captain Smith.

With best of good wishes for good luck from my sister, my son, and myself,

Sincerely,

Mrs. Dulah Llan Evans

PHONE: Park Ridge 691 J.

Note: The American Bar Association's vital issues with the Lindbergh "Circus" trial have been discussed before, but the move to revise trail rules in the future was not. A select committee was to be formed to ensure that such a flawed trial could never happen again.

Ellis Parker responded to Mrs. Dulah Llan Evans on 2-17-1936:

> February 17, 1936
>
> Mrs. Dulah L. Evans, Studio Place, Park Ridge, Illinois
>
> Dear Mrs. Evans:
>
> Your letter was received this morning, and I want to thank you for writing to me. Your deductions, in this case, is more common sense than most communications that I get. It is silly to think of this Dutchman doing such things that they claim he did. In fact, it is ridiculous. If this man's life is taken, it will, in my judgment, be a blot on the State of New Jersey, as I am satisfied, he is a victim of circumstances, and where unscrupulous officials use to avenge a crime at any cost, which they sometimes do, and I have often seen where there would be one thing, (like the money being found on him), which would prove to them the guilt. They would go beyond all decencies, and try to put them across, and feel that they are justified. Thank God I never had this disposition, because when a life was a stake, I always felt that there should be no doubt on the guilt before you take away what God gave.
>
> I intend to always pursue my investigation of this case, no matter what happens, and you can rest assured that that course will be pursued by me.
>
> Again, thanking you, I remain, very truly yours,
>
> Ellis H. Parker
>
> Chief of County Detectives

Note: The nation was shocked by the kidnapping of hero Charles Lindbergh's young son. Flyer-Pilot Lindbergh had become a symbol of American ingenuity to the public. The media's hour-by-hour coverage of his child's abduction was overwhelming. The public prayed for the triumphant return of the unharmed child to his famous parents. The world demanded information and debated within itself about who the suspects were. Family and neighbors discussed the case daily at their breakfast tables. Celebrities, Politicians, Law Enforcement Officers, and even the US President were quizzed routinely for their insights. The case was front-page news in countries around the world, and it was being discussed repeatedly on the radio and watched in Movie News Reels that would lead with the story. No case in American history had ever been more closely followed than that which became known as "The Crime of the Century."

Detective Ellis Parker's mailbox was filled with letters from all types of people. He received leads and suggestions from countless Americans. The list of potential suspects and plots was overwhelming, but Ellis was equal to the task. Many of those writing had become successful in their lives. Some of them can be described as "salt of the earth."

Dulah Llan Evans was one of those that had become famous, and she added a theory of her own to Ellis Parker's list. She wrote of the possibility that young Japanese patriots had stolen the Lindbergh baby in retaliation for the forming of the American Boycott Association. They had supposedly done this to promote arbitration in the Sino-Japanese crisis.

Dulah Llan Evans (1875-1951), also known as Dulah Marie Evans and then later as Dulah Marie Evans Krehbiel, was a woman of exceptional talent. She was an American painter, photographer, illustrator, and etcher. Her use of different names depended on how she was signing her artwork at the particular time she created the piece.

The Verne Sankey mentioned in Dulah's letter was a Depression-era outlaw who had kidnapped two men in 1932 along with his accomplice Gordon Alcorn. The crime made them 2 of the most wanted criminals in the United States. The police eventually captured Sankey in a Chicago barbershop. He committed suicide in 1934 while awaiting trial. Alcorn was also arrested and sentenced to life imprisonment. Verne Sankey had previously been a suspect in the early investigation of the Lindbergh baby kidnapping. The FBI cleared him.

The mention of S. Ben Lupica is interesting. The only place I am aware of his involvement in the Lindbergh case is from a letter Detective Ellis Parker wrote to Governor Harold Hoffman. Ellis interviewed Lupica, who the police had questioned after claiming to have seen the kidnapper in a car with the ladders. Lupica told the police that he couldn't identify Hauptmann's car as the one seen or Hauptmann as the driver. Lupica was called before the grand jury, where he would not identify Hauptmann. Dulah also mentioned Amandus, the 87-year-old man who swore during the trial that he had seen Hauptmann driving a car with ladders in it at an intersection near the Lindbergh estate. Millard Whitehead, who lived near the Lindbergh home, stated that he saw Richard Hauptmann before the kidnapping of Charles Lindbergh Jr.

In her letter to Ellis Parker, Dulah wrote, "Violet Sharpe was harassed to death by Inspector Walsh and others because they thought she might know something about the case." As I have written before, the strange suicide of Violet Sharp is the single most perplexing fact I cannot put to rest. It will never be fully explained or stop casting doubt on the real reason for the Lindbergh baby's kidnapping and death. This issue has fascinated many of us that in 2013 the Off-Broad Street Theatre in Hopewell, NJ, staged a play titled "Violet Sharp" written by William Cameron. In the play, the character Inspector Walsh conducts two intense investigation scenes of Violet Sharp, who the police had decided was a suspect.

Dulah Llan Evans again writes to Ellis Parker on 3-8-1936:

Mrs. Dulah Llan Evans, Studio Place, Park Ridge, Illinois

March 8, 1936

THE LINDBERGH KIDNAPPING CASE-THE BABY'S BODY WAS FOUND FACE DOWNWARD

Dear Mr. Parker:

I have just finished an article purported to be by Mr. Hicks, who is conducting the investigation at the Hauptmann apartment. He may reach some scientific conclusions, and I hope that he does. But I cannot believe, after reading the article, that he has a natural ability as a detective. Or that he has the ability in securing facts that are important. I hope that I am mistaken.

I cannot believe that either Gaston Means or John Curtis had any actual contract of any kind with the actual kidnappers; although they may have heard rumors connected with the EXTORTION plot that went about in the underworld. I do not believe they are worth wasting time on. What Gaston Means has to say is purely an expression of THEORY. He can present no actual facts.

I am interested in checking on all activities of Rosner, Spitale, and Bitz. It is my understanding that Bitzis now in prison for a long period. There were certainly some CRAZY things done in the investigation of this kidnapping case, and sometimes I have felt that there was an attempt to keep Colonel Lindbergh actively occupied, rushing about so that he would not have time to use his brain in connection with the kidnapping. To begin with, the THREE trained bloodhounds from Wilburtha ought to have been immediately placed on the trail of the kidnappers. WHY WERE THEY NOT? That is something for Colonel Schwarzkopf to answer. If you will study police history in this and other countries, you will find that DOGS have played their part in discovering criminals and in the solving of crimes. Nor would Colonel Schwarzkopf accept the services of a fine dog from Boston brought there by a couple who offered the dog without remuneration. This dog had a record for successfully tracking criminals. WHY did Colonel Schwarzkopf not use this animal? WAS he afraid that the kidnappers would be discovered? It looks that way to me. There is certainly SOMETHING wrong somewhere. I have checked on all facts that I have been able to learn of the movements of all persons in the Lindbergh house at the time of the crime. There are several matters that ought to have been investigated, but it is now too late for that.

Your theory that the body of the baby found was not that of the Lindbergh baby was formed largely on the fact that the body was treated so uncivilized a way. If you have watched the many peculiar things that Colonel Lindbergh and the Morrow family have done, you will find that this act toward the baby's body fits in with other things they do. Now they have taken a house that is said to be haunted, and this gives an opportunity for further trouble for them. Just how it may come, one can't say.

My theory has been and still is that the body was placed at the spot where it was found either shortly before the Japanese butler KILLED the groom on the Boice estate and committed suicide, or immediately afterward by some confederate in the kidnapping crime. The FACT that the body was found at so conspicuous a place only FIVE days after the suicide of Yamashito helps me to believe that the body was that of the Lindbergh baby because I regard this Yamashito as one of the most logical suspects in the kidnapping. Then the fact that the autopsy states that "there was a perforated fracture about a half-inch in diameter on the side of the skull posterior to the right ear." Dr. Mitchell had earlier stated, according to reports, that this hole seemed to have been made by a bullet. You will remember that NO stress was made in the Hauptmann trial of the 25 calibers German automatic found in the Hauptmann garage. This Japanese butler did his killing and suicide with a 25-caliber automatic of German make, a SIMSON make. I was told at Penn's Neck Station that this Yamashito's automatic made a "small hole, about the size of a lead pencil." On the witness state, Inspector Walsh of Jersey City stated that he made the hole in the baby's head referred to with a stick when he attempted to turn the baby over. I'm sorry that I don't believe him. The type of hole that a stick would make and that a bullet would make are so different that no physician would make a mistake. BESIDES, I WAS TOLD THAT THE Hopewell police were the ones that handled the baby's body. It is my belief that this small hole in the baby's skull back of the right ear was made by the 25-caliber automatic used by the Japanese butler.

I have all along tried to find the reason for the FACT that the body of the baby was found lying FACE DOWNWARD. I HAVE GONE THROUGH A LOT OF AUTHORITIES TRYING TO FIND IF THIS WAS ANY SORT OF A RACIAL CUSTOM OF THE Japanese, and I have asked many people who had knowledge of Orientals. I have learned that it is a RACIAL CUSTOM for the Japanese to SHOOT A VICTIM in the BACK OF THE HEAD as an act of mercy, and to ensure that their victim is really dead. It is referred to as a "mercy shot."

Mrs. Boice told us that her Japanese butler had been acting "strangely" for some time before he "went to pieces." From that, I assumed that he was disturbed in regard to the Lindbergh crime; and that his morose attitude might have been occasioned by remorse. If it were remorse, then it would be natural to treat the baby's body with as much kindness as possible. I have now learned that the "face downward position is the honorable position of death" with the Japanese. This may or may not account for the FACE DOWN position of the Lindbergh baby's body; and this interests me because I believe so thoroughly that all facts point to a RETALIATION by young Japanese patriots because of the BOYCOTT that was planned against Japanese imports by prominent persons in New Your City of March 1, 1932. I have NOT been able to learn if Colonel Lindbergh was present at that meeting of the AMERICAN BOYCOTT ASSOCIATION. I regard it as an important matter to be learned.

IF the red ink bottle which Mrs. Boice had when she resided at the Cedar Grove estate could be found, it might show the cork to be the one used when the actual kidnaper pressed it on the nursery ransom note when he made the FULL RED CIRCLE of the SYMBOL. This cork might settle the case. I had hoped to secure this cork and would have returned for further investigation the next summer, and business comes along better for us.

I regard this as something important for investigation. Then I believe that S. Ben Lupica is a suspect in this kidnapping case; and that his movements ought to be checked on. His story did not feel right to me. WAS he one of the "harmless prowlers" that were said to occasionally be on the Lindbergh estate? Whately, the Lindbergh butler, and his wife, are dead. Betty Gow is the only one left outside of the Lindbergh's who could tell this.

I regard this case as more serious than other people. I believe that to electrocute Hauptmann for this crime when he has NOT been proved guilty by any logical sequence of reasoning or by any witness who can be considered reliable and when some of the evidence resembles an attempt at a frame-up, will be the bringing of DISASTER on our country. I have a very strange feeling that the German people mean to make this execution a cause for VENGEANCE of their nation against our own. They are cooperating, it seems, with the Japanese.; and the Japanese are reported pleased with the recent action of Hitler in occupying the Rhineland. I cannot believe that it will be wise for our country to permit the execution of Hauptmann.

With good wishes from all of us – Miss Evans is still in Iowa.

Sincerely,

Dulah Llan Evans

Note: Dulah's research on the position of the Lindbergh's baby was surprising. She confirmed that it was a social custom of the Japanese people to honor the dead. Also, Dulah's theory that the hole in the Lindbergh child's head and that of the Japanese butler could both have been made by a 25-caliber bullet is surprising.

Ellis Parker responded to Dulah Llan Evans on 3-11-1936:

March 11, 1936

Mrs. Dulah Llan Evans, Studio Place, Park Ridge, Illinois

Dear Friend Mrs. Evans:

I received your letter this morning, and I agree with you 100% concerning the loose ends unconnected around this whole case. There is so much doubt, and I think it would be unsafe to sacrifice any life. The character of witnesses that were used to convict Hauptmann, and the whole trial, which has been branded by the American Bar Association as being a disgrace. These things alone make every decent person shudder when they think that a person's life is going to be snuffed out to satisfy a crime. It doesn't in any way clear up the affair. Of course, being an officer myself, and realizing that at that time that the case attracted so much attention, and that thousands of things came in that no doubt impeded progress, as a lot of things that should have been done that would no doubt have brought it to a successful conclusion, was omitted owing to the above just stated, therefore we have to reconsider those conducting the investigation, and not judge too harshly.

Again, thanking you for writing to me, and wish to be remembered to your family and trusting someday the real solution will be found. I remain, very truly yours,

Ellis H. Parker

Chief of County Detectives

Mrs. Dulah Llan Evans responded to Ellis Parker's letter on 6-5-1936:

Mrs. Dulah Llan Evans, Studio Place, Park Ridge, Illinois

June Fifth, 1936

Mr. Ellis Parker

Chief Detectives, Burlington County, Mt Holly, New Jersey

My Dear Mr. Parker:

My sister and my son join me in expressing sympathy for you and your family because of the annoyance to which you and your son have been placed because of your investigation of a suspect in the Lindbergh kidnapping case.

We remember with pleasure the two visits which we had with you in your office at Mt Holly, and we were impressed with your sincerity in your work.

It does not seem to us possible that your state and your country will permit any neighboring state to attempt to take custody one who has given so much faithful service to your community for so long a number of years. We were impressed with your upstanding young son when he came to your office door.

Your arrest may connect with the effort on the part of the Governor to not retain Colonel H. Norman Schwarzkopf as head of the State Police. Those persons responsible for the "legal murder" of Hauptmann are seemingly determined to retain their power.

The testimony of Colonel H. Norman Schwarzkopf at the Hauptmann trial was wholly unsatisfactory. He did not evince a readiness to assist in seeing that the case was brought to the light of public and judicial appraisement. He stated, as a witness, that he followed all leads in the case. Yet he refused to investigate a Japanese butler who was the most logical suspect in the case. In his refusal to make this investigation, Colonel Schwarzkopf placed himself in the position of being criminally negligent of responsibility as an officer, and he placed himself in a position where he should be tried for this criminal dereliction before a court of legal jurisdiction.

I place a high estimate upon the effort of Governor Harold G. Hoffman in the Hauptmann case, for he faced a most difficult situation. Colonel Schwarzkopf and Attorney General David Wilentz were determined, for some undetermined reason, to close the case with the execution of some person.

With our best wishes for your welfare and that of your family, I am, very sincerely yours,

Dulah Llan Evans

Ellis Parker writes to Dulah Llan Evans on 6-15-1936:

June 15, 1936

Mrs. Dulah Llan Evans, Studio Place, Park Ridge, Illinois

My Dear Friend:

Your letter of June 5 is received, and you have the right solution. The attack against me was solely to keep Colonel

Schwarzkopf head of the State Police, but they have failed. He is now out entirely, and it won't be long before his successor is confirmed.

No doubt you have seen by the press where they are trying to expedite me to New York, and I'm going to beat them because I wasn't there.

Thanking you for writing to me, and wishing to be remembered to all your people, I remain,

Very truly yours,

Ellis H. Parker

Chief of County Detectives

Note: H. Norman Schwarzkopf was the 1st colonel of the New Jersey State Police, serving over 14 years. His highest-profile case was the Lindbergh baby kidnapping. Schwarzkopf was replaced by Mark O. Kimberling on 6-17-1936. Kimberling was well known as the Trenton prison warden, where Bruno Richard Hauptmann was incarcerated and executed.

It had long been rumored that Ellis Parker wanted the position, but those that know him well knew that was not true.

After Paul Wendel rescinded his confession to the Lindbergh baby kidnapping, Ellis Parker was charged with his imprisonment and torture. Wendel, who had been allegedly held in the Bronx, had accused Ellis of his abduction, but Ellis had never left Mount Holly. He could not be expedited to New York.

FROM THE ELLIS PARKER LOST FILES

OFFICE OF PROSECUTOR OF THE PLEAS OF BURLINGTON COUNTY, MOUNT HOLLY, NEW JERSEY

HOWARD EASTWOOD Prosecutor Telephone—Mt. Holly 103

ELLIS H. PARKER Chief of Detectives

Telephone DAY—Mt. Holly 144

Telephone NIGHT—Mt. Holly 145

February 17, 1936

Mr. Gustave Arenson

Savannah, Georgia

Dear Friend:

I received your most interesting letter, and I wish to thank you for writing to me. Many of your thoughts are very good. You can rest assured that I am doing everything that lies in my power to run this crime down. The fact of his having some of the ransom money convicts him in a lot of people's minds, but not in my mind, as I am convinced that the kidnapping is one thing, and the extortion was another. Dr. Condon acting as a go-between in handing over this money, got himself in a devil of a mix-up, and it might be his identification of this man was brought about by his thinking that Hauptmann knew who did it, and whereas a matter of fact, I don't think he did, and that Hauptmann didn't tell him, that was somewhat of a revenge on Condon's part to identify him.

You can rest assured that I am doing everything I can for this man, although I do not know him, and he is nothing to me. I am only interested on the side of justice, I remain, Very truly yours,

Ellis H. Parker

Chief of County Detectives

Note: Interestingly, Ellis Parker was now included with Prosecutor Howard Eastwood (1884-1976) on the same letterhead. Eastwood, Parker's former boss, would soon have to decide on replacing Ellis Parker after his guilty verdict in the Wendel kidnapping charges. The execution of Bruno Richard Hauptmann was only two months away. Eastwood and Parker had enjoyed a close and friendly relationship during their lifetimes. Eastwood went on from Prosecutor to become a member of the New Jersey Senate from Burlington County (1940-1944). There he served as president in 1944 before resigning.

Eastwood became a circuit judge from 1944 to 1946. He then became a Justice of the New Jersey Supreme Court from 1946 until 1948.

FROM THE ELLIS PARKER LOST FILES

February 26, 1936

Governor Harold G. Hoffman

Trenton, New Jersey

Dear Mr. Governor,

Your kind letter to me 23rd 1935 encourages me to present to you a few more points relating to the Hauptmann case, which may be of some use in your noble work, which may ultimately purge American courts of improper methods.

1. Might it not be a good policy to ask Rev. Burns to go to a local court and make a sworn affidavit concerning the truth of his story? Other people who have come forward after the trial at Flemington may do the same thing. In the interest of science and justice, some of them may even be persuaded to tell their story both with and without the use of truth serum.

2. Wilentz said that he would after the trial start proceedings against some of Hoffman's witnesses, accusing them of perjury. Since he has not done this, those witnesses may demand that he immediately do so, or else himself face trial for defaming their character in public. I suppose Wilentz hopes that his bluff will be of no consequence after Hauptmann's eventual execution, but from the standpoint of justice and truth, it is clear that such proceedings should be done before it is too late to find the truth. If Wilentz can be forced to start perjury proceedings at once, Hauptmann's witnesses may themselves present additional testimony to confirm their statements and protect their honor. Certainly, there should be some legal means of protection against the despicable language and actions by Wilentz and others at the trial.

3. The public cannot be particularly interested in a new trial so long as they think Hauptmann is deeply involved in the crime, and the question is simply one of finding eventual accomplices. The possibility of his complete innocence should be pointed out, not perhaps by you since that might imply contempt of court, but by some mutual outsider. I enclose a little note, a slight improvement of a previous note I sent you, which may be given as a scientist's view of the case to some interested newspaperman. I am not afraid to have my name mentioned if you think it advisable. The force of the arguments presented depends greatly, however, on Hauptmann not having definitely stated that he had written Condon's address and telephone number in the closet.

4. It might have good effects if a reward was promised for information regarding any party involved in the actual kidnapping and murder. I suggested this to Mrs. McLean a week ago, and a hint from you may influence her. Many, who otherwise would remain silent, might be tempted to tell about things they know, in particular, if they do not need to have their names published immediately.

5. My wife, who was extremely interested in the case, and convinced of Hauptmann's complete innocence, has from several independent sources heard an amazing story, which I would never think of repeating if an innocent man's life were not at stake. The late Senator Morrow is said to have an illegitimate son, who was envious of Lindbergh. This son, the rumor says, committed the crime, with the help of somebody in Morrow's house. Perhaps Violet Sharp and the Butler knew of it and had to pay the price for their knowledge. Mrs. Morrow is said to know of him and has tried to protect him. Later Lindbergh himself has suspected him but did not want to tell about it.

There are some facts that may corroborate this story. In the letter to Rev. Burns, the writer, who may be Morrow's son himself, says, "When I heard a dear old lady like Mrs. Morrow committing perjury all on account of us, I felt like doing away with it all." According to Condon's story, Mrs. Morrow, at Condon's visit to Hopewell, had written a little verse which runs as follows bold.

H_____, Spitale and Bitz
Took dinner at the Ritz.
They met face-to-face,
Discussed the great case,
And put everything on the fritz.

Offhand it seems inconceivable that Mrs. Morrow would write a verse like that immediately after the tragedy. On the face of it, it seems that H- means either a swearword or Hauptmann. If it is true, it shows that Mrs. Morrow was happy that the crime was safely in on "the fritz," that is on a German. At the time, she probably did not know that Hauptmann was already selected and framed as an "emergency scapegoat," but she could tell from the spelling of the original ransom note that the kidnapper had intentionally used German spelling and idioms.

Certain spelling seems to indicate that a non-German writer has supposed that a German would spell as he pronounced a word. I doubt even a very ignorant young German, who has been in this country a couple of years, would spell so badly and inconsistently, especially not on a note which would be used as a clue by the Police.

There are other things which point in the same direction. Whited said that Lindberg did not want to tell Police that he saw a man in the woods. Finn says that Lindberg prevented the Police from searching the woods immediately after the crime. Both sections, if true, seem extremely strange, and the first is actually against the law.

It may be possible to find this alleged son of Morrow and obtained his fingerprints. I have called Mr. Parker's attention to it.

I had hopes that Lindberg was entirely ignorant of the perpetrator of the crime, and I wrote him a letter of February 18, 1935, a copy of which I enclose. I received no answer, and I never saw any statement from Lindbergh, where he expressed any desire to have all the facts in this case finally revealed. It might have been a conflict on his side between loyalty and duty.

6. Condon says that Lindbergh himself suggested that Condom sleep on the floor in the nursery. If true, it seems strange, indeed. If not true, it indicates that Lindberg and Mrs. Morrow do not dare to challenge Cordon's statements, since he may know too much about the actual perpetrator. If Mrs. Morrow did not write the verse, which seems more probable, then Condon wants to show his power over her and the family. The departure of Lindbergh and Mrs. Morrow on the eve of Hoffman's execution may have many reasons, one of which may be a dislike of questioning with regard to Condon's story.

7. It is too late to obtain fingerprints in the attic of the house where Hauptmann lived? Very few people may have been there, and Hauptmann may never have been up in the attic. He could not have use gloves since then he would have realized the importance of the attic board and never used a piece of board from the house where he lived in the first place. Hence the absence of Hauptmann's fingerprints is a very strong indication that he did not cut out the attic board.

Other points are contained in the enclosed note. I would like to know if the experts actually testified that the body found had been embalmed. If so, Hauptmann could not have done it. If it is not the body of the Lindberg baby, there is no evidence that a murder has been committed, and, I suppose, Hauptmann cannot be executed in accordance with the law in force at the time of the crime.

A copy of this letter has been forwarded to Mr. Ellis Parker and to Mr. Lloyd Fisher.

Respectfully yours,

Gustaf Stromberg

Note: The writer of this letter was Gustaf Stromberg (1882-1962). He was born in Gothenburg, Sweden. For over 30 years, Gustaf worked researching at the Mount Wilson Observatory. He became a well-respected astronomer, new-age thinker, and successful writer. Gustaf's most famous book, "The Soul of The Universe," was a brilliant study of the Cosmos' rational nature. Gustaf's book examined the relationship between mind and matter, the meaning and nature of human life and death. He believed in human immortality, the Quantum theory, and the theory of relativity. He saw the material universe as a uniform and interrelated whole.

If you are not impressed by the quality of those who wrote to Ellis Parker and Harold Hoffman by now, you never will be.

Stromberg suggests Reverend Vincent S. Burns, who had interrupted the Hauptmann trial by announcing from his seat that Hauptmann was innocent, be asked to create an affidavit confirming the truth of his claim.

Stromberg felt that David Wilentz defamed the character of witnesses during the Hauptmann trial by accusing them of perjury. He labels it as despicable language and actions by Wilentz.

Stromberg also raised the question of Dwight Morrow's son being illegitimate. He asks if the son could have committed the crime with someone's help from the house. Dwight Morrow Jr. was jealous of Charles Lindbergh with good reason as he was left out of his father's will. The help, he suggests, may have come from Violet Sharpe and Oliver Whatley. Charles Lindbergh may have suspected Morrow's son as well. Stromberg noted it was not too late to obtain Dwight Morrow Jr.'s fingerprints.

Stromberg also points out that Charles Lindbergh did not want to tell the Police that he saw a man in the woods and prevented the Police from searching there the night of the kidnapping.

FROM THE ELLIS PARKER LOST FILES

March 2, 1936

Mr. Ellis Parker, Mount Holly, New Jersey

Dear Sir:

The Following may be the information Governor Hoffman, and you need so badly to assist you in solving the Lindbergh case or in apprehending the real perpetrators of this awful crime. I believe Hauptmann to be criminally involved, but by no means alone in the planning and carrying out of this crime. But I believe that the real criminals, in this case, are a notorious, nationally known kidnap gang, and the following information may lead to the solution, and finally, the arrest of the real kidnappers and murderers of this Lindbergh child. He may even be found to be alive.

If this information proves to be of importance or value, I wish to urge the extreme importance of avoiding any publicity, and particularly of shielding, disguising, and protecting from "leakage" any news until after you have rounded up and securely apprehended the guilty parties. This gang I have reference to is large in number, and because of the numerous delays in execution of Hauptmann, they would now be extremely cautious and watchful, and would probably have several informers among both guilty and innocent groups, whereby they could easily detect danger, and act to further thwart the ends of justice.

I believe that the reason that Hauptmann has so stoically and persistently refused to render assistance or furnish information is that he fears the anger and consequent action not only of the officials, the German people of this country who have financed his impressive and strong defense, but he also fears the revenge of this criminal gang who he feels would not only frustrate his efforts to implicate them but would probably also harm his wife and child. He probably feels that they have connections (the gang) in high places and are not only very numerous but also very powerful. Perhaps, although he dealt with them, he does not really know their names or identities, and fears that he could not prove any charges he might make against others, and perhaps could not even place or locate them. That is why he is so eager to see and speak to Dr. Condon now. The following may explain what I mean more fully. He has no doubt been threatened and cautioned in gangster fashion, perhaps thru Mrs. Hauptmann, and he goes by maintaining an attitude that will leave a reasonable doubt in the minds of those officially in power to continue to get delays, reprieves, mistrials, etc. Naturally, his defense attorneys are laboring along these lines, too.

The enclosed 'ITINERARY" is an exact copy of a multigraph or mimeographed note I recently received (on Feb 5th), and the man whose name appears at the to, I will refer hereafter as Mr. X. It might be wise after you have noted the name, to cut it off and destroy it, so that it will not appear anywhere on this letter or the Itinerary, in order to further the secrecy so very important, and which I cannot stress too often or too much.

Now, I read that Dr. Condon did not return on the cruise ship on which he left but remained in Panama. The ship returned to New York on Feb 18th, and the chief steward remarked about Condon's evident intention of remaining in Panama until after the execution of Hauptmann, and that the steward stated that he gathered from Dr. Condon's general conversation that he was eager and hoped to have Hauptmann out of the way. I think Dr. Condon's behavior and attitude show that he fears meeting Hauptmann, and he also is chafing at the delay in his execution. Normally, a man would not be so eager for the execution of a man he had helped to condemn. I have never felt entirely sure of Dr. Condon's innocence, whom I believe to be a clever schemer and conniver. All of the foregoing leads up to what items I wish to inform you of. Since I am writing this in a sort of off-hand way (after much deliberation, however), some of the statements may not seem connected or in their proper order, but out of this maze, you may see many points of extreme importance. I do not wish to add to the confusion already existing in this case, so I will endeavor to state salient points, with whatever remarks I can make to give information or help on each point.

1. Referring to the enclosed Itinerary, please note that the ship, Steel Traveler" reached Panama on Feb. 11th, and departed on the same day. Dr. Condon, I believe, was in that vicinity then (In Panama) and that he and Mr. "X" may have met there by appointment (and others, also.) I do not know whether Mr. "X" is traveling alone or with a party, and I am aware that thousands of people take such voyages and stop at Panama but following are some of the reasons I believe that there may be a strong connection between Mr. "X" and Dr. Condon and others I suspect.

2. A more or less casual acquaintance with Mr. "X" for a period of about 16 years, during the first few years, I saw him occasionally

and corresponded with him. During the past 10 years, however, although I have seen him but a few times and received occasional notes from him, I have during all of the time, I believe gained a quite accurate estimate and insight into his character. During the first few years of our acquaintance, I knew nothing of his personal life, affairs, or connections, but regarded him as a very fine man whom I considered a constructive friend. But, about ten years ago, because of certain seemingly mysterious (but I thought at the time, unimportant) things he said and did, I came to regard him with extreme distrust and suspicion. It was, at first, intuitive, but later events tended only to strongly confirm my suspicions that he was a very unwholesome character, with some sort of underground or undercover connections. Inasmuch as I still know nothing about his personal life or affairs, I can tell you nothing pertinent to it. (We met in a business way). When we met, I understood that he was unmarried, but about in 1924 or 1925, I read in the New York Times that his wife had died. It was shortly after that that certain events led me to regard him with great distrust. I do not know if he has remarried or has any children. I purposely avoid all contact with the man,

3. He owns, and I believe lives in, a house in Little Falls, New Jersey. It is situated in a remote section, very rural, and there is another larger and older house standing almost right in front of it, near the road, in a most unusual manner, so that at first approach, only the older house near the road seems visible. I once drove by but would not have entered it for the world. He once stated to me that he was building a tunnel from his house to the garage, and not having seen the grounds, I presumed that the garage was underneath the house in California fashion. However, when I drove by, I was surprised to notice that the garage was only a few feet from the house, and on level ground (about 20 feet), so I could see no apparent reason for a tunnel, and thought it very strange,

if true. He stated that he had for many years a Japanese manservant, whom he wanted to discharge because he was becoming disrespectful, but he somehow kept him on. A few years ago, he stated that he was giving shelter to an unemployed man, wife, and several children. They were caring for the place.

4. I am not familiar with New Jersey geography, but I judge that this man would be familiar with the vicinity of the Lindberg residence. He was always a "Celebrity worshipper." By that I mean, that he always was attracted strongly by people who do startling things and become famous overnight, and who by sheer imitative, nerve or courage, make a great deal of money. He often cited such people to me, when he urged me to write, what he thought I could do, particularly along certain lines. But although his suggestions were most praiseworthy and respectful, I could not enthuse about his suggested medium of expression, so I never wrote the book. He seemed to admire and respect me greatly, as several letters from him attest, and I felt that he merely wished to offer encouragement to one who felt was doing complicated things, under challenging circumstances. So, I appreciated what I thought at the time was his kind interest. I know, Mr. Parker, that I am now rambling, but I am bringing out the "salient points, I hope that you will see that the last thing in the world I wish to do is injure anyone in any way, especially someone whom I once believed to be a fine person. So, you will understand that it was not easy to bring myself to the point of writing you this.

5. This Mr. "X" has taken trips along the Chesapeake Bay. He likes fishing, hunting, etc. They may have been perfectly harmless, ordinary trips, and one of them may not have been. In a later paragraph, I will render more of such activities.

6. He may be the J.J. Faulkner you are looking for. I state this for the following reasons. I was strongly impressed with the similarity

in the handwriting of this person and the printed bank deposit slip with the Faulkner name on it. Even the numeral looked like his. I don't know what made me see a similarity because the man was not even in my thoughts. A man might subconsciously choose a name similar to his own in some ways. Please note that the initials "J.J." are the same, likewise the last two letters of both names. I have tried to dismiss this thought from my mind as a coincidence, but the idea keeps recurring, so I am sending it on to you. It may be important, in view of what follows. Specimens of his handwriting today and at the time of the kidnapping could, I am sure, be obtained at his office (he was, or is, a traffic manager, with the Atlas-Portland Cement Co, N.Y.C. He has been with them for a great many years, but I do not know if he is still connected with them. A handwriting expert (New York or New Jersey) (but not Chicago) could easily analyze the writing. He owns, I believe, an auto, and that may give you some information. It is of the greatest importance that the handwriting expert be cautioned to secrecy. The steamship Co. could also furnish information, I am sure. If the man is innocent, I hope that nothing will be done to hurt him at his office.

7. A few years ago, during the Chicago World's Fair, he was here for a week or two, and I saw him once. At that time, he stated that he had gone "down, down, down." I did not question him about what he meant, as I did not consider it any of my concerns. Still, I thought that he meant financially, as he mentioned having had several cuts in salary, which his concern was making every year due to the depression. He stated that he was then receiving a small fraction of the income he had had when he first met me. I thought he acted as though he felt called upon to say something about his condition because of our long acquaintance, and also because he did not appear as well dressed as I had formerly seen him. I even got the impression that his trip was being financed

by someone other than himself. Now he essential item which led
to finally to write you all this was that he mentioned the alias of
the leader of the notorious kidnap gang as being a member of
his party. It happened in this way, Mr. "X" telephoned me upon
arrival here, telephoned me several times, in fact, and urged me
to join him and a party of friends from New York who were here
to see the Fair. He mentioned that he was particularly anxious
for me to meet a "Mr. & Mrs. Harold Cobb" who were in his
party, and who were also eager to meet me. I could not understand why he should have spoken of them or why they should be
eager to meet me. (He sometimes called him Harry Cobb.) Now
Mr. Parker, HAROLD COBB, is one of the aliases used by Roger
Touhy, the notorious kidnapper and gang leader, who was convicted of kidnapping John Factor, and who was or is suspected of
many other kidnappings and similar crimes. The Name of Harold
Cobb was printed in the Newspapers at the time of the Factor
conviction, and I looked in the telephone book and saw that it
was listed in the suburb, which the authorities gave as his residence. Therefore, when he mentioned this name (which I remembered at once because of the above), I naturally was suspicious
and would not have dreamed of joining them. But I pretended to
be busy, ill, indisposed, etc., every time he phoned. This kept on
for over a week. On one occasion, they phoned me about 10 P.M.
and not only Mr. X, but some woman in the party, and finally
"Mr. Cobb," was introduced on the phone, and very gently and
sweetly, urged me to join them. I told them that I was not worth
making such a fuss over and would be dull company, and when
they finally saw that I would not join them, Mr. Cobb snarled
and seemed to growl a threat (as though he thought I knew who
he was). Now, I have felt for years that an underground gang was
peculiarly interested, and persistently so, and that is the gang
I have suspected. I have made many memos thru the past ten

years, giving names, etc., of all people and events which aroused my suspicions along those lines, and it all harks back to about 10 years ago. There is no need to tell you more about this now, since the Mr. X information may not prove of value, but I have stated as much as I have, to bring home the connection between Mr. X and the gangster chief, at least, by the alias. Mr. X's own conduct and many tangible and intangible things have for years convinced me that much was wrong in the man's secret life. However, the "Colonel Harold Cobb" (the complete and exact alias) incident may have been a coincidence, or Mr. X may have been an innocent and unwitting tool in this incident. It was after that that I even ceased the exchange of greeting cards at Christmas and ignored all cards he sent me. I wished no further, even remote connection with Mr. X. I had heard the snarling, growling voice of the "Mr. Cobb" once before, when someone phoned me, who I thought sounded intoxicated, and asked me to call (on an extremely foggy day) at a remote, isolated, suburban spot, to give an estimate to a Mr. Smith, for some business transaction. It was all so flimsy and transparent that I would not have thought of going. But I made a note of the incident. It was the same voice. Of that, I am sure.

8. Frankly, Mr. Parker, I have long felt that Mr. X was somehow associated with a criminal gang, or syndicate, with far-flung ramifications and connections with people in "high places. Economic reasons may have prompted Mr. X to such an association. He once wrote to me that he was terribly depressed and TOO, TOO, INVOLVED. I don't know what he meant. I have the letter. It was three or four years ago, I think, or may have been earlier. He may have become involved with criminals without realizing what he was doing, and he may have deliberately done so. I have been wondering about his being able to take an extended and expensive ocean voyage, lasting about six months, after many years of

diminishing income, and how he could spare the time from the business unless it is for his health. I have thought that he may very easily be acquainted with Dr. Condon, and he may have seen him in Panama when they were both there (Feb 11th). Does he also, like Dr. Condon, wish to be far away until after the execution? Had he become acquainted with Dr. Condon thru fishing trips to City Island. He may have met Hauptmann there, and he may have, at one time, employed Hauptmann to do some carpenter work at his home. You may find some of the ladder wood on Mr. "X" premises, who knows? I was surprised to notice that the Itinerary was mailed to me on the very day of the departure and reached me on the 5th of Feb. It seemed as though he did not wish to make known his intended departure, but could not resist the show-ff streak, which is vital in him. There was a penned note at the foot of the Itinerary sheet, which said, "It is years since I have heard from you, even indirectly. I hope this reaches you. Au revoir. (I do not believe that even indirectly). Although I do not know why. I was much surprised to receive this notice, as of recent years, I had even stopped sending Xmas cards, and did not reply to his cards, as formerly, feeling that I did not want even a remote a connection with this man.

9. He may have been acquainted with Violet Sharpe and her friends, whom he may have met in roadhouse parties. I believe that he does that sort of thing a great deal. (I mean dining and drinking parties).

10. Now again, Mr. Parker, I wish to ask you to please stress the confidential nature of this data and any investigation you may make, as I feel that there may be something to it. The slightest whisper would speak volumes to the many connections that I believe this gang has. They will know, I feel sure if the investigation touches any one of them. Better for you to let your "opposition" feel that you cannot produce anything further until you are

ready to "close-in" than to risk anything. They would not hesitate to destroy anyone who endangered them. I mean the gangsters. They learn much by the grapevine method, but particularly by seemingly innocent connections and acquaintances with lesser and higher officials, police, troopers, and residents in the vicinity of the investigation. If my hunch is correct, you will not only uncover the real criminals but many other things of importance.

As for myself, I can hardly believe that I am writing you, but think it apropos to tell you that I was impelled to do so because of a newspaper article I read a few weeks ago, about you, in the Chicago Tribune, by a feature writer. What he wrote made me feel that I could trust you implicitly not only to keep my confidence but to protect me from the danger I would naturally feel from this criminal element. I have wondered about the seeming interest of some such people in me. I hope to find out someday. In the meantime, I prefer to be a "live Indian, rather than a dead general." I had once thought of sending this information or these suggestions to the Department of Justice, but according to the papers, they consider the case as closed, so I felt that they would surely ignore it. Should you also decide to ignore it. I will not feel hurt. I will know that I followed the dictation of my conscience and the "wee small voice" in writing to you. I have been following the Lindbergh case in the papers, and although I at first felt Hauptmann to be alone and guilty, I have since had a change of mind and heart. I do not believe his Fisch story, although Fisch may have obtained some of the4 ransom money innocently or otherwise. But Mrs. Hauptmann may have disposed of much in Germany.

I hope that I am not running any risk of danger or unpleasantness from the criminal element. I feel that some of them are aware of my suspicions, and this does not make me feel very comfortable, either.

I wish to re-integrate, I have no desire to injure anyone, and certainly do not wish to add to the confusion and babel now existing in the case. Any publicity or indications in my direction would prove very harmful. After the apprehension of the really guilty parties, I would not care. If you knew me and my circumstances, you would, I feel sure, be very careful to shield me from harm or publicity. You would, I think, deem me worthy of the greatest protection. I am young, respectable, in business for myself, and unfavorable or puzzling publicity in such a case could be very harmful to me and my interests. Naturally, people would be surprised and look with suspicion upon my writing you this way. But I feel that I am running no risk in trusting you completely. Having been thru much trouble, naturally, I do not wish to invite more. My life has always been clean and upright, and naturally, I wish to continue in such channels, unhampered.

Please do not try to trace me. Even should you learn my identity, please do not communicate with me in any way, as all means of communication can be intercepted.

Should you wish to hear further from me, will you please have inserted in the Chicago Tribune, daily or Sunday, the following advertisement in the personal's column. "L. JORGENSON, formerly chauffeur for Mr. Hopkins, please telephone. Position open." Do not mail or otherwise send in that advertisement from the East. Have someone in some Middle Western city place the advertisement, leaving the name of Hopkins, and giving the Morrison Stevens or Sherman House Hotels as their address. Have them keep the matter strictly secret. Someone employed at the newspaper office may divulge where the advertisement came from. Should I see that advertisement, I will again write to you, the same address, but will not telephone or place an advertisement.

Your advertisement will indicate to me that the contents of this letter have proven of value and that you would like to communicate with me. Should I be able to furnish any further helpful information, I will, of course, be glad to do so. There are many things that are puzzling me concerning this matter, but they would seem too detached and irrelevant if I wrote to them now. Should you find anything in my letter of value to you, undue haste may spoil everything, just as the slightest publicity would. Also, please do not under any circumstances indicate to anyone from what locality this letter is sent. That would be as dangerous as "flashing your trumps" or waving a red danger flag to the real criminals. (Mr. "X" by the way, is about 60 years old.)

I have been debating with myself for the past few weeks about sending you this, as I realize that I could be made to appear very ridiculous by any publicity or seeming connection with the investigation of this crime, as it is certainly very far from my "field of action." It is because, in following the Lindbergh case, I have formed a high regard for you, and for Governor Hoffman and his courage, which mighty few Governors would have displayed or risked under similar circumstances. The criticism and accusations are raining thick and fast, and everyone knows it. I must add, however, that I do feel that the prosecuting officials and the police were and are sincere in feeling that Hauptmann is alone guilty. While much may have been done that could be criticized, no one can laugh off the incriminating evidence of the money and other items.

I hope this may be valuable and wish you every success. Please protect all investigations of the above from prying and from publicity, and please pardon my colossal nerve in being so persistent on the subject, even to you, whose ability and character I admire and respect.

UNSIGNED

<u>Note</u>: "Unsigned" believed that a nationally known kidnap gang was responsible for the abduction of the Lindbergh child. They were described as large in number with many resources and being experts at kidnapping and extortion. Charles Lindbergh was afraid of them, and he feared revenge. "Unsigned" believed Roger Touhy might have led the gang. He was well known as being interested in kidnapping for profit. Charles Lindbergh was also afraid of losing the support of German patriots in America. Charles wanted to delay the ongoing investigation of the case initially. Still, later, he may have been anxious to see the execution of Hauptmann to force an end to the case.

"Unsigned" suspected that Mr. X that he wrote about might have been the J.J. Faulkner that had received so much publicity. Mr. X lived in Little Falls, N.J., which was not that far from the Lindbergh mansion. Mr. X may have been the J.J. Faulkner considered a suspect in the Hauptmann case. "Unsigned" also suspected that Mr. X might have been acquainted with Violet Sharpe.

"Unsigned" sensed that he could trust Ellis Parker. That is why he wrote to him.

<u>The following is the "ITINERARY" for a J. J. Collister. J.J. Collister is the "Mr. X" referred to in the above letter numerous times:</u>

J.J. Collister

ITINERARY

S. S. "Steel Traveler"

Captain J.J. Flannery.

	SAIL	ARRIVE
Leave Pier 17, Brooklyn		2/3
Colon, Balboa, Canal Zone	2/11	2/11
Honolulu, T.H.	3/1	3/3
Manila	3/19	3/20
Shanghai	3/25	3/26
Manila	4/1	4/5

VIA PHILIPPINE ISLANDS & DUTCH

EAST INDIAN PORTS

Singapore, S.S.	4/20	4/27
Port Swettenham	4/28	4/28
Bela wan Deli	4/30	4/30
Penang	5/1	5/3
Cape Town	5/23	5/23
Trinidad	6/12	6/12
Boston	6/21	6/22
New York	7/20	

AGENTS:

Honolulu, T.H.	-Castle, Cooke Ltd., Castle, Cooke Bldg.
Shanghai, China	-Isthmian S.S. Co., Union Bldg., 17 Canton Road.
Manila, P.I.	-International Harvester Co., of the Philippines, U.Y. Chaco Bldg.

Singapore, S,S,	-McAlister & Co., Ltd., Gresham House.
Cape Town, So. Africa	-Mann George & Co.
Trinidad, B.W.I.	-Trinidad Leaseholds Ltd.

Allow from New York.

	REGULAR MAIL	AIRMAIL
Forward Mail to Honolulu	12 days	6 days
Forward Mail to Manila	30 days	15 days
Forward Mail to Singapore	30 days	3/3
Forward Mail to Cape Town	25 days	
Forward Mail to Trinidad	14 days	10 days

FROM THE ELLIS PARKER LOST FILES

March 4, 1936

Mr. John L. Parr

Leipzig Ave., Germania Gardens, Cologne, N.J.

Dear Friend:

I received your letter and partly agree with you. You say I've got one chance in a million, it looks like one chance in a hundred million.

The Lindbergh place is occupied by some kind of a home, and for your information, I know there were fingerprints obtained, but they didn't correspond with Hauptmann's, therefore they say they got none because they could not afford to say they did get any.

You are like myself, and thousands more who do not feel that the case is solved, by any means, all of my work on the case has been prompted entirely by JUSTICE. I am thoroughly convinced in my own mind that Bruno Hauptmann hadn't a thing to do with the kidnapping.

I want to thank you for writing me, and any time that you're in this vicinity, stop in and see me.

I remain, very truly yours,

Ellis H. Parker

Chief of County Detectives

Note: This is a significant letter. It was written over four years after the Lindbergh baby kidnapping. Ellis Parker not only divulges that he knew fingerprints were obtained during the Lindbergh home investigation but that they did not match those of Bruno Hauptmann!

This very damaging evidence was withheld by the investigation team being led by Norman Schwarzkopf and the Bruno Richard Hauptmann prosecution team. It would have created considerable doubt of Hauptmann's guilt if they had acknowledged this. Probably enough to save Hauptmann from execution. The withholding of this evidence may be among the most criminal acts in history. State Executives and Law Enforcement officials should have higher values than this. There is only one conclusion. An innocent man was sent to his death because this evidence was hidden from the Defense.

FROM THE ELLIS PARKER LOST FILES

Portland, Oregon

March 6, 1936

Dear Mr. Ellis H. Parker:

I have yours of recent dates and in reply would say that since receiving the same, I have a very important discovery.

In this week's Liberty, the telephone and address number of Jafsie in Hauptmann's home was published for the first time, and in making an examination of the same, I find that the two items were written by two people and neither one by Hauptmann. Also, one of these wrote the J. J. Faulkner deposit slip. I now know who wrote these as well as the ransom notes.

I would like to send you more detailed information, but there are two reasons why it is best at present that I do not. The collateral evidence is so great it would take a large amount of writing, and without seeing the evidence itself, it would be difficult to get the real significance of the same. And I must be careful and avoid any possible danger to myself as attempts have been made.

I have every confidence in Governor Hoffman and yourself, and if you will see him, I think you can work out a plan of procedure- but I would urge a personal interview here or there. I am POSITIVE THAT I HAVE THE COMPLETE SOLUTION OF THE MYSTERY.

I have maintained from the first that Hauptmann was innocent, but with this new evidence, it is not so clear, but he can be tested out quickly. If he will describe the friends, he was with during the part of 32, I will be able to pick them out.

Believing in your pledged statement of confidence, I will be glad to cooperate with you and Governor Hoffman to the end that we may do justice to all and serve humanity in the highest sense.

Very sincerely Yours,

W. W. Williams

8520 Willamette Blvd.

Detective Ellis H. Parker replied to the above letter as follows:

March 9, 1936

W. W. Williams

8520 Willamette Blvd., Portland, Oregon

Dear Friend:

Your letter of March 6 received, and I again appreciate your writing me. As to a personal interview or paying expenses for you to come here, it is utterly impossible, as I have borne all expenses for my investigation myself and was only interested on the side of Justice in what I have been doing. I am satisfied myself that neither Hauptmann nor Fisch wrote any of the notes, not only the original that was left by the kidnapper but the others that followed as they are an older type of writing. All of the notes were written by a person who wrote the Spencerian or vertical type, both Fisch and Hauptmann write the Palmer Zone system. Any opinion that you might have as to who wrote these notes will be kept strictly confidential by myself. I imagine that your thoughts are concurrent with mine.

Again, I want to thank you for writing me, I remain, very truly yours,

Ellis H. Parker

Chief of County Detectives

Note: The Spencerian script mentioned by Ellis Parker in his letter was an oval-based writing style used in the United States from approximately 1850 to 1925, before the invention of the typewriter. It was gradually replaced by the Palmer method of script, which became the most popular handwriting system in the United States. It is entirely feasible that individuals could have been skilled in both.

In Ellis Parker's response to W. W. Williams on March 9, 1936, he reveals once again that he has been bearing all his investigation costs personally. He very candidly infers that he feels the pressure.

W. W. Williams writes once again to Detective Parker March 14, 1936:

March 14, 1936

Mr. Ellis H. Parker

Mount Holly, New Jersey

Dear Mr. Parker:

Yours of March 9 received, and I am going to answer promptly.

I appreciate what you say in regard to writing in ransom notes and your renewed pledge of confidential relations. I am going to place complete information before you in a series of letters and will ask you to acknowledge each promptly with your approval or criticisms. We are dealing with serious evidence, and we have a common viewpoint to start with, and I believe our mutual respect will increase as we discuss my evidence. Did you write an article as Investigator No. 3 for one of McFadden's magazines? If so, I congratulate you. It is a very able article.

In order that I may present the correct picture without being too prolix, I am going to set out four periods of my activities in relation to the Lindbergh-Hauptmann cases and to the parties implicated in the kidnapping.

Period No. 1. Before the Lindbergh kidnapping. This is the period I testified against and made examinations of writings and became acquainted with the parties or at least three of them. I now have seven listed. Four were added in '34. Thus, the standards of writings were in my files and had, of course, been subjected to the most rigid examination, as is the case with all my work.

Period No. 2. From March 1, 1932, when the kidnapping occurred to Jan. 20, 1933, the period immediately after the kidnapping, when I read the papers and followed the case with no greater interest than a general interest in criminology.

Period No. 3. From Jan. 20, 1933, to the arrest of Hauptmann.

Period No. 4. The trial of Hauptmann to the present time.

I am setting these out so you can see the proper sequence of time and events and that I did not have to have any writing of Hauptmann to base my opinion on at all. Likewise, the modus operandi is important, and I became very familiar with their disguises, which I will set out later. Period No. 2, we can pass with no further comment and go on to Period No. 3.

In January, I saw in the papers the reproduction of the Schlesinger ransom note. Schlesinger was a local man and disappeared Dec. 28, 1932. It was printed throughout. I immediately recognized the printing as similar to a case I had in '31. I got out my files, and it proved to be the same. A week after, I had access to Lindbergh printed postal cards, "Baby will die,"

"Baby safe," etc., and that printing lined up with it. It also corresponds with printing on envelopes of letters sent to Jafsie as published recently in Liberty. This is the writing of a local man prominently connected here. I went to the officers here and reported it to the Federal Authorities. I also wired Lindberg and wrote him a letter, which was answered by Schwarzkopf. Some correspondence took place between Schwarzkopf and myself when I was dumbfounded to receive a letter from him that no printed postal cards or postal cards of any kind had been received in the Lindberg case. From that time, I became conscious of the thwarting and suppressing of evidence, and this through several channels. Soon thereafter, I received the last two ransom notes and connected the ransom notes written in script and highly disguised with the writings of a woman against whom I had testified and have known her for many years. Violet Sharpe's ex-husband is an old acquaintance, if not a relative of the said woman. You will see a good description of her in Jafsie's article in February 15, Liberty, on page 47. She is approximately sixty years of age, not an Italian, and was educated in American schools.

In Liberty, October 12, Page 12, you will see an account of Geissler and Weigner, as well as the reproduction of the Faulkner deposit slip. You will note the manner of averting suspicion by having families and marriage licenses and certificates. Note also there are two husbands and two wives. This tallies with my information also. That is a strong card that they play. Notice also their clever get-away. They are artists at disguises, get-away, and breaking the chain of evidence by changing names with false documents and planting of evidence. They pass as man and wife with children. The two mentioned here are the two leaders which with the two sisters to get in with men, are an unbeatable quartette in crime. Jafsie would be easy dope for them. After reading this, I would be glad to have your opinion of Jafsie if you care to express it. I have no fixed opinion except that he is a child in criminology and is a peculiar character.

In my next move, I will give my version of what the relation of the two women likely was to Hauptmann and more evidence as to suppressing of my evidence by C. Lloyd Fisher. You may be a friend of his, but that will not change the documents I have to sustain my charges.

Later I will give you the real names of these parties on a separate piece of paper. I will also prove I think that the writing used in trial with Richard Hauptmann's name signed to it was planted and was written by the woman set out above.

With best wishes for your honorable desire to aid justice in this case. If Hauptmann is electrocuted, it will be legal murder in a double sense – lack of any evidence to convict – and the suppression of evidence. Regardless of our own personal interest, let's use every honorable means to prevent it. I am with you until we kick the goal.

Very sincerely yours,

W.W. Williams,

8520 N. Willamette Blvd., Portland, Oregon

FROM THE ELLIS PARKER LOST FILES

March 10, 1936

Mrs. S. E. Mount, Wrightstown, New Jersey

Dear Friend:

I received your letter and was glad to hear from you. I wish that you had put your maiden's name down so that I would know exactly who you are. I imagine I'm the fiddler that you speak of.

As to this case you speak of, there are so darn many things around that are unexplained. In my judgment, it would be unsafe to snuff anyone's life out for the sake of trying to satisfy some particular crime. I have never yet been able to see Bruno Hauptmann in the kidnapping or murder. I only interest myself in this case on the side of Justice. I have been severely criticized, but that comes to every person who stands by their conviction. I have learned in life that there are many people who, when once form an opinion, and if anybody dare challenge it, they are ready to go out and crucify them. I am very slow on making expressions in public, and always weigh every fact because I realize that I am going to be challenged.

There isn't the first bit of evidence in this case that would convince any fair-minded person that this man Hauptmann is guilty of kidnapping and murder.

The witnesses used by the State unquestionably perjured themselves with a promise of remuneration or thought of getting paid. The latter would seem more likely to me.

Thanking you for writing me, and the next time put your maiden's name down so I can recall you. I remain, Your friend,

Ellis H. Parker

Chief of County Detectives

Note: Ellis has pointed out some important points again. The thing that jumps out to me is, *"The witnesses' used by the State unquestionably perjured themselves with a promise of remuneration or thought of getting paid. The latter would seem more likely to me."*

FROM THE ELLIS PARKER LOST FILES

March 12, 1936

Mr. Ellis H. Parker, Mount Holly, New Jersey.

My dear Mr. Parker: -

Your very, very belated letter to-hand. It is a pity that you have procrastinated your reply for so long because I believe that the financial difficulties of the defense would have been solved long ago had I been informed of its predicament.

I cannot think of what can be done now, since the date of the execution of Hauptman is set for the end of the month, but, if by the grace of "God" the Governor will grant a reprieve, the money trouble, I trust, will be of the least importance.

I suggest that you arrange for a conference between his excellency, Governor Hoffman, yourself, Attorney Fisher, and myself at the earliest possible opportunity.

I believe that we can raise $50,000 in no time to assist us in our work.

I am more than ever convinced of Hauptman's innocence.

In the last two installments of Jafsie's story, he has given himself completely away. There is no doubt in my mind that he has planned the crime. You will readily see how handicapped I am as I am "groping in the dark," not having had an opportunity to see any of the exhibits or to talk to you.

I have sent my latest suggestion to Governor Hoffman last night. It is a long shot, but who knows? I might hit the bull's-eye.

I am praying to God that, in his own way, he will bring us together very soon. I feel that a meeting between yourself and me will be of immense value in exonerating an innocent man who, at present, is in the "shadow of death."

Very truly yours

Dr. Louis Joffe
417 Lockhart Street, Pittsburgh

Ellis Parker responded to Dr. Joffe on March 23, 1936:

March 23, 1936

Dr. Louis Joffe

417 Lockhart Street

Pittsburg, Pa.

Dear Dr:

I am returning the enclosures as you requested, and as the time is close, and Hauptmann will have to prepare to meet his redeemer, it is impossible to undertake to do much. I have spent many days and months investigating this case at my own personal expense, as I felt there was something wrong, and I still feel that he is a victim.

Again, thanking you for the interest you have manifested, and it would seem to me that the only thing we can do now would be to pray for him. I remain,

Ellis H. Parker

Chief of County Detectives

Note: Bruno Richard Hauptmann did meet his redeemer on April 3rd, 1936, just 11 days after Ellis Parker wrote this letter. Hauptmann, a carpenter, was only 36 years old when he was strapped into the electric chair at the Trenton, NJ prison, where he had been incarcerated. Hauptmann insisted he was innocent until the end. His last words were, "I am absolutely innocent of the crimes with which I am charged."

I learned from the Lindbergh Kidnapping Discussion Board, Michael Melsky's fascinating website that Dr. Louis Joffe visited with Charles Lindbergh at his home on March 18th, 1932, for a discussion about the case. None of the Doctor's ideas were ever used by Charles Lindbergh.

FROM THE ELLIS PARKER LOST FILES

3-16-1936

From: Toledo-OH

Written by N.B. Rowe

Ellis Parker responded to this letter telling the writer that he didn't think the person described would fit the picture. Ellis thought that the person that did this job was along in years and had a distorted mind. The first note and those that follow are entirely different, which leads me to believe that the kidnapper is one individual, and the extortionist is another.

FROM THE ELLIS PARKER LOST FILES

Note: the Beatrice Potter story was much too large to tell all here. I am giving you a synopsis of the more exciting parts.

March 15-1936

Beatrice Potter

Worcester, Mass.

Synopsis

Beatrice Potter wrote a total of 24 letters to Detective Ellis Parker. 4 letters in 1935, 14 letters in 1936, and 6 letters in 1937. They were all in a long-hand script that was very difficult to read. Beatrice's letters were lengthy, sometimes as long as eight pages as they rambled on. She wrote all those letters while an inmate at the Worcester State Hospital in Worcester, Mass. The facility was managed by the Commonwealth of Massachusetts Department of Mental Diseases.

She once wrote to Ellis Parker, "Please don't let the hospital know I have sent this as they threatened to lock me in a back yard if I sent anymore."

She also wrote that she feared being put in the "Violent insane yard" at the asylum.

Ellis saved all of Beatrice's letters and envelopes, yet he never responded to her. That is understandable.

After writing 24 letters, I think Beatrice has earned having her story told, as hard to believe as it is:

Beatrice believed that her next-door neighbor, Joe Snyder, was the real kidnapper and was responsible for the Lindbergh baby's death. Snyder was the assassin of the Lindbergh child, she boasted. Beatrice believed that the child was killed with Snyder's cobbler's hammer. She was sure that Joe Snyder buried the Lindbergh baby in the rabbit coup he had built near her property. This, for her, explained the horrible smell coming from it. "Funny how the smell went away after the Lindbergh baby was found in the woods."

She declared that the repulsive, cunning criminal Joe Snyder framed Richard Hauptmann and that he was a German military agent. She saw Snyder bring the real ladder back to hide in his basement the night of the kidnapping. She believed that the same man who had built the rabbit coup had made the kidnap ladder. Beatrice also noticed "the real criminal limped, and so did Joe Snyder." She also informed Ellis that Snyder knew J. J. Faulkner.

Beatrice told Ellis, "The Snyder's were strange people and jealous of everything I have in my house. Mrs. Snyder wanted everything. They were jealous of my flowers, so they crept in the yard at night when nobody was around to pour rye or lime on them. That's why they all died. My rose bush too. My windows all burned loose because the putty was chipped off, and I believe that's what they must have poured down that poor child's throat. That's why there were no internal organs, as the medical examiner said."

Beatrice charges that she was being kept in the Worcester Asylum against her will to keep her from proving Snyder was guilty of the Lindbergh baby abduction. She was demanding her release.

Beatrice begged Ellis Parker in her letters to have her released while describing the horrible conditions she was enduring. She hated that her husband was living in adultery with "that Nellie Brown."

"No wonder Snyder bragged of his smartness, "I smart guy, and I can fix anything." Perhaps he fixed it so I would be railroaded to the nuthouse. People are so simple, and no wonder he picked that convenient back yard for the spot."

I think I was also framed so that if I realized what I was all about, and told, they could get me railroaded to a Lunatic asylum as people would think me crazy. What a pity as I was quite sane but frightened a little, that's all.

<u>Note</u>: No wonder Ellis Parker never responded to Beatrice's 24 letters!

FROM THE ELLIS PARKER LOST FILES

March 17, 1936

J. T. McGuire

3852 Calumet Avenue

Chicago, Illinois

Dear Friend,

Your letter of March 14, received. On the baby found in the woods near the Lindbergh estate, the fontanelle is about an inch in diameter. The baby being twenty-two months old would show that the baby found was subnormal. This corresponds with the Doctor's report of the baby that was examined prior to its disappearance.

The clothing found on the baby that was identified as being on the Lindbergh baby at the time it disappeared.

I wish to thank you for writing me because suggestions sometimes are very helpful, and I always feel that a person that is enough interested to express their views does it with the thought of assisting.

Again, thanking you, I remain, very truly yours,

Ellis H. Parker

Chief of County Detectives

<u>Note</u>: That the child's fontanelle was subnormal is concerning. It lends credibility to the theory that Charles Lindbergh Jr. had developmental issues that his father may have found embarrassing.

Lindbergh's belief in Eugenics could explain the abnormal fontanelle. A fascination that continued throughout his life up to his death. Eugenics is the practice of arranging reproduction to increase more desirable characteristics. The Nazi party adopted this doctrine as a reason to justify their extermination of the Jews. Eugenics was later discredited as immoral and racist after the Nazis were defeated in World War II.

FROM THE ELLIS PARKER LOST FILES

829 Orange Street, Yuba City, Calif.

March 26, 1936

Hon. Ellis Parker, Mt. Holly, New Jersey

Dear Mr. Parker; -

I have writer's itch to say one more thing about Hauptmann, whom I rather expect will be alive after March 30th. However, my point may be one you already canvassed.

I wonder if it were not just possible the "kidnap ladder" when built was not intended nor designed for the window of the child's nursery at Hopewell, but perhaps for a room of the Morrow home at Englewood.

That possibility I have not seen advanced in the press or anywhere at any time. But I have read that the ladder was too short.

Well, dead men tell no tales. With Hauptmann electrocuted, the investigation would perhaps shut up shop.

Yours truly,

M. A. Carpenter

<u>Note:</u> This idea that the ladder was designed for the Morrow home in Englewood, New Jersey, has been discussed in other letters. It was the perfect design and length for the Morrow home but not optimal for Hopewell's new Lindbergh home. This leads us to believe that Charles Lindbergh Junior's kidnapping had been planned for some time. The perpetrators may have grown tired of waiting for Charles to move his family to Hopewell. Isn't it strange that the kidnapping occurred on the earliest possible day? One of the first days that Charles and his wife Anne decided to stay overnight with their newborn in their completed new home? Or was Charles Lindbergh waiting for the optimal time? His new Hopewell home was isolated.

FROM THE ELLIS PARKER LOST FILES

March 29, 1936

2: 40 am

Mr. David Wilentz, Trenton, NJ

Dear sir,

This is to inform you that I knew nothing about the kidnapping and murder of Charles Lindbergh Jr. and was never on the Lindbergh property.

I know nothing about the crime except what I read and heard.

I did sign several statements which were false, which implicated me. I was forced by torture and brutal treatment In New York where I was detained from February 14 to February 24, 1936, from that date until today, I was detained by Ellis Parker Jr., at the State Colony at New Lisbon, N.J., under guard, two in day and extra at night.

I pleaded with Ellis Parker Jr., Dr. Jones, to get in touch with the Attorney General of New Jersey, Colonel Schwarzkopf, and Pros. Hauck and I ask if he did not deliver me to the above to return me to Mercer County, he kept telling me when he got ready, he would act and not before. Ellis Parker, who I thought was my friend, tried to tell that Pros. Hauck and Attorney Wilentz would be superseded by any he would name because Gov. Hoffman assured he would do so, that I was to plead guilty with a lawyer that confession would be used and I could write a story that I had been out of my mind and suddenly come to and realized what I had done which startle not only the medical but would make me a million dollars and my family could live easy the rest of their lives. Parker promised me that the Attorney General Wilentz, Pros. Hauck or Justice Trenchen would not try the case that the Governor Hoffman was Governor, and he would appoint anyone Parker asked him to. He said he would appoint Pros. Eastwood and have a special Grand Jury appointed to indict me, and then if it were tried in Hunterdon that he would speak to Judge Robbins about it, and I would get the benefit of it (meaning his friendship with Judge Robins). I knew that Parker was trying to do me harm, so I built up a defense for myself. I could show Pros. Hauck and Attorney General Wilentz just what was going on. I ask for law books which were brought to me, and I wrote to showing him that Governor Hoffman could not supersedes Pros. Hauck or Wilentz. I told Parker that the lie wanted me to plead to something I did not was out of question. I told him after he had informed that I want to plead guilty so that the Court would look ridiculous and make a laughingstock out of Attorney General Wilentz and Col. Schwarzkopf and State Police.

Sg. Paul H. Wendel

H. W. Bradley, Sheriff

Under Sheriff C. J. Milltop

Thomas Conrad, Special Deputy, Mercer County, Trenton, N.J.

<u>Note</u>: This letter is significant because Paul Wendel clearly created it after meeting with David Wilentz five days after leaving the State Colony in New Lisbon, New Jersey. Wendel had gone to the Colony willingly to rest at the suggestion of Detective Ellis Parker. Wendel had requested that he be taken directly to Detective Parker in Mt. Holly after his release from the New York City basement, where he claims he had been held against his will.

The grammar of the letter has not been corrected. It reads exactly as the copy we retain except for the addition of a few commas.

We believe that David Wilentz convinced Paul Wendel to repudiate his confession and write the above letter during their meeting either at the Colony or shortly after leaving there.

If you compare this letter and Wendel's confessions, it is hard to believe his claims of torture. It reads like a calculating, guilty man looking for a way out after he has confessed the truth. Notice that Wendel is still looking for "The Big Score" of a million dollars. That was always his goal throughout his whole life—the life of an evil con artist, fraudulent pharmacist, suspected bootlegger or organized crime associate, and disbarred lawyer. It is also interesting to note that after Wendel repudiated his confession and wrote this letter, all his outstanding criminal charges and warrants disappeared.

FROM THE ELLIS PARKER LOST FILES

April 1st, 1936

Detective Ellis Parker

Mt. Holly, New Jersey

Dear Sir:

In the January 15th, 1936, issue of the New York Daily News, there was printed copies of letters written by Dr. John F. Condon. We wish to call attention to the fact that the majority of the "I"s were not dotted, and most of the "T"s are not crossed. This similarity to the writings in the ransom notes is significant as these were some of the principal points brought out by the prosecution against Bruno Hauptmann. Kindly look into this matter.

Yours truly,

Anonymous

<u>Note</u>: As has been pointed out in my past notes, Detective Ellis Parker was suspicious of Dr. Condon's role in the case. Here, only two days before Bruno Richard Hauptmann's execution, Anonymous is questioning if Condon could have had a hand in composing the ransom notes.

FROM THE ELLIS PARKER LOST FILES

<u>Note</u>: This is the first letter of 7 total in this file. There is a separate Confidential report on Paul H. Wendel that Howell S. Cresswell wrote. A newspaper clipping was enclosed identifying the man who presented himself to Howell S. Cresswell as an ex-attorney. It is Paul H. Wendel.

This information is an essential addition to the **Ellis Parker Lost Files** because Paul H. Wendel was the only person to sign a written confession to the Lindbergh baby kidnapping and murder. Detective Ellis H. Parker obtained the confession.

But that is not all that is revealed. This is quite a ride. Please stay until the end.

<u>The following is the first letter:</u>

117 N. College Street

Ottumwa, Iowa

April 1, 1936

Mr. Ellis H. Parker

Mount Holly, N.J.

Dear Mr. Parker:

Have followed with interest your work on case. Also, read story in Chicago Tribune about chasing down 70 NELLY'S (Boat). Result was interesting and, to a certain point, evidently needs contributing data and facts. However, it leads in direction one would supposed to be logical one, i.e., to Fisch and that he or persons present with him saw that boast in harbor of Stonington, Conn. Thank you for developing that lead. A great deal of work even if result was or is not as yet conclusive.

Have your information as to whether Paul H. Wendel was in Paris about the month of October 1933?

I met in a small restaurant-café (called "Chez Jaques") in the Rue Delambre, Montparnasse section, a man strikingly resembles photos in yesterday's papers.

It was about 2 a.m. This early hour was due to my work as a newspaperman with Paris edition of Tribune. I was seated in the rear of the café. Place was full, and I only had one seat to take. This was next to a man answering the description of Wendel, who was talking with a young man in '20s (say about 24) whom I took to be either his son or friend introduced to him. The crowd moved out, and I was left next to the two. As my rule is to make my nationality known when conversation takes place in English, I did so. (I have had embarrassing things happen by not doing so).

Gentleman was very friendly. Gave me his card, which I should still have somewhere and which I remembered as Kiendle or such. It read that he has former legal advisor or ex-legal Dep't of Central R.R. of N.J.! I spoke of difficulties arising from the death of my mother and of perplexing letters from the administrator, by all means. His advice proved only too true.

So, I wrote about four months ago to the legal Department of central N.J. in Philadelphia, to find out who their former associate might be as his advice turned out overwhelmingly correct. (One of the items is that a bank employee tried to steal my mother's savings account of $847!) But legal department made an inquiry and could locate no one. They were sure they knew them all. They wrote they were highly interested. For what reason, I do not know, unless they suspected an imposter.

May tell you that conversation between this ex-lawyer and the young man was very much undertone, paper and pencil being used and careful pondering of whatever the scheme or plan was they had under consideration.

Hence my desire to avow my nationality to prevent what seemed to be a very confidential matter being overheard.

Now this man was medium height. He talked by jerks, first thinking and then talking snappy and rapidly, then stopping and repeating a rapid, precise opinion. He was inclined to be heavy built, but not excessive. I believe he emphasized his thoughts by a jerk of right hand downward.

I hope I find his card here. If this helps you in any way, I shall be happy. One can never tell. He certainly was a retired lawyer, insisted he was not looking for money.

Yours Very Sincerely,

Howard S. Cresswell

Note: Howard S. Cresswell's description of Wendel is dead on. Wendel was a con man his entire life. Could the man in his 20's with Paul Wendel have been his son? Cresswell mentions the card given to him by Wendel. What a lost opportunity.

<u>Ellis Parker responded to the above letter on 4-4-1936, the day after Bruno Richard Hauptmann was executed:</u>

April 4, 1936

Mr. Howell S. Cresswell

117 N. College St.

Ottumwa, Iowa

Dear. Mr. Cresswell

I received your letter, and I would be glad to have anything that you might assist me with. At present, I am unable to give any information about Paul H. Wendel, as the Grand Jury of another County is at present, making an inquiry about him.

Again, thanking you, I remain,

Very truly yours,

Ellis H. Parker

Chief of County Detectives

<u>Note</u>: Unfortunately for Ellis Parker, Paul Wendel would rescind his signed confession accusing Detective Parker of imprisoning and torturing him until he would sign the confession. Wendel was assisted by the ever-willing David Wilentz, who was deathly afraid of seeing his Hauptmann conviction overturned.

<u>M. Howell S. Cresswell wrote again on 4-7-1936:</u>

<u>Note</u>: Please be reminded again that anytime Cresswell writes of "X," he identifies Paul Wendel.

117 N. College St., Ottumwa, Iowa.

April 7, 1936

Mr. Ellis H. Parker, Mount Holly, New Jersey

Dear Mr. Parker:

Your letter of the April 4th here. I understand the circumstances. For your use, I enclose a more detailed repetition of data in my other letter. This you can file in an appropriate place or reference.

Newspapers give little information RE Paul H. Wendel to allow me to connect him with Paris in October 1933. I say October 1933 as administrator wrote the two letters which X handled shortly after my mother's death on September 7, 1933. These arrived in Paris and of September., So it was not long after that and certainly not as late as November as I had subsequent letters from the administrator. At that moment, ONLY TWO. Hence X could have seen only these first two. Hence, I place it in early October or at the very end of September.

Up to you to delve this out. Not me. I have no machinery here. Only State Department would have record of issue of passports. Maybe he used the other name, as mentioned in papers of Alpert.

His presence in Paris may or may NOT be of importance. I can't tell with lack of facts, movements, etc. We all know Paris was a hotbed of headquarters in Europe for bootlegging. There was a woman there who was a cover for them and who acted as paymaster for incorporated bootleggers. This was common knowledge in Paris.

The enclosed photo is an ABSOLUTE IMAGE OF THE MAN I TALKED TO. He seemed heavy or chunky for his height, which I put at 5 foot 10 and no more.

Perhaps you have a friend in the legal department of Central of J a Phila (Jersey Central Railroad)? You have the liberty of mentioning my correspondence. But I would not care to make a mistake to be regretted. But I may tell you that fellow I met had a murky psychic smell about him in spite of his wish to advise me.

I would be willing to send you the two letters for finger-prints if there are any and enclose my own. About five people handled those letters, including myself, X, etc. But your work would be to see if he was in Europe in 1933 in October. You may know without having recourse to other ways. If his presence had any bearing on the case, I really do not know. Police in Paris can give you information unless the passport was mutilated. Many hoarders and money changers are holding on to U.S. gold certificates. Hoping for revaluation of the dollar or having their own governments force the U.S. to honor gold clause. A cryptic place for ransom notes!

I am leaving for a trip to Ozarks Re some zinc mines we have there and may be away for nearly two weeks but would see that any urgent letter from you would be forwarded or contents wired to me.

Very Sincerely yours,

Howell S. Cresswell

This following confidential report on Paul H. Wendel was attached:

CONFIDENTIAL
April 6, 1936
Paul H. Wendel.

In early October 1933, a person answering description and photo, as published in newspapers last week, conversed with me in a small cafe' restaurant in the Rue Delcambre, Paris, (XIV arrondissement, called Montparnasse). The name of the cafe' is "Chez Jacques," at approx. Nr. 9 on the same street.

This is a place for rendezvous for late-night habitués, including those called by profession to be up at late hours. (I had been working on morning edition of Chicago Tribune, Paris Edition, had given up job because of death of my mother and forced return, but retained the habit of late hours.)

Chez Jacques is a small place, differing from the large boulevard cafes, and is well suited for a private conversation.

I was sitting at the rear of the room. The place was full. I occupied only vacant seat left. In the corner was gentlemen answering the description, as mentioned. With him, a young man, say about 24 years of age, air of college boy of good breeding and well dressed. X was explaining something very private to a young man with paper and pencil on the table. The room somewhat emptied, and it became possible to overhear the conversation.

As I always declare my nationality under such circumstances, I did so. This to avoid embarrassment to myself if I overheard what was supposed to be private or secret and also not to embarrass the other party.

I explained my position as about to return because of death in the family. Let it out that I was perplexed by vague letters from the administrator of my mother's estate. Whereupon X said, "I am a lawyer though not practicing now. I'd like to see those two letters that trouble you. I am not going to charge you for services but am sure I could let you know something."

He either gave me or showed me his card. It read "??????" ex-legal counsel to the Central of New Jersey (or Jersey Central Railroad).

X expressed extreme doubt as to the integrity of my administrator and advised I should change him immediately and by cable. To get another man.

Though I agreed, it was awkward because of the intimate family friendship for the administrator. But X was more than right. They tried to swindle me of most of the estate, crooked up accounts, watered estate figures to get fees in excess, attempted to steal a savings account of $847....but this is not the line with what you want as to X.

X is identical with the photo enclosed. Can't say so for other photos shown in papers. But this one to the dot! Unless it is a coincidence and a double. He was around 50 or over in looks, heavily built, but not tall.

X had a manner of regarding these two letters attentively, grunting or humming a bit, then firing a volley of thought. Emphasized with a jerk of hand and arm a bit.

Now some 5 months or so ago, I tried to locate X through the legal department of the Central of Jersey. They wrote back that they were much interested and more than interested and amazed. Led me to think they knew and suspected a man flying under false colors! They asked me for further data, but I could supply none. I seemed to recall the name of Kiendle or Kendall but as a Germanic name. I wished to tell him his prediction came true as to my administrator of estate and to thank him, believing he would be pleased.

He must have had powerful hypnotic power as the young man with him seemed in a daze and looked so attentively at his paper and pencil.

Note: "X" is, of course, Paul H. Wendel. Wendel is doing what he would do for his whole life. Run a con, for profit. Long after the Lindbergh case was being forgotten, Wendel was still doing it. The term "Bootleggers" is referenced several times in the above letter. In this era, the term "Bootlegger" is interchangeable with "mob," "mobster," "organized crime," or "underworld."

Ellis did mention that there was a space of time that he did not know Wendel's whereabouts. We know now that Ellis was overwhelmed with his fight over the doubtful accusations that he had imprisoned and tortured Wendel.

In this letter, Howell Cresswell continues:

117 N. College St., Ottumwa, Iowa.

June 11, 1936

Mr. Ellis Parker, Mount Holly, N.J.

Dear Mr. Parker:

Thoroughly disgusted with the developments RE your case. It has all the earmarks of a scandalous frame-up. The names of those gangster kidnapers sound in spelling and atmosphere of the last dregs of a paid under-world that will do anything at the request of politicians or others interested. The fact that they were SO EASILY OBTAINED in a mere 24-hour hunt proves that.

Trust my other letter reached you. I have no means of knowing if the party can really be checked up as being in Paris end of September 1933 or the first week of October of that year. Even if so, it may have no weight. But if that was not the same man from facts and photos, it must be a double.

Yours Very Sincerely,

Howell S. Cresswell

Hope to see this last affair exposed as it should be. Papers say very little, which proves there is not much in it.

Note: Howell Cresswell continues with his analysis of the Lindbergh crime. He is right on. In his opinion, it was a frame-up, and gangsters were involved. The underworld was accessible to the politicians. And Bruno Richard Hauptmann was a "Scapegoat" as Anthony Scaduto would famously name him many years later in his brilliant work, his bestselling book "SCAPEGOAT."

Ellis Parker responds to Howell S. Cresswell on 6-15-1936:

June 15, 1936

Mr. Howell S. Cresswell

117 N. College Street, Ottumwa, Iowa

Dear Friend Mr. Cresswell:

Your two letters received, and I certainly appreciate your writing to me. You have the right deduction in this affair. All the people involved against me are crooks, even to some of the so-called enforcement officers.

I see by this morning press that the acting Governor of New York has signed extradition papers for my return to that State, but I'm going to fight the papers here when it comes to a hearing before our Governor because I know I can lick them because I was not in New York State as they claim. My indictment was nothing but to cover up some of their own shortcomings, and to keep their name off the front page, as some of the officers in New York are under investigation themselves, that is back of this proposition.

In regard to the photograph, you sent me in the first letter, which is of Paul Wendel, I could not ascertain whether he might be the one or not because there was a space of time that I had no knowledge of his whereabouts, but I doubt really whether it was him or not, as I'm sure he wasn't away long enough to go from here, there, and back. If he did, it couldn't have been over a month that he was away.

He has brothers, but I have never seen them and do not know very much about them.

Again, I want to thank you for writing to me and assure you that I appreciate everything that you have said. With best wishes, I remain, very truly yours,

Ellis H. Parker

Chief of County Detectives

Note: In this letter, Ellis clarifies that he is fighting crooks that are even enforcement officers. He understands his enemies have no scruples. Ellis tells of being busy fighting off the attempts to extradite him to New York, where Ellis would be tried for kidnapping Paul Wendel. He moved to have it held in New Jersey, which was his right, preferably in his Mount Holly hometown.

Hauptmann was executed on April 3, 1936. Wendel had rescinded his confession on February 10, 1936. Wendel claimed he was tortured until he agreed to falsely write and sign the confession that Parker would use to delay the Hauptmann execution.

The Hauptmann prosecution team was behind the effort to expedite Ellis to New York. The David Wilentz-led team could ill afford to have Detective Parker back at work on the Hauptmann case. Even though

Hauptmann had been executed, they were still afraid that Ellis would continue his investigation to prove that Hauptmann's death was unjust and engineered fraudulently. Wilentz and his team greatly feared losing the celebrity and rewards of the fame they gained for their successful prosecution and execution of the Lindbergh baby killer. The rewards and recognition set them up for a comfortable future. However, many believed they had done it with Hauptmann's innocent blood on their hands.

Howell S. Cresswell responds on August 21, 1936:

> August 21, 1936
> 117 N. College St., Ottumwa, Iowa.
>
> Mr. Ellis H. Parker, Mount Holly, New Jersey
>
> Dear Mr. Parker:
>
> I have followed with increasing interest the Curtis story in Liberty Magazine now running. As it coincides so closely with all my own doping out of the case, I could not help but write you to point this out. I just hope private investigation will follow up more closely the clues, unfortunately, disregarded, as mentioned by Curtis.
>
> I believe the Larsen episode is parallel to my idea of the "BOAT NELLY," which some friend of yours evidently chased down and found a connection with Isidore Fisch. I would say again that whoever spoke of Larsen also were in same vicinity at Cape May, and I believe nearly all these names may have been faked, and they (he, Larsen) used the name Larsen because he saw of or knew of these Larsen's in Cape May.
>
> They all turn out to be ex-bootleggers as I thought they were in my first letter to you. My conjecture of the "split gang" is also brought out. I got that idea not from my imagination but from things said in so-called ransom notes. (I agree with you that there was just ONE real ransom note and the rest were extortion notes, though the public and others classify

all those notes as "the ransom notes.") Also, there were happenings which could not be explained except by a split in the ranks of the gang. The split (unless proved to the contrary) was due to fear at the probable death of the baby, at first perhaps not known to all the gang but learned by them later.

I cannot help but express my indignation at the attitude of Schwarzkopf and am glad Hoffman got rid of him. His police not only gave third degree and extorted a false confession from Curtis but also even attempted to blackmail and extort a confession from that contortionist, Condon. And how many more! Certainly, it is not a proper way to get at the truth by hiding it. It appears more like cowardice, fear of aroused public sentiment at his failure to get the kidnaper, followed by his breaking down and letting anything pass as the truth to satisfy the public and Lindbergh and finally do away with Hauptmann and end it all, and collect the reward!

Of course, you know of the many other shortcomings of the Jersey police under Schwarzkopf.

It is also too bad that the personal prominence of Lindbergh cast a hypnotic daze over so many, including Condon. Schwarzkopf frankly admitted his impotence by bowing to ideas and directions of Lindbergh. But I do not believe Lindbergh personally intended it to be so. He was the greater man, Schwarzkopf, and Condon, the little men. I also believe that Schwarzkopf realized that Curtis was on the right trail, and to cover his failures, he was glad of the opportunity to seize upon Condon amateur work and finally force the blame on Hauptmann at all costs.

I may have overlooked, but it would seem strange that work was not also done to try and find that house in Trenton, where Curtis talked with Hilda and others. They tried to find the house in Newark but failed. Perhaps you or others will run down the Trenton house.

The whole affair seems to boil down to one of a story of mass intimidations, including your own affair, which I know of. I am just hoping Governor Hoffmann will act with an iron hand and put those responsible where they belong.

I again repeat that I am so glad that what I wrote you previously seems to be borne out of this Curtis story. I find my mixtures of nationalities just as I conjectured, not to speak of the split gang. I can easily understand why you became interested in my ideas as you likely knew these facts secretly though I did not until Liberty began the series of Curtis stories. Now I realize why you took the trouble to write me. My only source of information was the setting and the to-and-fro or backwards and forwards sort of wishy-washy tell-tale in the language of the notes.

I may add that I heard a Professor Leslie of the Department of Justice school of Chicago lecture here last Fall. He spoke at length of the Lindbergh case, likely because it was a la page. He stressed the sketch of Hauptmann as taken down by an agent from the description given by Condon. I let him know that I could go in New York and find nearly 1,000 answering the same sketch tomorrow. He looked at me in surprise.

Also, the mention of other $10 notes being found in Canada as sent from Norfolk seems to have been left in the dark.

I hope you will discover something before long and that you will be rewarded by a similar series of stories in Liberty to denounce those irresponsible and vindicate Hoffman, not to speak of Hauptmann.

Yours Very Sincerely,
Howell S. Cresswell

<u>Note</u>: Cresswell again brings up the John Hughes Curtis story and a connection with ex-bootleggers. He also points at the relation to these individuals had with Isadore Fisch. A relationship that is still suspicious. Olaf "Dynamite" Larson is also mentioned.

<u>Ellis Parker responded on September 18, 1936:</u>

> September 18, 1936
>
> Mr. Howell S. Cresswell
> 117 N. College Street, Ottumwa, Iowa
>
> Dear Mr. Cresswell:
>
> Your letter of August 21 received, and as I was away on a vacation, did not get the opportunity to answer sooner.
>
> I appreciate the thoughts contained in your letter, and although I am not in a position to make a statement at this time, I hope that there will be a time when I can express myself as I would like.
>
> Again, thanking you for your interest, and hoping that someday this matter will be adjusted to the satisfaction of everyone, I remain, very truly yours,
>
> Ellis H. Parker
> Chief of County Detectives

<u>Note</u>: The writer of these letters is Howell S. Cresswell. He was born in 1885, and at the time of these writings, he was 51 years old and living in Ottumwa, Iowa. He was a graduate of Cornel University. After graduation, he had lived in Paris, France, for seven years.

I have addressed the John Hughes Curtis story in another letter. To summarized, Curtis tells Charles Lindbergh that he knows the location of Charles Lindbergh's son. Curtis supposedly is acting on behalf of a Norfolk, Virginia seaman who has the baby. Curtis kept the ruse going until the Lindbergh baby was found in the woods near the Lindbergh estate on May 12, 1932. Before the baby was found, several airplanes and boats were used to comb the seas off the coasts of Delaware and Maryland, searching for the vessel that held the Lindbergh baby. Unbelievably the ship always eluded them for one reason or another. Cutis kept telling Lindbergh that he was in touch with the kidnapper's gang. When the Lindbergh baby's body was found, the gig was up. No money had ever exchanged hands. John Hughes Curtis signed a confession on May 16, 1932, admitting it was all a hoax. Curtis was later tried for the scheme and convicted of obstructing justice. He was fined $1000, but the story didn't end there. Curtis later repudiated his signed confession. Curtis was put on trial in the same courthouse as Bruno Richard Hauptmann would later be sentenced to death. Amazingly and unexplainably, the transcripts of Curtis's trial were lost! Who would profit from their loss or destruction?

FROM THE ELLIS PARKER LOST FILES

April 2, 1936

Long Island, N.Y.

Dear Sir –

Have heard as has others that the Lindbergh baby was deaf and dumb.

If so, that would account for quietness in being kept or being taken.

Please investigate.

Yours truly,

Unreadable signature

Note: Many Americans have questioned the health of Lindbergh's baby. Charles Lindbergh's embracement of Adolph Hitler and his philosophies was well known. Lindbergh would later acknowledge his belief in Eugenics that would become an essential proponent of Hitler's ideals. He would later campaign to keep the United States out of WWII. Sadly, his son, Charles Junior, may have been an embarrassment to him. Lindbergh's interest in politics was growing. He may have pursued Dwight Morrow, Elizabeth, and Ann's daughters to enhance his profile as an electable politician and align himself with the Morrow's family fame. Who better to be the father-in-law of a President? Dwight Morrow had been a friend of Calvin Coolidge, a U.S. Senator, an Ambassador to Mexico, and a partner in the prestigious firm of J.P. Morgen.

FROM THE ELLIS PARKER LOST FILES

J. George Dages

REALTOR

308 THIRD STREET

BEACH HAVEN, N.J.

MEMBER, LONG BEACH N.J.

STATE AND NATIONAL ASSOCIATION OF REAL ESTATE BOARDS

TELEPHONE 158

April 4, 1936

Mr. Ellis Parker

Mt. Holly N.J.

Dear Mr. Parker:

Just a few lines to commend you for your noble efforts to save Hauptmann, and I am sure sorry that he was sent to the chair as I do not believe for a minute that he was guilty of this crime, and I consider this whole episode a disgrace, and I am by no means alone in this opinion, almost every person to whom I spoke about it to in the past few days thinks the same way.

WHY DID NOT THEY PUT YOU ON THIS JOB AT THE BEGINNING?

This is what most people want to know.

Why was this Russian, Wilentz, in such a hurry to put Hauptmann out of the way? Is this Russian Justice?

I only hope that we will get this rotten mess cleared up sometime soon, and if there is one man that can do it, it is you. Best regards to your son.

Sincerely yours,

J. George Dages

Ellis Parker responded to J. George Dages on 4-7-1936:

April 7, 1936

Mr. J. George Dages
308 Third Street, Beach Haven, N.J.

Dear Friend Mr. Dages:

I received your splendid letter this morning, and I am glad to hear that some other people think as I do. I was only interested in this case on the side of Justice.

Immediately after it occurred, I was requested by the Governor to interest myself, which I did. Today I am being severely criticized for what little part I played. I never had the advantage of getting any information from the inside. Therefore, I was somewhat handicapped, but I have no complaint to make because it was their affairs and their case, not mine.

Again, thanking you for writing me, and my son Ellis, Jr. wants to be remembered to you and your family. With regards, I am,

Ellis H. Parker
Chief of County Detectives

Note: Ellis Parker owned a home on New Jersey's Long Beach Island. He took his family there often. From the numerous pictures that Andy Sahol (Ellis Parker's Grandson) shared with me, it is evident that he and his family loved their seashore home. From his letter's warm tone, I suspect that J. George Dages may have helped Ellis find his beloved home on the Island.

Ellis explained his work on the Lindbergh case to his friend in his letter. Ellis wrote of the problems he faced when doing an investigation from the outside and of having information withheld from

FROM THE ELLIS PARKER LOST FILES

Parker Sisters

347 Whittington Ave., Hot Springs, Ark.,

April 4, 1936

Dear Mr. Parker: -

What a sorry spectacle Governor Hoffman has made of the Hauptmann case, and any further investigation on his part will be a mockery. After all the hard work you have done to bring to justice to the real kidnapper, and they let you down on the last go around. That is the most disastrous blow that could have been handed out to a person. It looks like you are at a dead end. We never knew a person by the name of Parker that was a quitter, and that would not fight to hell froze over then fight them 40 years on the ice.

Accept our wishes,

We are sincerely yours,

Parker Sisters

Ellis Parker responded to the Parker Sisters on 4-9-1936:

April 9, 1936

Parker Sisters

347 Whittington Avenue, Hot Springs, Ark.

My Dear Sisters:

I received your letter, and I want to explain the Governor's position on this matter. Under the circumstances, the Governor couldn't do a thing other than to refuse to grant another reprieve as the law doesn't permit him to do it.

I fought until I had nothing to fight with, and today his spirit is to go on and show the others that they made a mistake. I am sure if the law gave him the power, he would have continued to grant reprieves until this case was closed, but the court's decisions were all against him, and he went as far as he could. I am only telling you so that you will not place him wrong. Since this has happened, I haven't been able to see him, but I have spoken to others close to him, and I think he felt worse than any other person in this state when he knew he couldn't grant another reprieve, however as long as my health permits, I intend to go on, and perhaps one-day things will break my way, and I'll be able to show this world that this was a bad mistake.

I wish to thank you for writing me the splendid letter, and I want to assure you that even though I was alone in my stand in this case, I would still stick to what I thought was right, and Justice, I remain,

Very truly yours,

Ellis H. Parker

Chief of County Detectives

Note: I doubt there is any family relationship between the two Parker families, but I am not sure of that. The Parker Sisters wrote their letter the day after Bruno Richard Hauptmann was executed.

Ellis writes to the Parker Sisters to defend his friend New Jersey, Governor Harold Hoffman. Ellis's longtime and robust loyalty to the Governor as a friend and inspiration is well-spoken. Ellis also makes it clear that his investigation is not ending. He vows to continue seeking justice as long as his health allows. Unfortunately, Ellis will be attacked by the Hauptmann prosecution team for this, and his health issues will worsen. Eventually, the Hauptmann prosecution team will be successful. Ellis H. Parker will be sentenced to a 6-year prison term on June 30, 1937. His son,

Ellis Parker Jr., will also be sentenced to 3 years for Paul H. Wendel's supposed abduction. Wendel had signed a confession admitting kidnapping and causing the death of the Lindbergh baby. Wendel later rescinded his confession after meeting with New Jersey Attorney General and successful Hauptmann prosecutor David Wilentz. Ellis Parker's health deteriorated until his death, attributed to a brain tumor, in Lewisburg Prison on February 4th, 1940. A posthumous pardon was immediately sought but never confirmed.

FROM THE ELLIS PARKER LOST FILES

April 5, 1936

Dear Ellis Parker,

I'm writing to you in regard to a sea captain, which I know, by the name of Captain Reiholdt DeLein. I have always suspicioned this man as having something to do in the Lindberg Case. I base my suspicions on the fact that he and his wife moved here from East Orange, New Jersey, in August 1932, a few months after the kidnapping, with quite a few thousand dollars on his person. According to his relatives, he had never had any money before this.

During the time he was around this neighborhood, a supposed-to-be broker from New York came to visit them quite often. Now I suspect that probably this man might have been Wendell.

This Captain DeLein has disappeared ever since the day that Hauptmann was arrested and hasn't been seen since. His wife claims that she does not know where he is. Now since Hauptmann is dead, she is thinking about moving back to New Jersey.

If you would come to see me, I could send you to two different people who have seen and talked to this broker and could tell you his name.

I am giving you my name and address on a separate sheet of paper. Please keep it confidential, but do not delay in coming to see me. I don't want my name mentioned until the case has been investigated, and my suspicions have been found to be true., as I don't know to what kind of a gang he may belong. Until then, I wish my name to be kept quiet. Please.

Yours,

Louis Dreyer

R.D. #3, Sewickley, Pa.

PS: As I work in Midland, Pa., you can see me from Monday to Friday between the hours of 10 A.M. to 2 P.M. each day at 649 Penn Ave., where I room, or if not there at the City Restaurant on Midland Avenue, where I eat. Please keep this personal.

Ellis Parker responded on 4-14-1936:

April 14, 1936

Mr. Louis Dreyer

R.D. #3

Sewickley, Pa.

Dear Friend:

Your letter of April 5 was received. It is utterly impossible for me to get up to see you at this time, as you undoubtedly realize just how busy I am. I would like you to see the people you mentioned, and get this broker's name, and any information you care to send me will be kept strictly confidential.

Thank you for writing to me, and trusting that I may hear from you in the very near future, I remain,

Very truly yours,

Ellis H. Parker

Chief of County Detectives

<u>Note</u>: By now, after reading many of these letters, you know of the many sightings of Paul Wendel told by those writing Ellis Parker, including the one in Mr. Louis Dreyer's letter above. We can only hope you see why we are so confident of his cowardly acts.

This has only increased our belief that Paul H. Wendel, most likely accompanied by Isador Fisch, took the baby from the Lindbergh home. Once again, we will point out that we believe that Detective Ellis Parker, America's Sherlock Holmes, solved the case and presented the only signed confession, that of Paul Wendel, to the world.

FROM THE ELLIS PARKER LOST FILES

105 Harding Park, Clason Point, Bronx

April 7, 1936

Mr. Ellis Parker

Burlington Co., New Jersey

Dear Sir:

For three years, I have interested myself considerably in the Lindbergh case about which I know much. The angle on which you are now making fits absolutely into a story I heard, so I am going to tell you the story as briefly as may be. Then I believe you would be interested in talking with me and hearing my contacts with Col. Lindbergh and his lawyers, the New Jersey State Police, the Department of Justice, the New York Police Department, and the New York Daily News.

I am a woman of sixty-three, born in New York on Manhattan Island. A series of misadventures left me financially flat. Some of these happenings may eventually be traced to the desire for my effacement from the Lindbergh case. In February 1934, I was recovering from rheumatic fever and was still lame.

On the day that the mercury dropped to fifteen below zero, I went to my church (Episcopal) and got a card admitting me to S. Barnabas House, 304 Mulberry St. I was privileged to occupy a cubicle which gave me the privacy of a locked door and many comforts. We, of the cubicles, were permitted to use a large upstairs recreation room, with piano, large chairs, etc. smoking was also allowed. In this room were two or three couches. After I had been there a week or two, one evening, a woman, Mrs. Mary Rooney, was brought in by the New York Police Department for shelter. She was accompanied by her daughter Kathleen, twelve or thirteen years old. As there were no dormitory accommodations available, Mrs. Rooney and Kathleen were to sleep in the recreation room on couches. Therefore, they sat there through the evening.

Mrs. Rooney and I fell into conversation. It turned on the Lindbergh case. She had been living in Yorkville, within 89th or 87th Street. At the time of the kidnapping. Now here is where the story details into the Wendel story. From the house where she lived, Mrs. Rooney had seen the Lindberg baby carried out of a laundry wagon in a laundry bag. He was in a man's arms. His head was exposed, but his body in the bag. She saw the child several times then one night, she heard a man curse, heard the child scream, and she never saw the child again. She heard through an open window a telephone call made by the captors. She traced the call, and it was to a man named Wilson in East 121st St. I believe No. 129. Among the captors was a red-haired man. One of the men was named Maurer.

Later Mrs. Rooney went to live at that 121 St. home. She said a woman from Hackensack brought there who had knowledge of the Lindbergh case was taken out by Italians (whose names Mrs. Rooney told) and killed. She knew the place of the killing. The man named Wilson seemed to be connected with the Lindbergh lawyers. There was a G man named Wilson working on the case. I do not know whether he was the man that Mrs. Rooney went to Englewood and tried to contact the Morrows. She did contact a woman named Sullivan in Englewood who may have been the one who employed and recommended Betty Gow to the Lindbergh's. Mrs. Rooney was a woman in her thirties of striking appearance. She was tall and slim with blue eyes and a remarkable head of black hair, worn in two braids wound round and round to form large wheels covering her ears.

She was a rather loose woman. I imagine for a while she could speak well when aroused, she used gutter language. Her maiden's name was Shangnessy, and her sister Loretta married to a man named Purcell, had been framed by vice cops and killed for letting of it. Mrs. Rooney testified to this at the first Hofstadter investigation. She knew Irving Ben Cooper, but she had known from that time that she was on a spot. At the time I saw her, the Police were evidently keeping her undercover so she would not spread her story.

Miss Chambers, the Superintendent of St. Barnabas House, told me that when Mrs. Rooney left there, it was the Detective Bureau who telephoned for her.

I know the story of her stay at St. Barnabas might be hard to get at. The child Kathleen has been in school, and they might be traced through the Dept. of Education, if someone appeared merely as a friend If still living, Mrs. Rooney would be only too glad to tell. The fact that Wendel said he used a laundry bag made me feel that you should hear this laundry bag story. If this were true, it would be a N.Y. murder. I own and occupy a small waterfront bungalow on rented ground. I am living on home relief and have been checked, re-checked, and checked to such an extent that I can recite my life history at a moment's notice. I do not know whether the Jersey Trooper I know is Aurthur Keaton or not, but as he was working with Detective Finn the last time I saw him in police headquarters, Manhattan, I assume he is.

Very truly yours,
Mrs. Marie A. Clarke

<u>Note</u>: This is quite a story and very well written just four days after Bruno Richard Hauptmann's execution. Twice, Mrs. Clarke mentions Paul Wendel. She has been inspired to come forward by the publishing of Wendel's confession to the Lindbergh baby kidnapping.

The fantastic thing disclosed by the writer, Mrs. Marie A. Clarke, here is that a woman she has met, Mrs. Rooney, had seen the Lindberg baby carried out of a laundry wagon in a laundry bag and that she saw the Lindbergh baby several more times that night. It is a shame that Detective Parker did not respond to Mrs. Clarke and investigated her story of an eyewitness to the Lindbergh baby's kidnapping.

Unfortunately, Ellis was never busier than during this period. He was busy defending himself against Paul Wendel and Attorney General David Wilentz's attacks over their claims that Detective Parker had ordered the kidnapping of Wendel.

FROM THE ELLIS PARKER LOST FILES

395 Lafayette Ave., Brooklyn New York,

April 8, 1936.

His Excellency—
Gov., Harold G. Hoffman,
Trenton, N.J.
State House.

Dear Excellency:

Although Bruno Richard Hauptmann has paid the debt society demanded of him, I am one among millions who believe the State unjustly convicted him for the sole purpose of closing the case. Also, I heartily approve your actions and offer my congratulations for the stand you have taken and trust you will have the courage to continue the investigation to the bitter end, regardless of the obstacles that you are combating.

From a careful perusal of the sworn testimony given by Dr. Condon and Betty Gow, the following thought occurred to me:

Dr. Condon admitted that he spent the night of March 8, 1932, sleeping in the baby's nursery and that he took two safety pins from the nursery—unbeknown to the Lindbergh's. Betty Gow, in her sworn testimony, stated that there were four or five sleeping garments identically alike and that two or three of them were unaccounted for.

While in the nursery, could he have also concealed one of the said garments beneath his clothing and cunningly placed it in the hands of the man or gang to whom he paid the ransom money?

Respectfully yours,

George Gates, Jr.

The following is a copy of the letter George Gates wrote to Harold Hoffman:

395 Lafayette Ave.,

Brooklyn New York,

April 8, 1936

Mr. Ellis Parker:

Congratulations, and best wishes for the attitude you're taking in the Hauptmann case! DON'T GIVE UP! I HOPE YOU BEAT THEM TO A FRAZZLE!

Attached hereto, please find a copy of a letter of even date, which I'm mailing to Governor Hoffman. It might be of interest for you to investigate the angle of the case, which I have enclosed in ink.

If I can be of any assistance to you in offering suggestions – I'm at your command!

Yours for success,

George Gates, Jr.

Ellis Parker responded on 4-14-1936:

April 14, 1936

Mr. George Gates, Jr.

395 Lafayette Ave.

Brooklyn, New York

Dear Friend:

Your letter of April 8, and enclosure of the copy of the one you sent to the Governor received. I wish to thank you for the kind expressions and assure you that letters like this are always appreciated, I remain,

Very truly yours,

Ellis H. Parker

Chief of County Detectives

Note: Dr. Condon (aka Jafsie) never received much love from the public. They did not trust him just as the writer of the above letter, George Gates Jr., did not. Condon's actions and demeanor may have warranted it. The missing baby garment story was covered by many of the newspapers.

FROM THE ELLIS PARKER LOST FILES

Philadelphia, Penna.

April 9th, 1936

Ellis Parker
Chief of County Detectives
Mt. Holly, N.J.

Dear Friend Ellis: -

Knowing you for the upright, kind consideration in your questioning Subjects to obtain information. I feel it is my duty as knowing you and coming in close contact with you on several occasions in the past several years to offer my services to assist in clearing the great wrong done to a man who has built up a wonderful reputation.

There is no doubt in my mind that all of this contention has been caused by a lot of sore heads to discredit your ability and ruin your reputation, and I, as well as my friends, know you as one person in our chosen line of work to employ the cleanest methods.

I have been in your office at times when you have questioned suspects, and I know of your clean kind of methods. It sure does seem a darn shame ANY PERSON or PERSONS would make the slightest effort to ruin your reputation.

My sincere feelings also go out to your considerate Governor Hoffman.

I only wish that I had the use of my leg and the cash to carry on, and I, for one, would of given my services toward solving that mystery. It would be a great pleasure for to help a regular fellow like the Governor, for he sure has shown what a real human being should be.

Well, Ellis, I and all my friends are 100% for you, and we all hope that nothing serious will come toward the ruin the of your wonderful long experience, and I honestly wish the best of success in cleaning this dirty mess.

Have you considered resigning your present position and going in business for yourself? I ask you this question for the reason that you have more than a national reputation as to great success and ability, which is known all over the World. Have you ever stopped to think what all that would mean as to getting a wonderful business? Well, I do. I managed the Superintendent of Police J.B. Taylor's office. I know what it did for him, then there was William Burns, Bob McKenty, Captain Lindon (whose office I also managed), Jimmie Tate (late ex-Captain of Philadelphia Detective Bureau), and there are a number of others, none of whom were as successful as you have been and all of them made a great success at Private Detective.

If you have not given the latter a thought at any time, think it over and let me know what you think of the proposition, in fact, I would like to have a talk with you on the subject in the near future.

Wishing you the best of health and success and that I would at any time give you any assistance in my power and that I would deem if a pleasure to do so.

P.S. I moved to be nearer to Town.

I remain as always
Your Sincere Friend,

J. J. Watson
1625 West Oxford Street
Philadelphia, Penna.

Note: A interesting letter, and obviously, the writer is very knowledgeable about Detective work. I get the feeling that J.J. Watson's main issue was pitching that he and Ellis start an agency. Andy Sahol, Ellis's Grandson, has told me many times that Ellis was all about family. Ellis had countless opportunities to move on from his County Detective job, but it was always known that he never would. Ellis would never leave or consider moving his family from Mt. Holly. He had no interest in branching out, not for additional fame or fortune.

J.J. Watson was Ellis's friend, and he did make a meaningful comment. Watson had read about Paul Wendel's claims that he had been tortured until he signed his confession. It was later revealed that Wendel might have injured himself on purpose to support his lies when rescinding his signed confession to New Jersey Attorney General David Wilentz. Watson knew that Ellis would never have allowed a prisoner to be mistreated, and he wanted to make that clear by telling of his participation when Ellis was questioning suspects.

FROM THE ELLIS PARKER LOST FILES

Note: There is not a lot here that I can agree with because "A. Sincere Friend" made so many racist comments. They were not necessary and should be distasteful to anyone of dignity. At least "A. Sincere Friend" got one thing right. Ellis Parker and Ellis Parker Jr. solved the Lindbergh kidnapping case. Paul Wendel was guilty. He signed a confession. Case closed.

May 7, 1936

Hon. Governor Harold G. Hoffman, Trenton, New Jersey

Dear Sir:

For your information: During the trial of Bruno R. Hauptmann, I noticed all newspapers of Jewish extract, such as the Philadelphia Daily News, the Philadelphia Record, The Courier, that I believe is published in Camden, N.J. and part of the Philadelphia Record and a number of newspapers which I have every reason to believe are controlled by Jewish parties, in New York City, came out with some of the most damnable statements concerning you as Governor, I also noticed whenever Mr. Hirstberg and Boake Carter came on the sir they would always say something of a foul or rotten remark concerning you. Now it looks like the Jews came out to get you and Mr. Ellis Parker Sr. Particularly you.

I would advise that you get a number of copies of these different papers published during the trial, this last trial, just note yourself these different statements. They, I sincerely believe, feel that you have a chance of being our next "President of The United States" and have made up their minds to kill all those cases if they can, they also have a fear Ellis Parker Sr. would become Superintendent of the State Police.

I feel the same as a number of my friends do, is that if you could only get to the "Rock bottom of this Wendel case," you would find it is the works of the Jews, who planned to get you and Ellis Parker Sr.

If Mr. Ellis Parker Sr. or his son should go to New York, they should object to any Jews being allowed to have anything with or connections with the trial of then the Jews arrested in this case. They must also realize I believe the Jews can pull anything in New York and get away with it least looks that way according to latest events.

GOD HELP ANY-ONE WHO DOES ANYTHING FOR A "GERMAN" IN THIS COUNTRY IF THE JEWS HAVE ANYTHING TO SAY.

JUST LOOK AT THE PICTURES OF THE ONES WHO ACCUSE ELLIS PARKER JR. AND PERHAPS SR.

P.S. I would have done the same thing as Mr. Parker's son did if I positively believed this man Wendel was the kidnapper. Who would not have done this for a Governor like you? I stake my right arm on Mr. Ellis Parker or his son. They are 100 Percent, and regardless of how much they desired to help you, they never would lower themselves to crooked work, that's what burning everybody else up. The solution is, as I sincerely believe it was well laid on "God" only knows who was in on it to?

From, A. Sincere Friend

FROM THE ELLIS PARKER LOST FILES

May 6, 1936

Mr. William Heckheimer

373 Central Park West

New York, N.Y.

Dear Friend:

Your letter addressed to the Governor was sent to me, and also the telegram, but as my wires are tapped, I have refrained from attempting to contact anyone until this storm blows over. I would certainly love to see you, but at the present time, I have been advised by counsels to stay in this county and not contact anyone for the time being, as you know this whole thing is directed against the Governor when he has nothing to do with it whatever, and the whole thing is a bunch of mush. It is a red herring being drug across the trail by some people as a smokescreen for themselves.

Later on, I will communicate with you, and I will make an appointment. Thanking you, I remain,

Very truly yours,

Ellis H. Parker

Chief of County Detectives

Note: Ellis is obviously under tremendous pressure. The Hauptmann prosecution team, led by David Wilentz, is concerned with Ellis's next move, so they are watching and monitoring Ellis's movements. This is not the first time that Ellis has complained about phone taps.

Something that Ellis points out here is often overlooked. That is how political the Lindbergh case was. Sides were taken, most often by political party affiliation. Ellis points out, "this whole thing is directed against the Governor." The Governor, Harold Hoffman, was a republican. The Attorney General, David Wilentz, was a Democrat.

FROM THE ELLIS PARKER LOST FILES

THE DETROIT FREE PRESS
DETRIOT, MICHIGAN
May 19, 1936

Jersey's Governor Fells Writer for News Service

New York, May 18, 1936—(AP)—Gov. Harold G. Hoffman of New Jersey tonight knocked down Lou Wedemar, a writer for Universal Service, outside the Rainbow Room in Radio City where dinner was being held in connection with the first National Exhibition of American Art.

Spectators rushed between the two men and prevented the continuation of combat.

The Incident took place after Hoffman and Wedemar walked from the room toward the elevators discussing the New Jersey political campaign. Gov. Hoffman later returned to his seat, and Wedemar left the dinner.

Note: This disagreement and confrontation were most likely caused by Governor Hoffman's move to dismiss Col. H. Norman Schwarzkopf from his position as Superintendent of New Jersey State Police and replace him with Col. Mark O. Kimberling, a state prison warden. The change would need to be ratified by a New Jersey Senate vote, and the division was along party lines. Governor Hoffman's move to replace Schwarzkopf was seen as political payback for handling the Lindbergh case that he did not feel was correct.

Lou Wedemar had a successful career as a news reporter and writer. He even created a comic book based on the Lindbergh case in later years.

FROM THE ELLIS PARKER LOST FILES

ELLIS H. PARKER AND THE LINDBERGH CASE

(BY UNKNOWN AUTHOR FROM THE ELLIS PARKER LOST FILES)

On April 3rd, 1936, Richard Hauptmann was electrocuted for the murder of Charles Augustus Lindbergh, the young child of Anne and Charles Lindbergh. The "Crime of the Century" had been solved to almost everyone's satisfaction. The world celebrated Hauptmann's death. The same public that had been horrified by the crime's details could now relax and rejoice in Hauptman's death, condemning anyone that suggested that Hauptmann was innocent or not the only person involved in the kidnapping.

Ellis Parker was unfairly criticized for his attempts to prove that Paul H. Wendel was a kidnapper or maybe the sole kidnapper. Ellis Parker, who had been investigating the Lindbergh case for over four years, was ironically accused as a kidnapper. Not of the baby, but for that of Paul H. Wendel.

Now, here we should evaluate the life and career of Ellis Parker. Ellis Parker devoted his life to law and order. He solved more than 300 crimes of violence, in NJ and other states. His 45 years of exemplary performance and experience had won him a national reputation as a law enforcement officer. He was loved by many, nearly everyone he met, and his neighbors from all over Burlington County turned out at his trial to testify in his defense

Initially, the only thing Ellis Parker wanted to accomplish was the return of the baby, as did millions of American citizens. He was determined to solve the crime and reunite the baby and its parents. Not long after the baby's abduction, Ellis was visited by Colonel A. J. MacNab, who was Dwight

Morrow's attaché. MacNab and Parker began to correspond to obtain the safe return of the baby.

Harry A. Moore, then the NJ governor, wrote to Ellis on March 15th, 1932, asking him to join the investigation with New Jersey State's full cooperation

Ellis Parker ran a newspaper statement that he hoped would lure the kidnappers into exposure. He informed that if he were in Colonel Lindbergh's place, he would deal directly with the kidnappers and not the police for the return of the baby. Paul Wendel, a disbarred Trenton Lawyer, read these newspaper articles and called Ellis on the telephone. Wendel was a man of questionable character and had been convicted of perjury. The conviction was never reversed. He did eventually obtain a Pardon, and his rights were restored. He next was stricken from his law practice, then subsequently reinstated only to be barred again from practicing. Numerous indictments for embezzlement and for obtaining property under false pretense were filed against him. During his telephone call, Wendel asked Parker if he meant what he said in the newspaper. Ellis confirmed that he did. A short time later, Wendel visited Ellis's office. During the meeting, Parker realized that it had been Wendel on the phone. He recognized his voice. Wendel told Ellis that he could get the baby returned because he had the right contacts. Parker doubted that Wendel was truthful and that he, Wendel himself, was the baby's kidnapper. Ellis decided to lead Wendel on until he could obtain the safe return of the baby. Ellis asked Wendel to work for him, with an offer of payment. Four years passed as Wendel traveled about always keeping in secret communication with either Ellis or Anna Bading. Wendel made many promises, but in the end, the child was never found. During these years, Ellis Parker became certain that Wendel was guilty of the Lindbergh baby's kidnapping.

FROM THE ELLIS PARKER LOST FILES

Aug. 6th, 1936

Dear Mr. Parker:

Don't you think that the Jews are the cause of all your trouble? I think that the Jews are at the bottom of most of the troubles that we have. Look at Spain, how would you like to have such a condition in this country, the Jews started it in Spain. We have too many Jews in this land of ours, and if we are not careful, we will have them doing the same here as they have done in all countries, where they have got a hold.

Have you noted the vast number and the awful looking Jews you see on the streets of our cities today? Roosevelt and his Jew boss Frankfurter are letting them come into the United States at the rate of four or five hundred a week. How do you like this Jew influx into the country? I do not like it myself. Let's put a stop to it.

"My friends."

A vote for Roosevelt is a vote for the Jews

Make the United States Jew conscious, put everybody wise

Do you know?

It is here at the door

Bolshevism in the United States

Drive Roosevelt and his Jew out of Washington

Eliminate the Jew from our national life

Protect our women form the lascivious Jews

Do not buy from the Jews, it is dangerous

Vote and buy Gentile

Yours very sincerely,

American Gentile

Note: This is a frightening and horrible letter for Ellis Parker to have received. How can someone hate a whole race so wholly? Racism is unacceptable. It is an example of what you do not want to allow. If you allow it, you are just as responsible for its existence as the writer of this letter. I have known the Grandson of Ellis Parker, Andrew Sahol, for some years. From what I have learned from him, I can guarantee you that Ellis Parker disagreed with this garbage.

FROM THE ELLIS PARKER LOST FILES

December 20, 1935

Mr. Ellis Parker,
Burlington County Court House
Mt. Holly, New Jersey

Dear Sir:

Several weeks before the discovery of the Lindbergh baby's body, I was told by a bartender in an Orange Tavern, that he had overheard the plotting of the baby's kidnapping. He went into some details, saying that the baby was buried and that the kidnappers were going to demand $25,000 from Mr. Lindbergh. He said that they decided at the time the plot was formulated not to return the baby, as it would be too risky to find a hideout.

I wrote to Colonel Lindberg, also visited his lawyer's office, and a young clerk there, by his actions, thought that I must be seeking notoriety. I gave up trying to aid them because they disgusted me.

A woman reporter for the Newark Evening News went with me on Sunday evening, and the bartender reiterated what he had told me. Later, when the body was found, she phoned me and was very much excited, as our man had told of later developments at our previous interrogation. His manner at the time was very excitable, and he evidently did not wish to discuss it for fear of being overheard. Italian boot-leggers owned and operated the Tavern. They are a syndicate that covers several states.

I feel, as do most people that I talk with that the case was fearfully bungled, and if you believe that there may be something beneficial in talking to this bartender, who is an ex-convict, I would be very glad to help you get in touch with him. My opinion is that Hauptmann used the money that others implicated in the plot thought "too hot" to circulate at that time.

I have worked for the past ten years with different agencies, Hargrave Secret Service of Chicago, Burns Detective Agency, Cosgrove Detective Agency, Newark, and with some lawyers of divorce cases. At the present time, I find a better living in selling Burners and Air-conditioning.

Trusting that I may be of some use in assisting you to unravel something different and tangible to further your success, and also, having a great admiration for Governor Hoffman's fairness in this case.

I remain,

Yours very truly,

Lavinia B. de Forest

P. S. I have discussed the case with a Newark lawyer with whom you are acquainted, and he thinks favorably of my writing you this letter.

Note: I think there was reason to believe this story because it originated from a known Bootlegger hangout, the Orange Tavern in Northern New Jersey. Ellis Parker suspected the involvement of Bootleggers in the Lindbergh crime. At the core of the Bootlegger's syndicates were powerful and aggressive criminals, fueled by illegal profits. Robbery, kidnapping, and embezzlement were planned and completed by the members of these criminal organizations. They had the resources to be capable due to the illegal Bootlegging profits easily obtainable during Prohibition.

FROM THE ELLIS PARKER LOST FILES

Ellis H. Parker, Esq.,

Chief of Co. Detectives,

Mt. Holly, N.J.

Dear Chief; -

I came to see you today but missed you. You know how I feel about the result of the trial, as we have talked that over several times.

In all of my conversations with newspapermen and lawyers, they all tell be that you will win the appeal. Of course, I am only too sorry that you have to go to all this trouble and expense. The nicest part about this whole unfortunate circumstance has been the way your friends, both here and in other parts of the State, have stood back of you. After all, one can stand a lot of trouble and suffering when you know you have real sympathy and help.

Now, I want to write you very seriously about another matter- that is, your health. I certainly do not wish to be a pessimist and frighten you to death, but I do feel it is my duty as your physician and friend to give you some very good advice.

For a long time, you have been in failing health. I realize you have been under a terrific strain, that you have had very little sleep at night and that your appetite and digestion have both been very much interfered with. I am not only now recommending, but insist upon you getting a good, long vacation along the lines I talked to you recently at Newark. I want you to spend a lot of time out in the open, sitting in the sunshine and fresh air, fishing, and anything that will occupy your attention, but which will not be work or anything to worry you. As you know, you are suffering from blood vessel changes; also, low blood pressure and the former condition has apparently caused trouble to your kidneys and bladder – at least, the X-ray pictures and cystoscopic examination made some time ago showed an interference in the passage of water from the kidneys to the bladder.

I was very much worried about you and thought perhaps you would have to have an operation; however, it is my earnest desire that you avoid an operation at this time of life, and I believe if you had sufficient rest, the right kind of diet, proper elimination, that these measures would at least restore you part of the way to your former health and vigor.

Now, I want you to take this letter to the proper authorities and permit them to read it in full so that you may be granted a vacation.

In conclusion, I want to ask you to relax and not worry and count upon the right, winning out in the end. I believe you have so many good friends that with their aid, things will begin to look rosy son again.

Sincerely your friend,

Dr. Harold E. Longsdorf

Note: Unfortunately, there was no date on this letter to be sure, but I would estimate it was composed sometime in late 1937. The writer, Harold Longsdorf, was more than Ellis's Doctor. He was a friend. A friend that supported him and wanted to testify for him during his trial. Dr. Longsdorf was concerned about Ellis's health because he was under tremendous pressure. Detective Parker had the double burden of continuing his investigations and of defending himself.

FROM THE ELLIS PARKER LOST FILES

WENDEL DENIES HIS KIDNAPPING WAS PREARRANGED WITH PARKER

Charges New Jersey Detective Was Brains of Plot.

Aided in Lindbergh Probe

NEW YORK, Feb. 10 (AP)... Paul H. Wendel, former Trenton N.J. lawyer, testified that Ellis H. Parker Sr., chief of Burlington County N.J. detectives, had assigned him to establish some "contact with the underworld" in the investigation of the Lindbergh kidnapping. Wendel, complaining witness in the trial of three men charged with kidnapping him and torturing him into confessing falsely to the Lindbergh kidnapping, said he agreed to help Parker.

"I told him." Said the middle-aged witness, "that I had one contact in Chicago." He said he had another contact in New York.

"And why." queried Defense Counsel Burton Turkus on cross-examination, "did Parker want to know your contacts with the underworld?"

"Because he wanted to get the baby back." Responded Wendel.

Wendel, on the stand a second day, had told the Kings County court and jury that he considered the defendants, Murray Bleefeld, Harry Weiss, and Martin Schlossman, mere "dopes" for Parker, whom he called the "brains" of a plot to kidnap him early in 1936 and delay electrocution of Bruno Richard Hauptmann, who died April 3, 1936, for the Lindbergh slaying. Wendel denied that his alleged kidnapping was "prearranged" with Parker.

"I took Parker and his secretary, Anna Bading, to Leonia, N.J. to see a man named Frank Calabrese in 1932 before the body of the Lindbergh baby was found."

He informed Parker of this, Wendel told Burton B. Turkus, defense council, shortly after the Lindbergh kidnapping in March 1932 when Parker conferred with him about the case. Sometime in March of that year, he admitted he got $200 from Parker for expenses for himself and Calabrese. The money was given with the understanding that they were to go to Chicago, but they did not go.

Wendel said through Calabrese "made contact there."

"Why did Parker want to know your contacts with the underworld?" Turkus asked.

"Because he wanted to get the baby back," Wendel replied.

Wendel testified yesterday that he was forced by torture to "confess" kidnapping the Lindbergh baby.

<u>Note</u>: I believe this (AP) article (found in the lost files) was created in May or June of 1937, shortly before the beginning of Ellis Parker's trial. Calabrese is a name long associated with the Chicago mob, but Frank Calabrese Sr. wasn't born until 1937, and his father's name was James. Possibly Wendel knew a Calabrese relative in New Jersey? Ellis Parker's long relationship with Paul Wendel was based on Wendel's ability to contact the underworld for information to help the Detective's investigations. I suspect that Wendel's motivation was the same as it always was, easy profit without concern for legality.

FROM THE ELLIS PARKER LOST FILES

From: Providence, Road Island

To: Ellis H. Parker, Sr

Dear Sir,

I am writing you again hoping to convince you that what I told you about the Lindbergh boy being alive is true. It seems unbelievable. That three more men can be sent to jail, and Wendell, the guilty man, can get away. I was in New York for three weeks and talked to Mrs. Hauptmann and some of her former neighbors, and from what I learned about the gang that stopped at the rooming house at West 86th St. the night of March 1, 1932. They answer the description of Wendell and his daughter. The young woman, tall and Autumn blonde, she avoids looking at people. That answers to Dariy Ogbon, and the child was gone early next morning. The boy they call Bobby Ogbon was supposed to go to school this term at Miami Fla. he told to me he attended the Herdugarden thru last year surely, if he is entered at any school, its Miami Fla you could find him. I wish you would look for the boy the Ogbons pass as their son. He would be recognized at once. I hope you don't let them put you two in jail too, there is a gang of them here in Providence. I am followed every time I go out, I got the registration number of the Machines and know who they are please believe me when I tell you the boy is alive.

M. Guane

<u>Note</u>: This was a tough letter to read and difficult to understand and believe completely. It was handwritten, not typed. The spelling and some words are illegible. However, the gist of the letter can be understood. The writer, M. Guane, believes that the Lindbergh baby was alive in 1937. He has a problem with the three men accused of kidnapping Paul Wendel going to jail while Paul Wendel goes free. M. Guane fingers Paul H. Wendel for the Lindbergh baby kidnapping. When he states that he has the machines' registration numbers, he means the cars that are following him. One thing is sure, M. Guane leads an exciting life.

FROM THE ELLIS PARKER LOST FILES

<u>Note</u>: The below was written on a postcard mailed to Ellis Parker on April 27, 1937, from Birmingham, Alabama. Ellis is vigorously attacked by the anonymous writer for the kidnapping and torture of an innocent man. The innocent man is presumably Paul Wendel. My research has uncovered numerous times where Detective Parker could have profited from writing books, making appearances, or supplying stories to newspapers. He consistently turned these opportunities down. Ellis had no desire to be a hero or make a significant sum of money by writing a book. Ellis consistently repeated for much of his life that he was only interested in Justice.

That was the most beastly crime of the century that you committed on an innocent man. Such torturing was never done by a wild Indian. Al that you might be a hero and make money by writing a book about it. You are due the same treatment, and the American people hope you get your deserts, together with that son of yours. Gov. Hoffman was not innocent, for he was a plotter with you. I guess you convicted many an innocent man or woman by torturing them into a confession. An investigation of all your convictions should be made and free the many convicted people now suffering from your efforts. May you get your deserts with a double dose. Your name is a horror to the American people, and they will shudder every time it is mentioned for many years.

Signed,

Anonymous

FROM THE ELLIS PARKER LOST FILES

Mr. Ellis Parker

Mount Holly, New Jersey

Detective, Burlington County

You are a wonderful Corn Cob Detective of 44 years of experience. Do you know where you live? You don't know where the Statue of Liberty is located, Dumbbell. Only in Jersey man of your bright brains be found same as your Dutch Governor, another bright light. All from Jersey Swamps, some good officials a disgrace to Jersey State. I hope all of you get a good send off to jail. Why not drown yourself? You are ashamed of yourself. Brainless dog.

Note: Needless to say, this postcard was postmarked in New York, N.Y. The anonymous writer could not have been from New Jersey. Could he? The writer did call Ellis "a wonderful Corn Cob Detective," but after that, it was all downhill before ending with the warm closing of "Brainless Dog."

FROM THE ELLIS PARKER LOST FILES

WENDEL: PAUL H., (CONFIDENTIAL Personal Report)

Brooklyn, NY 94 Hicks Street, Brooklyn, NY 94 Hicks Street

This supplements our report of 8-19-39 and is additional information concerning Paul H. Wendel not included in our original report.

We find that in 1931 Wendel was under mental observation in Trenton State Hospital., and, in addition, was a disbarred N.J. attorney. These two facts are stated to have been the chief reasons that Wendel was selected as the victim at the time he was kidnapped, and a confession to the Lindbergh baby kidnapping wrung out of him by torture. It will be remembered that Wendel was kidnapped and held for several days in a New Lisbon, NJ institution, and beaten and tortured until he confessed. This confession was later repudiated before Attorney General Wilentz.

The investigation of the Wendel kidnapping later involved Ellis Parker, a well-known detective, and resulted in Wendel being held in the Towers Hotel in Brooklyn as a material witness at the expense of New York City. It was Parker to whom Wendel made his "confession."

Then in May 1939, Commissioner of Investigation Harland of N.Y.C. announced that he obtained evidence of hotel bills padding against Wendel and intended ordering his arrest. The expense of maintaining Wendel at the Towers Hotel grew to about $10,000. In going over records of these expenses, Harland noticed a large number of dinner and luncheon checks were forged, indicating some checks originally marked for two people were changed to one, showing that Wendel had a guest who dined on the city. In addition, evidence pointed to the fact detectives who dined at home permitted their names used (or had it done without their knowledge) on checks against the expenses for Wendel. It was estimated that about 20 percent of Wendel's total was the result of such forgeries.

Note: More evidence of Paul Wendel's very questionable character. Why was his behavior tolerated? He was never charged with these crimes, and many long-time warrants for his arrest disappeared. Is it because David Wilentz was concerned that he would change his mind about testifying against Ellis Parker? Without Paul Wendel's or Murray Bleefeld's testimony Detective Parker would not have been found guilty. Wendel's motivation was that he wanted to avoid prison or a death sentence. Bleefeld turned against Harry Weiss and Martin Schlossman to accept a deal offered to avoid a long-term prison sentence. Bleefeld was the quickest to accept the Wilentz offer. The primary condition of the agreement must have been to secure his testimony at the Parker trial. As a free man, Ellis Parker would have proven that the State had executed an innocent man, Hauptmann, of anything except passing the ransom money. Career suicide for those on the prosecution team.

FROM THE ELLIS PARKER LOST FILES
STATE OF NEW JERSEY
OFFICE OF THE ATTORNEY GENERAL

HIS EXCELLENCY, FRANKLIN D. ROOSEVELT
President of the United States,
Washington, D.C.

My Dear President:

I am writing in behalf of Ellis H. Parker, Sr. who is confined in Leesburg, Penna. Prison on a Federal charge. I have known Mr. Parker for thirty-five years, and during the time that he was County Detective of Burlington County, he was one of the best officers in the State of New Jersey.

Mr. Parker is very ill at the present time, and he has a large family to support, who are in destitute circumstances. Regardless of his guilt, he has certainly served sufficient time and punishment for his offense.

I trust that you will use your good offices in granting him a pardon so that he can spend the balance of his days, which in my opinion, will be few, outside prison walls.

Sincerely yours,
ROBERT PEACOCK,

Assistant Attorney General of N.J.

Note: I estimate that this letter was written in early January of 1939 as Ellis Parker's health deteriorated rapidly in the weeks before his death. His many friends, admirers, associates, and family members wrote to elected officials seeking a pardon for the famous Detective. They reached out as high as President Roosevelt's office, as New Jersey Attorney General Robert Peacock did in this letter. Unfortunately, Ellis never received the pardon he deserved before he passed on February 4, 1940.

FROM THE ELLIS PARKER LOST FILES

Note: This letter, more of a paper, is dated 1-1-1937. It was written by Dr. Fred C. Swartz (1913-2009), who calls himself the Antagonizer of Crooks, a Masonic Struggler for Justice and the Old Horse and Buggy Day Political Sleuth. Dr. Schwartz would have been 24 years old when he wrote this paper. Read thru until my notes at the end of his paper to learn more about this complex man and his plausible Lindbergh case theory.

A 1937 NEW YEAR GREETING:
WHEN OPPORTUNITY RAPS AT YOUR DOOR:
GRASP IT AND DO NOT LET IT SKIP GALORE.
YOU HAVE HAD A CHANCE, BUT YOU LET IT SLIP:
SO NOW TAKE HEED OF THE ANNEXED
INFORMATION TIP.

A REPEATED STATEMENT:

As soon as I saw the picture of the LINDBERGH kidnaped boy and the picture of the ladders in the NEWSPAPERS, I knew who the GANGSTERS were who kidnaped the boy; and when I read the description of the man who passed LINDBERGH when the RANSOM MONEY was passed, I had positive proof that I was in possession of the knowledge that that man was one of the GANGSTERS who rode away in the truck with the ladders.

As soon as I saw WENDEL'S picture in the NEWSPAPERS, I recognized him as one of the MEN who was with ISADORE FISH and another tall man, with a FISH truck at the time when CURTIS made the expose that the LINDBERGH boy was on a boat.

And when I read in the NEWSPAPER that WILENTZ and HAUCK had hurried to the JAIL to interview WENDEL, I knew that they would concoct a plan for to protect ISADORE FISH and the OTHERS who perpetrated the LINDBERGH boy kidnaping.

And when I was told that the woman who had the LINDBERGH boy was J. EDGAR HOOVER'S concubine, then I knew that there was a great political scheme connected with the kidnapping. – For HOOVER and LINDBERGH had in the late WORLD WAR time played a dirty trick.

Some PRO and CONS, which INFORMATION ought to of been taken into consideration in the LINDBERGH kidnapping case, and, in the HAUPTMANN prosecution case.

This reliable information was sent to LAWYER FAWCETT; To MRS. HAUPTMANN; to MRS. GLOEKNER; for them to send a detective to WASHINGTON, D.C., to secretly run down the LINDBERGH boy kidnapers.

They having failed to pay any attention to the advice, then LAWYER POP was informed of what was known about the ladders, ETC., no attention paid to this information. Then PREACHER "WERNER" and the NEW YORK DEFENSE FUND of HAUPTMANN was informed of what was known about the kidnapping of the LINDBERGH boy. No attention paid to it. – Then, REV. JOHN MATHIESON was informed; he sent a man here to investigate. Then MATHIESON asked for a statement. – He got a statement, with a copy of an affidavit attached. He wrote that he would put the matter before ELLIS PARKER.

I had tried to get HEARST to expose the political rascality plied in the case, the said MANUSCRIPT was sent in DECEMBER 1935; it was returned the following JULY 1936, with a slim excuse that HEARST was too busy to attend to such matters.

The registered letter with a SPECIAL DELIVERY STAMP thereon to GOVERNOR HAROLD G. HOFFMAN took several days to reach him. ---On the day it was mailed, ATTORNEY GENERAL WILENTZ made a hurried trip to WASHINGTON, D.C.----ETC., ETC., ETC.

Here the paramount questions arise: "Why was there no attention paid to the reliable information which was sent to the HAUPTMANN LAWYERS; to HAUPTMANN'S wife, relatives, and friends, and OTHERS? ---They followed up all clues which was sent to them by EX-CONVICTS and by DAYDREAMING VISIONARIES; but they deliberately neglected to pay any attention to reliable information sent to them by an INSPECTOR GENERAL and by a graduated GRAND SAGE.

THE FACTS as they stand, are: The LINDBERGH kidnap ladders were owned in WASHINGTON, D.C., by —— ——; they were first stored at ——; they were next stored at ——; they were transported away before the LINDBERGH kidnapping in an OLD FORD TRUCK into which FIVE or SIX GANGSTERS got, one Looked like ISADORE FISH; one was the MAN whom LINDBERGH described as passing him when the RANSOM MONEY was paid. – This truck, with the

GANGSTERS in it, was followed by a greenish SEDAN with a woman in the back seat.

The LINDBERGH boy was brought to WASHINGTON, D.C., on a boat said to be owned by -----; the kidnapped LINDBERGH boy was seen alive after the kidnapping in WASHINGTON, D.C., in custody of a woman who it was said was J. EDGAR HOOVER'S CONCUBINE. ---Thereafter, a man resembling WENDEL was seen with ISADORE FISH and another tall man – at three different mornings- standing beside a FISH truck when CURTIS made the exposure that the LINDBERGH boy was on a boat. They each time came from the direction where the LINDBERGH boy was kept. ---A man who looked like WENDEL was seen coming out of the HOUSE where the LINDBERGH boy was kept. ---

Your orator gave reasons why he could not openly appear as an INFORMANT in the case because he was suspicioned by the GANGSTERS of knowing too much.

So, you see, the LINDBERGH kidnapping case is no more solved today than as too what it was the day after the kidnapping.

Your orator has kept track of the corrupt practices I the LINDBERGH kidnapping and Hauptmann framing case, and he wrote an ESSAY thereon called "AN EX PARTE PROCEEDINGS." This is a four-fold book, to wit: On RELIGION, on CREEDISM, on POLITICS, and on SCIENCE. ---This ESSAY of DISSERTATIONS upsets all the trumped-up claims in the HUAPTMANN prosecution case by 'WILENTZ and the GOVERNMENT EXPERT witnesses." ---How they misled GOVERNOR HOFFMAN; how they led the PARKERS into a trap; how they offered $10,000 for this

MANUSCRIPT then raised it to $20,000, then to $35,000; and when this offer was refused, they threatened to send NEW YORK GANGSTERS to WASHINGTON, D.C., for to do up the AUTHOR and the PUBLISHER if they printed the said book. This was in mid-summer of 1935.

Since the execution of HAUPTMANN, there was an outright offer made for the MANUSCRIPT of $35,000, which offer was rejected.

Your orator tried to get REPUBLICAN PARTY LEADERS in 1935 to help publish the political trickery plied in the LINDBERGH-HAUPTMANN case. - Slim excuse from one U.S. SENATOR. Others snubbed the appeal. ---The expose of the corrupt practice in the LINDBERGH case, and the NATIONAL and INTERNATIONAL politics connected therewith would have been worth MILLIONS of DOLLARS to the REPUBLICAN PARTY in their 1936 campaign; for it would of exposed all the seditious under-takings that was back of the F.D.R. NEW DEAL OBJECTIVES.

All attempts to get HAMILTON and his AIDES to help make an expose in 1936 was snubbed. ---RESULT. The REPUBLICAN PARTY was snowed under; whereas an expo-sure of the LINDBERGH political kidnapping game would of snowed under the NEW DEAL PARTY. And MILLIONS and MILLIONS of DOLLARS of wasted campaign FUNDS could of ben saved.

Understand, this WRITER was an old HORSE and BUGGY day SLEUTH, and as a life-long SCIENTIFIC STUDENT and EXPERIMENTER – knows what he is writ-ing about, and what OFFICIAL "HIGH-YOU-MUCKS" he is tackling and indicting. --- Already deliberate attempts at pro-catarctic dispatching have been plied to get rid of your orator by the heart disease racket. ---The political GANGSTERS are getting desperate. ---And unless GOVERNOR HOFFMAN and ELLIS PARKER SR., are not careful, they will be pro-catarctically dispatched by the customary racket of: "He died from APOPLEXY."

It is up to GOVERNOR HOFFMAN and ELLIS PARKER SR., to wake up out of their trance and secretly run down the real CRIMINALS in the LINDBERGH kidnapping case; and vindicate their attacked character.

P.S. Three men who knew something about the LINDBERGH boy having been in WASHINGTON, D.C., and who have seen the three men with the FISH truck have already been procatarctically dispatched., And, your orator has been deliberately doped up so that he got HEART DISEASE in order to get him out of the way.---The woman who had the LINDBERGH boy has been moved out of the DISTRICT, and her name is changed.,---"The LADDER-man is ----" ---The MAN who passed LINDBERGH ------?

Spotters of all kinds have been around in order to get information; but they were recognized as SLEUTH'S the moment they came into the place and started to talking.

It is now up to GOVERNOR HOFFMAN and ELLIS PARKER to pick up the trail of the LINDBERGH KIDNAPERS, and of their POLITICAL ENEMIES as revealed here, not only for to vindicate their character; but also, to help make an exposure of the seditious undertaking which I know is connected with the LINDBERGH kidnapping case, of overthrowing the UNITED STATES GOVERNMENT with the NEW DEAL OBJECTIVES.

Your orator tried to get BOLTON, KNUDSON, FESS, and OTHER REPUBLICAN LEADERS interested to help make an exposure. But it seemed that they were all mesmerized into inactivity. --- Even HAMILTON failed to pay any attention to make use of what could of slugged F.D. R'S POPULARITY.

SIGNED: DR. FRED C. SWARTZ

217 INDIANA AVE. N.W.,

WASHINGTON, D.C.

ADDENDUM: DECEMBER 26, 1936 --- There was brought to me a NEWSPAPER Item of the 22cnd instant, which states that GUNNAR SVEDBERG, a deported NEW YORK PAINTER, reported that the LINDBERGH boy was held for ransom by five men and a woman, who gave it narcotics from which the baby died.

Here I must say: "I do not know where this SWEDE got his information from; but it "co-hitches-up" with the C. MARTIN letter sent to LAWYER FAWCETT.

Here a moot question arises: "What connection had this GUNNAR SVEDBERG, with one of the FIVE GANGSTERS?"- Or: "With one of the government witnesses against HAUPTMANN?" --- I see that there are some TRUTHS and some FALSEHOOD in this SWEDE'S statement.

THE "WOLVERINE POST:" ...-. SENDS A 1937 NEW YEAR GREETING.

The GOVERNOR made a mistake by not calling upon the old BARD:

For had he introduced himself; he would of found he was not interviewing and UPSTART:

But that he was conferring and confraternity with a man of uprightness: Who is fighting for RIGHTS and JUSTICE; - upon this lay a solemn stress. And ELLIS PARKER, SR., ought to of came along and started on the right track: Of the LINDGERGH kidnapping case, which could have been picked up in the BARD'S shack. Now then it is up to YE to correct your errors of the past:

And to regain your former prestige; and win out in the game – at least.

Understand, your orator is not presenting any daydreams nor any imagination:

But he is presenting the FACTS and the TRUTH in full realistic ration.

When HE says: The LINDBERGH kidnapping "has not been solved:"

By any J. EDGER HOOVER'S tactics, nor by NEW JERSEY POLICE, has it been golfed.

For the kidnap ladders were made and owned in the city of WASHINGTON, D.C.:

And CHARLES LINDBERGH, JR., was seen here alive, after the heralded kidnapping spree.

And CHARLES LINDBERGH, SR., described one of the hired kidnap GANGSTERS in todium:

And "JAFSIE" CONDON sustained this description of that very LINDBERGH recognized BUM.

Dated this 1st day of JANUARY, A.D. 1937

(SIGNED:) DR. FRED. C. SWARTZ. - THE OLD HORSE AND BUGGY DAY POLITICAL SLEUTH.

THE "WOLVERINE POST:" ...-. IS NEAR HIS LAST DAY ON EARTH.

The "GRIM REAPER" has been after me for some time; but MR. "FATE" stood in his way:

That is why I am yet alive; and I may be able to live yet another day.

But my old "GORE PUMP" is playing out, which spells: Your days are numbered now:

And the old SOUL will depart from your body; and forever fly in the IONIC "MOW."

And, centuries in the "HEREAFTER," your SOUL ION'S – on the follow-up PLANET will again build-up:

Yourself, as you have been on this EARTH. And you'll have to go through the same kind of "drub."

MISTER "FATE" was kind and liberal to me, in making me rich in GRAND KNOWLEDGE:

But the DEVIL got into my mate and forced me- at times – to live on starvation porridge.

I have been in quest for the CHIEF DEVIL – for many a long year:

But devil a bit could I find him – for to trumpet something into his ear.

This left me to alone, fight a lot of COURT DEVILS, which was an uphill job:

But as long as there is life in me, at this battling, I shall never stop.

For as an 'INSPECTOR GENERAL," I have vowed to fight for JUSTICE and for RIGHT:

And as a graduated "GRAND SAGE," I am bound to hit the CROOKS in the fight.

They all talk and preach "RIGHTEOUSNESS" and "JUSTICE" to be dished out to all:

But many U.S. GOVERNMENT OFFICIALS have deliberately driven me to the wall.

DATED this 1st day of JANUARY, A.D., 1937

(SIGNED:) DR. FRED. C. SWARTZ. ...-. A MASONIC
STRUGGLER FOR JUSTICE. -99:.

THE "WOLVERINE POST:" ...-. FORENSICS
A FORENOTICE.

Understand, your orator has written an exposure in
prose and in rhyme:

Of how GOVERNMENT OFFICIALS – against
HAUPTMANN- perpetrated a fearful crime.

At this assertion, the GOVERNMENT OFFICIALS may
start in to hoot and hiss:

But they will discover that those charges are not made
by a dreaming MISS.

Bear in mind, your orator has not presented a tale
of fiction:

But he has presented all the accused to try and "alibi"
the accusation:

For they will be caught as devilish OFFICIAL CROOKS
in this NATION.

Your orator is not a writer of fiction nor of wild rev-
erie dreams:

But his is an ESSAYIST of FACTS – which are not hidden behind screens.

TRUTH and JUSTICE is your orators creedistical
upright – PASS-WORD:

And this is expounded at length, and not in a way –
so curt.

If the WORLD could know what the ESSAY of "AN EXPARTE PROCEEDINGS" contains:

They would all be converted to the TRUTH, and they would have rejuvenated brains.

For this   MANUSCRIPT also contains the true story about the "a priori" evolution.

Which will upset all FALSE DOXOLOGY; and eradicate all religious confusion.

Dated this 1st day of JANUARY, A.D. 1937.

(signed:) DR. FRED. C. SWARTZ. …-. THE ANTAGONIZER OF CROOKS.

NOTE: On the internet (Wikipedia), I discovered that Dr. Swartz lived from 1913 to 2009. He was 24 years of age when he wrote this letter. Born a Jew, he converted to Christianity. Dr. Schwartz was a passionate anti-communist and actively supported the movement with his writings and speaking tours in the United States and his native Australia in a time when Americans felt that communism was a threat to our survival. Most Americans thought it needed to be contained throughout the world. Dr. Swartz wrote the internationally bestselling book, *You Can Trust the Communists (to be Communists)*, in 1960, and he later wrote more successful books and a newsletter.

He founded the Christian Anti-Communism Crusade (CACC), which he initially based in Sydney, Australia, before moving it to Long Beach, California. In California, his television network saw his fame explode in the US as he gained friendships with presidents (Ronald Reagan) and other writers (William F. Buckley). One of his rallies filled the 16,000-capacity Los Angeles Memorial Sports Arena. Roy Rogers, John Wayne, James Stewart, and Senator Thomas J. Dodd of Connecticut appeared with Dr. Swartz at subsequent events.

It was no surprise to me to find that Dr. Swartz communicated with Detective Ellis H. Parker. I have seen other letters from other less known anti-communists in his files.

His writing style is impressive, entertaining, and intelligent. He has a unique flair. The paper starts with a poem he wrote that warns the reader not to ignore an opportunity or the tip contained in his paper.

The Lindbergh babies' body was discovered accidentally near the estate on 5-12-1932. It was severely decomposed, and it was never forensically determined that it was Charles Lindbergh's son. Dr. Swartz does not tell us the dates of the baby's Washington, DC sightings.

The combination of very interesting accusations and theory is at first questionable, but when the writer's identity is fully revealed, you pause to wonder. In his paper, Dr. Swartz calls himself the "orator" a few times. This confirms to me that the writer of this paper was, in fact, Dr. Swartz, who went on to become a very rich and powerful "orator."

Dr. Fred Schwartz's main points in his paper are astonishing. They support Ellis Parker's opinions, particularly his belief that Paul Wendel and Isidor Fisch were the kidnappers. I read their names too many times in this paper. The following is a review of his main points:

- When he heard that **Wilentz** and Hauck had hurried to the jail to interview the detained **Paul Wendel,** he knew that someone was concocting a plan to protect **Isadore Fish** and the others who had perpetrated the kidnapping.

- When Dr. Swartz learned that the woman who had been caring for the Lindbergh baby was **J. Edgar Hoover's concubine,** he knew that there was a tremendous political scheme connected with the kidnapping. He knew that **Hoover and Lindbergh had collaborated during World War I** to play a dirty trick.

- David Wilentz had made a hurried trip to Washington, DC.

- The **Lindbergh kidnap ladders were stored in Washington, DC.** They were **driven away long before the kidnapping by five or six gangsters.** One of them looked like **Isadore Fish,** who Lindbergh described as the man he had passed the ransom to. The ladder truck was followed by a greenish sedan with a woman in the back seat.

- The **Lindbergh boy was taken to Washington DC by boat.** He was seen alive in Washington in the custody of a woman. It alluded again that she was **J. Edgar Hoover's concubine.**

- The Doctor Swartz states that **Wendel** was one of the men recognized with **Isadore Fish** standing next to the fish truck (holding caught fish for sale). A man named Curtis that was standing next to a fish truck, said that the **Lindbergh baby was on a boat.**

- Paul Wendel was seen coming out of the house where the Lindbergh boy was kept.

- **Wilentz mislead Governor Hoffman and then set a trap for Ellis Parker.**

- **Wilentz** (in 1933) so feared the release of a new manuscript that he offered up to $35,000 for the book. When the offer was refused, the author and publisher in Washington, DC, were threatened with a visit from New York Gangsters. If they went forward with the book's printing, they would be "done up."

- Dr. Swartz believed that the **Lindbergh kidnapping was connected to the Republican party** and political Gangsters who were getting desperate. He warned that Governor Hoffman and **Ellis Parker** should be careful, or they could be dispatched by the customary racket of "He died from APOLEXY." It said that it is up to Governor Hoffman and Detective Parker to pick up the trial of the Lindbergh kidnappers and their political enemies as revealed here. Not only to vindicate their character but also to expose the seditious undertaking which Dr. Swartz knew was connected with the Lindbergh kidnapping case—**being the over-throwing of the United States Government with NEW DEAL objectives.**

- A newspaper article stated that **Gunnar Svedberg, a deported New York painter, reported that the Lindbergh boy was held for ransom by five men and a woman. The Lindbergh baby was given narcotics that resulted in his death.**

- **Ellis Parker was on the right track.** The Lindbergh case has not been solved by J. Edgar Hoover's tactics nor the goofs of the New Jersey State Police. **The kidnap ladders were made and owned in the city of Washington, DC, and Charles Lindbergh Jr. was alive and seen in Washington DC after the kidnapping.** Charles Lindbergh's description of the man he gave the ransom money to **match that of Isadore Fish**).

FROM THE ELLIS PARKER LOST FILES

Cora E. Parker, 509 Garden St., Mt. Holly, N.J., July 4th, 1939

My dear Wife: -

I was very glad to receive your letter (you write just like Hannah Lippincott) a lot in a few lines, as soon as we get out of quarantine it will be better.

We are now undergoing thorough examinations, which is a good thing for us. Tell Dr. Longsdorf I am getting along better than I thought possible. I will never forget him.

I am receiving the Herald and the Courier. Thanks to them. I have not received any letter from Mr. Ryan as of yet. Find out from Hannah what became of the two bills at Trenton. I am anxious to know. Remember us to Prosecutor and all down the line and to all our friends.

Congratulate Charles Hansbury on the new baby and tell him to keep going.

The following in the family can write whenever they want to but put your name and address in the corner of the envelope and when signing a letter inside put son, daughter, or wife. Charlotte put her mother's name on the outside of the envelope instead of her own. (Cora E. Parker, Edward S. Parker, Mrs. William Charlotte Fullerton, Lilyan Sahol, Harry Green (Lawyer), Anna E. Bading, Secretary and Senator Cliff Powell). These are the names listed here to receive mail from. Tell Edward to write one or the other of us a letter at once. Hannah will help him. Tell Mildred she is a real daughter, and God bless her.

Your Loving Husband, Ellis

Note: In the above letter, Ellis Parker is writing to his wife and his children's mother. He seems to be of sound mind and spirit. Unfortunately, he has only seven more months to live. Cora was an extraordinary woman that supported her husband and family during the difficult times of his imprisonment at Lewisburg. It was a stressful period. The Lindbergh investigation and the defense of her husband Ellis and her son, Ellis Jr., had extracted a high financial toll on the family and Ellis's health. The injustice of the father and son's conviction and imprisonment was also crushing. The family all knew that Ellis had solved the Lindbergh case with the delivery of Paul Wendel's confession. Detective Parker and his son were imprisoned for a crime using weak and manufactured evidence supplied by David Wilentz and his Hauptmann prosecution team. The real purpose of the Parker prosecution was to protect the false conviction of Bruno Hauptmann. He was only guilty of extortion and money laundering, not the kidnapping of Charles Lindbergh Jr. The result is that Paul Wendel, the only person ever to confess to the Lindbergh crime, was released to continue living a free life. Simultaneously, one of America's most significant law enforcement officers was incarcerated to suffer his death.

FROM THE ELLIS PARKER LOST FILES

July 12, 1939

Cora E. Parker, 509 Garden Street, Mount Holly, N.J.

Dear Wife –

Imagine my surprise when I received two letters from you and one from Ed on Monday afternoon. I was so overjoyed I read them all over twice and then let Ellis, Jr. see them. To tell the truth, I had a good cry.

Ellis, Jr. will be 29 next Sunday but says he don't think he will bother celebrating until he gets home.

You spoke of Lilyan's writing. When? Tell her to get busy and also tell Charlotte and Ed to keep writing. You know, I can only write two a week, and you can keep them all posted.

Kiss all the kids for us and tell Hannah to be sure and write Frank Ryan and thank him 1000 times for the paper. It certainly keeps us posted throughout that district. Also, tell Frank to remember us to all down there.

Tell Hannah to tell Howard, if he decides to run (on account of the great pressure brought to bear on him &) for God's sake don't make any campaign pledges – just meet the issues as they come and say he is going to do what the people whom he represents want done. Also, tell him not to let any one newspaper represent him as Manager, as that is bad business, but select a good campaign manager and let him distribute the bologna that goes with the game. Remember in that district you have Daily's, as well as weekly newspapers, and he has got to watch his step, or some will put him on the back page with a? Never mention any other candidate's name, as you only advertise them.

Well, Cora, tell Ed. to write and let me know how he and Bob are making out down shore. Hannah will write if he runs up there.

Also, write me the news, especially the families. It is only 9 more days, and we will be out of quarantine.

Our lawyer, Harry Green, can come any time.

I am glad Anna and Hannah are on the job down to the office, as I know with Florence's help, they can run the whole shebang.

With love and prayers for all, we remain, Your husband and son, Ellis H. Parker #8735

Note: This letter is a very poignant look at what Ellis Parker and his family endured for his participation in the Lindbergh case investigation and then the subsequent case brought against the Detective for allegedly kidnapping Paul Wendel. To be jailed on the testimony of such a flawed man, Paul Wendel, is a crime. A crime carried out by those in power who had much to lose if the case against Richard Hauptmann was proven fraudulent or organized by men who only desired the fame and fortune that would result from Richard Hauptmann's execution. Even if it was at the cost of the innocent man's life.

FROM THE ELLIS PARKER LOST FILES

November 1, 1939

Re: Parkers Hoffman v. Wendel (New York)

On October 20, 1939, I spoke to Prosecutor Duch, who told me that an FBI man, sent directly from Washington to get full particulars of the criminal record of Paul H. Wendel, called at his office about two weeks ago, spent about 2 hours with him, went over all the indictments with him, particularly the indictments of the proofs in the Schrader Estate and the FBI man was very much impressed, intimated that this gave them an entirely different picture of Wendel and that he proposed to so report to his superiors.

Duch also stated that he tried a case with John J. Quinn the previous week and that he expressed himself as very sympathetic towards the Parkers, that he blamed J. Mercer Davis and George Silzer to a great extent for the outcome of the trial and that the result might have been a tougher battle if I had tried it, and upon the theory that I had intended to try it. He also said that Wendel was absolutely no good.

H. G.

Note: This document was found in Ellis Parker's lost files. I am confident that H.G was Harry Green, a New York attorney that represented Ellis Parker during their trial for Paul H. Wendel's kidnapping. Paul Wendel is the only person who confessed to the Lindbergh baby kidnapping and the baby's death during the commission of the crime. In this letter, Harry is lamenting that Prosecutor Duch didn't try the case. He felt that the outcome would have been different if he had.

It is revealing that John Quinn felt that Paul Wendel was "absolutely no good." Yet Ellis Parker and his son were found guilty based on Wendel's testimony. The form of this letter may have been a report rather than a letter of correspondence. Interestingly, the FBI was investigating Wendel's conduct. It is easy to believe that this was done at J. Edgar Hoover's request and that he was following the case against Ellis Parker closely.

The criminal record of Paul Wendel is significant. It was whitewashed by the Lindbergh prosecution team to entice Wendel to accuse Ellis Parker of imprisoning him and withdrawing his confession of kidnapping the Lindbergh baby.

FROM THE ELLIS PARKER LOST FILES

LAW OFFICES

HARRY GREEN

SUPREME COURT COMMISSIONER, SPECIAL MASTER IN CHANCERY

26 THIRTEENTH AVENUE, NEWARK, N.J.

Phone Mitchell 2-1804

January 20th, 1940.

Hon. Daniel M. Lyons, Pardon Attorney, Department of Justice, Washington, D.C.

Re: Msc. 39 – Parker

I last wrote to you about this matter on August 14th, 1939, and received a communication from you dated August 23rd, 1939.

The condition of Ellis H. Parker, Sr, has taken a turn for the worse – he has suffered a stroke and is partially paralyzed. He is now confined to the hospital and is in very bad shape, as the authorities at Lewisburg will confirm.

I have prepared an application for a pardon for Ellis E. Parker, Sr. only, expect to be in Lewisburg tomorrow (Sunday) and have it signed, and I would like to come to Washington on Wednesday and present the same to you with letters and petitions urging the President to grant Chief Parker Executive Clemency. I realize, of course, that you have to follow a certain routine and obtain certificates or reports from the trial Judge and from the U.S. Attorney who tried the case. In view of the exigency, may I suggest that you telegraph to the Judge and U.S. Attorney for their reports.

I feel that I have fully complied with the rules and that "unusual circumstances" are set forth in the petition for pardon, and I believe that the trial Judge and the U.S. Attorney will recommend the granting of the pardon in this case.

In whatever way the consideration of the application can be expedited, it will be greatly appreciated because the Chief is close to 70, by reason of the stroke and his condition, he has only a short time to live, and we would like him to spend his few remaining days at home and not in prison.

Please, Mr. Lyons, do whatever you can to accelerate the matter.

Appreciating very much the courtesies which you have extended to me and your cooperation, I am Respectfully and sincerely yours,

HARRY GREEN

Note: Detective Ellis H. Parker died on February 4, 1940. He had only 15 days left to live when his attorney Harry Green wrote this letter. Unfortunately, that was not enough time for the Pardon Harry Green was requesting to be issued. The celebrated Detective did not get to return to his loving family and hometown of Mount Holly, N.J., where he had become famous. Ellis succumbed in the Lewisburg Federal Prison after seeing his health rapidly deteriorated. His wife Cora and his family were in transit to Lewisburg but did not arrive in time to say goodbye.

We, Ellis Parker's Grandson Andy Sahol and Russ Lloyd, believe that Ellis Parker was sentenced to prison on fabricated testimony. The testimony of Paul H. Wendel, used to convict Ellis Parker, was most likely fraudulent and created to discredit the Great Detective so that he couldn't return to his investigation of the Lindbergh case. The prosecution team members who had successfully campaigned for a death sentence in the Hauptmann trial had a lot to lose if the conviction was reversed by Ellis Parker's investigation when and if he was released.

Wendel's life and character were hardly one of dignity and honor. Wendel was a scoundrel that lived his life on the edge of respectability, using fraud and criminal endeavor for his enrichment. Wendel planned on authoring a book about his role in the Lindbergh saga to great profit. He was encouraged to do so by the same people who convinced him to rescind the confession he gave to Ellis Parker of the Lindbergh kidnapping and murder.

Wendel, who met with New Jersey District Attorney David Wilentz immediately after being released from his supposed imprisonment by Detective Parker, was encouraged to rescind his confession and accuse Ellis Parker of masterminding his kidnapping and his torture to write the confession. It is no coincidence that all Wendel's warrants, charges, and indictments disappeared when he turned state's evidence against Parker.

FROM THE ELLIS PARKER LOST FILES

February 9, 1940

Harry Green, Esquire, Attorney-At-Law

26 Thirteenth Avenue, Newark, New Jersey

In regards: Ellis H. Parker, Sr.

Dear Sir:

This is to acknowledge your letter to me of February 5, 1940, and your telegram to the President of February 6, 1940, which was referred to this Department for acknowledgment.

Some of the observations made in your letter and telegram seem to be based upon the assumption that a pardon would have been granted to Mr. Parker in a few days if he had not died. I do not know upon what you base such an assumption and wish to make it clear that it should not have been based upon any statement made by me.

At the time of Mr. Parker's death, no ground for pardon had been established, and no expression had been made by this office of any opinions as to the probable outcome of the petition, which had been therefore filed. No such expression is ever forthcoming from this Department prior to the filing of an application or during its pendency. The pardoning power is the sole prerogative of the President, and no other officer of the Government will presume to predict the President's action.

As to your suggestion of a posthumous pardon, you are advised that pardon applications are not considered by the Department after the death of the convicted person.

In your letter, you also refer to a proposed application for pardon for Ellis H. Parker, Jr. Applications for executive clemency are not ordinarily entertained prior to the parole eligibility date of the prisoner. The records of this Department show that Ellis H. Parker, Jr. will be eligible for parole on June 21, 1940.

Very truly yours,

Daniel M. Lyons,

Pardon Attorney

Note: Ellis Parker died just four days before this letter was written by Daniel Lyons. The great detective died behind bars in Lewisburg Prison on February 4, 1940. Ellis Parker never received a pardon from the US Government, although many were championing it. He certainly deserved one, but we are still waiting for a posthumous one. Ellis was one of the finest law enforcement officers that ever lived. His record of achievement is unparalleled in American history. Except for accepting the task of investigating the Lindbergh baby crime, he would have retired with a celebrated life and a wonderful family to enjoy. Ellis was known as "America's Sherlock Holmes." When questioned about this title, he was known to respond, "The difference is, I am a real Detective, Flesh and Blood, and Sherlock was a fictional one."

Ellis Parker deserved more consideration than this cold letter offers. The investigation of the Lindbergh case was called the worst example of American Justice in history. The President should have at least taken action to bring Ellis home when he fell ill. Someone was blocking this. The writers of this book, Andrew Sahol, and Russell Lloyd, believe it was those who had a lot to lose if Richard Hauptmann's execution was proven a miscarriage of justice and that Ellis Parker had been framed. Their fame and fortune would be taken away from them if Ellis Parker was released. The irony of this is that Detective Ellis Parker solved the crime. He produced the only signed confession to the crime, by Paul Wendel.

In 1941 Ellis Parker Jr. was released from prison. A full Pardon was issued to him by President Harry Truman on January 30, 1947. He would never speak of the Lindbergh case again.

FROM THE ELLIS PARKER LOST FILES

Note: The following is a list of miscellaneous and random letters found in the "Ellis Parker Lost Files." It is an interesting look at what type of information was being sent to Detective Ellis Parker during his investigation of the Lindbergh case.

FROM THE ELLIS PARKER LOST FILES

3-15-1936 Ellis Parker's letter to Mr. Harold Wolf, New York City

Of course, your article, like many others, is very interesting, but having not made a study in my life of any code, I am really unable to pass on that part of it. I would also say that your article shows that Dr. Condon, who has spent more or less time on such things might have more knowledge than what he has given concerning the extortions.

FROM THE ELLIS PARKER LOST FILES

FRED'S LETTER TO ELLIS PARKER 3-2-1936 RE: ISIDOR FISCH'S HOT MONEY

This letter written by a "Fred" was found in Ellis Parker's personal files. It talks about "Hot Money" and mentions Isidor Fisch. Ellis had asked Fred to investigate Fritz Karger, who had purchased a steamship ticket for Germany.

Fred tells Ellis of Arthur Trost. A man who introduced Fritz Karger to Isidor Fisch for the purpose of purchasing "Hot Money."

It is probable that Ellis Parker was trying to tie Isidor Fisch to Paul Wendel and also wanted evidence to prove that Isidor Fisch's occupation was money laundering. Ellis suspected that Fisch and Paul Wendel were deeply involved in the conspiracy to kidnap the Lindbergh baby.

12-14-1935
From: Fort Worth-TX
Written by: C.L. Traxler

Traxler, an investigator, knows of a prisoner that had information. Wants someone to come to Fort Worth.

2-10-1936
From: New York
Written by: Josephine Kinel

Write to tell Ellis Parker that a man named Fritz, who knew Hauptmann, will help solve the case. Ellis writes back that Bruno Hauptmann only knew one Fritz, Fritz Hammell, and he went back to Germany in 1931.

3-27-1936
From: New York
Written by: George R. Barnett

Writes that three of the five men that kidnapped the baby have died since it was done. Hauptmann is not guilty.

5-7-1936
From: Philadelphia-Pa
Written by: A Sincere Friend

The writer sees the newspaper coverage and the case against Hauptmann as a Jewish crusade.

12-17-1935

From: Mendota-Wisconsin

Written by: Mrs. Florence Dow

Mrs. Dow is a patient at the Wisconsin State Hospital. She can provide the "low down" that was written for a person that was dying in the hospital. She can also get a letter from a nurse having the Lindbergh baby. The man that drove the baby to Canada is also working at the hospital. She closed the letter asking that Ellis keep her name secret. She suspects her mail is being held up, but she gets news on the radio nine times a day soon to be increased to 11 times a day.

12-13-1935

From: Mobile-AL

Written by: Mrs. Inez Braswell

Mrs. Brasell's question was, did the man who said, "Hey Doctor," in that cemetery know Dr. Condon was anyone other than "Jafsie" at that time? Ellis Parker noted the "good logic" of this question in his response.

12-10-1935

From: New York

Written by: Anonymous

The board matching with one from Hauptmann's attic is questioned.

12-9-1935

From: Aurora-IL

Written by: Anonymous

There is another person who claims to have seen the kidnappers with the Lindbergh baby.

1-21-1936

From: Springfield-Mass

Written by: J. P. Martini

Ellis Parker responded to J.P. Martini's telegram asking him to find out where Michael Lakey (residing on Lombard Street) gets his mail. With this information, Ellis says, then I can find out something about him.

12-10-1935
From: Pittsburg-PA
Written by: Humble Sympathizer

The writer asks if all members of Dwight Morrow's (Charles Lindbergh's father-in-law) family was happy with his will? Also, were there lawsuits started to break the will? Isn't their vengeance in the best of family's? Do you believe that John Hughes Curtis made a confession through fear or remuneration?

UNDATED LETTER
From: No Postmark
Written by: Mrs. Mask

A woman calling herself "Hell Hath No Fury Like A Women Scorned" wrote that Elizabeth Morrow had the baby taken to avenge herself on her sister Ann for being jilted by Charles. The baby was to be taken to England by Violet Sharp. The baby was carried down the back stairs by Betty Gow while the Butler held the dog. The child died thru accidental neglect, it was then thrown from the car, which caused the hole in its skull. Violet Sharp became hysterical, so she was poisoned by Elizabeth to shut her up. The Butler was also dealt with in the same way.

EPILOGUE

Now that you have read our book, you can understand that my grandfather was made a scapegoat just as Bruno Richard Hauptmann had been. Ellis H. Parker was prosecuted by the same men that had extensive roles in the prosecution of Hauptmann. They were New Jersey Attorney General David Wilentz, New Jersey Judge William Clark, and New Jersey Prosecutor Anthony Quinn.

I hope you are convinced, as my grandfather was, that Paul Wendel and Isidor Fisch were responsible for the kidnapping and the horrible death of Charles Lindbergh Jr.

I am confident that my grandfather was not healthy enough during his trial to defend himself properly. He died soon after he was convicted, and I doubt he would have been if he were of sound mind. I hired a forensic scientist to confirm that he had been suffering from a brain illness during his trial. The condition is called "Thrombosis of the brain." It severely limited his abilities to defend himself. He was a shell of the man he had been. I believe in my heart that he should have been declared "Innocent by reason of insanity" or just Innocent of the crime fabricated by Wilentz, Clark, and Quinn for their fame and profit.

Thanking you for your support,

Andrew Sahol

FINAL CONCLUSION

There is no final conclusion on who is responsible for the Lindbergh baby's abduction and death, and there most likely never will be. Too much time has passed. Since then, countless books, newspaper editorials, magazines, movies, and television stations have presented alternative conclusions and suspects.

The multiple theories and evidence presented are massive and impressive. Creating a book based on a new theory is lucrative and rewarding. It is the American way, and it works. These books can change opinions. America's thirst for more information about the Lindbergh case rivals that of the Kennedy Assassination, the Manson Family Murders, and the OJ Simpson case, to name a few. The internet is full of websites where these cases are discussed daily.

What we have done here is present another alternative theory. We are loyal to this theory because it is Detective Ellis H. Ellis Parker's theory. It is supported in his letters, his writings (presented in this book), and his presentation of Paul Wendel's confession.

There is a historically recorded conclusion that Bruno Richard Hauptmann was given a justifiable sentence for his crime. But now, in modern days, we believe that there is a consensus that the Flemington-NJ "Trail of The Century" was an unfair miscarriage of justice. There exists great doubt that Hauptmann had received a fair verdict.

We hope that if you read our book and the miraculously found Lost Letters of Detective Ellis H. Parker you will be convinced our conclusion is possibly the best one. His letters are the only place you can learn what many Americans of the time were thinking.